Longman Co-ordinated
S-C-I-E-N-C-E

PHYSICS

David Brodie

with

Wendy Brown
Nigel Heslop
Gren Ireson
Peter Williams

Series Editor
Terry Parkin

LONGMAN

Addison Wesley Longman Limited
Edinburgh Gate, Harlow, Essex CM20 2JE, England

First published 1996   Second impression 1998

© Addison Wesley Longman Limited 1996

Designed and produced by Gecko Limited, Bicester, Oxon

Produced by Addison Wesley Longman Limited,
Hong Kong.   GCC/02

ISBN 0582 279844

Acknowledgements

We are grateful to the following for permission to reproduce copyright material:

Folens Publishers for extracts from *What is Science? (Press for Action Series)*; the Controller of HMSO for extracts from *The Highway Code* Crown Copyright and an extract from 'Model Rules for Laboratory Office Staff' from *Model Rules for Workers (1991) Safe Working and the Prevention of Infection in Clinical Laboratories* Crown Copyright.

We are also grateful to the following for permission to reproduce photographic material:

Front cover
Sidney Moulds/Science Photo Library
Polarised micrograph of crystal of vitamin B12

The photographs reproduced on page 6 centre right,150 centre and 207 are crown copyright

Ace Photo Agency, pages34 bottom left (photo Jason Burns), 210 top (photo Eric Pelham)
Allsport, pages 16 top, 16 left, 83 (photo Tim Defrisco), 86 top (photo Adrian Murrell), 101 top, 101 bottom, 104 (photo Tony Duffy), 126, 127 centre (photo Pascal Ronderu), 127 bottom (photo Clive Brunskill), 130 top (photo Vandystadt/M Masculin, 130 bottom (photo Vandystadt. P Patoulidou), 135 (photo David Cannon), 142 right (photo Pascal Ronderu), 143 (photo Bob Martin), 200
Anglesey Borough Council, pages 19 centre, 34 top
Audi, page 98
Catherine Blackie, pages 2, 147 botom left, 149, 152, 184 bottom
British Geological Survey, page 39 centre
British Maritime Technology, page 6 left
British Sky Broadcasting, page 48 centre
British Waterbed Company, page 147 below right
BP, pages1 top right, 93 top left
David Brodie, page 167 right
Bubbles Photo Library, pages 77 top right and left (photos F Rombout), centre (photo Jacqui Farrow)
Cable and Wireless, page 198 bottom
Cern, page1 bottom right
Chatsworth House, page 146
Chubb, page 221 bottom right
Trevor Clifford, pages175 top, 175 centre right, 176, 177, 179
Bruce Coleman, page 129 (photo Kim Taylor)
Collections, pages 77 bottom right (photo Anthea Sieveking), 77 bottom left (photo Gary Smith), 80 (photo Paul Watts), 86 centre (photo Brian Shuel), 174 centre right and centre left (photos Neil Calladine)
Colorsport, pages 159 top, 196 (photo Fred Carol/GLMR)
Diamond International Magazine, page 18
EEV, page 87 top
Mary Evans Picture Library, page 191 top
Chris Fairclough Colour Library, pages 153, 199, 203 bottom
Ronald Grant Archive, page 56
Sally & Richard Greenhill, page 32 top left, 161
Robert Harding Picture Library, pages 15 centre right (photo John Gardey), 23 bottom (photo J Lightfoot), 33, 95, 97 (photo Ian Griffiths), 99 (photo Ian Griffiths), 145, 174 top, 174 centre (photo James Green)
John Hawkins, page 127 left
Holt Studios, page 89 bottom (Mike Flood)
Hydrographic Office, page 207
Image Bank, pages13 (photo Juan Silva), 14 top right, 15 top (photo David Vance), 16 bottom (photo Tim Bieber), 29 (photo Colin Molyneux), 93 top right (photo David Hamilton), 125 (photo Stockphotos/ U Wallin), 158 (photo Gabriel M Covian), 160 (photo Peter Grumann), 189, 198 centre right (Anne Rippy), 237 top (photo Grant Faist)

JCB, page 148 top
LPU, page 14 centre right, 38 bottom
Andrew Lambert, pages 4 centre, 38 top, 38 centre, 117 bottom, 151 top and bottom, 159 bottom left and bottom right, 164, 180, 184 top
Frank Lane Picture Agency, pages1 left (photo Phil Ward), 87 bottom (photo H Hantala), 128 bottom (photo S Jonasson)
London Electricity Board, page 182
LFDCA, page 25 top
Mansell Collection, page 223 top right
NASA, pages 63, 66 bottom, 116, 150 bottom
National Grid, page 103
National Meteorological Office, page 6 centre right, 150 centre
Natural History Photographic Agency, pages 20 (photo L Campbell), 144 (photo Norbert Wu)
Newcastle Chronical and Journal Ltd, page 210 bottom
Open University, page 72
Oxford Scientific Films pages 4 (photo Henry R Fox), 32 bottom (photo Stephen Dalton), 128 centre left (photo Henry R Fox)
Panasonic, page 157
John Paul/ The Telegraph plc, London 1995, page 79
Range Pictures, page 17, 227 bottom
Rex Features, pages 39 top (photo Roy Garner), 61 bottom (photo Nils Jorgenson), 84 (photo Tony Larkin), 86 bottom (photo Peter Brooker), 93 bottom, 101 centre (photo Nick Bailey), 109, 111 top (photo Sipa), 111 centre (photo Sipa), 115 bottom (photo DPPI), 117 right, 118 (photo DPPI/Michel Pissotte), 120, 127 centre (photo Clive Dixon), 133, 137 top (photo O, Reck/ATP), 142 left (DPPI), 147 top right, 173 (photo Barry Norman), 191 bottom, 194, 203 top, 227 centre right, 230
Tim Robertson, page 85
The Royal Institution, page 211
Jack Sealey Ltd, page 148 bottom
Seiko Europe Ltd, pages 4 top, 115 top
Science Museum, page 55
Science Photo Library, pages 6 top right (photo Cern), 14 left (photo Adam Hart-Davis), 14 centre (photo Martin Dohrn), 16 centre right 19 top (photo BSIP Bajande), 21 (photo David Parker) 22, 23 centre right (photo Simon Fraser), 24 top (Dr Jeremy Burgess), 24 bottom (photo NASA), 25 bottom (photo Mehau Kulyk), 26 (photo Simon Fraser), 32 top right (photo CNRI), 34 bottom right (Science Source), 45 centre (photo NASA), 45 bottom (photo Steve Percival), 48 top (photo Dr Gene Feldman), 50 (photo NASA), 51 top & bottom (photos NASA), 53 (photo John Sanford), 57 (photo Dr William Keel),61 top, 62 top (photo John Sanford), 62 centre (photo J Baum & N Henbest) 66 top (photo Imperial College Physics Department), 70 (photo NASA), 71 (photo Royal Observatory, Edinburgh), 89 top (photo Roger Ressmeyer, Starlight), 93 centre left (photo Alec Bartel), 105 (photo Dr Jeremy Burgess), 111 bottom (photo NASA), 131 top (photo NASA), 131 centre (photo Kaj R.Svensscon), 137 bottom (photo NASA), 141 (photo Ron Church), 162 below middle, 167 left (photo Joseph Nettis), 190 (photo Will & Deni McIntire), 191 (photo Dr Mitsoo Ohtsori), 195 (photo keith Kent), 205 (photo Tim Beddow), 208 (photo Alex Bartel), 221 top (photo Department of Clinical Radiology, Salisbury District Hospital) 221 bottom left (photo Starlight), 222 left, 222 right (photo Geoff Tompkinson), 223 bottom left (photo Will Mcintyre), 223 bottom right (photo Starlight/Roger Rossmeyer), 226 (photo Simon Frazer), 232 top (photo Chris Priest/ US Department of Energy), 232 bottom (photo US Department of Energy), 237 centre left (photo Geoff Tompkinson), 237 bottom left (photo Fred Espenak)
Telegraph Colour Library, , pages 5 (photo Milan Rodes), 112 (photo Mark Pepper),162 below left 189 inset
John Walmsley, pages 214, 228, 237 right

Contents

How to use this book   iv

1   Experiments and investigations   1

2   A spectrum of light   13

3   Different waves   29

4   Earth and space   45

5   Time and space   61

6   Energy and resources   77

7   Energy measurements   93

8   Moving, falling and stretching   109

9   Measuring motion   125

10   Pressure   141

11   Circuits and components   157

12   Mains electricity   173

13   Particles, charge and current   189

14   Electromagnetism   205

15   Radioactivity   221

16   Physics help   237

Index   250

How to use this book

In Chapter One (Experiments and investigations) you will find out how to do experiments and what to think about when planning and carrying out investigations. In Chapter Sixteen (Physics help) you will find general information and hints which you might need for your practical work.

All the other chapters are organised in the same way. The first page of each one is an introduction to the subject which you are going to cover. The second page is designed to remind you what you might have learned before. There are some questions to help test what you remember. The remaining pages cover what you need to know for your exam.

Experimental science

This book also contains introductions to the practical work which you might do. There are detailed worksheets to help you carry out your experiments. Use the practical summaries if you miss a lesson or need to revise.

The icons show you which skills you will be using;

planning   obtaining evidence

analysing   evaluating

▶ *There are questions marked with an arrow head like this. These are designed to help with your understanding of the text. For example you might be asked a short question to check if you have understood the paragraph you have just read.*

Your teacher will tell you whether you need to cover material which is marked like this.

These boxes contain extra information

You will find a summary at the end of each chapter.

Finally, there is a selection of graded questions at the end of each chapter. These are similar to the questions that you might get in your exams. You may be asked to do the questions in class or as homework. Your teacher will tell you which questions to do.

We hope you enjoy using this book.

CHAPTER ONE

Experiments & investigations

◼ How scientists work

Scientists collect and use information in many different ways. A biologist might observe the behaviour of an animal in its environment and then compare these observations with others of the same animal under different conditions. Statistics, a form of mathematics, can help to analyse the results and to discover if the differences observed mean anything.

Studying animal behaviour.

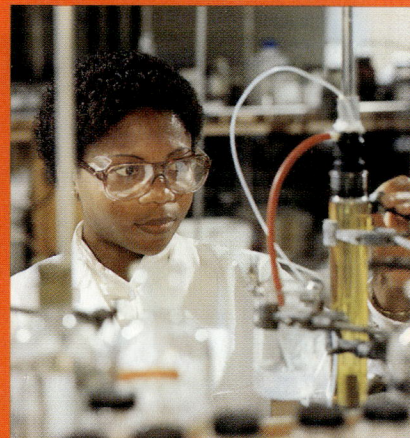

Investigating a group of newly discovered chemicals.

A chemist might try to solve a particular problem. For example, she might be trying to design a new type of antifreeze using a group of newly-discovered chemicals. She might have to analyse the chemical properties of all the members of this group before a suitable antifreeze can be produced. The scientist might have to run hundreds of separate tests, each involving the careful control of variables so that the results can be compared fairly. In this case, the scientist would have a good idea what to expect, but would not know exactly what the answers to the questions she was investigating were going to be.

A physicist might be trying to discover exactly what is in the centre of an atom. He might be part of a team of over a hundred scientists, working in different laboratories in different countries. Each of his experiments might cost millions of pounds and so his team cannot afford to do more than one a year.

An aerial view of the huge loop near Geneva where scientists study atomic structure.

The people on the previous page are all scientists but they all work in different ways. This book does not suggest that scientists work in the same way. Nor does it suggest that one method of working is better than any other. Instead, it suggests a range of methods that can be used in studying science. Some of these methods might be useful in other situations – at home or in a maths lesson, perhaps.

▶ *Make a list of some of the skills you think a scientist would need.*

Things to think about

Use practical work to help your learning. Try to explain the results you get from practical work in terms of **models**. Models are systems that can be used to help understand other problems and to predict what might happen in other situations. Using information from many different sources will help you understand your classwork better. Do not be afraid to ask for help, or to ask a friend to explain an idea to you. You may be given the chance to use computers to collect or to handle data, or to write up notes or experiments. Computers are very good at finding patterns in data.

▶ *Write down a list of all the possible sources of information you might use for a project in science.*

Try to apply what you learn to a real-life situation. Do not think of science as just something learned in a classroom. Look for it in your everyday life, but do not think that science can solve all the world's problems. Some problems seem just too difficult for even the greatest of scientists and others are just too expensive to solve.

▶ *Think of some problems that science has yet to solve. Can you think why we have failed to find a solution?*

Just as we study different types of scientific problems in different ways, you might like to write up your notes in different ways. Graphs, tables and diagrams help to explain complicated information. Presentations, models and posters can help to make the information more interesting.

▶ *Write down all the ways you can think of for showing data from different experiments.*

▶ *Copy the list of words below and discover their meaning. You might need a dictionary. Two are done for you as examples.*

- *fair test*
- *accurate*
- *reliable*
- *precise*
- *hypothesis*
- *variable*

Hypothesis *Based on earlier tests or some background research, this is an idea which can be tested by experiment. Usually, a hypothesis will involve predictions.*

Variable *This is a factor that can affect the outcome of an experiment.*

Experimental work

Scientists spend much of their time collecting and analysing data. To do this effectively they must have a clear idea of exactly what they are trying to discover or test. Following a series of steps is helpful for many people. You might like to use these general headings when planning your practical work.

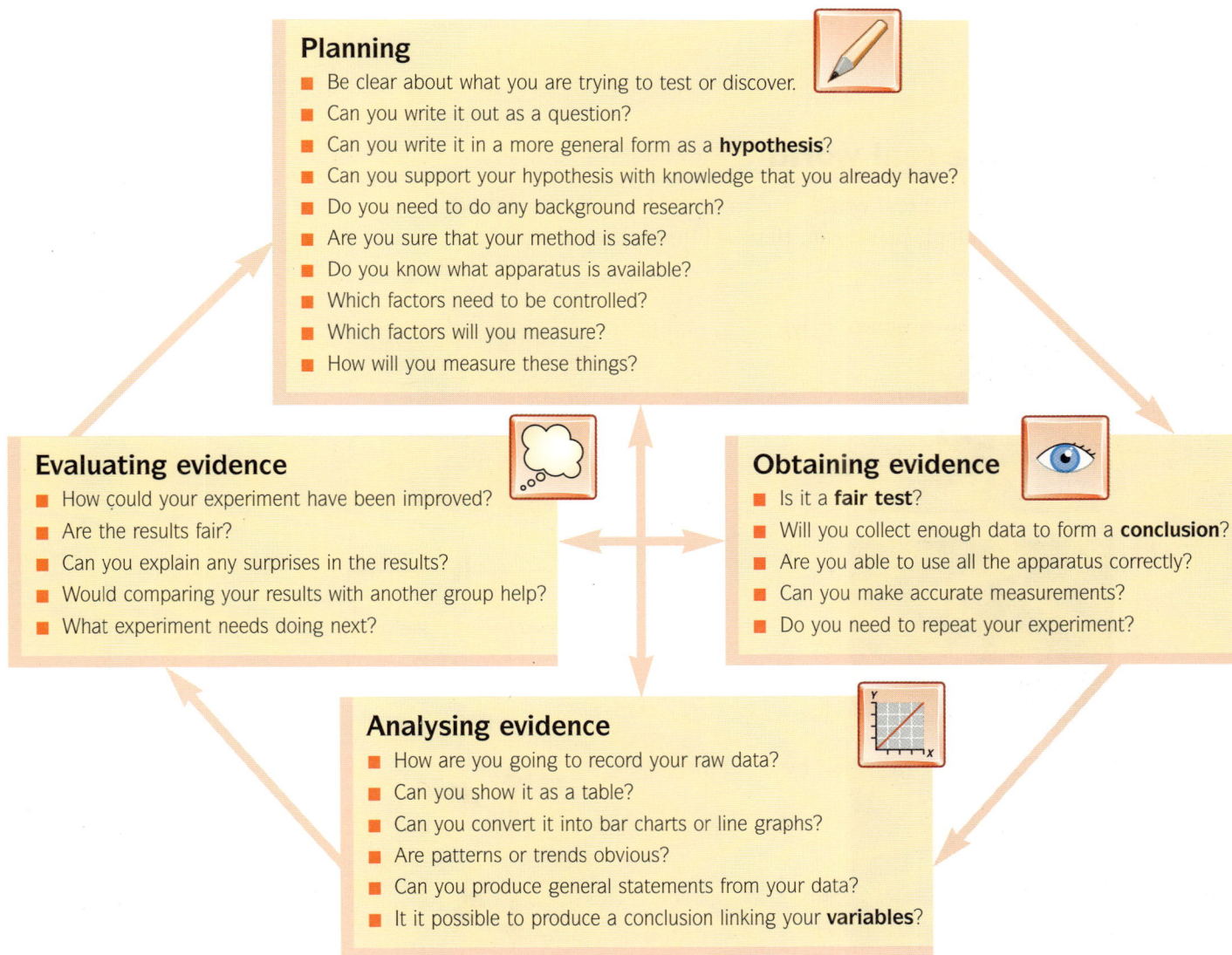

Planning
- Be clear about what you are trying to test or discover.
- Can you write it out as a question?
- Can you write it in a more general form as a **hypothesis**?
- Can you support your hypothesis with knowledge that you already have?
- Do you need to do any background research?
- Are you sure that your method is safe?
- Do you know what apparatus is available?
- Which factors need to be controlled?
- Which factors will you measure?
- How will you measure these things?

Evaluating evidence
- How could your experiment have been improved?
- Are the results fair?
- Can you explain any surprises in the results?
- Would comparing your results with another group help?
- What experiment needs doing next?

Obtaining evidence
- Is it a **fair test**?
- Will you collect enough data to form a **conclusion**?
- Are you able to use all the apparatus correctly?
- Can you make accurate measurements?
- Do you need to repeat your experiment?

Analysing evidence
- How are you going to record your raw data?
- Can you show it as a table?
- Can you convert it into bar charts or line graphs?
- Are patterns or trends obvious?
- Can you produce general statements from your data?
- It it possible to produce a conclusion linking your **variables**?

▲ Things to think about when planning and carrying out experimental work.

Safety

Remember, you will be doing a great deal of practical work. You, just as much as your teacher, will have to be responsible for your safety, so do not start any practical activity unless you are sure of what you are doing. You should carry out a **risk assessment** for each practical. One simple way of doing this is to write down each step of the practical, highlight any dangers and find a way of reducing your risk. Your teacher may give you a worksheet to help you each time you need to do a risk assessment.

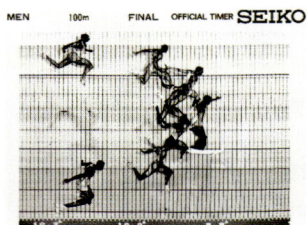

Danger   Biohazard   Flammable   Wear gloves

Corrosive   Toxic   Irritant or   Wear eye
                      harmful   protection

▲ Hazard signs.

Representing the real world

In Physics we think about the real world, and to do this we have to put our ideas down on paper as simply as we can. Here are three ways of representing real events in the world:

1 *Motion* 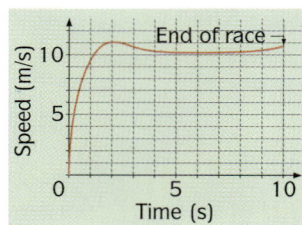 by *graphs*

2 *Circuits* 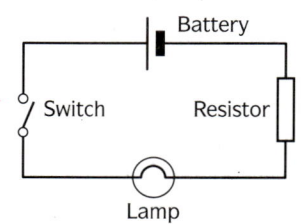 by *diagrams*

3 *Forces*  by *arrows*

Investigations with stage lighting

Stage lighting is science applied to art. All sorts of effects are possible. The people who can create the most stunning effects are the people who know most about how light behaves.

This chapter uses stage lighting as an example of a subject that you might investigate through practical work. Suppose that you want to investigate the sharpness of the shadow created by a spotlight.

Safety with stage lighting

Safety comes first in any scientific investigation. All practical activity requires a risk assessment before starting. Once you have done a risk assessment you are aware of what could go wrong.

In a theatre or hall there are three special hazards linked to lighting.

The first danger is that lights can fall if they are not properly clamped, so lights should have a secondary chain or similar fixing to make sure that it can't happen.

The second hazard is fire. Stage lights often have high power. Supertroupers, for example, are bright spotlights which run at 2 kilowatt. That's 20 times more powerful than an ordinary light bulb. The lamps can become very hot. Plastic filters placed in the light beam can create colour effects, but they can cause a fire hazard if they are not used according to the maker's instructions. Cables can also get hot, especially if they are too thin to carry big currents. Cables must be of the right thickness.

Thirdly, lamps are electrical devices, and there is always a danger of electric shock. To minimise the danger, theatre lighting runs at lower voltage than the domestic mains electricity. The lower voltage, usually 115 volt, can generally only drive a low current through a large resistance, such as the resistance of a human body. You can read more about the safe use of electricity in Chapter Twelve (Mains electricity).

▶ *Write a list of safety rules for use with a stage lighting system.*

Using models

▲ Models act like the real thing, in some ways at least.

▲ Models can be in your head, or they can be pictures. This nuclear scientist invented ways of picturing how forces act between very small particles. The pictures are not the real thing – they are just models that help people to think about the actual particles.

It is often safer, more convenient and cheaper to investigate stage lighting in a lab and not in a hall or theatre. Scientists very often use 'models' of real situations to help them to think about aspects of real behaviour. Modelling can be very useful, but you have to be careful. It is easy to use models that do not behave like 'the real thing'. Then you get the wrong answers.

▶ *Look through this book to find models of the Solar System. Are the models identical? Do you think that it is possible to use different models for the same thing?*

The following pages show how you could work on stage lighting to cover the various points on which you will be assessed on 'experimental and investigative science' in your science course.

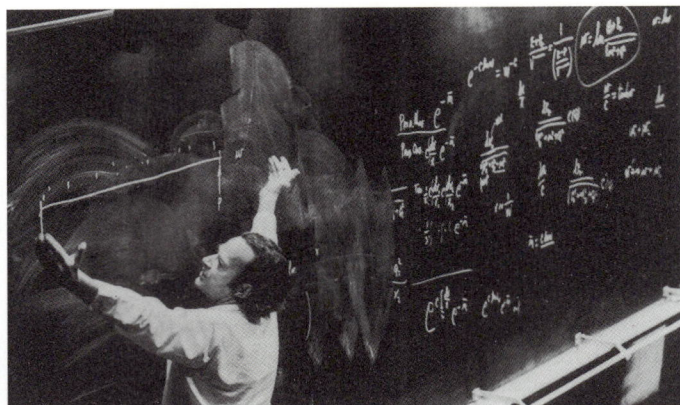

▲ Clever computer programs can predict what will happen next. A computer program can 'behave' like the real weather – it is a model.

Planning your investigation

Think about what you already know (using scientific knowledge)

You could start by brainstorming some key ideas. You can do this best if you work in a small group. Write down some important words, including the names of **variables** that influence the sharpness of shadows.

A variable can be measured. When a variable changes it may or may not influence other variables.

▶ *Which of the words in the student's list are variables?*

Talk about your ideas to get it clear in your mind how much you know and how much you need to find out more about.

Research (using secondary sources)

Find out more about the key words. Use this book, encyclopaedias and CD-ROM. If you are working in a group then each person could look up a small number of the words and then report back to the group.

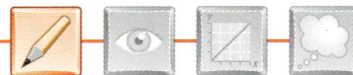

shadows
brightness
darkness
reflection
light rays
angle
distance
measuring distance
measuring brightness
measuring angles

▲ A student's list of key words for investigating stage lighting.

Decide which variables to investigate

Be clear about what you are trying to find out about. Write it down in a short and simple form.

Suppose that some students do an investigation and set up the light so that the beam hits the floor at a certain angle. They mark a line through the length of the patch of light on the floor. Then they are free to make measurements anywhere they like along the length. They are in complete control of this variable. It is the **independent** variable.

The students measure the brightness of the light. They have no control over this once they have set up the lamp. They just measure it. The brightness of the light is different in different places. It depends on position. In this investigation, the brightness of the light is called the **dependent** variable.

All other variables, such as the angle of the lamp or the current in the lamp, must stay the same all the way through the measurements. Otherwise you won't know whether the changes in brightness are caused by changes in position, or by some other factor. If you work with just *one* independent variable and *one* dependent variable and all the other variables are fixed, then you will be making a fair test.

▶ *In an investigation, a student measures out some lengths of wire, and then measures the resistance of each length. Which variable is the student changing? Which is the dependent variable?*

An investigation in the variation of brightness of light along the length of 'spot' on a stage floor

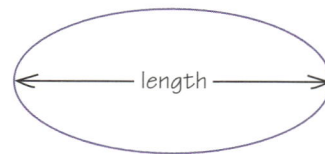

length

There are two variables involved in this investigation.
They are:
• the length along a line through the patch of light on the floor
• the brightness of the light.

🔺 Length is the independent variable. Brightness of light is the dependent variable.

Decide on your task – practical considerations

Be realistic. Think about:
- How much time you have got
- What equipment is available
- Whether you will work with a model or with actual stage lights.

🔺 A 'model' stage is simpler to work on.

🔺 Complex systems present more problems.

Sort out details of measurements and equipment

Decide roughly how many measurements you will need to make. If you try to take too many measurements you could run out of time before you have gathered the really important information. If you don't take enough measurements you might not discover some important patterns.

It helps if you have a rough idea of what the results will be like before you start. Your guesses might turn out to be wrong, but that doesn't matter. If you have some idea about what you are looking for, you stand a better chance of finding it. For example, if you expect that there will be a lot of variation in brightness of light around the edges of the spot then you might choose to make measurements there that are close together.

Decide what equipment you will use to measure the length of the spot of light – a tape, a short ruler, or a metre rule. Think about how precise your measurements should be – to the nearest millimetre, the nearest centimetre, or the nearest metre.

▶ *Why would it be silly to measure to the nearest metre?*

Consider how you will make a useful measurement of brightness. You would need to use an LDR (light dependent resistor) in a circuit. You might need to try this out before you begin your actual investigation. Scientists often need to do such preliminary work.

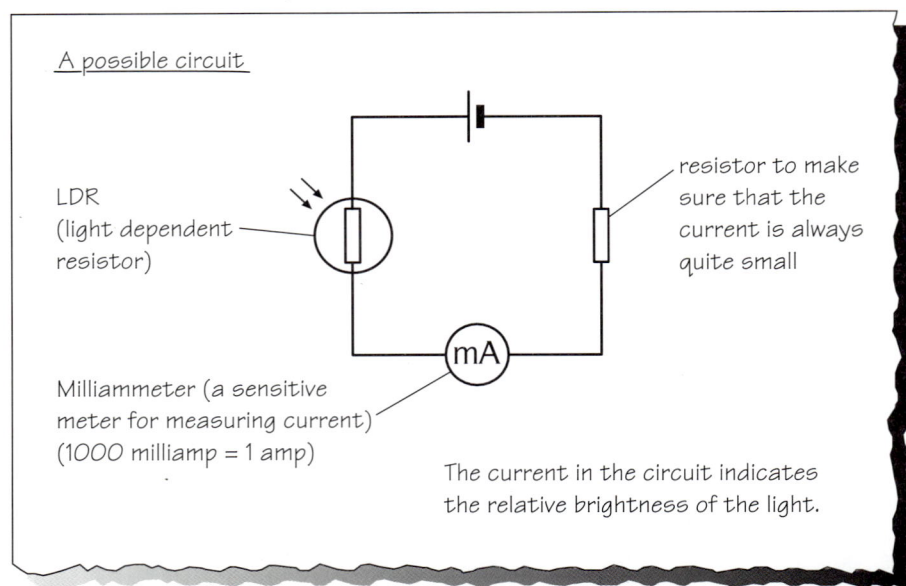

A possible circuit

LDR
(light dependent
resistor)

resistor to make
sure that the
current is always
quite small

Milliammeter (a sensitive
meter for measuring current)
(1000 milliamp = 1 amp)

The current in the circuit indicates
the relative brightness of the light.

🔺 Preliminary investigation – ideas for an LDR circuit.

Obtaining evidence

Precision of measurements

Make your measurements to a sensible precision. An answer of 1. 6581 m for the length of a spot of light is not sensible. Your rule or tape will not measure to so much precision. And there would be no point because your brightness detector is much more than one ten-thousandth of a metre across. There is no way that you can know the brightness at an area that small. A sensible level of precision would be 1.66 m.

▶ *How precisely do you need to know the time right now – to the nearest millisecond (thousandth of a second), to the nearest minute, to the nearest day?*

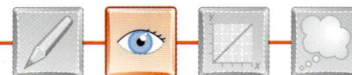

Relevance of measurements

Make sure that your measurements are relevant to your task. There is no point in measuring the *width* of a beam if your investigation is about *length*. The extra measurements just make life more complicated for yourself and for anybody who reads your report.

Enough measurements

Make sure that you have enough measurements. It would be silly to measure the brightness of a 1 m long spot of light every centimetre. The brightness changes only slowly along the length, and so measurements taken at points 0.1 m (or 10 cm) apart will be enough for most of the time. But if you want more detailed information about the rapid change in brightness that takes place at the *edges* of the spot then you should make closer measurements in those areas.

distance from front of spot in m	current in circuit in milliamp
0.1	
0.2	
0.3	
0.4	
0.5	
0.6	
0.7	
0.8	
0.9	

🔺 Measurements can be recorded in a table.

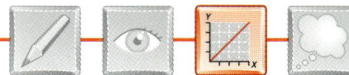

Uncertainties in measurements

Be aware that measurements have uncertainties. For example, if your brightness detector is 1 cm across then you cannot be certain of its position to the nearest millimetre.

Repeating measurements

It is often a good idea to check measurements. That means doing them again. It is particularly important if measurements are fluctuating randomly, or if you are not sure that you made the measurement carefully enough.

Recording measurements

Write down your measurements in a usable form as you go along.

Analysing the evidence

Presentation

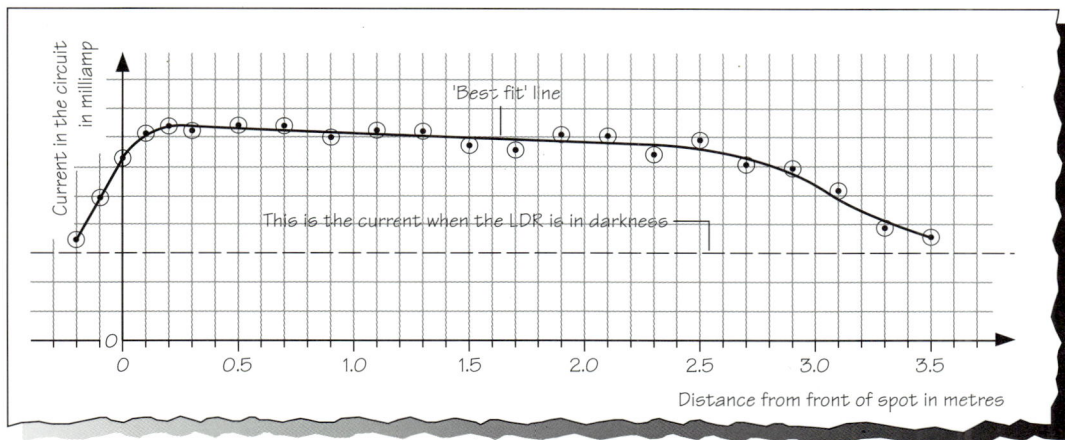

🔺 Data presented in a graph can show trends or patterns between variables.

In your final report, show your data clearly. Use the right unit for each quantity. Use tables, charts and graphs. (You can read more about units and about using graphs in Chapter Sixteen – Physics help.)

Graphs make trends and patterns easier to see. For a spot of light, for example, a graph can show clearly which parts are brighter and which parts are duller. It can also show how quickly the light fades out at the edges. In some investigations, a graph will help you to recognise particular relationships (such as proportionality).

▶ *Which normally goes on the x-axis, the independent variable or the dependent variable?*

Valid conclusions

The conclusion is the end result of all your work. It should agree with the evidence that you have collected.

Conclusion

The brightness of the light changes more sharply at the 'front' of the spot than at the 'back'.

front of spot   back of spot

The brightness of light decreases slightly as you go from the front of the spot to the back.

Checking predictions

You might have made a prediction about the outcome of your investigation. If your conclusion agrees with your prediction then that is fine. If it doesn't agree, that is just as good. Some of the most important scientific experiments in history are ones which gave conclusions that were not expected.

Explaining conclusions

Does your conclusion fit in with what you know about the subject you have been investigating? Find out if it agrees with what the books say. It could be that books don't deal with the details of your own particular investigation. The important thing is to make sense of what you already knew and what you found out in the experiment, and to write down your explanation.

Evaluating evidence

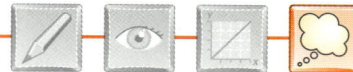

Be critical

Be critical of your own work as well as other people's. Be sure that you really have enough evidence to justify your conclusion. Think about what you would do that would be different if you started the investigation over again. Also think about what other investigations you could do if you had time.

Watch out for unreliable results

It is easy to make mistakes, and results that stand out from the general pattern are usually wrong. But you need to be careful that you have taken enough measurements to be reasonably confident that an 'odd' result really is a mistake and not some special part of the real pattern.

More ideas for investigations

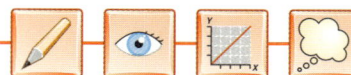

An investigation of brightness of light at the edge of a shadow in a spotlight.

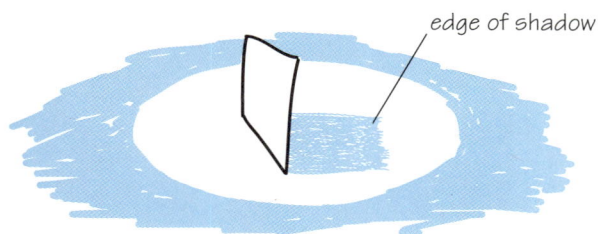

edge of shadow

An investigation of brightness of light across the width of a spot.

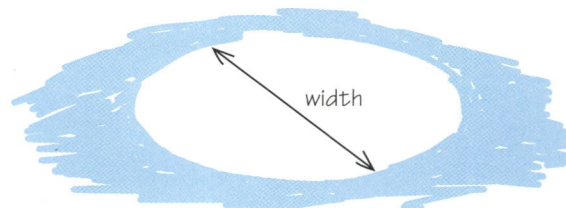

width

An investigation of the effect of angle of tilt of the beam of light on the brightness at the centre of the spot.

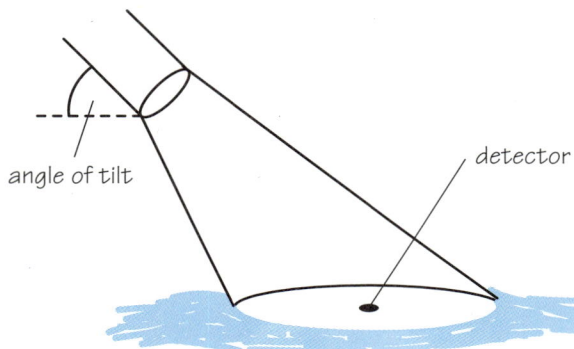

angle of tilt

detector

An investigation of the effect of distance from spotlight to spot on the brightness at the centre of the spot.

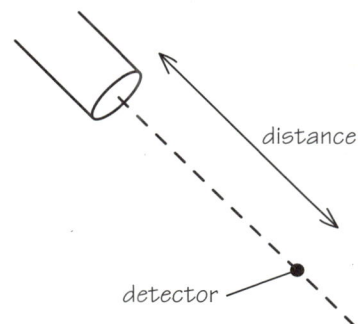

distance

detector

A spectrum of light

The colours of light are just part of a whole range of radiation that comes from the Sun and other sources. Most of this range, or spectrum, is invisible to our eyes. But we can detect it in other ways. This chapter is about this whole spectrum of radiation.

The sky is blue and the sunset is red. It is the air, and tiny water droplets and dust specks in the air, that cause the colours. The red light from the Sun is better at going in a straight line. The blue light bounces from the droplets and specks in the air. So blue light reaches your eyes from all directions in the sky – the whole sky looks blue. At sunset the light has to skim across the Earth. It travels through a lot of air before it reaches your eyes. There is more scattering of blue light, so it is mostly just the red light that gets through to you.

Review

Before going any further, read this page and attempt the tasks. Write the answers in your notes.

▲ Some objects give out light (as a candle flame does) and these are called luminous. Light is reflected, or scattered, from objects and some of it reaches our eyes. Look at your hand. It does not give out visible light. You see it because light reflects off it.

▲ The speed of light has been worked out to be very close to 300 million m/s. Light only takes 2.5 s to travel to the Moon and back. Sound only travels at 330 m/s in air – about one millionth of the speed of light.

▲ Light travels in straight lines, so it makes sharp shadows.

▲ Surfaces between different materials can reflect light, or let light pass through. If the light crosses the boundary, it can change its path – that is refraction. Some materials absorb (soak up) energy from light, and the light ceases to exist. White light is a mixture of colours. Filters can be used to remove some of the colours from the mixture. A red filter will only let red light through – it absorbs all the other colours.

CHECK TWO

1 Solve the anagrams:

deeps – much bigger for light than for sound

a silent right – the kind of path that light follows

do wash – a place where light doesn't reach

sum in lou – giving out light

left creed – scattered from a surface

traced ref – it happens when light crosses boundaries between materials

trifle – it absorbs some colours

2 Which of the following are luminous sources of light?

Sun   Moon   light bulb   candle   mirror

3 An explosion causes a flash and a bang. Roughly how far does the sound travel in the time it takes the light to go 1 000 000 m?

4 Imagine what life would be like if light could travel around corners. Write down some examples of what might happen.

5 Material can reflect light which hits it, or it can absorb it, or it can let it pass through. A lot of materials do more than one of these things. Which do each of these do:
- a white book?
- a thin sheet of tissue paper?
- clear glass?
- dark coloured glass?

Smooth and shiny

If a thin beam of light hits a very smooth surface, all the light is reflected in the same direction. So a lot of light enters your eye and the surface looks shiny. This kind of reflection is called **regular reflection**.

Rough and dull

When a beam of light hits a rough surface it is scattered. You can't see clear images in rough surfaces. Only some of the rays go into your eye and so the surface looks dull. This is known as **diffuse reflection**.

▶ *What must you do to make a metal trophy shiny? How does that work?*

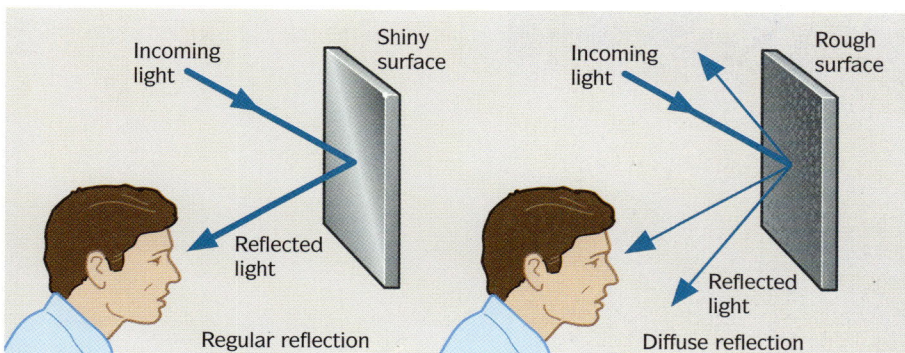

▲ Light bouncing off a very smooth surface keeps its original patterns. An image in a mirror looks like the original object.

▲ Regular reflection keeps the rays in the same pattern, but diffuse reflection scatters them in all directions.

Reflection from a plane mirror

Everyone has at some time played with a mirror or shiny object reflecting the sunlight in a particular direction. It takes little skill to direct the beam where you want it to go. Physics shows us how light behaves so that we can predict what will happen in certain situations. Patterns of behaviour are called **laws of nature**.

▲ Water surfaces are good at reflecting light. But waves make bumps on the surface that send the light strongly in some directions and not others. As the waves move, the water sparkles.

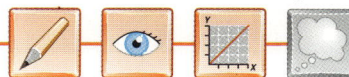

A law of reflection

A **normal** is a line drawn at 90° to the surface of a mirror. You can measure the angle between the incoming thin beam (or ray) of light and the normal. You can also measure the angle between the reflected beam of light and the normal. Then you can try different angle sizes, and compare the two angles each time.

Your results should show that the two angles are equal.

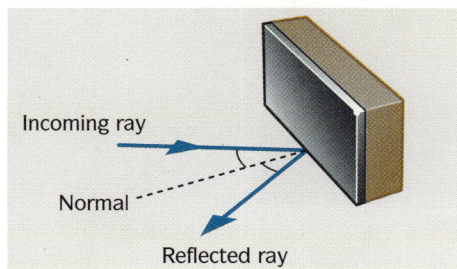

Angle between normal and incoming light	Angle between normal and reflected light
6°	6°
17°	18°
28°	27°

Reflection rules

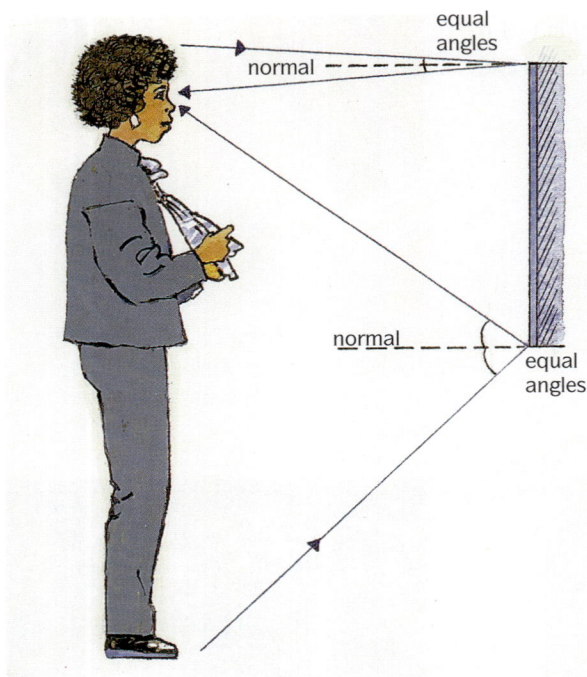

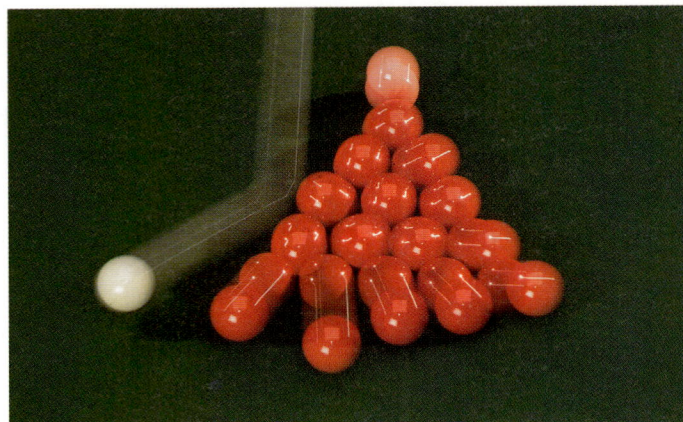

🔺 The path of the incoming snooker ball, the path after it is reflected and the normal are all in the same flat plane as each other. The incoming angle and the reflected angle are roughly the same.

🔺 Many people have a mirror that gives a full-length view of themselves somewhere in their home. The mirror must be at least half the height of the person looking at it. The top must be level with a point half the distance from the eyes to the top of the head.

Some uses of mirrors

▶ *How many uses will you find for mirrors today?*

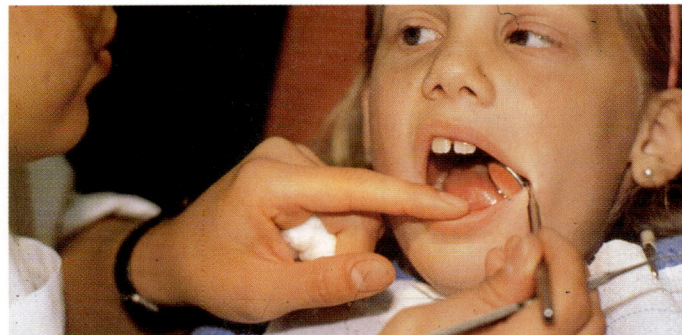

Light travelling through glass

Glass surfaces reflect light, but most of the light travels into the glass from the air. Inside the glass, some of the light is absorbed, but you only really notice that when the glass is thick. Most of the light usually passes through the glass and back out into the air.

As it crosses the boundaries between air and glass, the pathway of the light is bent. It is an example of a process called **refraction**.

Light can travel through many different transparent media. These include air, water, vacuum, glass, diamond and Perspex. Whenever light passes from one medium to another, refraction happens.

🔺 When glass transmits light it can change its pathways.

Refraction of thin beams of light

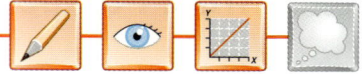

Incoming light

Normal

Angle in air

Angle in glass

Plan view

Emerging light

Very thin beams of light are sometimes called **rays**.

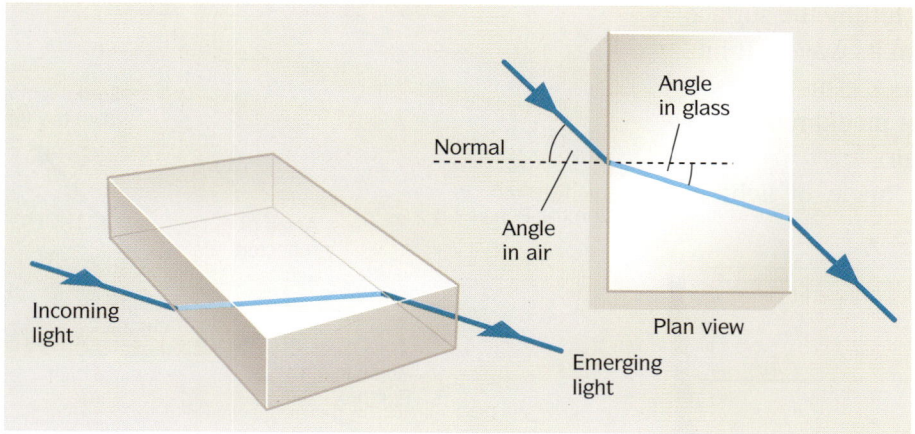

Refraction by glass is easiest to see when just a thin beam of light shines through it.

You can measure the angles that the beam of light makes with a normal. You can call them 'angle in air' and 'angle in glass'. Then you can try different angle sizes and compare the two angles each time.

The angle in the glass is always smaller than the angle in the air.

Angle in air	Angle in glass
9°	
18°	
25°	

Refraction by lenses

A lens is a curved block of transparent material such as glass. **Concave** (curved inwards) and **convex** (curved outwards) surfaces have different effects. The amount of curvature also makes a difference. Fat convex lenses, for example, focus a beam of light to a point that is quite close to the lens. We say that fat lenses have short **focal lengths**.

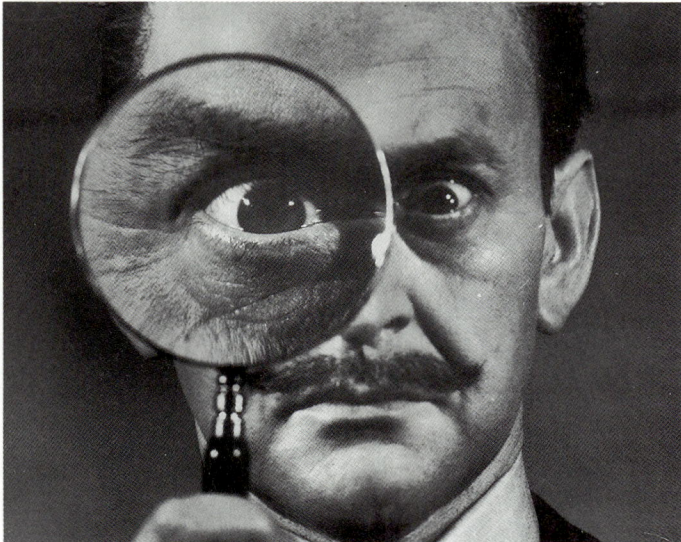

▲ Lenses bend light and change what you see.

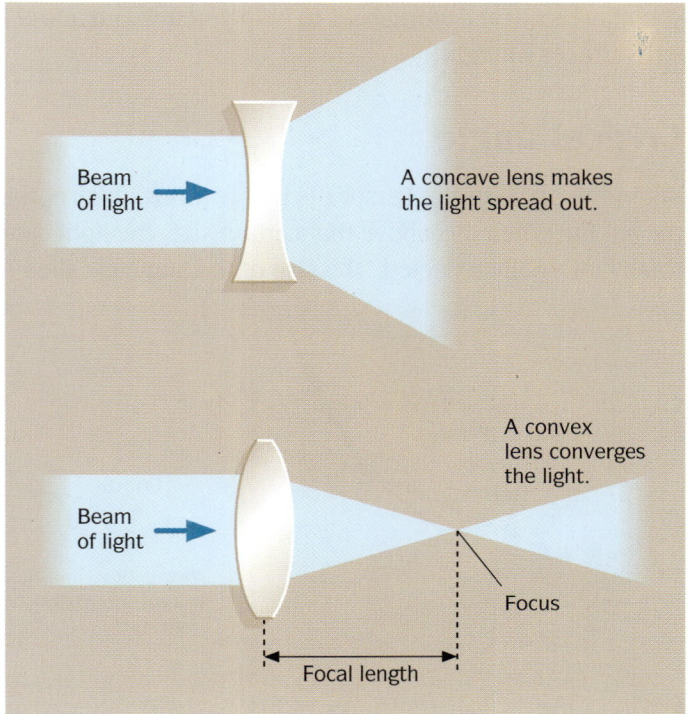

Beam of light

A concave lens makes the light spread out.

Beam of light

A convex lens converges the light.

Focus

Focal length

▲ Different shapes of lenses have different effects.

Refraction from Perspex to air

Light can shine into a D-block of Perspex, hitting the surface at 90°. That way, the light does not bend on its way in. It hits the middle of the straight edge of the block. This makes it possible to study light going from a denser medium (Perspex in this case) to a less dense medium (the air).

You can see what happens when the angle of light in Perspex is increased.

Angle of light in perspex (at perspex/ air boundary)	Angle of reflected light inside perspex	Angle in air
0°	–	0°
10°	–	15°
20°	–	31°
30°	Weak beam at 30°	49°
40°	Weak beam at 40°	75°
50°	Strong beam at 50°	No refracted beam
60°	Strong beam at 60°	No refracted beam
70°	Strong beam at 70°	No refracted beam
80°	Strong beam at 80°	No refracted beam

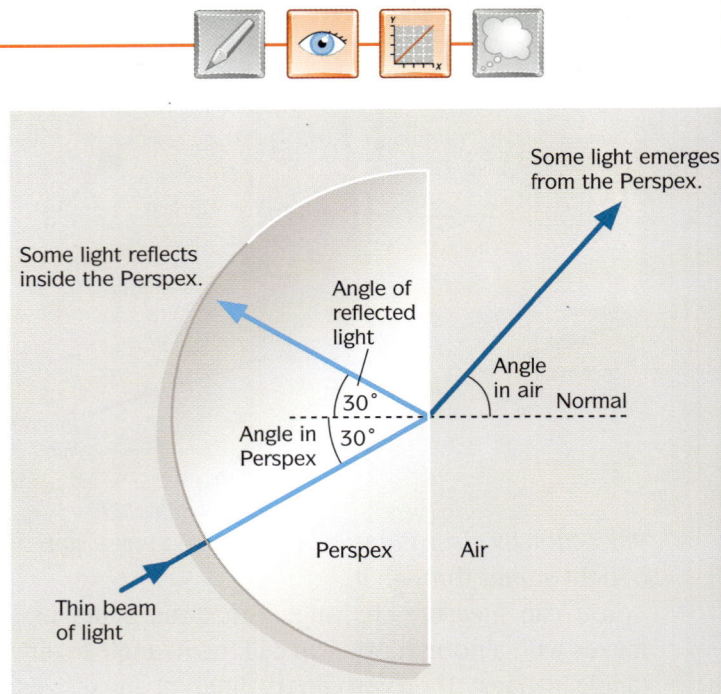

The angle in the air is always bigger than the angle in the Perspex. When the angle in the air reaches 90° the ray can no longer escape. Instead, it reflects completely back into the Perspex. That is called **total internal reflection**.

Light control

You may be given a worksheet to help you find out about the effects of different surfaces on light.

Critical angle

When the angle in the Perspex is below a certain size, the light emerges into the air. But when it is above that certain size, the light cannot emerge and it is totally internally reflected. The size of the angle is called the **critical angle**.

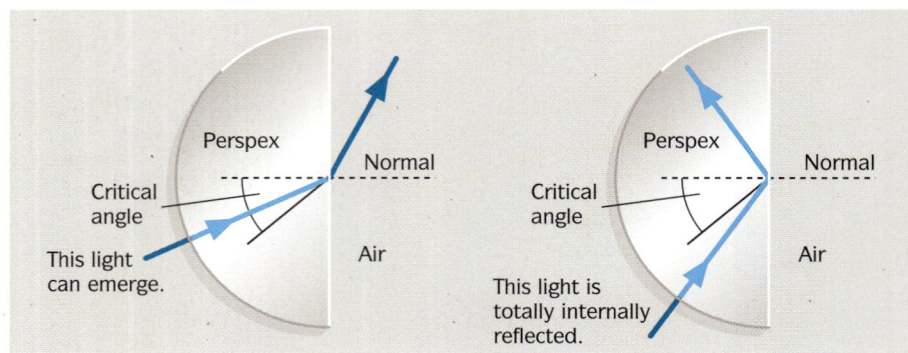

▶ *Why is the critical angle always inside the Perspex or glass and not in the air?*

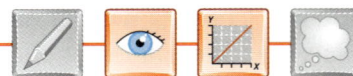

▲ In diamond, the critical angle is much smaller than it is in glass. A lot of total internal reflection takes place in diamonds – so they sparkle more than glass.

Optical fibres

An **optical fibre** is a thin fibre of glass. Inside, light hits the side of the fibre at an angle bigger than the critical angle. All the light is reflected. The light can be reflected many times, and it emerges from the other end of the fibre almost as bright as it went in. The fibres are very thin so they can be bundled together and used as a **light pipe** which can carry a clear image from one end to the other.

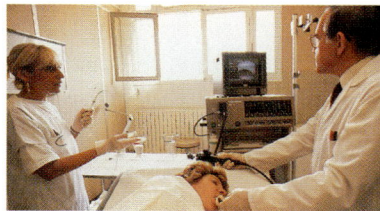

▲ Using a light pipe to inspect a patient's stomach.

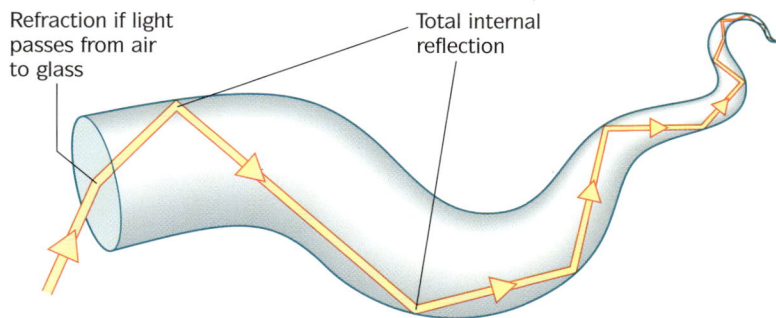

▲ The reflection of light through a glass optic fibre.

KEYHOLE SURGERY AIDED BY OPTICAL FIBRES

Very many surgical operations are now done by the keyhole technique. To operate on the inside of the chest, surgeons used to open up the patient's ribs to get their hands inside the body. That involved a long and painful recovery period. Now the same operation is done by making a few one-centimetre-long cuts. The long-handled instruments are manipulated through these holes and surgeons use optical fibres to see what they are doing.

Reflection and refraction of waves on water

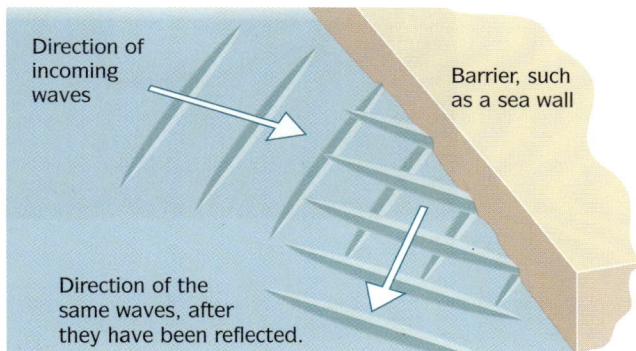

▲ Waves reflect off surfaces, just as light does.

▲ Waves bend as they move into shallow water.

Waves travel quickly across deep sea water. When the water begins to get shallower near the beach, the waves slow down.

The part of the wave that is nearest to the shoreline slows down first, and slows down for longest. The part of the wave that is still in deep water continues to travel at the same speed – so the wave changes in direction and arrives at the beach nearly parallel with it.

Note that as the waves slow down, they also get 'closer together'. The length of each wave from one peak to the next, called the **wavelength**, gets smaller.

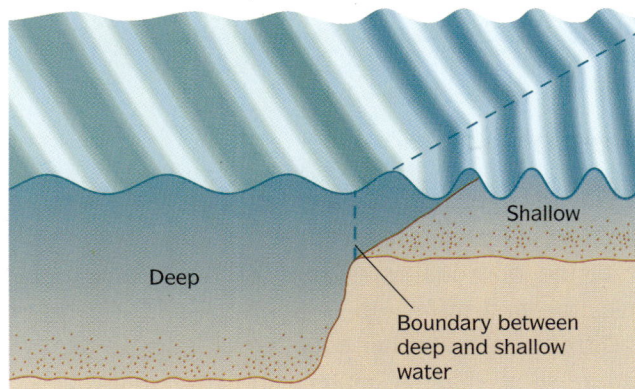

▲ The speed, wavelength and direction of waves change as the waves pass from deep to shallow water.

Wavelength and frequency

We can study waves travelling along a rope. Just as for water waves, the wavelength is the distance from peak to peak. High-frequency flicking of a rope produces short wavelengths. Low frequency flicking produces long wavelengths. **Frequency** is the number of waves produced every second.

We usually measure wavelength in metres, just as for any kind of distance. The unit of frequency is called the **hertz**, **Hz**. A frequency of 10 hertz means 10 complete waves every second.

▶ *What happens to the wavelength of waves on a rope as the frequency gets bigger?*

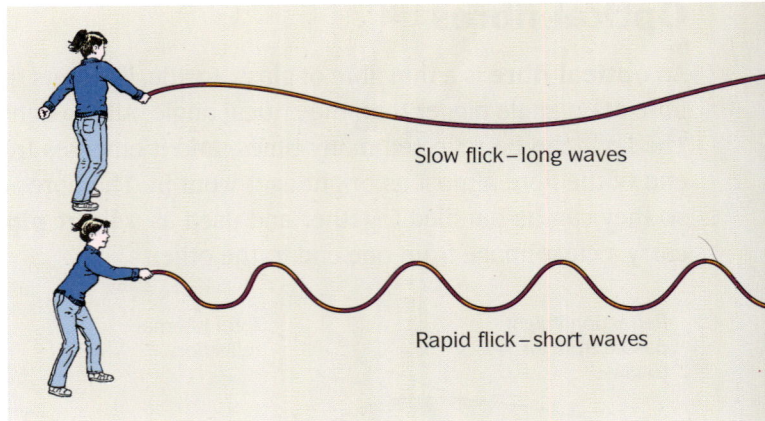

Slow flick – long waves

Rapid flick – short waves

🔺 The faster you flick a rope, the shorter the waves.

Amplitude of waves

Imagine that you are a seagull floating on water. As the waves pass underneath you, you bob up and down. Short waves carry you up and down at high frequency, and long waves make you bob less often. But there is another important measurement, and that is how far you rise and fall.

On flat calm water, you would not bob up and down at all. You would rest quietly on the surface. The maximum distance that a wave carries you, up (or down) from this rest position, is the **amplitude** of the wave. Amplitude is a distance, so its usual unit is the metre.

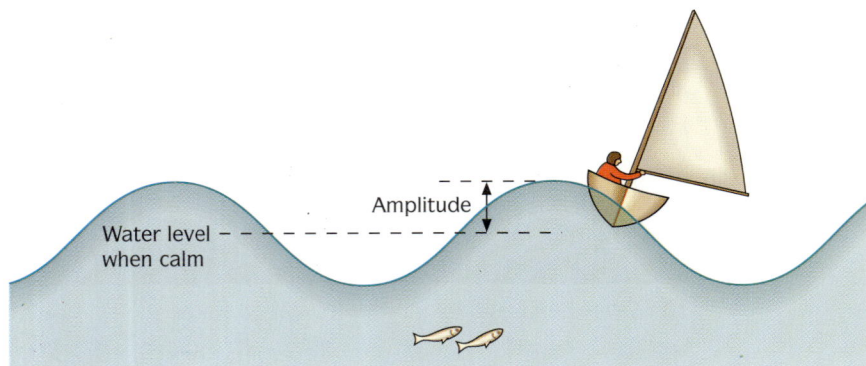

🔺 The amplitude of waves is important, as well as their length.

Amplitude

Water level when calm

▶ *Some radio stations send out AM signals and some send out FM. What do A and F stand for?*

Waves of light

Water waves can be reflected and refracted. Light waves can be reflected and refracted. That leads us to the idea that light travels in the form of waves. We can't see the individual waves, but that doesn't mean that they don't exist.

Reflection and refraction of light are evidence that there are waves of light. Diffraction is another effect which adds to the evidence, but you can read more about that in Chapter Three (Different waves).

If light travels by some sort of wave motion, then the waves must have wavelength and frequency. Some light waves will have short wavelength, and some will have long wavelength. Likewise, there must be light waves with high frequency and low frequency.

Explaining refraction of light

Refraction of water waves happens when the waves change their speed. It is the same for light waves. Waves travel more slowly in denser materials like glass than they do in air. As light passes from air to glass, there is a sudden change of speed. It is the change in speed that causes the change in direction, just like it is for water waves as they get near to a beach.

The spectrum of visible light

A prism **disperses** light – or splits it – into different colours. It happens because of refraction of some colours more than others.

Visible light has a range of wavelengths. The shortest visible light waves are about 0.45 micrometre long. The longest are about 0.70 micrometre long. Our eyes and our brains can tell the wavelengths apart. The different wavelengths give us different sensations. We call them *colours*.

Glass slows down the short wavelengths more than it slows down the long wavelengths. So it bends the shorter waves more. The shorter waves and the longer waves come out of the prism in slightly different directions.

Refraction causes the same effect in raindrops when the Sun is shining. Then we see a rainbow.

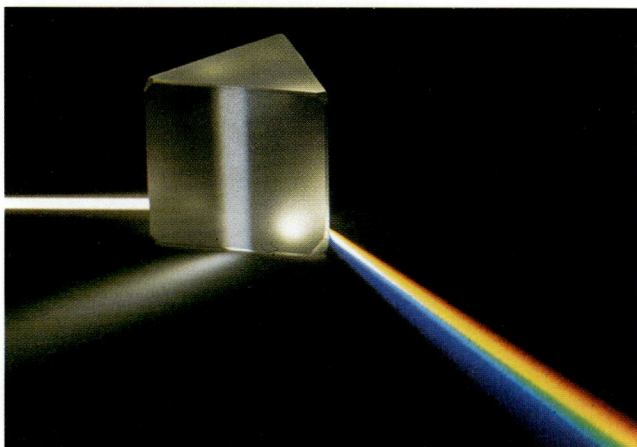

🔺 Light is refracted as it enters a prism, and again on its way out.

1 micrometre = 1 μm = 1 millionth of a metre

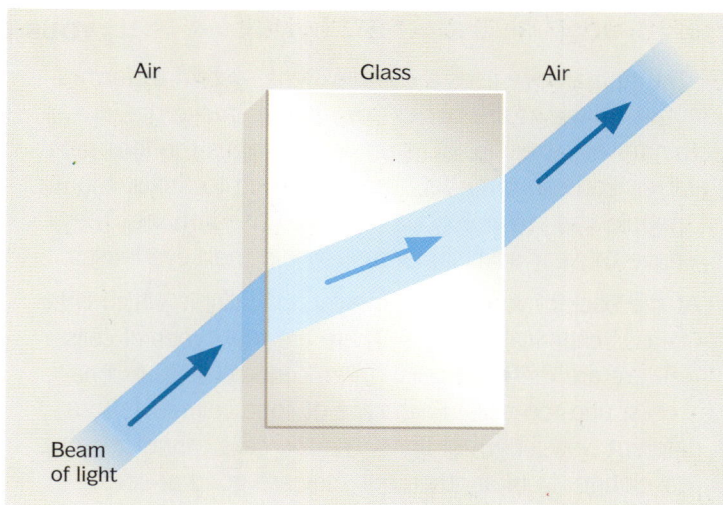

🔺 Light waves, as well as water waves, change speed, wavelength and direction when they pass from one medium to another.

SQUIGGLES IN YOUR BATH

You may have noticed squiggling patterns of light and dark on the bottom of a bath as you run the water in. It happens when cold water is mixing with hot water, and there is a strong source of light reflecting off the bottom of the bath. Light waves travel more slowly in cold water. As light moves from areas of hot to cold and back again, the paths of the waves change direction. So you seem to get no light from some parts of the bath, while other parts are quite bright. The patterns squiggle because the boundaries between hot and cold water are continuously moving.

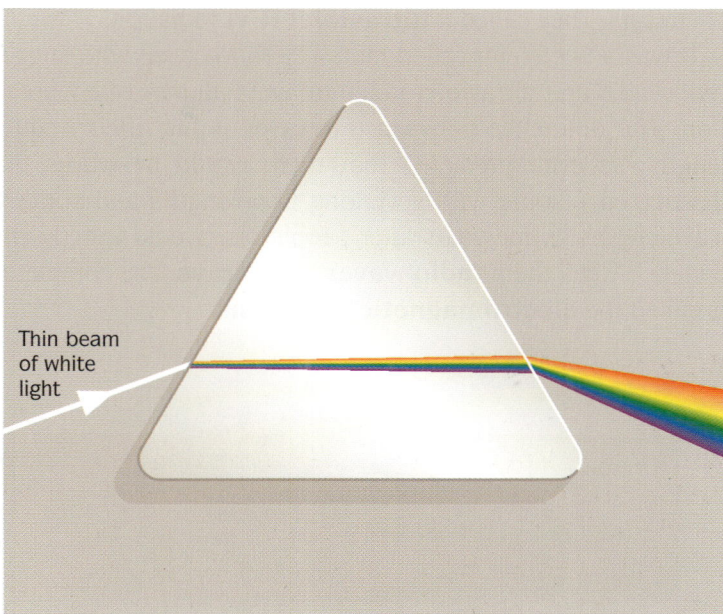

🔺 The shortest waves that we can see give us a sensation which we call violet. The longest waves make us see red, literally.

The human eye uses a complex lens system to form a tiny image at the back. Tiny muscles make the lens thinner or fatter. To focus on close images the lens gets fatter. You can often feel the lens strain to focus. Many people can still not get a clearly focused image. They have to wear artificial lenses to help their eye lenses.

At the back of your eyes are layers of cells, in which light causes chemical changes. There are four types of cells. There are red cone cells, green cone cells, blue cone cells, and rod cells. Each type of cone cell reacts to a different wavelength of light. The rod cells cannot tell one wavelength from another, but they are good at seeing in dull light. You can't see much colour when the light is low because your cone cells don't work in dull light.

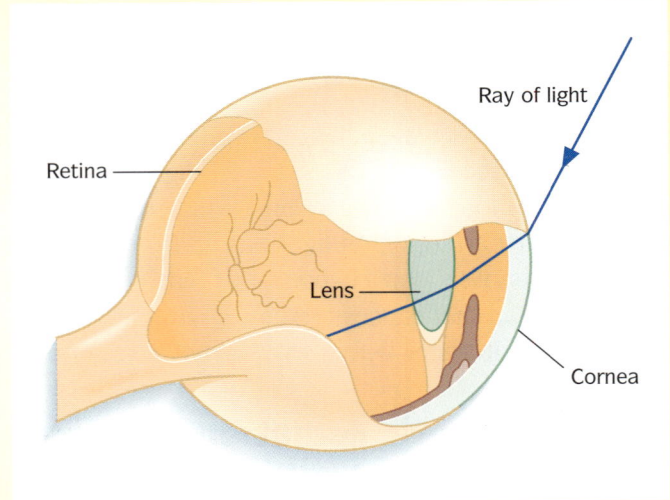

Ray of light

Retina

Lens

Cornea

The spectrum goes further

People using telescopes were the first to notice that just outside a spectrum of light, just past the red end of the spectrum, you can feel a gentle warming effect. They called this **infra-red** radiation. Sometimes it is called heat radiation. It was the first evidence that the spectrum of 'light' goes beyond what our eyes can see.

Not long after, people were experimenting with chemicals that change when light falls on them. Now we call them photographic chemicals. They found that some chemicals change faster in blue light than in red light, and faster still when they used 'non-existent' light past the violet end of the spectrum. They decided that there was some form of radiation affecting the chemicals. They called it **ultraviolet (UV)** radiation.

It was a Scotsman called James Clerk Maxwell who suggested that infra-red, visible and ultraviolet radiation were all part of a whole range of radiation. The difference between the waves is just their frequency and wavelength. He even predicted that there would be waves that nobody had discovered – some with very long wavelengths and some with very short wavelengths. Some years later people discovered exactly what he had predicted. We call them **radio waves** and **X-rays**. The complete range of waves is called the **electromagnetic spectrum**.

🔺 Chemicals were affected by light that was reflected from the face of James Clerk Maxwell – and made a photograph. He predicted that radio waves existed 15 years before anybody actually discovered them.

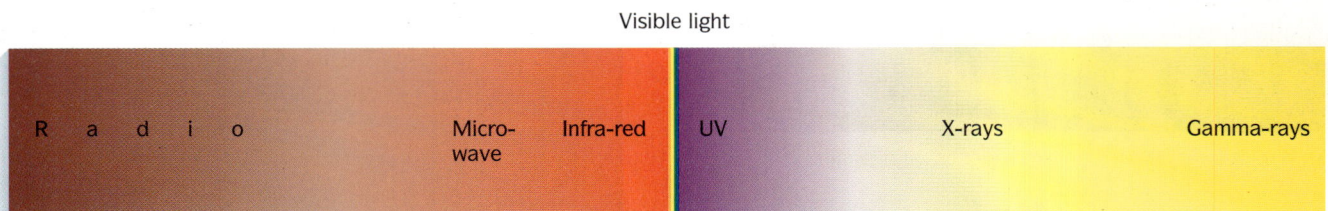

Visible light

| Radio | Micro-wave | Infra-red | UV | X-rays | Gamma-rays |

🔺 The whole electromagnetic spectrum

PHYSICS

Investigating fax paper

You may be given a worksheet to help you research the electromagnetic spectrum, using fax paper.

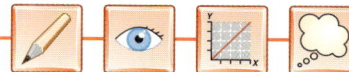

The speed of electromagnetic radiation

Light is a kind of electromagnetic radiation. So are radio, microwaves, infra-red rays, ultraviolet rays and X-rays. All electromagnetic waves move at the speed of light, which is 300 million m/s. They all travel through air and space at about this speed but travel more slowly in other things they pass through.

Electromagnetic radiation at home

Microwave ovens

Microwave ovens are very useful for cooking. The water molecules in the food absorb the energy from the microwaves and so the food heats up. This type of cooking is much faster than an ordinary cooker because the radiation penetrates the food, heating as it goes. Also, the energy goes into the food, and very little is wasted in heating the whole oven. Microwaves can cause damage to human tissue. For example, long exposure to microwaves can damage our eyes by causing cataracts. The radiation makes the eye lens become cloudy and blindness may result. Modern microwave ovens have a metal grid inside the glass of the door. The metal absorbs the microwaves so that they can't escape.

▶ *What is the speed of the microwaves inside an oven?*

Infra-red radiation

Infra-red radiation provides a heating effect. It can help in treating damaged muscles. Too much exposure, though, could cause overheating. That is particularly dangerous for your brain.

In domestic hot-water systems that use the Sun's energy, solar collectors (panels) are mounted on roofs facing the Sun. They have glass or plastic panels on top, with water circulating in pipes behind. The pipes are painted black to make them better at absorbing infra-red radiation to heat the water.

Ultraviolet light

Too much exposure to ultraviolet light can damage the skin and cause cancers. A dark substance called melanin in your skin absorbs ultraviolet light – it is a natural protection against skin cancer. Fair-skinned people have less melanin, and they are in more danger of getting skin cancer.

But ultraviolet light has benefits as well. It affects natural fats in the skin and turns them into vitamin D. Without vitamin D young children's bones do not form properly, causing a disease called

LIGHT AND LIFE

Human beings can only see a tiny slice of the whole electromagnetic spectrum. Snakes are good at sensing infra-red radiation, so that they can detect warm bodies that mean food or danger. Bees cannot see red light so they are not much attracted by red flowers. But they can see some ultraviolet radiation that is invisible to people.

Perhaps it is plants and algae that make the most use of light. They take its energy and use it in the process of building large molecules out of small ones. The process is called photosynthesis.

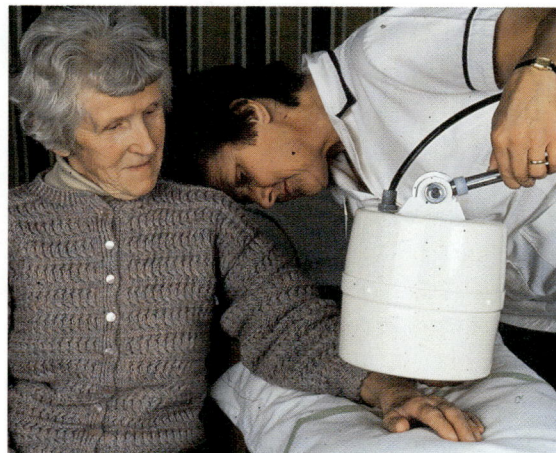

▲ Absorbing infra-red radiation.

▲ Gaining energy from electromagnetic radiation from the Sun.

rickets. However, if you get enough vitamin D from your food you do not need to make your own by using the effect of sunlight. You can read more about vitamins in Biology, Chapter Four.

▶ *Melanin acts as a filter. What type of radiation is it particularly good at absorbing?*

△ Protection from the ultraviolet rays in sunlight on an Australian beach.

Electromagnetic waves for communication

Radio waves

Radio waves can be produced by making an alternating electric current flow in the mast or antenna of a transmitter. Each radio station uses waves which have their own particular frequency and wavelength. Radio waves will bounce off the higher levels of the atmosphere and can travel all the way round the world.

△ Tuning a radio means picking the frequency you want, such as 96.8 megahertz.

'Television waves' are radio waves with high frequency and short wavelength.

Microwaves

Microwaves have wavelengths of a few centimetres. Like radio waves they can be used for communication. They can be directed towards satellites using specially shaped transmitting aerials. The satellite is in an orbit where it stays above the same place on Earth all the time. The satellite can then reflect the signal to receivers on Earth. One satellite can send signals across a huge area, so even though satellites are expensive to build and launch, they are a lot cheaper than building lots of transmitters on the ground.

Infra-red waves

Infra-red radiation can be useful for carrying information over short distances through air, or for long distances in space. It does not travel very far through air, because air

OZONE LAYER DAMAGE

Too much ultraviolet light would be harmful to living things on Earth, including people. We are protected by a layer of ozone gas in our atmosphere. Ozone molecules absorb ultraviolet light.

CFCs are substances which are used in some aerosol sprays and in refrigerators. CFCs destroy ozone, which means that more ultraviolet light can reach the Earth's surface.

△ A reflector of high frequency radio waves called microwaves.

absorbs its energy and it ceases to exist. A television remote control is an example of use of infra-red radiation for short distance communication.

Visible light

Nods, winks, waving flags and flashing lights can all be used for communication, and they all rely on visible light travelling from one place to another. We also use visible light to communicate in more high-technology ways, such as in optic fibres.

▶ *What type of radiation can be used for communication and for cooking?*

Electromagnetic waves for medicine

X-rays

X-rays have much shorter wavelengths than visible light. Because they can travel through materials, X-rays are used to investigate inside solid objects, including people. When they pass through substances they cause **ionisation** – they can tear electrons from atoms. If X-rays enter a human cell, this ionisation can damage or kill it. So we have to be very careful when using X-rays.

X-ray photographs are taken with the shortest exposure times possible to get a good image. Unless it is essential, X-rays are not taken of pregnant women, because of the possible damage to the developing fetus. People working with X-ray machines (radiographers) wear protective clothing lined with lead. Where possible the person taking the X-ray stands behind a protective screen.

A more complicated technique for detecting cancers in some parts of the body is called arteriography. The doctor injects a special material called a contrast medium directly into blood vessels, and this makes them show up on an X-ray.

Another special technique is Computerised Tomography or a CT scan for short. The patient has to lie very still as a fine X-ray beam passes through the body to a detector on the opposite side. The beam and the detector rotate around the patient's body while a computer builds up a cross-section picture of the patient's insides.

Gamma rays

Gamma rays are very penetrating rays similar to X-rays. You can read more about them, and how they are useful for 'seeing' inside human bodies, in Chapter Fifteen (Radioactivity).

🔺 All warm objects give out some infra-red radiation. The radiation from a human body can be enough to pick out a survivor in smoke or rubble.

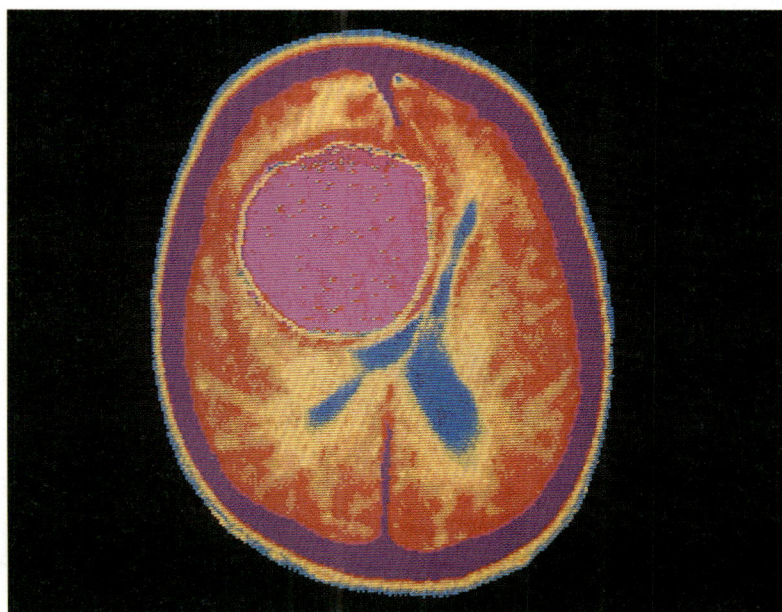

🔺 A CT scan of a slice of brain, showing a large tumour.

Summary

- Smooth surfaces reflect light in a regular way, so that rays of light keep the same pattern and they can produce clear images.
- Rough surfaces reflect light in an irregular or diffuse way, so that rays of light scatter in many directions.
- During reflection of a ray of light, the incoming angle is equal to the angle of reflection. The angles are measured between the rays and the normal.
- Curved mirrors can produce magnified or diminished images. Sometimes they produce upside-down images, and/or images which can be projected on to a screen.
- Refraction takes place when light passes from one substance or medium into another. It happens because the speed of the light changes and unless a ray is travelling along a normal the direction of the ray changes.
- Lenses are curved pieces of transparent material that can produce images which are magnified or diminished, sometimes upside-down, and sometimes able to be projected onto a screen.
- Total internal reflection happens when light hits a boundary with a less dense medium (such as when it is travelling in glass and reaches the boundary with air). Then, if the angle between the ray and the normal is above a 'critical size' the light cannot escape from the denser medium, but reflects back into it.
- Barriers reflect waves on water.
- Boundaries between deep and shallow water, where water waves change speed, refract the waves.
- It is because light behaves like waves on water (and other waves) that we believe that light travels in waves.
- Light waves, like water waves, have frequency, wavelength and amplitude.
- Visible light is made up of a small range of frequencies and wavelengths. Our eyes can detect the different frequencies and wavelengths to give us the sensation of colour.
- The light that we can see is just a small part of a very wide range of frequencies and wavelengths called the electromagnetic spectrum.
- Radio waves are at one end of the spectrum. They have the longest wavelengths and lowest frequency.
- X-rays and gamma-rays are at the other end of the spectrum. They have very short wavelengths and extremely high frequency.
- Microwaves of a certain frequency can be used for cooking. The microwaves must not escape from the oven, because they will 'cook' anything they meet, including people.
- Infra-red radiation has a warming effect, though over-exposure can cause burning.
- Ultra-violet radiation (UV) causes tanning as well as skin cancer.
- Radio waves and microwaves can travel for long distances through air and they are useful for communication.
- Infra-red radiation is useful for short-range communication.
- We use visible light to communicate whenever we use body language and signals, as well as in some optic fibre systems.
- X-rays and gamma rays can pass through human tissue, and so we can use them to produce shadow images of our bodies. They can also kill cancer cells.

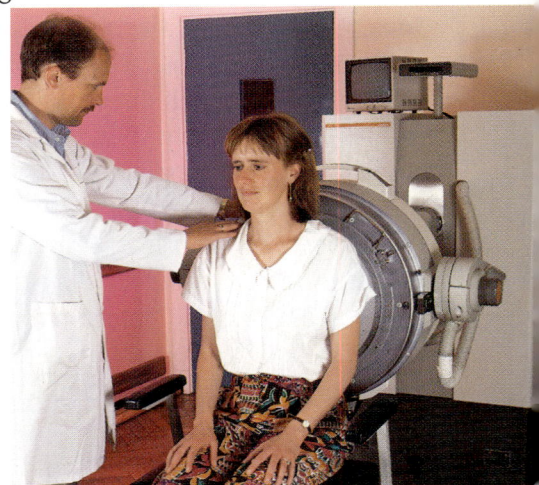

▲ This patient has drunk some radioactive material so that the 'gamma camera' can detect where it goes inside her body.

Revision Questions

1 If a caver's lamp stopped working would he still be able to see anything?
Explain your answer.

2 A single beam of white light shines into a triangular glass block (prism).
Use colours to draw a diagram of what you would see coming out of the prism.

3 a Copy the diagram and show how the 'ray' of light will be reflected in the mirror.

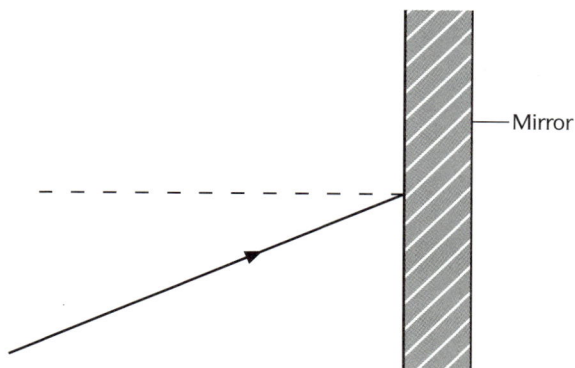
—Mirror

  b On your diagram mark the angle of the incoming light (i) and the angle of reflection (r).

4 You can see a good reflection of yourself in a mirror but not in a piece of paper. Copy the diagram and show why this is. Draw lines to represent rays of light.

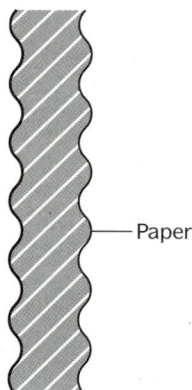
—Paper

5 The diagram shows the lamp on a bicycle. Copy and complete the diagram and explain why this shape of lamp gives a fairly narrow beam of light.

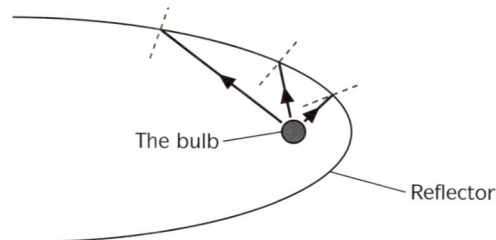
The bulb—
—Reflector

6 In hot weather, you sometimes see a mirage. A mirage is caused when light waves change direction as they pass from cool air to hot air.
  a What is the name given to the change in direction of the light?
  b Explain why the light changes in direction as it travels from hot air into cool air.

7 Microwaves, ultraviolet rays, radio waves, and infra-red rays are all parts of the electromagnetic spectrum.
Give one use for each of the rays mentioned.

8 Copy the sentences and fill in the gaps using words from the list below.

gamma rays   infra-red   microwaves   radio

  a The waves which have the longest wavelength are _____ .
  b The waves which have the highest frequency are _____ .

9 Copy the sentences and fill in the gaps using words from the list below.
gamma rays   infra-red   visible   microwaves   ultraviolet
  a Telecommunications and some ovens both use _____ .
  b A type of waves given off by an electric fire is _____ waves.
  c Our bodies make vitamin D when exposed to _____ waves.
  d Cancer can be treated using _____ .

10 The table shows the waves in the electromagnetic spectrum.

Radio		Micro-waves		Light		X-rays	Gamma rays

a Copy the table and fill in the gaps using words from the list below.

infra-red   sound   ultrasound   ultraviolet

b Electromagnetic waves are often used in medicine to find out what is wrong with a patient or to cure the patient.
Choose *three* electromagnetic waves and explain how they are used in medicine.

c Sometimes too much exposure to electromagnetic waves can cause medical problems. Choose *three* electromagnetic waves and explain how they can cause medical problems.

11 Microwaves, ultraviolet rays and radio waves are all part of the electromagnetic spectrum.
a List the waves mentioned in order of *increasing wavelength*.
b Give one use for each of the waves mentioned. In each case explain why the wave is suitable.

Different waves

■ Waves are everywhere

This trawler will locate shoals of fish by reflecting pulses of sound waves off the fish. The crew have a radio for communication and to listen to weather forecasts. They can locate where they are, using radio waves from navigation satellites. The radar on the mast will use different radio waves to keep track of where other ships are. And of course, the ship is surrounded by waves made by wind blowing across the sea. Waves are everywhere.

CHAPTER THREE

Review

Before going any further, read this page and attempt the tasks. Write the answers in your notes.

Sound is what we call a sensation – something we experience in our minds. There are many different kinds of sound sensation – loud and quiet, high pitch and low pitch, steady notes and sounds that change. Language, for example, is a pattern of sounds.

Sounds tell us about what is happening in our surroundings. They come from vibrating objects. In fact the kind of sound we hear depends on the kind of vibration. A bass drum is a large surface vibrating at low frequency. When it is hit gently the vibrations have low amplitude, and the sound is quiet. A powerful thump makes the drumskin vibrate with large amplitude. With a smaller drumskin, or if the drumskin is tightened, it vibrates more times per second. The higher frequency means that we hear a higher note.

The drumskin makes the air around it vibrate. Particles of air make each other vibrate, and so the vibration spreads out through the air. Vibration can travel through other materials. In fact it travels more easily through liquids than gases, and even more easily through solids. In a vacuum, there are no particles to vibrate and so sound cannot travel at all.

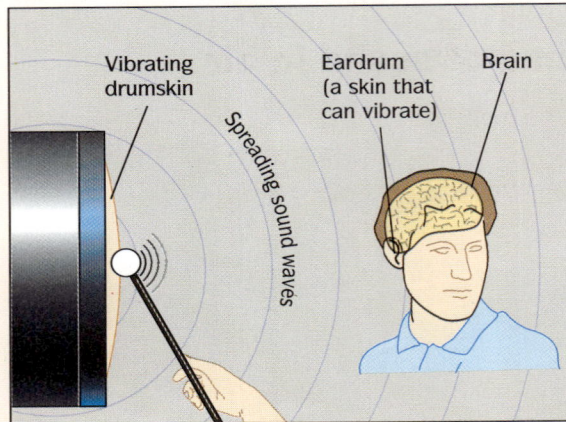

▲ The human ear can hear low-frequency sound (down to about 20 hertz) and high-frequency sound (up to about 20 000 hertz).

CHECK THREE

1 Copy the word puzzle into your notebook. Solve the clues and complete your grid.

Clues

1   the full name for the unit of frequency
2   a travelling vibration
3   all sound sources do it
4   sound won't travel through this
5   do this to set a guitar string vibrating
6   a lot of this makes a loud sound
7   if it is high, so is the pitch of the note
8   do this to set a drumskin vibrating

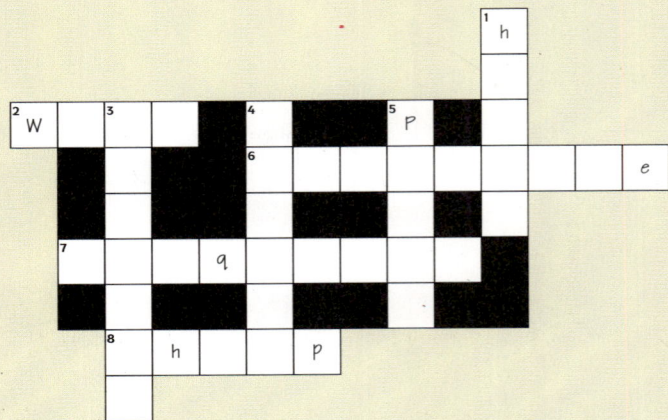

2 What is the lowest frequency that people can hear? What does it sound like?

3 What can you do to a drumskin to make it vibrate at higher frequency?

4 There is no air on the Moon. Write a list of different ways in which astronauts can communicate when they are standing on the Moon.

5 Why does sound become fainter as you move away from a source of sound such as a drum?

Reflecting sound waves

Light waves reflect off surfaces between materials. So do sound waves. A trawler's sonar system sends out short pulses of sound through a special loudspeaker or transducer.

The trawler's transducer turns an electrical signal into sound and sound back into electricity when the echo returns to the ship.

The sound travels at a speed of about 1500 m/s in water. That is nearly five times faster than sound travels in air.

The sound waves reflect off anything in their path. This could be the sea bed, or a wreck, a submarine or a shoal of fish. The sound pulse takes longer to get back to the ship if the obstacle is further away.

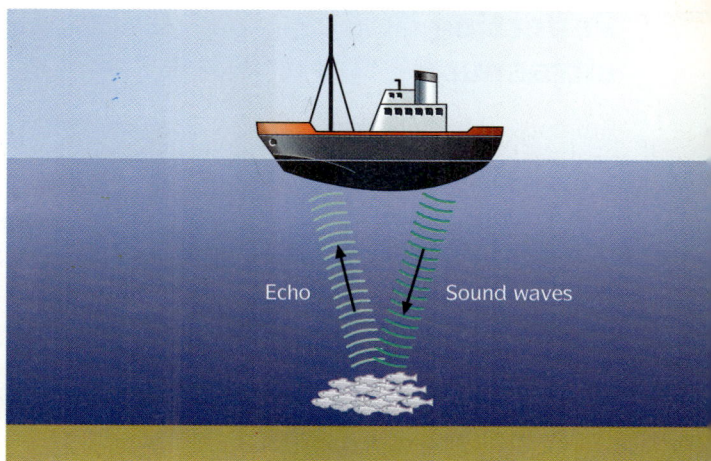

▲ Finding fish by sonar.

Echoes and the speed of sound in air

Shout at a mountainside and it sometimes shouts back. Or rather, the sound of your own voice returns to you. The mountainside reflects the waves. It takes a second or two for the sound to come back, because sound only travels at about 300 m/s in air.

The speed of sound

You can use reflected sound to get an estimate of its speed. You may be given a worksheet to help you with this activity.

Working out distance from time

You may read about measurements of speed, distance and time in Chapter Eight (Moving, falling and stretching). The formula that links the three quantities together is:

$$\text{speed} = \frac{\text{distance}}{\text{time}}$$

and speed is measured in metres per second, or m/s.

An alternative version of the same formula lets you work out the distance when you know speed and time:

$$\text{distance} = \text{speed} \times \text{time}$$

We know the speed of sound in water – it is about 1500 m/s. A sonar system first measures the time it takes for a pulse of sound to bounce back to a trawler. Sophisticated systems can use the times for pulses to come back from different places, to construct an image of the whole underwater scene. For example, if the time from sending a pulse of sound out from the ship until it returns is 0.2 s, then,

$$
\begin{aligned}
\text{total distance} &= \text{speed} \times \text{time} \\
&= 1500 \, \text{m/s} \times 0.2 \, \text{s} \\
&= 300 \, \text{m}
\end{aligned}
$$

The object is 150 m away (300 ÷ 2).

▲ Sound reflects well off mountainsides. You can hear good echoes.

▲ Measuring distance by sonar.

Reflecting ultrasound

Humans can only hear sounds with frequencies up to about 20 000 hertz, or Hz for short. Some other animals can hear much higher frequencies, but because we cannot hear them we give these sounds their own name – **ultrasound**. Sound, including ultrasound, travels quite well through human tissue. Reflected ultrasound waves give quite clear pictures of surfaces inside a human body. They are especially useful for making images of unborn babies. They are much better than X-rays, which can cause damage to a developing baby.

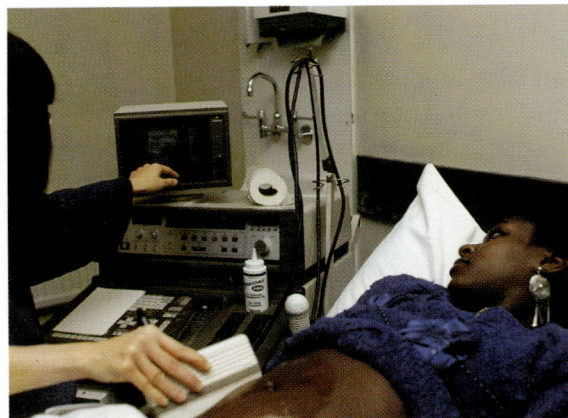

▲ An ultrasound 'scan' to produce an image of a baby.

For ultrasound scans, a special transducer vibrates to produce a burst of high-frequency sound waves. The same transducer picks up the vibrations of the reflected waves. The ultrasound has a frequency of about 1.5 megahertz and is reflected off different tissue layers inside the body. Ultrasound bounces back well where there is a big difference in density between neighbouring layers.

▸ *Were you ultrasound scanned before you were born? Try to find out.*

▸ *What is the short version for writing:*
- *hertz*
- *kilohertz*
- *megahertz?*

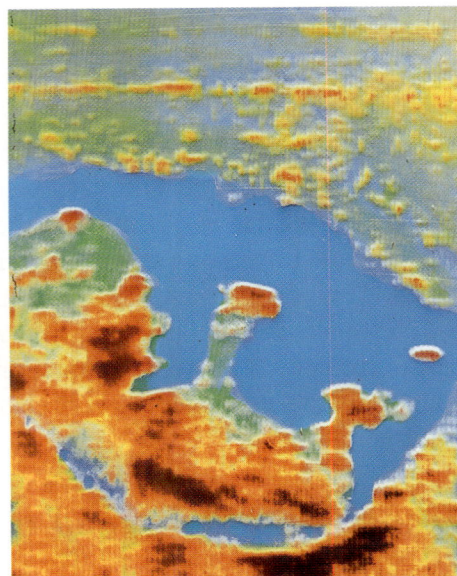

▲ A picture of a human fetus in the womb, made by reflected ultrasound.

1 megahertz = 1 million hertz
= 1 MHz

Ultrasound travels at about 1500 m/s in human tissue. This is almost the same as the speed of sound in water.

CLEANING WITH ULTRASOUND

Ultrasound is used to clean delicate items that could be damaged by rough treatment. The high-frequency sound loosens dirt. Jewellers clean necklaces and rings with tiny delicate stones, opticians clean glasses and contact lenses and electronics engineers clean circuit boards which have to be super-clean for use in micro-computers.

Bats and ultrasound

Bats can find their way on dark nights and even in the blackness of caves. People know where things are around them mostly by using light that objects reflect. But bats 'see' the world by reflected ultrasound, with frequencies roughly from 50 to 100 kilohertz. They make the sounds themselves, in short pulses. From the patterns of reflected sound they sense rocks, leaves and fluttering moths.

▸ *Why is ultrasound so called?*

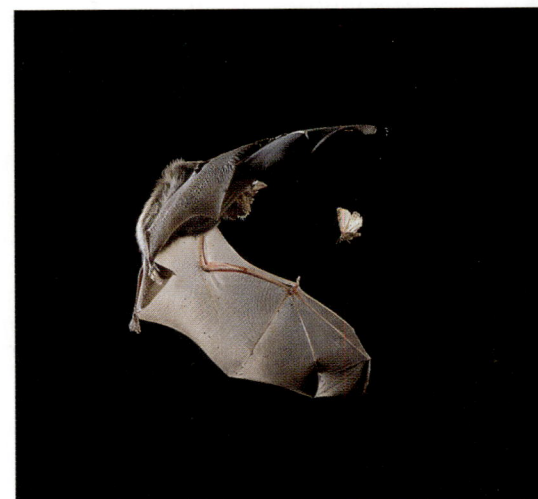

▲ A bat 'sees' the world in sound, not light.

1 kilohertz = 1 thousand hertz
= 1 kHz

Refraction of sound waves

In the airy world of humans, light travels long distances but sound quickly loses energy as it travels. Air absorbs the sound, and only the loudest of sounds can still be heard from a few hundred metres away. The watery world of whales is the other way around. The water quite quickly absorbs light, so that it is impossible to see many hundreds of metres. But sound travels much more quickly than it does in air, and it does not lose its energy so rapidly.

For most humans, sight is the most important sense. We have also developed the ability to use other kinds of electromagnetic radiation for communication. For whales, hearing comes first. Whales take advantage of water's ability to carry sound. They communicate across hundreds of kilometres of water with their complex songs.

Human eyes are very sophisticated. They focus the light to make sharp images on a layer of special sensing cells. Whales have sophisticated ways of focusing sound waves. Many species of whales have huge heads with shapes that seem strange to us. But their heads contain layers of tissue, and the pathways of sound waves bend as the waves travel from layer to layer. They bend for exactly the same reason as light pathways bend when they pass between the layers of the human eye. It is because they are changing speed. It is an example of refraction of waves. You can read about refraction of light waves and waves on the surface of the sea, in Chapter Two (A spectrum of light).

▶ *How does your brain know what is going on in the world around it? What is the most important way in which your brain gets information? Do you think that it is the same for whales?*

Refraction of sound in air

Sound travels more quickly in warm air than in cool air.

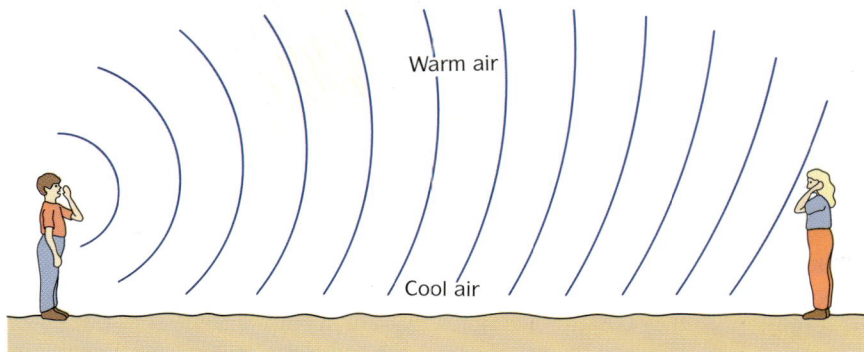

🔺 In water, sound travels further than light does. Whales have sophisticated hearing systems.

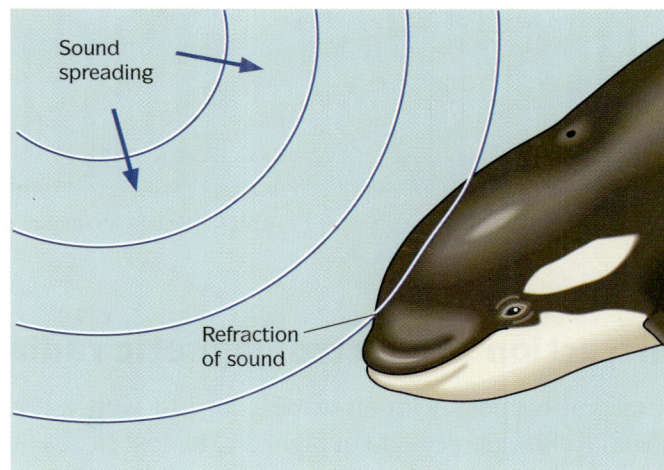

🔺 Refraction of sound waves in a whale's head. The waves change speed, wavelength and direction as they pass from the sea into the whale's head.

🔺 Sound travels at different speeds in cool and warm air. This distorts the shapes of spreading sound waves.

Diffraction – another kind of wave behaviour

All kinds of waves can reflect off surfaces and refract when their speed changes. Reflection and refraction are examples of wave behaviour. There is a third example, called **diffraction**.

When waves on water go past an obstacle they spread out into the space behind the obstacle, and become circular. This spreading out is diffraction.

Diffraction is most noticeable when the size of the obstacle is similar to the wavelength of the waves. Also, strong diffraction happens when waves pass through a gap which has a similar size to their wavelength.

▶ *Write down the names of three types of wave behaviour.*

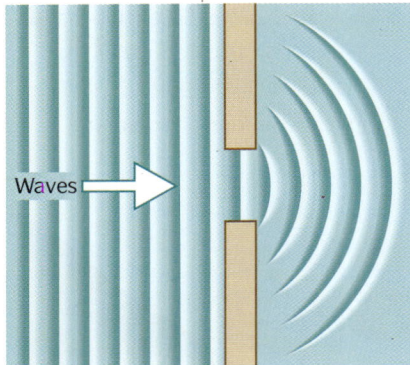

Diffraction through a gap.

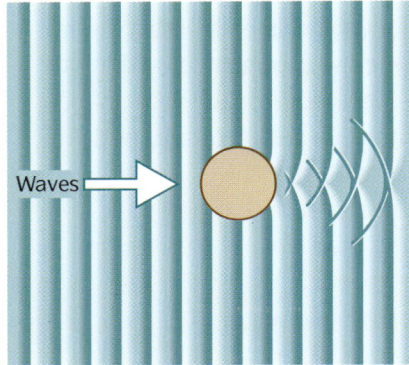

Diffraction around an obstacle.

Diffraction of electromagnetic radiation

Diffraction happens with all waves, not just with water. Look at a distant sodium (yellow) street light at night and almost close your eyes. The blurred pattern of light that you see is produced by light diffracting through the gaps in your eyelashes.

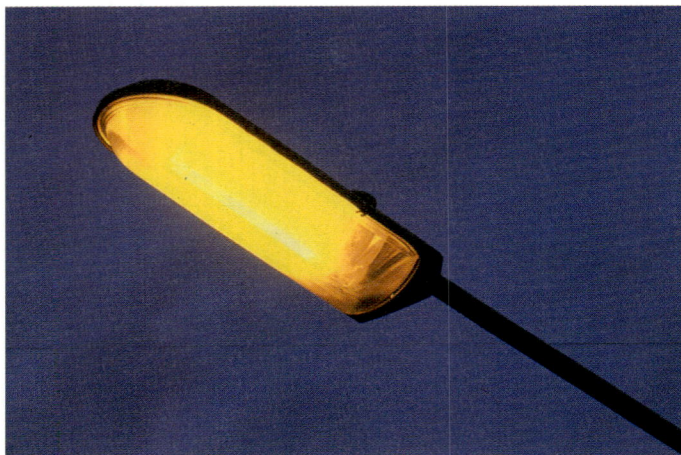

🔺 Visible light is electromagnetic radiation. You can see effects of diffraction with light of very pure colour (single wavelength, not a mixture) such as sodium street lights.

▶ *What do X-rays and visible light have in common?*

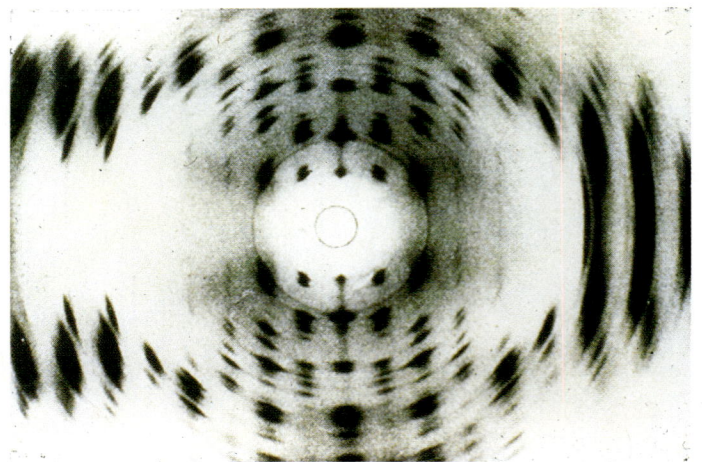

🔺 X-rays are electromagnetic radiation with very short wavelengths, and they make good diffraction patterns when they pass through gaps that are about the same size. Gaps between atoms are about the same size as X-ray wavelengths. X-ray diffraction is a way of finding out about the arrangements of atoms in different materials.

A SCIENTIFIC CONTROVERSY

In the 18th century, people argued about how light travels. Some said that it travels as a stream of particles, like tiny cannonballs. 'The pathways of cannonballs change when they hit water', they said, 'just like light bends when it goes into water or glass.' But the refraction of light is in the opposite direction to the deflection of cannonballs, so some people were not convinced. It was a scientific controversy.

Some scientists believed the particle theory, and some believed the wave theory. Some admitted that they weren't sure. The scientists knew about diffraction of water waves and sound waves, but they had never seen diffraction of light. The argument was settled when people discovered patterns of light when they shone pure colours through rows of tiny gaps. The patterns could only be caused by diffraction. The wave theory of light had won.

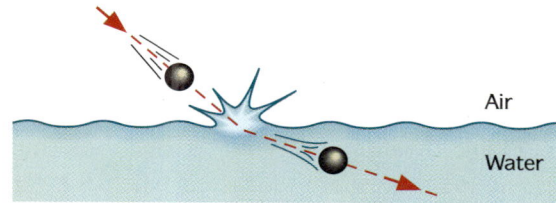

A cannonball changes direction as it passes from air to water

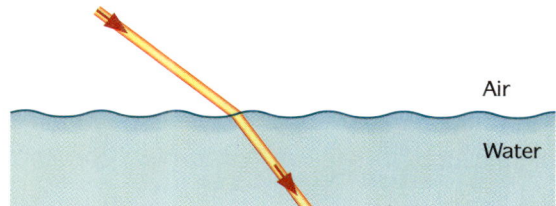

Light changes direction as it passes from air to water

Investigating diffraction

A pencil floating on water makes a good source of straight-line waves. The water needs to be well lit up so that it is easier to see the waves. Tapping the pencil regularly provides a steady series of waves.

A piece of card with a gap a centimetre or two wide, dipped into the water, will produce a diffraction pattern. It is possible to investigate the effect of using gaps of different size, and to make sketches of what happens in each case.

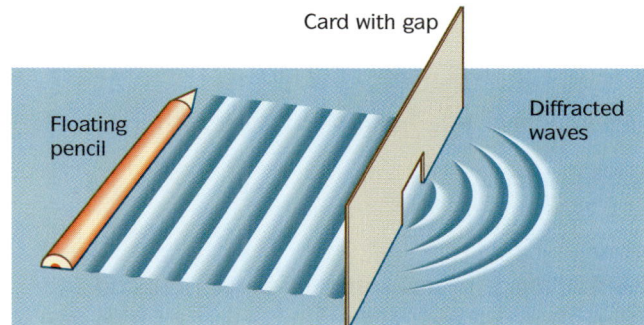

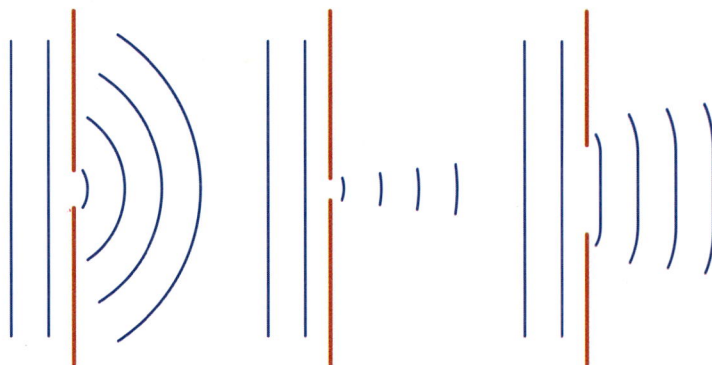

Diffraction is strongest when the width of the gap is about the same size as the wavelength.

Investigating diffraction patterns using gaps of different size.

Diffraction of sound

Sound travels by waves. So sound should also be diffracted when it travels through a gap of the right size.

A doorway is about 1 m wide, which is similar to the wavelengths of everyday sounds such as human voices. Sound waves are diffracted when they travel through gaps such as doorways. Diffraction makes it possible to hear around corners. You cannot see around corners because light waves have short wavelengths. With light waves you only notice diffraction effects with very small obstacles and gaps.

▶ *What would life be like if you could see around corners as well as you can hear around corners?*

🔺 Sound can spread out when it reaches corners.

Relating frequency and wavelength

The pattern of waves on the sea can look quite complicated. But a boat can bob up and down very steadily, and a windsurfer cutting through the waves will sense the regular patterns in the waves. In these regular patterns, the longer the waves, the less frequent they are.

For all waves, there is a connection, or relationship, between frequency, wavelength and the speed of the waves. The formula that describes the relationship is:

speed of wave = frequency × wavelength

In symbols the formula is:

$$v = f\lambda$$

longer waves, lower frequency

shorter waves, higher frequency

🔺 Long waves have low frequency. Short waves have higher frequency.

If the frequency is measured in hertz (Hz) and the wavelength in metres (m) then the speed of the wave will be in metres per second (m/s).

▶ *If you flick a rope at higher and higher frequency, what happens to the wavelength of the waves that travel along the rope?*

An example – water waves

Some water waves have a wavelength of 8 m and a frequency of 0.5 Hz (one wave every 2 s). So the speed of the waves is found using the formula:

speed of waves = frequency × wavelength

$$= 0.5 \text{ Hz} \times 8 \text{ m}$$

$$= 4 \text{ m/s}$$

The formula can be used for any sort of wave, not just for water waves.

▶ *A whistle produces a sound of frequency 2000 Hz and a wavelength of 0.165 m. How fast does the sound travel through the air?*

Hz = hertz

m = metres

m/s = metres per second

Electromagnetic waves

Light and all other kinds of electromagnetic radiation travel as waves, and they all travel at the same speed in a vacuum.

The frequency, wavelength and speed of electromagnetic waves are related together by the usual formula for all waves:

speed = frequency × wavelength

The speed of electromagnetic waves is often called the speed of light. It is very fast – 300 000 000 m/s. Because of this very big number most electromagnetic radiation has high frequency. For example, if you look at anything that looks yellow, then about 500 million million waves of light enter your eye every second. The frequency of the light is 500 million million hertz.

▶ *A sound wave with a 1 m wavelength has a much lower frequency than an electromagnetic wave with a 1 m wavelength. Why?*

Long wavelength comparatively low frequency — Short wavelength high frequency

🔺 The elctromagnetic spectrum – a range of frequencies and wavelengths.

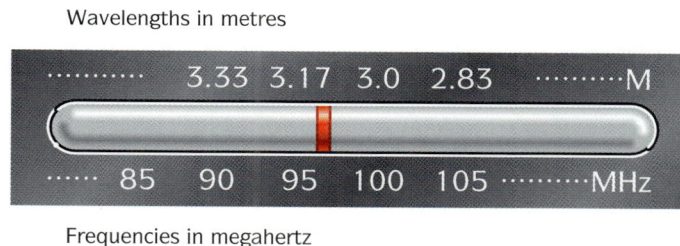

Wavelengths in metres

3.33 3.17 3.0 2.83 ·········M
85   90   95   100   105 ·········MHz

Frequencies in megahertz

🔺 Tuning a radio means choosing the frequency and wavelength that you want.

Radio waves

Every radio station sends out its signals using its own particular wavelength and its own particular frequency. A lot of radio stations use the numbers in their name, like Atlantic 252. The station's transmission frequency is 252 kilohertz, and its wavelength is about 1190 m.

Around the world there are thousands of radio stations. But for every single one, if you multiply wavelength by frequency you will always get the same answer, which is the speed of light. All the waves have this same speed, and they all obey the formula:

speed = frequency × wavelength

Frequencies and wavelengths

You have read how frequencies and wavelengths are related. You may be given a worksheet to help you discover that the same relationship works for all kinds of waves.

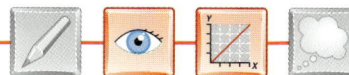

Moving energy

A wave can carry energy from one place to another without having to take any material with it. When sound crosses a room, no air moves from one side of the room to the other. When light travels from the Sun to the Earth, the material of the Sun stays where it is. Only the energy moves.

▶ *Think about a particle of water as a wave goes past. Where does the particle get energy from? Where does the energy go to?*

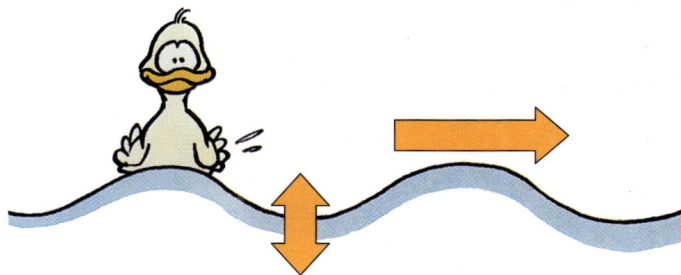

🔺 A wave can carry energy, but the material of the medium does not transfer along, it only vibrates. Particles of water move up and down. Energy passes from particle to particle.

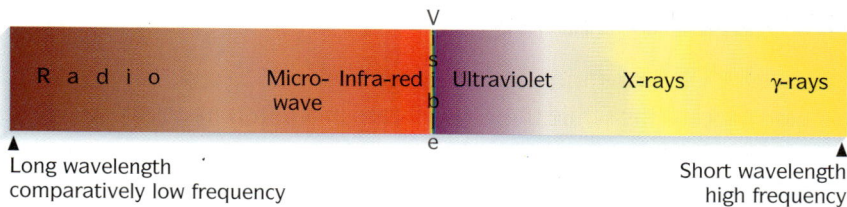

Two kinds of waves

A sideways flick on a spring sends energy from coil to coil. The energy transfers along the spring while the coils vibrate in a different direction. The angle between the two motions is 90°. A wave like this is a **transverse** wave.

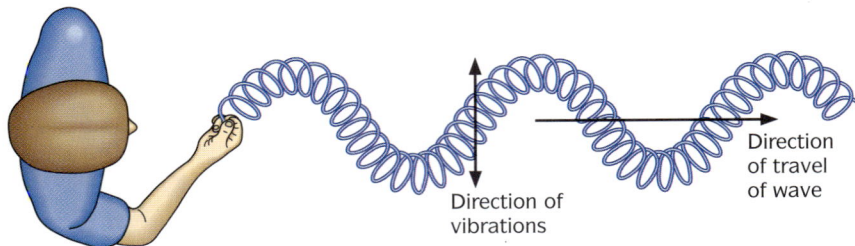

Direction of travel of wave

Direction of vibrations

🔺 A transverse wave.

A lengthways flick also sends energy down the length of the spring. This time, the coils vibrate along the same direction. The angle between the energy transfer and the coil vibration is 0°. It is called a **longitudinal** wave.

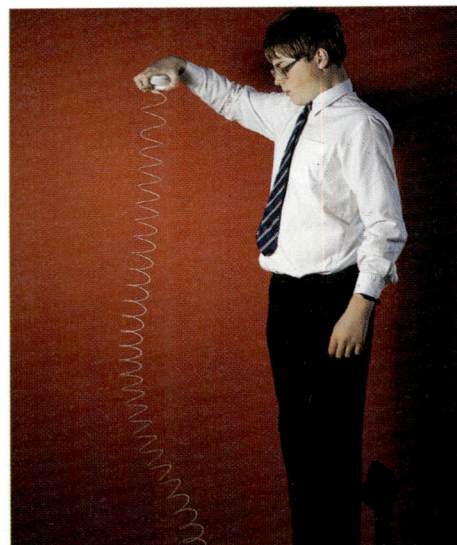

▶ *What is the difference between a transverse and a longitudinal wave?*

▶ *What sort of wave can you produce with a skipping rope?*

Direction of travel of wave

Direction of vibrations

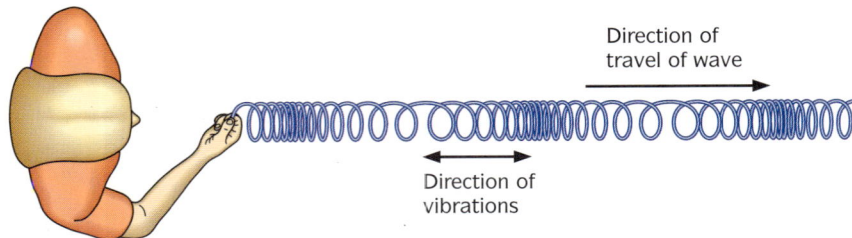

🔺 A longitudinal wave.

Waves through the Earth

Waves can be produced in any material that will carry them. If you tap a jelly, waves will travel through it as well as across its surface. Longitudinal and transverse waves are involved. Both kinds of wave are also involved in earthquakes. You can also read about the internal structure of the Earth in Chemistry, Chapter Seven.

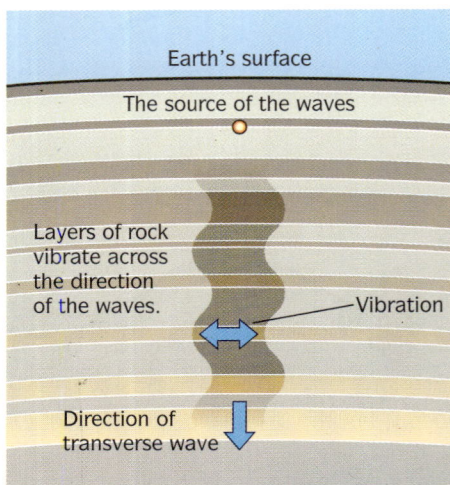

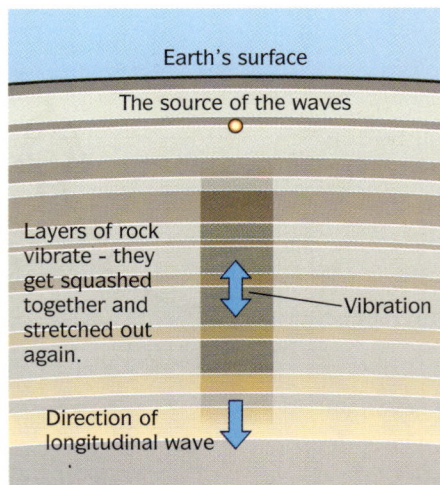

Earth's surface

The source of the waves

Layers of rock vibrate across the direction of the waves.

Vibration

Direction of transverse wave

Earth's surface

The source of the waves

Layers of rock vibrate - they get squashed together and stretched out again.

Vibration

Direction of longitudinal wave

🔺 A sideways flick produces one kind of wave.

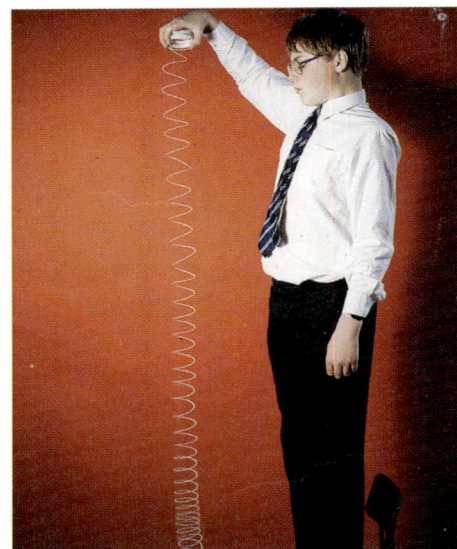

🔺 A lengthways flick produces another kind of wave.

🔺 When a jelly wobbles, waves travel across its surface and through the inside.

Seismic waves spread up through the Earth and shake the surface. The photograph shows the effect of an earthquake on the city of Kobe in Japan in 1995.

When an earthquake happens, rocks suddenly move and crack deep in the Earth. The place where this happens is called the epicentre. The rocks shudder, and vibrations spread outwards from the epicentre. The spreading vibrations are called **seismic waves**. Some seismic waves are transverse, and some are longitudinal.

▶ *How could you make*
a *a longitudinal wave,*
b *a transverse wave*
travel through a jelly?

Seismograms

Waves from earthquakes spread out and reach seismic research stations all around the world.

At the seismic research stations, sensitive instruments can pick up small vibrations. The instruments make records of the vibrations, called **seismograms**.

Some waves travel more quickly than others, and the faster waves reach the research stations first. So seismograms show vibrations that seem to go on for some time. The faster and slower waves produce separate bursts of vibration on a seismogram.

There seem to be three main types of wave with three different speeds. They have different speeds because they travel through or across the Earth in different ways. They are called **P waves**, **S waves** and **Love waves**.

▶ *Why do waves from an earthquake arrive at a seismic research station at different times?*

A scientist at a seismic research station studying waves that have arrived from a distant earthquake.

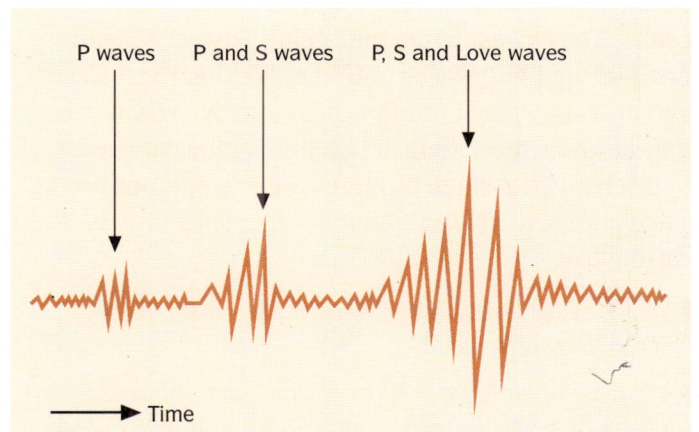

An example of a seismogram.

More about seismic waves

P waves are the first to be recorded and travel at about one and a half times the speed of S waves. They are longitudinal waves and are able to travel through the interior of the Earth, through both solids and liquids. S waves are transverse waves and can only travel through solids as they move through the interior of the Earth.

Love waves have the slowest speed and are the last to be recorded. They are also transverse waves, and they travel across the Earth's surface. They have large amplitude. In an earthquake, it is usually the Love waves which do the most damage.

Each year there are about a million earthquakes. Many are so small that nobody feels them and they are only picked up by seismometers. Most earthquakes last for less than one minute but the effects can be devastating. The worst record for earthquake deaths occurred in China in 1556 when 830 000 people were killed.

▶ *Which kind of waves are better at travelling through liquids, longitudinal waves or transverse waves?*

Using graphs to locate epicentres

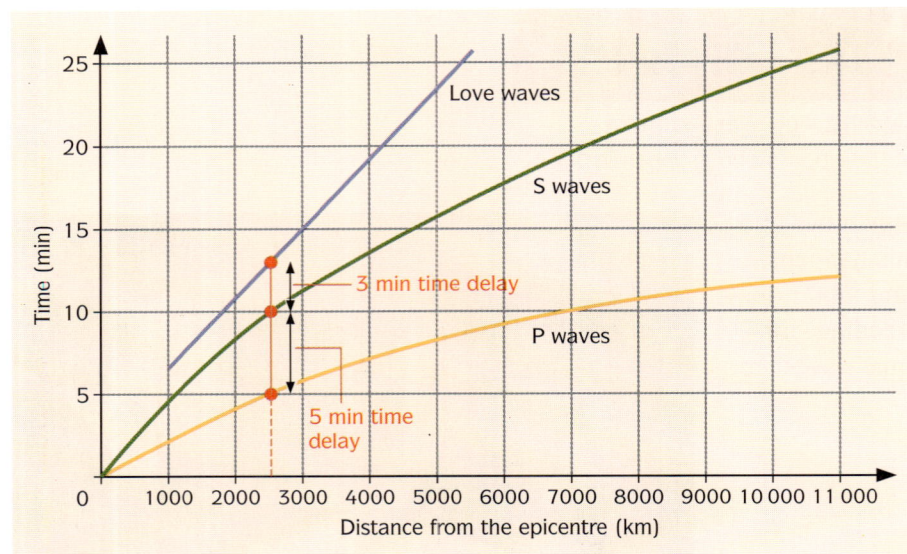

🔺 Travel-time curves for Love, P and S waves. At a station 2500 km away from the epicentre the S waves arrive 5 minuites after the P waves. The Love waves are another 3 minutes later.

Graphs can show how long it takes for the P waves, S waves and Love waves to travel different distances. Scientists use these curves to locate an earthquake epicentre. They measure the time delay between when they first pick up the P waves until they pick up the S waves, and also the delay until they pick up Love waves. Then they see how these time delays fit with the curves.

If scientists at three or more research stations do the calculations, they can pinpoint the epicentre of the earthquake.

▶ *Which waves will always appear first at seismic recording stations?*

▶ *What is the difference in time of arrival of P and S waves at a seismic recording station 5000 km away from the earthquake epicentre?*

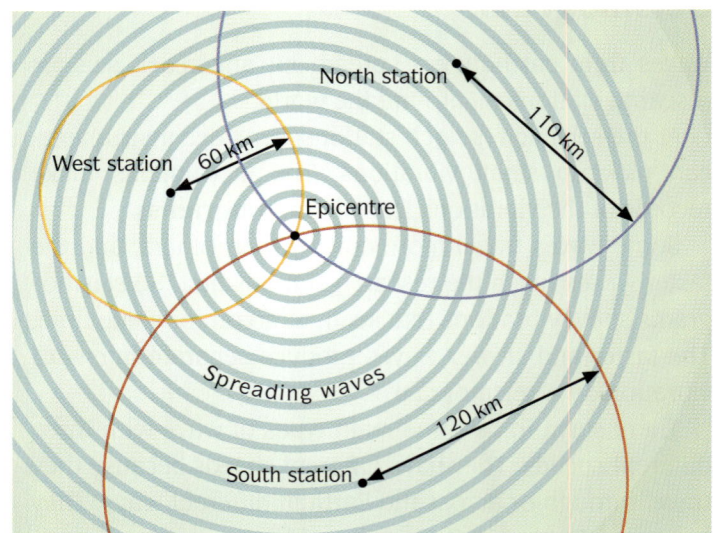

🔺 Scientists at three stations all know how far away they are from the epicentre. If they combine their information they can pinpoint the epicentre.

Reflection and refraction of P and S waves

P waves from an earthquake can be detected all around the world. But S waves don't reach the opposite side of the Earth. There is a large 'shadow'. It seems that there is a barrier to the S waves deep in the Earth.

S waves are transverse waves. They can travel through solids but not through liquids. The S wave shadow is evidence that there is a layer of liquid in the core of the Earth. This layer is called the outer core.

P waves are longitudinal, and they can travel through liquids and solids.

The velocities of the P waves and S waves within the Earth change as the waves pass through different layers. The changing velocities curve the paths of the waves. It is an example of refraction of waves. The refraction is a gradual process where the wave speed is only changing gradually. But where P waves move into the liquid outer core they slow down very suddenly, and their paths are sharply bent. Rays (pathways) of light are sharply bent in the same way when they pass from air to glass or water.

▶ *Why don't seismic waves travel in straight lines?*

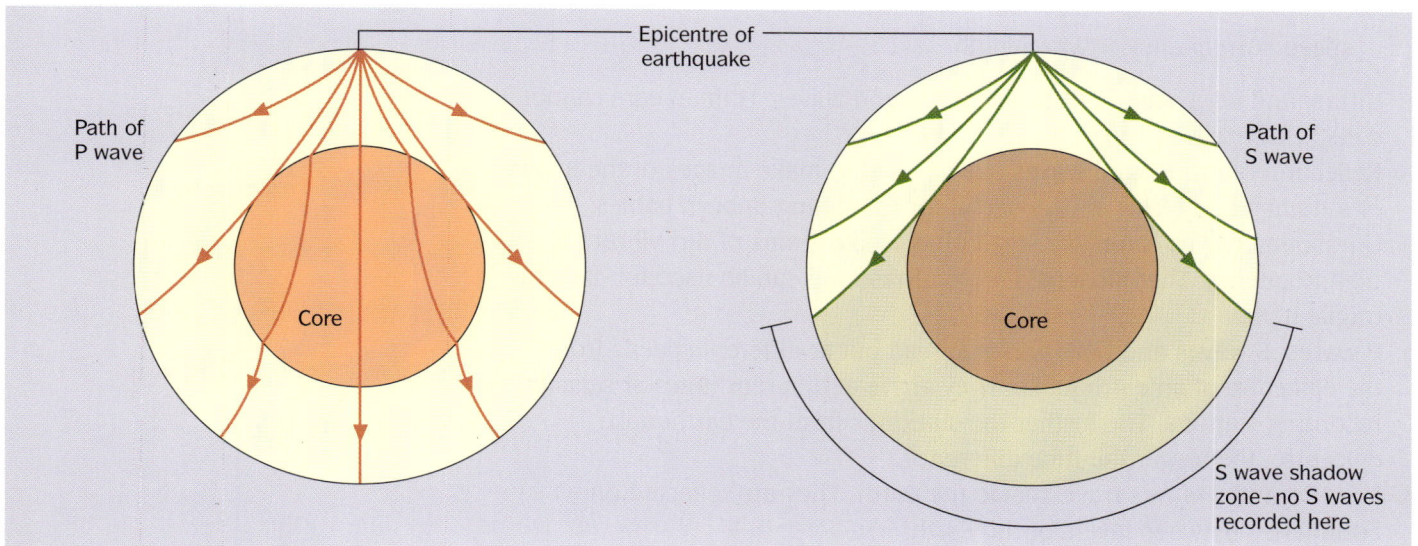

△ Wave pathways in the Earth.

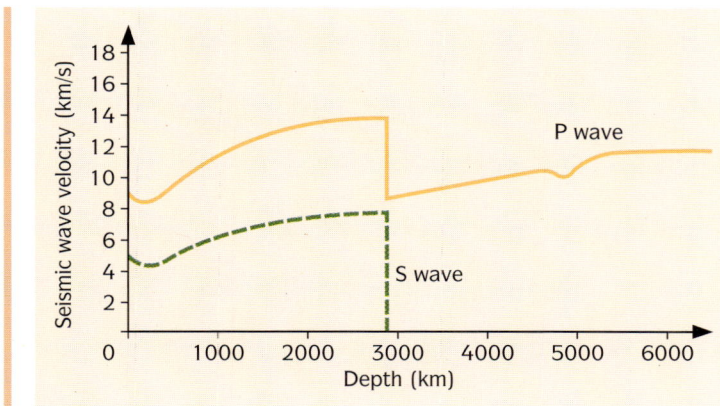

△ The graph shows the speeds of P waves and S waves at different depths in the Earth. The waves generally travel faster where the Earth is denser.

Summary

- Sound waves can be reflected from objects in their path.
- Sound waves can be refracted when their speed changes.
- Diffraction is the spreading out of waves after passing an obstacle or passing through a gap.
- All kinds of waves can be diffracted.
- Waves transfer energy without transferring any material.
- In transverse waves, the direction of transfer of energy is at 90° to the direction of vibrations.
- In longitudinal waves the direction of transfer of energy is parallel to the direction of vibrations.
- Transverse waves travel quite easily along ropes.
- Springs can carry either transverse or longitudinal waves.
- Water surface waves are transverse waves.
- Sound waves are longitudinal waves.
- Speed, frequency and wavelength of waves are related by the formula:

  speed = frequency × wavelength

- Ultrasound waves are high-frequency sound waves. Human ears cannot detect these waves.
- Reflection of ultrasound waves can be used to make images of the inside of a human body. This is very useful for examining unborn babies.
- Ultrasound waves can make small objects like grains of dirt vibrate at high frequency. That loosens dirt, so ultrasound can be used for cleaning fragile items.
- P waves, S waves and Love waves spread out at different speeds from the epicentre of an earthquake. They arrive at different times at seismic recording stations. The further the station is from the earthquake epicentre, the bigger the time difference.
- P waves and S waves travel inside the Earth. They are reflected off boundaries between layers of the Earth.
- Changes in speed of the waves inside the Earth causes them to be refracted.
- Study of P waves and S waves provides scientists with information about the layers of the Earth.

Revision Questions

1 Match each word with its description. Write the answer in your notes.

   reflection   *refraction*   *diffraction*

   - the spreading out of a wave when it goes through a narrow opening.
   - when a wave bounces back from a surface.
   - when light changes direction at the boundary between two substances.

2 Why are ultrasound scans better than X-rays for examining unborn babies?

3 How does the head of a whale do a similar job to the job done by a human eye?

4 Radio Blabla has a frequency of 90 megahertz. Radio Active has a frequency of 100 megahertz.
   a Write down the short version of megahertz.
   b How many hertz are there in 1 megahertz?
   c Which radio station has the longest wavelength?
   d What is the speed of the waves for both stations?

5 Which of these waves are transverse and which are longitudinal?
   - water surface wave
   - light wave
   - sound wave in air
   - seismic P wave
   - seismic S wave
   - seismic Love wave

6 Sound waves travel faster in water than in air.
   a There is an explosion just above the surface of the sea. Explain what happens to the sound waves as they travel from air into water.
   b A whale and a flying bird are 1 km from the explosion. Which one hears it first?

7 Why do ultrasound scans show sharp boundaries between bone and soft tissue?

8 Which is bigger, 100 megahertz or 1000 kilohertz?

9 Why can you see diffraction effects when you look at street lights through your eyelashes, but not when you look through your spread-out fingers?

10 How did the discovery of diffraction of light settle an old argument?

11

Copy this picture of some water waves. Complete your drawing by adding what will happen to the waves when they go through the two gaps.

12 Explain how X-rays are useful for comparing the structures of atoms in different materials.

13 Ultrasound waves of frequency 1.5 megahertz travelling in a human body have a wavelength of about 1 mm (which is 0.001 m). What is the approximate speed of the waves?

14 Make a table to show all of the different properties of P waves, S waves and Love waves.

15 What do S waves tell us about the Earth's inner regions?

16 In an experiment to measure the frequency and wavelength of sound, the following table of results was obtained.

Frequency (Hz)	100	500	1000	1500	2000
Wavelength (m)	3.40	0.67	0.35	0.23	0.18

   a Plot a graph from these results.
   b What would the wavelength be at 800 hertz?
   c What would the frequency be when the wavelength is 0.2 m?

17 a Victor, who has a heart condition, is in hospital for a check-up. The doctors are using ultrasound to find out whether his heart valves are leaking. Why would ultrasound be safer than using X-rays? How would doctors see what Victor's heart valves were doing?
   b Give one other medical use of ultrasound and one non-medical use.
   In each case say why ultrasound is used.

18 What size of obstacle will produce strong diffraction patterns with 1.5 megahertz ultrasound waves travelling in human tissue?

19 If a sound with a frequency of 2000 hertz travels through water at a speed of 1445 m/s, what is its wavelength?

20 Light moving down an optic fibre has a wavelength of 1 μm (0.000 001 m) and a frequency of 2×10^{14} Hz (200 000 000 000 000 hertz). How fast is the wave moving?

21 Study the graph on page 40, which shows the time vs distance relationships for different types of seismic wave. What will be the time differences between the three types of wave when they reach seismic detectors 5000 km from an earthquake epicentre?

22 Study the graph on page 41, which shows the variation of seismic wave velocities with depth in the Earth.
   a Describe in detail how the velocity of P waves changes with depth.
   b Why does the S wave velocity suddenly drop to 0 km/s at a depth of 2900 km?
   c What can you say about the matter in the Earth's core?

Earth & space

■ Looking both ways

Looking inwards

We can take pictures of the Earth from aircraft a few kilometres high, where the atmosphere is less dense than it is on the ground. Satellites can orbit the Earth, and take photos from above the thin layer of air. These photos help us to study the Earth's surface. A few people have even been way beyond our atmosphere, as far as the Moon. They have seen our planet from the outside, shining in the reflected light of the Sun.

Looking outwards

Other planets, such as Mars and Venus, would take years for people to reach. Only unmanned spacecraft have gone so far. Nobody from Earth has ever seen the Sun and its planets, the Solar System, from the outside. Perhaps they never will. All we can do is look outwards at these distant objects, and the stars beyond, from the neighbourhood of the Earth.

Most of us live flat lives, on the surface of the Earth. We can only imagine what the Earth looks like from space. But some people have been out there, and they have seen for themselves.

Review

Before going any further, read this page and attempt the tasks. Write the answers in your notes.

▲ The Galaxy or Milky Way – 100 billion stars spinning together.

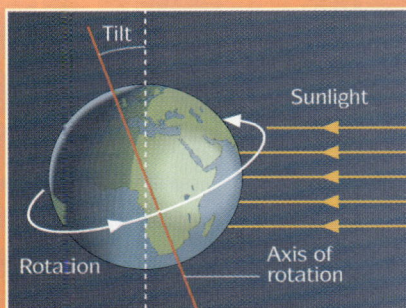

▲ The rotation, axis and tilt of the Earth.

Motion upon motion

Objects in space are all in motion, relative to each other. Galaxies of stars are moving apart. And the Sun is one star in a huge Galaxy which is spinning. We spin along with the rest of our Galaxy. We travel like passengers with the Sun, trapped by the pull of its gravity.

The Earth orbits the Sun with incredible regularity – one year for each orbit. For half of this time, the northern half of the Earth is tipped a little to face the Sun. For the other six months it is the turn of the southern half of the Earth. This gives us the yearly changes of the seasons. But that is not the only regular change that we experience. Every month, the Moon seems to change shape from a thin crescent to a full round ball and back again. The shape we see depends upon how much of the sunlit surface of the Moon is facing in our direction.

Perhaps the most important changes of all are the steady repetitions of night and day. The Earth has quite a rapid spin, turning once around every 24 hours. When we face the Sun we have the benefit of its light, and when we face out to the edge of the Solar System and beyond we have darkness.

Imagine your motion – spinning each day with the Earth, circling the Sun every year, turning once around with the Galaxy every 200 million years.

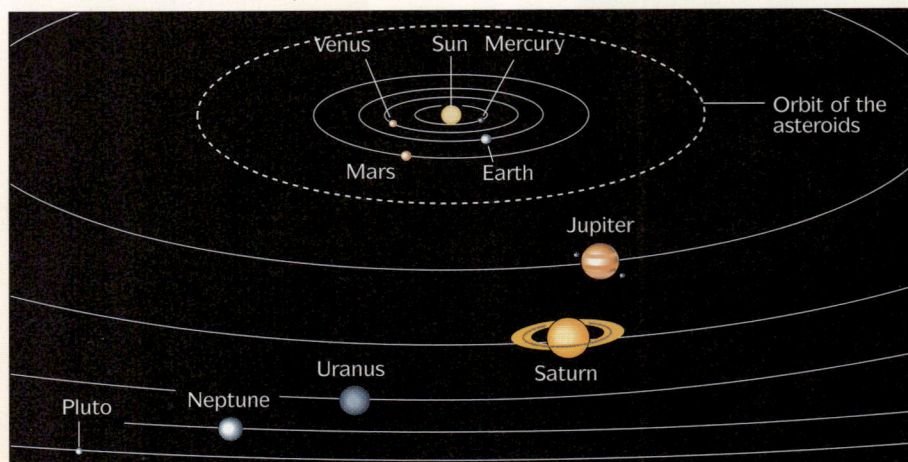

▲ The Solar System.

CHECK FOUR

1. Draw a simple circle sketch of the Earth. Shade one side to show night time. Show which side is facing the Sun.

2. How long does the Earth take for one spin around its own axis?

3. Which two planets are closer than the Earth to the Sun?

4. Gravitational force acts between your body and the Earth. What evidence is there to support this statement?

5. Gravitational force acts between the Earth and the Sun. What evidence is there to support this statement?

6. Name two objects in space which are only visible to us because they reflect the bright light of the Sun.

7. Which objects emit their own light, so that we can see them even though they are vast distances away?

The scale of the atmosphere

The first person to break free of the Earth's layer of air was Yuri Gagarin, a Russian. That was in 1961. But first the Russians sent animals, like Laika the dog. That solved the tricky problem of how to get safely back to Earth. In the case of Laika she was left to die up in space. We would not think of doing the same thing today, but people's attitude to animals was different in those days.

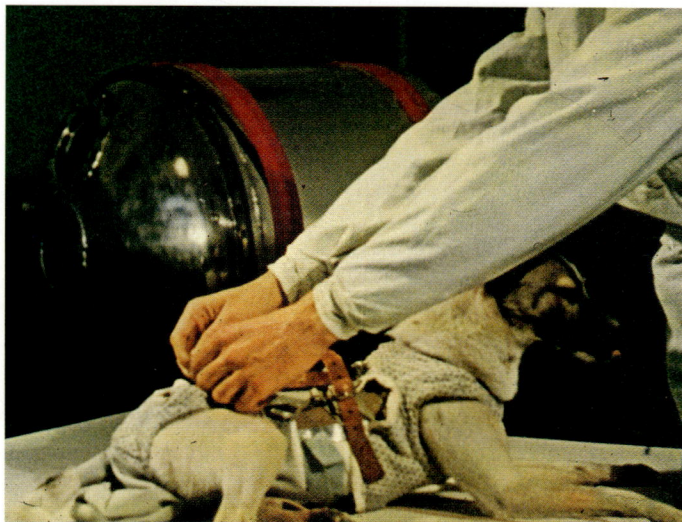
🔺 Laika the dog, ready for her one-way journey into space.

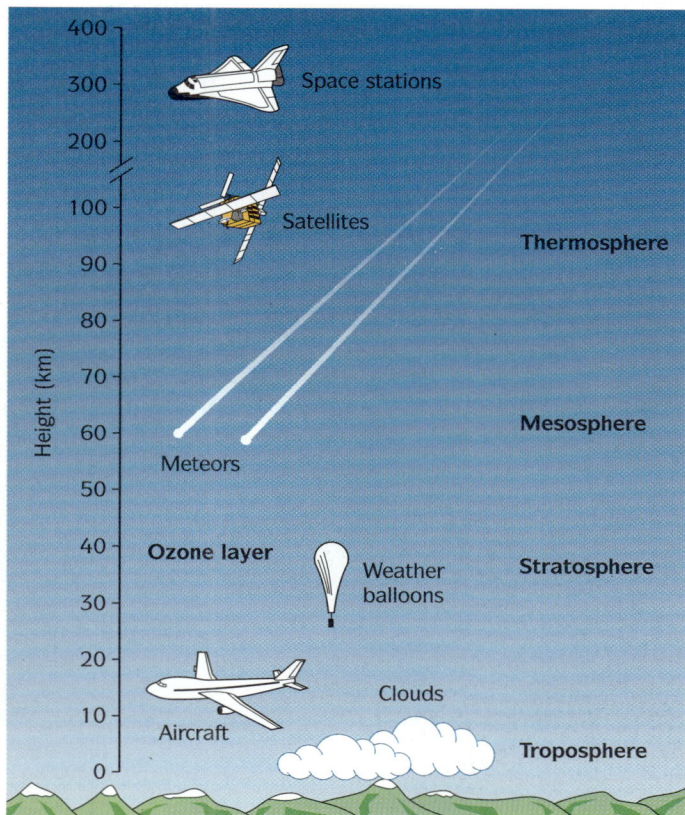
🔺 The distance from the Earth to the top of this diagram is about one thousandth of the distance from the Earth to the Moon.

Neither Laika nor Yuri Gagarin went very far outside the atmosphere. Even now, the space shuttle and space stations are only about 300 km above the Earth. Some people travel that far to go backwards and forwards to work every day. The difference is that they travel along the surface. It's a big difference.

The atmosphere is densest near the Earth's surface. But on high mountains, the density of air is so low that there is not enough to supply oxygen quickly to our bodies, and people easily get out of breath.

▶ *Why do athletes sometimes train at high altitude (up mountains)?*

Protection from the hazards of space

The atmosphere provides us with air to breathe. But it also protects us from harmful radiation, such as the ultraviolet radiation from the Sun. It is the layer of ozone in the stratosphere that is particularly good at absorbing these dangerous rays. So astronauts who go outside their space stations need to be well protected. Their suits must shield them from ultraviolet radiation, X-rays and the low-density stream of tiny particles from the Sun and from distant stars. And in the vacuum of space not only would they have no air to breathe but the pressure of their own bodies would blow them apart – a quick but messy end. Space is a hostile place, yet we live our lives just a few kilometres away from it.

▶ *Your body is pushing out strongly on your skin. Why does an unprotected astronaut blow apart, but you don't? What design feature of an astronaut's suit prevents this?*

Satellite images of the Earth

Satellites orbit the Earth at heights of 100 km or more. From those heights they can get pictures of huge areas of the ground. Then they transmit the pictures back to people on Earth by encoded radio waves. You can read about radio waves in Chapter Two (A spectrum of light).

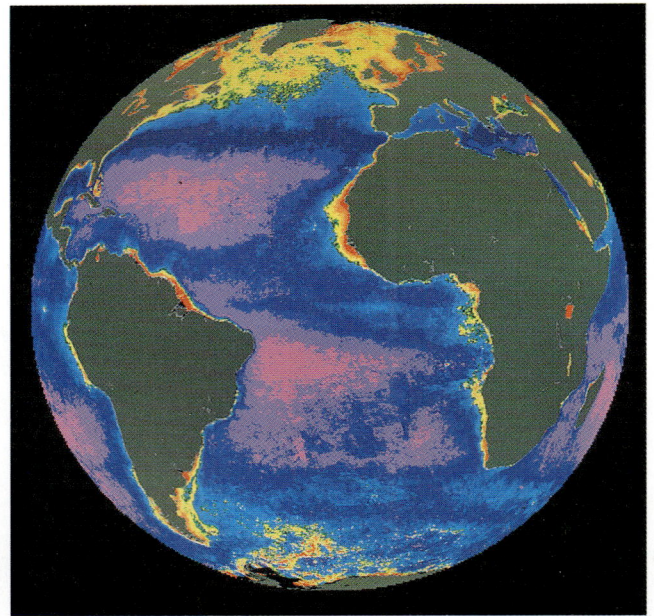

🔺 A satellite image of the distribution of phyto-plankton in the sea.

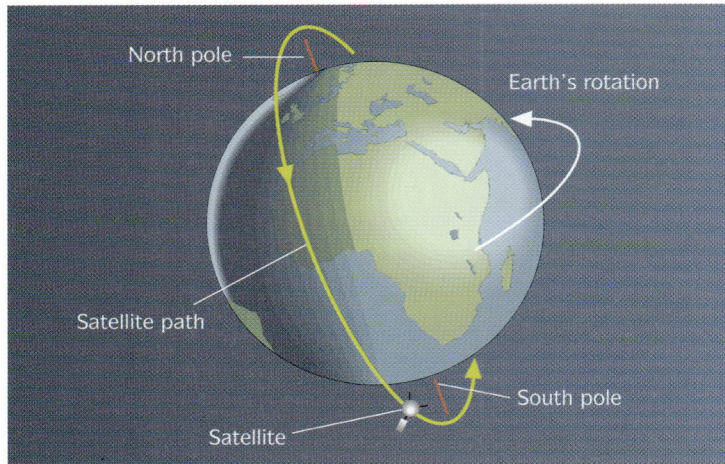

🔺 **Polar orbit** – a weather satellite moves in circles while the Earth spins beneath it. That way it can photograph different slices of the Earth's surface.

Satellites for studying distant objects

Satellites can be used to do more than just photograph the Earth. Cameras can be turned outwards into space. Some radiation from space – X-rays, and a lot of infra-red and ultraviolet – cannot penetrate our atmosphere. So scientists can't use instruments on the ground to detect that radiation. They can find out much more about stars and other objects in space by sending instruments above the atmosphere.

▶ *Visible light from stars reaches the Earth's surface. What does that tell you about the effect of the atmosphere on visible light?*

Satellites for communication

Satellite television uses radio waves, beamed up from a station on Earth, and bounced back down to receivers on houses across a wide area. The receivers point in a certain direction because the satellite is always in the same direction. The satellite is in orbit above the Earth, moving in a circle, but its rotation exactly matches the speed of rotation of the Earth.

▶ *What would happen to a satellite which made one orbit above the equator every 12 hours?*

🔺 TV journalists sending a message from a war zone via satellite.

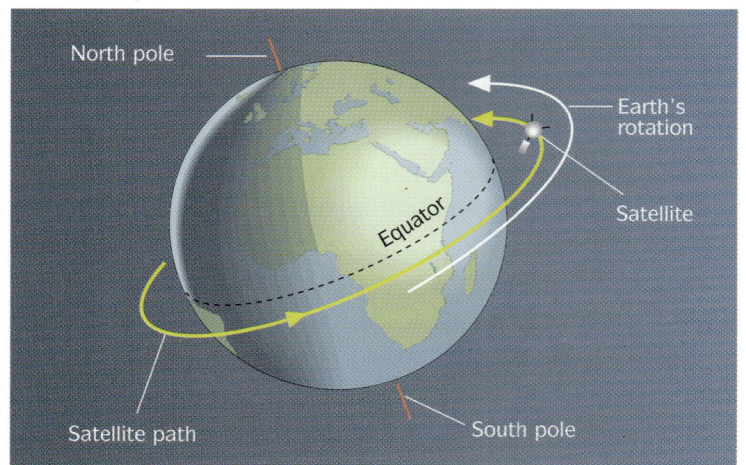

🔺 **Geosynchronous orbit** – the satellite makes one orbit every 24 hours, so it is always above the same point on the Earth's equator.

PHYSICS

Motion of satellites in orbit

At 300 km above the surface, the force of gravity acting on a satellite is almost as strong as it would be at ground level. A satellite in orbit around the Earth still feels the pull of the Earth's gravity. In fact, without the pull the satellite would not stay in orbit. It would travel in a straight line off into space.

It sometimes seems odd that a satellite can feel the pull of the Earth without ever tumbling to the ground. The satellite stays in orbit because it is going fast *horizontally*. The Earth's gravity pulls it but cannot make it stop. The satellite flies on, always turning towards the Earth but never crashing into it. Only if the satellite slows down will it start to lose height.

▶ *What would happen to a satellite that stopped?*

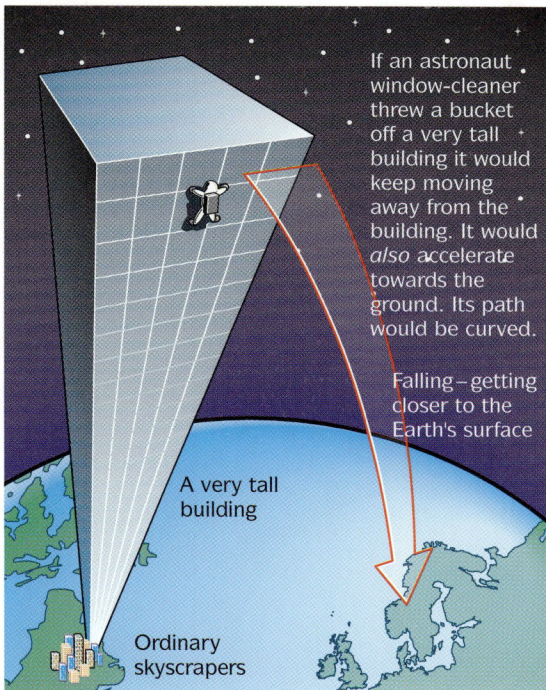

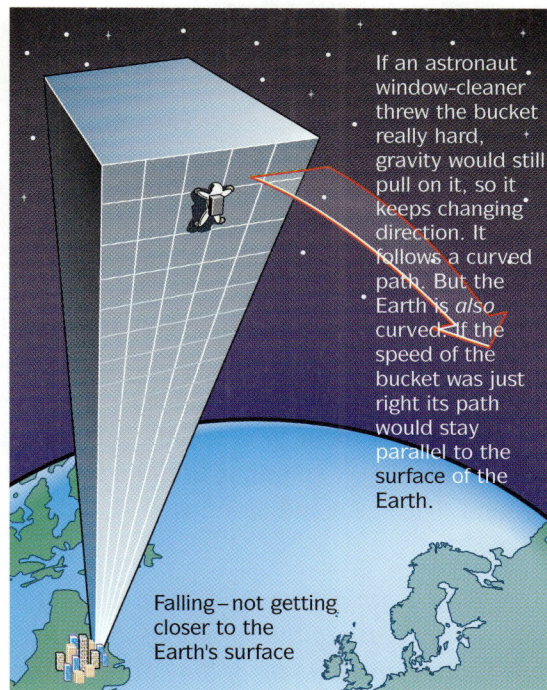

The planet Jupiter has 16 moons, one of which is Io. The moons are like prisoners trapped by gravity, just as the planets are trapped by the pull of the Sun. Io is about the same size as our own Moon, and its distance from the centre of Jupiter is about the same as the distance from the Earth to the Moon. But Io takes less than two Earth days for its orbit. It has a huge speed – more than 15 km/s relative to the surface of Jupiter.

If an astronaut window-cleaner threw a bucket off a very tall building it would keep moving away from the building. It would *also* accelerate towards the ground. Its path would be curved.

Falling – getting closer to the Earth's surface

A very tall building

Ordinary skyscrapers

If an astronaut window-cleaner threw the bucket really hard, gravity would still pull on it, so it keeps changing direction. It follows a curved path. But the Earth is *also* curved. If the speed of the bucket was just right its path would stay parallel to the surface of the Earth.

Falling – not getting closer to the Earth's surface

🔺 Understanding orbit.

Model orbits

You may be given a worksheet to explore the principles of orbit.

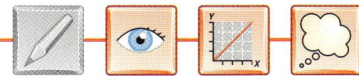

The Earth and the Moon

The Moon is the Earth's closest neighbour. Like the Earth it is a ball of rock. But it is not big enough to have a strong enough gravitational pull to hold on to any gas – it has no atmosphere. An astronaut standing on the moon is exposed to the dangers of vacuum and radiation.

It is a long time since the first human landed on the Moon. The race to the Moon cost a lot of money, but there has never been much reason to go back.

PHYSICS

▲ The Moon – a ball of rock which holds precious metals beneath its surface.

The Moon has no air and no life, only rock. The rock is like some of the rock on Earth, and it contains metals like iron and gold and titanium. But the cost of mining these in the hostile conditions of the Moon's airless surface would not be worthwhile.

The Earth and the Moon are large objects, so the force of gravity between them is strong even though they are 400 000 km apart. Yet they never get closer together. To think about this, picture two metal balls, one big and one small. Imagine that somebody joins them by a length of string, and then twirls them into the air. They could stay spinning, and the string could stay taut, until they hit the ground. The Earth and Moon are like these balls, with gravity acting as the string.

▶ *In very round figures, the Earth's atmosphere is 100 km thick. If the distance from the surface of the Earth to the surface of the Moon is exactly 400 000 km, how far is it from the top of the Earth's atmosphere to the Moon?*

The ultimate ride

You may have noticed that stars seem to change in the sky. You will certainly have noticed that the positions of the Sun and the Moon seem to change. You may be given a worksheet to help you to understand why.

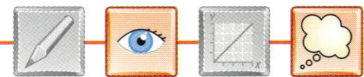

Space missions to another planet

You can see Venus from Earth. It looks like a bright star, though it does not shine with its own light. We see it because it reflects the strong light of the Sun, just as the Earth and Moon do.

Venus is the planet closest to our own. When the paths of Earth and Venus bring them to their closest points, they are just 41.5 million km away. At a

The surface of Venus.

speed of 1 km/s you could cover that distance in just over a year. It is little wonder that Venus is not much more than a speck in the sky.

Machinery built by humans has been to Venus. Automatic space probes have descended through its atmosphere to send back information about the planet. The space probes did not last for very long once they got close to the planet. It is not a very nice place. The atmosphere contains a lot of carbon dioxide. That creates a strong greenhouse effect and makes Venus very hot. There is also a lot of sulphuric acid in the 'air', and the atmospheric pressure is 90 times stronger than at the Earth's surface.

People used to wonder if Venus could be a new home for people. They dreamed of new colonies, that could provide a base for life if anything goes wrong here on Earth. But the space probes showed that there is no chance of that. Earth is all we've got.

▶ *What effects does carbon dioxide in the atmosphere have on the planet Earth?*

Spacecraft in the Solar System

The spacecraft Voyager 2 was launched a long time ago – in 1977. It went past Jupiter in 1979, Saturn in 1981, Uranus in 1986, and Neptune in 1989. Like Voyager 1, it took photos of the planets and their moons. Both of these space probes have now gone beyond Pluto, the furthest planet. Eventually they will go beyond the reach of the Sun's gravitational pull.

The Voyager probes gave close-up pictures of the rings of Saturn. The rings are made of boulders and smaller fragments of rock, like the shattered remains of a moon.

Planet data

Study the table and complete the tasks below.

Planet	Average distance from the sun, in millions of km	Surface temperature, in °C	Time to spin once, in Earth days	Density, in kg/m³	Time for one orbit, in Earth years
Mecury	58	−85 to −30	59	5600	0.24
Venus	108	350 to 475	243	5200	0.62
Earth	150	−80 to 50	1.0	5500	1.0
Mars	228	−180 to 420	1.0	3950	1.9
Jupiter	778	−150	0.4	1300	12
Saturn	1430	−200 to −150	0.4	700	30
Uranus	2870	−220	0.4	1200	84
Neptune	4500	−220	0.7	1700	165
Pluto	5900	−250	6.3	2000	248

▶ *Name a planet with oxygen in its atmosphere.*

▶ *Which is the hottest planet?*

▶ *Why do we talk about 'Earth days' and not just 'days' when dealing with planets other than Earth?*

▶ *Make a bar chart of the densities of the planets. Use the chart to divide the planets into two categories.*

▶ *Plot a graph of distance from the Sun (x-axis) against time for one orbit (y-axis). What conclusion can you make from your graph?*

The temperatures of the planets

Space is cold, but the Sun is very hot. Planets, including the Earth, would be cold if it were not for the Sun. They reach steady temperatures when they receive energy as quickly as they lose it. Planets which are furthest from the Sun receive energy slowly. They do not become hot.

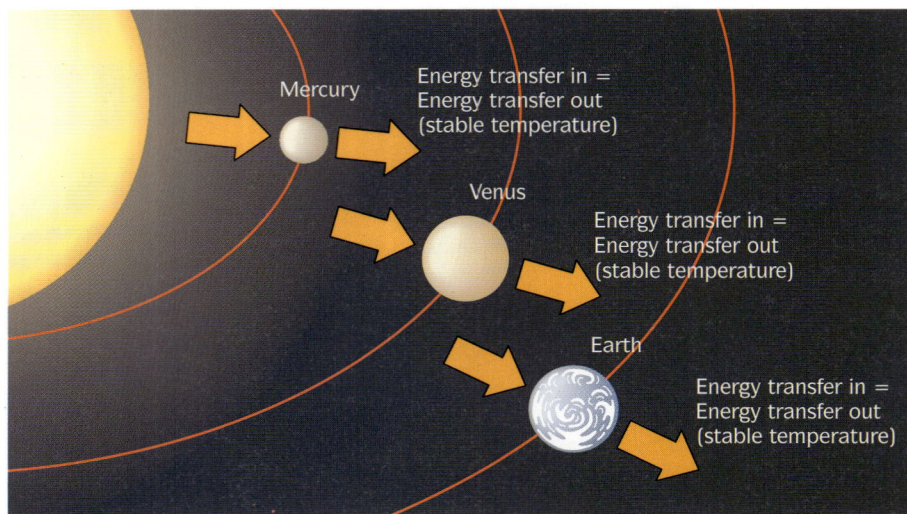

Mercury

Energy transfer in =
Energy transfer out
(stable temperature)

Venus

Energy transfer in =
Energy transfer out
(stable temperature)

Earth

Energy transfer in =
Energy transfer out
(stable temperature)

🔺 Energy flows for Mercury, Earth and Venus.

Modelling how the Sun warms the planets

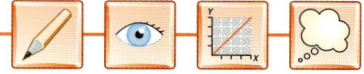

It is not always possible to make all the measurements that we would like. But it is possible to use *models* to learn something, if not everything, about a real situation.

We can use an electric lamp as a model Sun and test tubes of water as model planets, warmed by the Sun. That provides useful understanding of the way in which different planets reach their fairly steady temperatures.

The test tube 'planets' should be at different distances from the 'Sun'. Their temperature can be measured, say every minute. Eventually they stop heating up. That happens when the rate at which they receive energy from the 'Sun' equals the rate at which energy transfers away from them.

A graph of temperature against time for the different 'planets' will show what happens. The planets closest to the Sun are at higher temperatures.

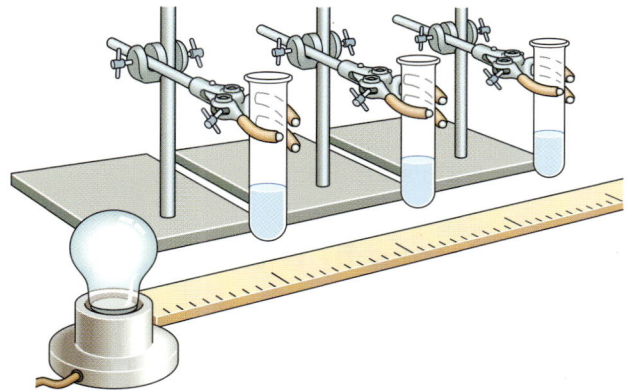

The paths of comets

Comets are small icy bodies that are trapped by the Sun's gravity, just as the planets are. But comets have orbits that take them out to the furthest planets and beyond. They also come in much closer to the Sun. They gain speed on their way in, under the influence of the Sun's gravitational pull. Then they swing around the Sun and fly back out towards the darkness.

▶ *Why do comets speed up as they get closer to the Sun?*

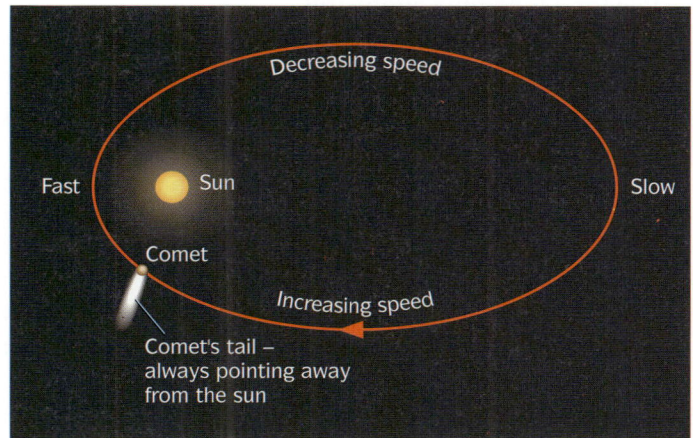

A comet in orbit.

Meteors and asteroids

Collisions of tiny grains of stone with our atmosphere happen every day. At night, if you look carefully, you sometimes see a fast streak of light. People call them **shooting stars**, or **meteors**. They hit our air at such high speed that the collisions with molecules are so hard that the meteors reach enormous temperatures and glow very brightly. They evaporate – their molecules mix with the air molecules – and only the very biggest ones ever hit the ground. There is a crater in Arizona where there was one such a collision.

▶ *Why are there a lot of craters on the Moon but not many on Earth?*

Meteors are probably left over from the early days of the solar system. Perhaps two planets collided, or a planet began to form but was pulled to pieces by the strong gravitational force of nearby Jupiter. Whatever happened,

The Arizona Crater – made by a meteor collison.

to this day there is a band of dust and rocks of different sizes between the orbits of Mars and Jupiter. The band is called the **asteroid belt**.

Some of the rocks, or asteroids, are as big as small moons. The biggest ones have names, like Ceres, which is about 1000 km across. Asteroids, large and small, do not all stay within a neat belt of space. They have elliptical orbits, and at some times they are much closer to the Sun than at other times. Sometimes they pass through the path of the Earth. That is the source of all the dust and small stones that hit the top of the atmosphere, and occasionally hit the Earth's surface.

Major collisions in the Solar System

You can look at the planet Jupiter through a powerful telescope and see detail of its surface. Back in 1994 many astronomers watched a spectacular event. They saw a comet crash into Jupiter. The strong gravity of Jupiter pulled the comet into fragments, and when they hit the planet they must have created huge shockwaves. The disturbances created scars which were visible for a long time afterwards.

If the same thing ever happened on Earth nobody knows what the damage would be. Scientists' favourite theory for the extinction of the dinosaurs is that it was caused by a collision of the Earth with a comet or asteroid.

Skywatchers have spotted a comet that will pass quite close to the Earth in the 22nd century. Its exact path is hard to predict, but it will probably pass within a few million km, and there is an outside chance of a collision. Space is not a very safe place to live!

▶ *It is possible to predict the motion of objects in the Solar System. Where will the Earth be, relative to the Sun, exactly a year from now?*

Revolutionary ideas

Learning something new can be hard. But unlearning something old can be harder still. Very often, getting rid of an old idea from your head, and replacing it with a new one, is the real challenge. You are used to the old idea. You feel comfortable with it. Up to now, it has made sense. But sometimes you have to 'change your mind'.

Changing your mind is most difficult of all when people you trust all seem to believe in the same old idea.

The centre of the Universe – early ideas

In the 1500s, everybody in Europe believed that the Earth was the centre of all of the Universe. They believed that the Moon, the Sun, the planets and the stars all went around the Earth. It was an idea that seemed to fit the facts. The Sun moves across the sky every day, for example. It always rises at one side of the sky, and goes down at the other. That is exactly what it would do if it went once around our planet every 24 hours.

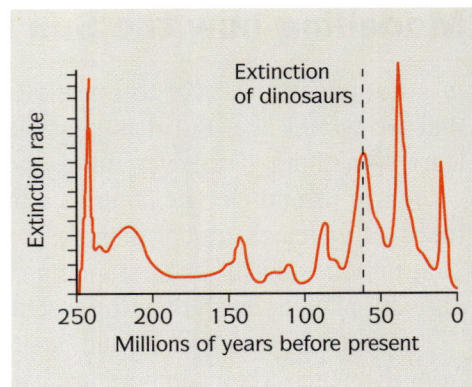
▲ A space collision may have caused the extinction of the dinosaurs, 64 million years ago.

In 1937, an asteroid called Hermes passed less than 800 000 km from Earth. That sounds like a long way away, but compared to the distances between most objects in space, it was a close shave.

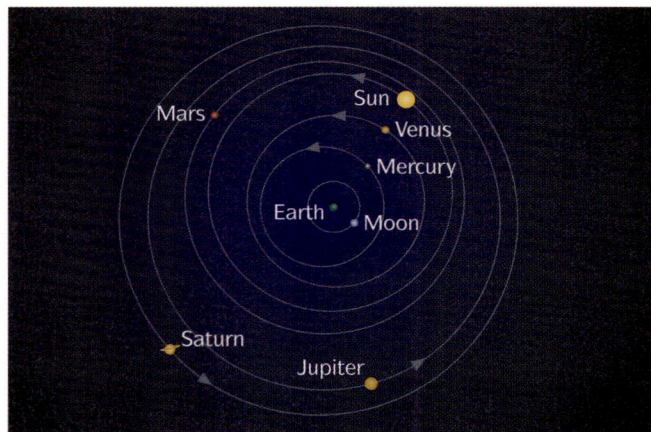
▲ The Geocentric Universe, with the Earth at its centre – an old idea.

An alternative explanation

Then some people came up with a different way of explaining things. They said that the motion of the Sun across the sky could be explained by the spin of the Earth. It was just as if you stand in one place and turn round and round – everything you see moves across your vision once for every turn that you make.

The people who came up with these alternative ideas about revolutions of the Earth and other objects were regarded as too clever by half. The first one to write that the Sun might be at the centre of the Earth's motion, not the other way round, was Nikolai Koppernick (also known as Copernicus). He was so scared at the thought of challenging ideas that were centuries old that he did not dare publish his ideas until he was dying.

A philosopher monk called Giordano Bruno publicly said that there might be some truth in Koppernick's 'revolutionary' ideas. Priests and politicians in Italy, where Bruno lived, did not like someone upsetting their old ideas. Bruno was burned to death.

Evidence from telescopes

Later, another Italian, Galileo Galilei, used a newfangled device called a telescope to show that the Moon was not a perfect sphere but had mountains. He also showed that there were objects in the sky which do not go around the Earth but go around Jupiter – it was Galileo who discovered the moons of Jupiter. He thought that these observations supported the new idea more than they supported the old one. He said so, and got locked up for his trouble. But within a few years people made more observations of the motions of the planets. The idea that they were all in orbit around the Sun and not around the Earth fitted the facts much more simply.

Older generations hung onto their ideas of the Earth at the centre. Many could not get the idea out of their heads – they could not change their minds. Newer generations accepted the new notion – that the Sun, not the Earth, is at the centre of the Solar System. That idea is the one we still have today.

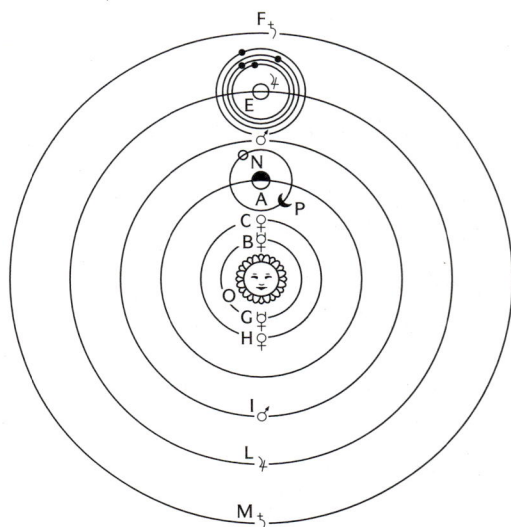

Galileo – once regarded as a dangerous revolutionary.

Galileo's picture of the Solar System, showing the orbit of planets and their moons. It was Galileo who discovered the moons of Jupiter.

▶ *How did the discovery of the moons of Jupiter show that not every object in space goes around the Earth?*

▶ *Think of a time when you have changed your mind about an idea. How easy was it?*

Problems of interstellar travel

A fast human being can run 10 m in 1 s. A fast spacecraft can travel 10 km in 1 s. At that speed it can make it to the Moon in just over 11 hours, and to the Sun in about 23 weeks. To get to the nearest star other than the Sun would take about 30 thousand years. It seems impossible.

Yet science fiction stories are full of ideas about visits to far-away star systems, or of 'extra-terrestrials' who come to Earth. The writers of the stories make up their own new 'technology' to deal with the distances. But they are just stories. They are not real.

The reality is that space is bigger than we can ever imagine. Unless there are some 'revolutionary' new ideas, there is little hope of people reaching other star systems.

▶ *If you could travel at 10 km/s, how long would it take you to get from home to school?*

▶ *Think of another science fiction story about space travel. What ideas did the story writer use to make it possible for the characters to travel between stars and their planets?*

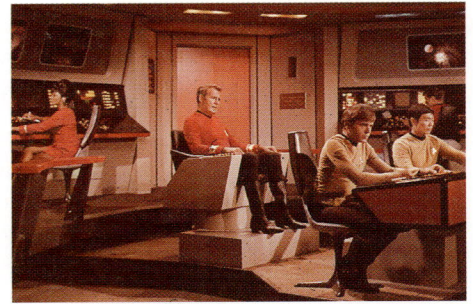

🔺 The Star Trek stories are classics of television and film science fiction. 'Warp factor' is the story writer's idea for getting over the problem of travel in the enormous distances of space.

Constellations and distances

If you are lucky, you might get away to a beach, or to camp in a field, far away from the glare of city lights. Then you might get the chance to lie under the stars and look at the night-time sky. It takes your breath away.

There might be a planet like Venus or Mars, just a little bit brighter than the stars. There will be the Pole Star, always in the north. There will be other patterns made by the scattering of stars – a saucepan shape, a W, or a bright little cluster of stars.

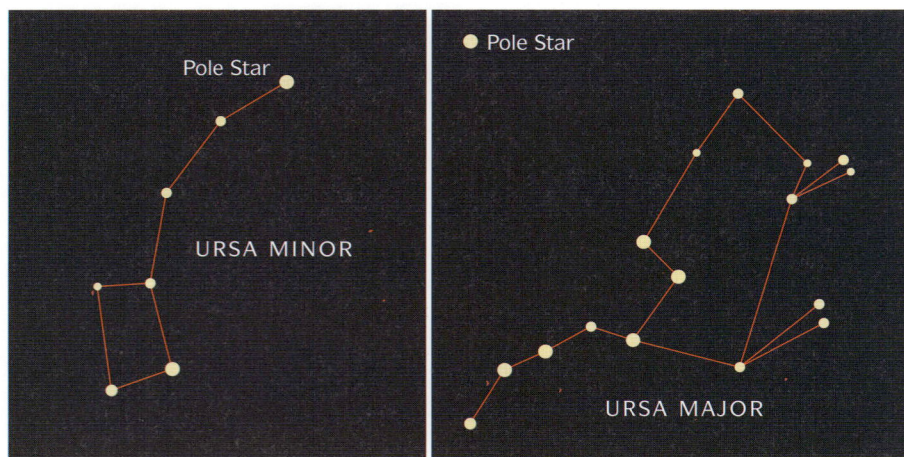

🔺 Patterns of stars have ancient names.

People have wondered at the stars for thousands of years. They have made up stories about the patterns – about warriors, bears and goddesses. Ten thousand years ago, people saw the same star patterns as we see now. The patterns are called **constellations**.

But stars in the same constellation are not necessarily close together. The Sun is so far from the next nearest star that it takes 4 years for light to travel the distance. We say that the star is 4 light years away. A light year is a unit for measuring very big distances.

If you look at two stars in the sky they may seem close together from where you are. But if you went close to one star then the other one could still be several light years away.

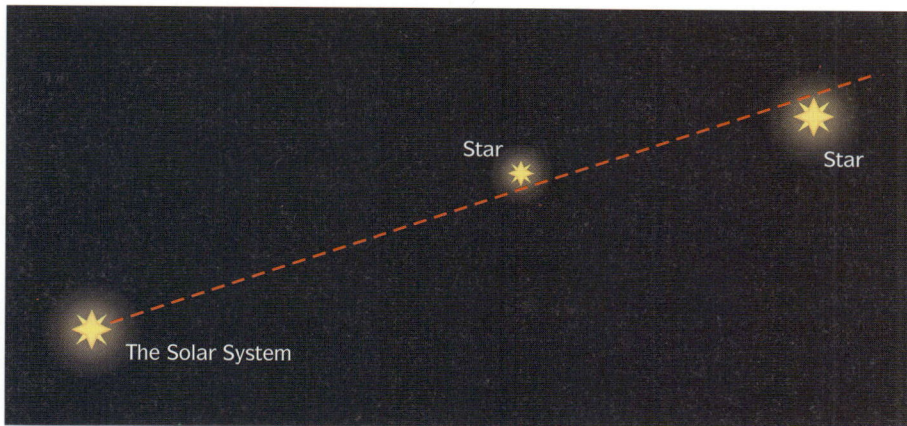

Stars that seem close together can really be a long way apart.

▶ *It takes light 190 years to travel to the Solar system from the star called Betelgeuse. How far away is it?*

Galaxies

Without telescopes we can only see a thousand or so stars. But on a really clear night we can see a faint band of light going all the way across the sky. People called it the **Milky Way**. Telescopes show that it is packed with distant stars. It goes all around us, though it is brighter on one side than on the other. It seems that we live in a galaxy, a spinning disc of about 100 billion stars. It is often still called the Milky Way, but some people also call it the *Galaxy*.

Telescopes help us to see other galaxies. They are all enormous collections of stars – often billions of stars in each one – and they are a very long way from us. We can only see distant galaxies because the stars together make a very bright object. Some of them are balls of stars, and many are spinning discs. The nearest galaxy to us is *Andromeda*. The light we see from Andromeda took 2.2 million years to reach us. When that light began its journey there were no people on Earth.

▶ *Why is it impossible for us to see all of the stars in the Milky Way?*

The Galaxy is big. Light that we see from the far side began its journey to the Solar System 100 000 years ago.

A spinning spiral galaxy, far away in space.

PHYSICS

Summary

- The Earth is one planet in orbit around the Sun.
- The Moon is much closer to us than are the planets and the Sun.
- The Moon is the only natural object which is in orbit around the Earth.
- People have launched many artificial satellites into space.
- Artificial satellites can be used for studying the Earth's surface and atmosphere, for studying space from outside the atmosphere, for communications, and for war.
- The Sun is a star.
- The Earth, other planets, moons, asteroids and comets are trapped by gravity in orbit around the Sun.
- Gravitational attraction combines with high speed motion to produce stable orbits.
- The Sun is much closer than other stars to us.
- The Sun is one star in the Milky Way.
- The Milky Way is one galaxy, but there are many others.

Revision Questions

1 The tops of the world's highest mountains are about 8 km above sea level. Why do mountaineers often carry oxygen tanks when they climb these mountains?

2 Do you think that satellites make the world a better place or a worse place? Explain your answer.

3 Why will it never be possible to live on Venus?

4 Why is the planet Pluto very cold?

5 Is the Earth flat or round? Make a list of reasons for saying that it is flat. Make another list of reasons for saying that it is round. Which do you believe?

6 Make up a story about space travel. How do your characters travel between star systems?

7 Why can't we see all of the stars of the Milky Way?

8 Why is your skin in more danger from ultraviolet radiation in high mountains than on low level ground?

9 Make a list of the hazards faced by an astronaut outside a spacecraft in space. Write down how each hazard must be dealt with by the astronaut's spacesuit.

10 Why is it impossible to study X-rays from stars using detectors on the surface of the Earth?

11 There are many satellites in orbit around the Earth. What would happen if gravity was suddenly switched off?

12 Do you believe that any extra-terrestrial intelligence will ever find the Voyager 2 spacecraft and wonder where it came from? Explain your answer.

13 Explain what *shooting stars* are and where they come from.

14 Make a list or table to compare the evidence for the idea that the Sun goes around the Earth with the evidence for the idea that the Earth goes around the Sun.

15 Bruno and Galileo were punished for their ideas. Do you think that it can ever be right to punish people for talking about ideas?

16 What is a constellation? Why would you see different constellations if you went to another star?

17 Where on Earth would you expect the natural air to be densest?

18 Imagine that some disaster caused the Earth to lose half of its air. What changes would you expect to happen?

19 a What is the ultimate source of the visible radiation that reaches a satellite from the surface of the Earth?
   b What is the source of a lot of the infra-red radiation that reaches a satellite from the ground?
   c Many satellites are equipped with cameras that detect infra-red radiation from the ground. Suggest what information this might give about the surface of the Earth, that might not be detected using visible radiation.

20 Explain why geosynchronous orbit is only possible above the Equator.

21 The Moon and the Earth attract each other with a very strong force. Why don't they crash into each other?

22 a Explain why the planet Venus has a high but steady average surface temperature.
   b What could cause the surface temperature of a planet to become unstable?

23 a How many hours does it take for light to cross the Solar System?
   b How many Solar Systems, side by side, would it take to match the diameter of the Milky Way?
   c How many Solar System diameters are there between here and Andromeda?

24 The Sun is about 25 thousand light years from the centre of the Milky Way.

   a If the diameter of a circle is $2\pi r$, how far does the Sun travel during one spin of the Galaxy?

   b What is the speed of this motion of the Sun? How does it compare with the speed of the Earth around the Sun?

Time & space

■ Star material

Clouds of particles in space, from stars which blaze and then die.

People – made of particles which were once scattered across space.

Space is cold, but the Earth has a non-stop supply of energy from one of the hotspots of the Universe, a star which we call the Sun. Across the unimaginable emptiness of space there are other concentrations of matter like the Sun. From Earth we can look out and see these stars, and we can also see clouds of very thin gas. It could be that a long time ago a cloud collapsed to make the Sun and its planets. On one planet, material that was once part of the cloud now forms into trees and turtles, poppies and people. The particles of your body were once scattered across space.

Review

Before going any further, read this page and attempt the tasks. Write the answers in your notes.

There is only one large object in our Solar System that glows with its own light, and that object is the Sun. It is 140 million km away, yet its energy can burn our skin and dry up rivers. But without this energy the Earth would be cold – far colder than the deepest ice of the Antarctic. There would be no life.

There are billions of other stars, and many of them are a lot like the Sun. They are vast distances away. Light travels across a room more quickly than we could ever notice, yet light from stars that we can see takes tens or even hundreds of years to reach us. When we look at most stars, we are looking at light that began its journey before our parents were born.

Telescopes show stars, and there are whole galaxies of stars still further away. Some galaxies are so far away that their light must have taken billions of years to reach us. Their light set off across space before there were people, before dinosaurs, bacteria, or the Earth itself.

▲ There are billions of suns in space.

▲ A galaxy of stars.

CHECK FIVE

1

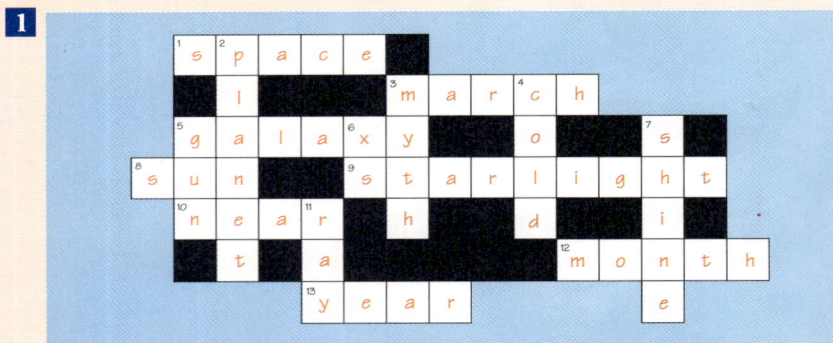

Make a list of clues for this word puzzle. The challenge is to see how many clues you can write that have something to do with space.

2 What is the difference between a star and a galaxy?

3 When you feel the sunshine on your face, how far has the light had to travel? What did it have to travel through?

4 Jupiter is the second biggest object in the Solar System. What is the Solar System? How is it possible for us to see Jupiter from Earth?

5 The nearest star outside the Solar System is 4 light-years away. How old were you when the light reaching Earth today set off from that star?

6 Do you think that it is likely that there are other stars like the Sun, with planets going around them? Do you think that there could be living things in other star systems? Explain your answers.

7 Use a CD-ROM, an encyclopaedia or a textbook to find out about nuclear fusion. Why is it so important to life on Earth?

The age of the Earth

A lot of people believe that the Earth is just a few thousand years old. They claim that the Earth has not changed much in that time. They say that people and all the plants and animals that we see now were made at the same time. These people call themselves 'creationists', and they believe that the Earth was made for the benefit of people.

Other people claim that the planet is billions of years old (see Chemistry, Chapter Seven). They say that people have not been on Earth for very long, but that people developed from other living things. They claim that the rocks wear away, become squashed and folded, so that the rock of the Earth is constantly but slowly changing. These people call themselves scientists, and they have ideas about *how* the Earth was formed, though they do not claim to know whether there is a reason *why* it was formed.

▶ *Do you think that the Earth was made for a reason? If you do, what do you think the reason is?*

Moving mountains to the sea

Geologists look at piles of silt that rivers have deposited. Out at sea from New Orleans in the southern United States, for example, the Mississippi river has dumped layers of worn-down rock that are several kilometres deep. It must have taken millions of years for the river to carry so much material out to sea. In that time the mountain streams have carved out valleys, and washed away the dust.

🔺 The Mississippi river carries mud (worn down rock) from the mountains to the sea.

🔺 As the flowing waters of the Mississippi river reach the sea the mud settles to the bottom.

Radioactive Earth

The inside of the Earth is hot. Perhaps the Earth was once hot like the Sun, and has been cooling down ever since it formed into a ball. But without a source of energy inside it, the Earth would have cooled to its present temperature in just a few million years. That would mean that the Earth is not old enough to have existed in the time of the dinosaurs.

So the Earth must have its own source of energy. When scientists first thought about this they were puzzled. They could not understand where the Earth could get energy from, other than from sunlight. Then they discovered radioactivity. Radioactive processes transfer energy, and they heat up their surroundings. The whole Earth is slightly radioactive.

The material that you are made of has come from your food. The material of your food comes from air and water and rock. All of these materials contain some radioactive substances. So you are radioactive. You can read more about radioactivity in Chapter Fifteen (Radioactivity).

It is radioactive energy which makes the Earth so hot inside. But radioactive materials become less radioactive as time goes by. From the radioactivity left in the rocks of the Earth, the Moon and meteorites, scientists can calculate that the Earth, the Moon and meteorites are about 4.5 billion years old.

▶ *What two reasons are there why the inside of the Earth is cooler than it used to be?*

An idea about how the Earth began

Imagine a mass of gas and icy, rocky dust spread thinly across space. In places it is not quite so thin, and is dense enough to be called a cloud. About 4.5 billion years ago, there was a cloud like this, and it was big enough for gravity to start to play a big part. The force of gravity acts between all objects, even ones that are quite far apart. It causes objects to attract each other. So different parts of the cloud attracted each other, and the cloud began to squash together into a smaller and smaller space. The energy of this collapse was huge. It was enough to set off nuclear processes that release still more energy – nuclear fusion of small atoms in the gas. (You can read more about nuclear fusion later in this chapter.) This was the beginning of the Sun. Nuclear fusion is still going on in the Sun today, providing the energy by which we live.

There must have been a disc spinning around the new Sun. Material in the disc gathered together in lumps. Some lumps pulled each other together, by the force of gravity. There must have been collisions, and sometimes these lumps of rock must have joined together, and sometimes they may have smashed each other apart. The Earth and Moon may be the remains of a tremendous collision.

▶ *What would make a cloud of dust and gas squash together into a smaller space?*

1

A random swirl of gas collapses under its own gravity.

2

Nuclear fusion starts in the centre of the cloud – the Sun is 'set alight'.

3

'Baby planets' start to form near the Sun. Further out there is a ring of gas.

4

Mercury
Venus
Earth
Mars

Jupiter

Saturn

The 'baby planets' collide and join together to make the inner planets. The ring of gas gathers into a few gassy balls.

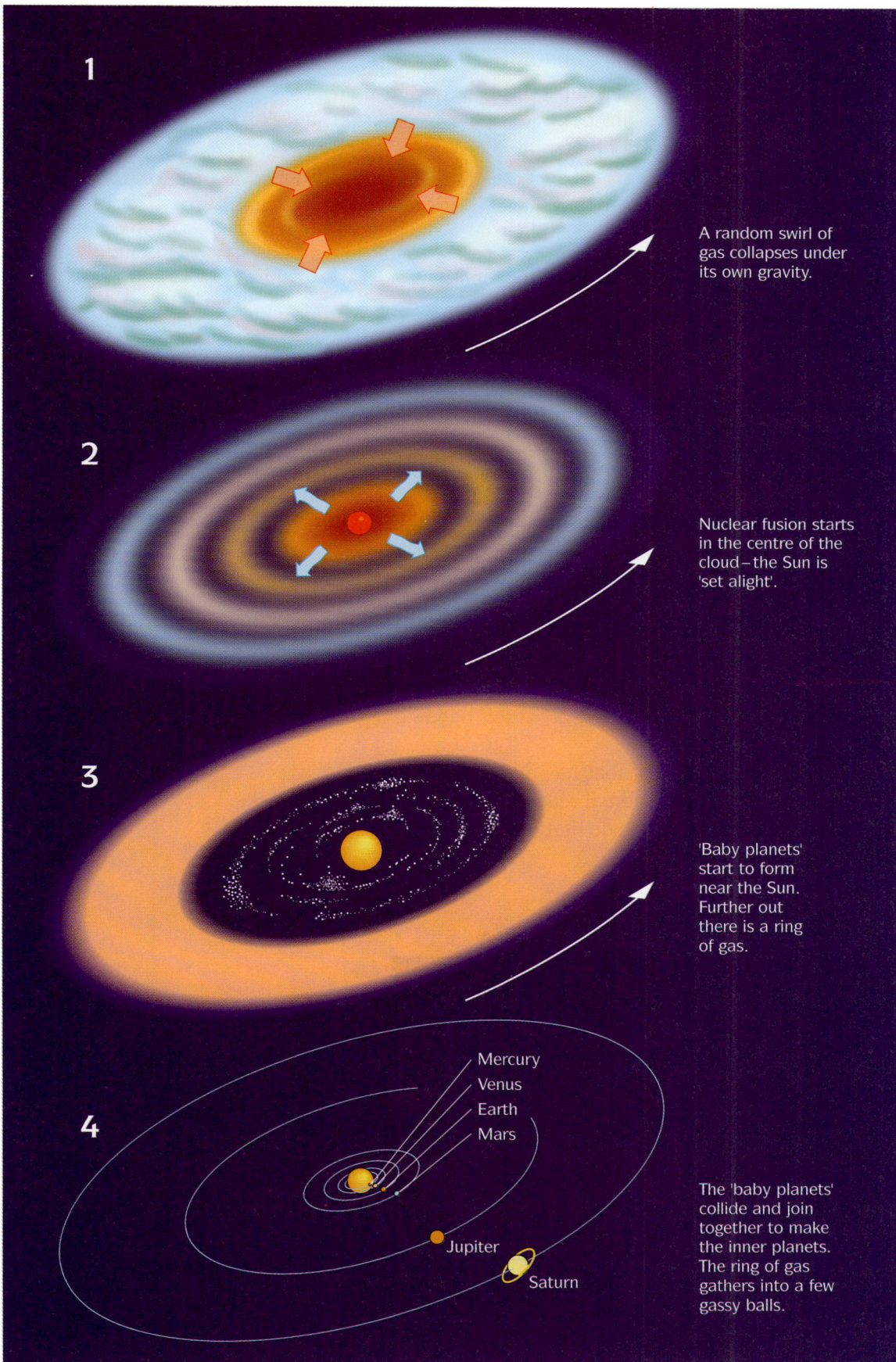

🔺 An idea about how the Earth began.

Sunlight

We see by the light of the Sun. It warms us and, thanks to plants, it provides us with food. Its ultraviolet rays can kill us, but fortunately most of this radiation does not get through our atmosphere. We can use prisms and other devices to separate sunlight into different colours, or different wavelengths. You can read about the wavelengths of light in Chapter Two (A spectrum of light).

If we look carefully at the spectrum of sunlight, we can see that it does not run quite continuously from colour to colour. There are small bands of colour missing. We can see this whether we look at the spectrum from the surface of the Earth or from satellites in orbit above the atmosphere. The Sun gives us light with certain wavelengths missing.

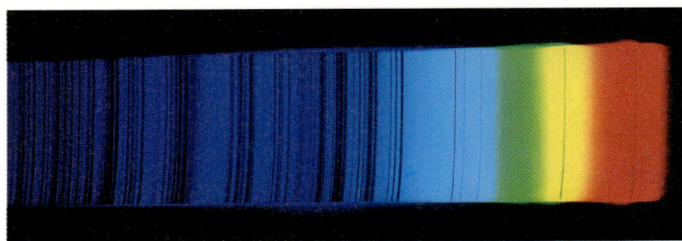

▲ The Sun's absorption spectrum. The photograph shows light from the Sun, dispersed into separate colours. The pattern of lines tells us that there is a lot of helium in the outer layers of the Sun.

Matching sunlight with helium

We can do experiments with electric light sources. The light from them does not have patterns of missing wavelengths like the pattern in sunlight. But if we shine the light through helium gas, we begin to see the same patterns. The helium absorbs certain wavelengths. These wavelengths of light go into the helium but they do not come out again. Other gases also absorb some light, but different gases absorb different patterns of wavelengths. Each gas has its own absorption pattern, like a fingerprint.

▶ *What are the colours of the strongest dark bands in the absorption spectrum of the Sun?*

Light from the Sun has the same pattern as light that has passed through helium. So sunlight must pass through helium before it reaches us. There is hardly any helium in empty space. Scientists conclude that the outer layers of the Sun must have a lot of helium in them.

Light from the stars

▲ The colour of stars shows up on film. This picture was taken by leaving a camera with its shutter open for several hours. The turning of the Earth causes stars to appear as curved streaks of light.

Stars have many different colours, which show up on photographs. We do not see the colours because of the way our eyes work. The colour-sensitive cells in the backs of our eyes only work in bright light. So we see little colour at night, except from bright sources of light like street lamps. The stars are not bright enough for us to see their colours.

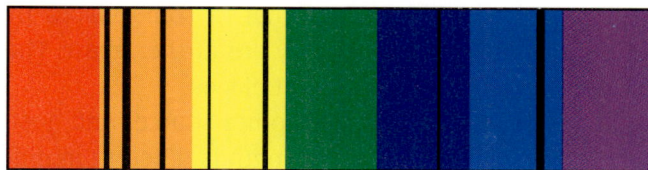

A spectrum of light from the Sun.

Some stars are reddish. A piece of coal in a fire glows red when it is hot. It is emitting electromagnetic radiation. A blast of air to the coal will make it burn more quickly. It gets hotter, and glows more brightly. It also changes colour, from red to orange or yellow. Really hot burning coal, such as in a power station furnace, glows white. A hotter object emits light that is further along the electromagnetic spectrum towards the blue end of visible light. That is true of whole stars as well as small pieces of coal. Stars that are comparatively cool are red; hotter stars are more blue.

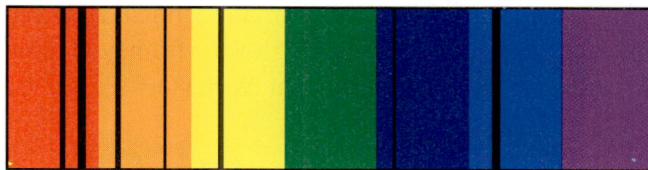

A spectrum of light from a distant star. The pattern of lines caused by helium is shifted towards the red end.

The spectrum of light from a star shows the same helium 'fingerprints' as in light from the Sun. But there is one difference that you only notice if you look very closely. The pattern in the spectrum of the star is shifted along a bit, towards the red end of the spectrum. This is called **red shift**.

▶ *How do we know that stars contain helium?*

▶ *Red dwarves and blue giants are the names for different types of star. Which stars do you think are hotter?*

Understanding the cause of red shift

Light behaves like waves on water in many ways. Light and water waves can be reflected, refracted and diffracted – you can read about this in Chapter Two (A spectrum of light) and Chapter Three (Different waves). To understand light it is very often helpful to picture water waves.

Ripples on a pond spread out from their source. A fish nibbling on the surface creates circular waves. If the fish slowly swims as it nibbles, each ripple is still a circle, but the centres of the different ripple circles are

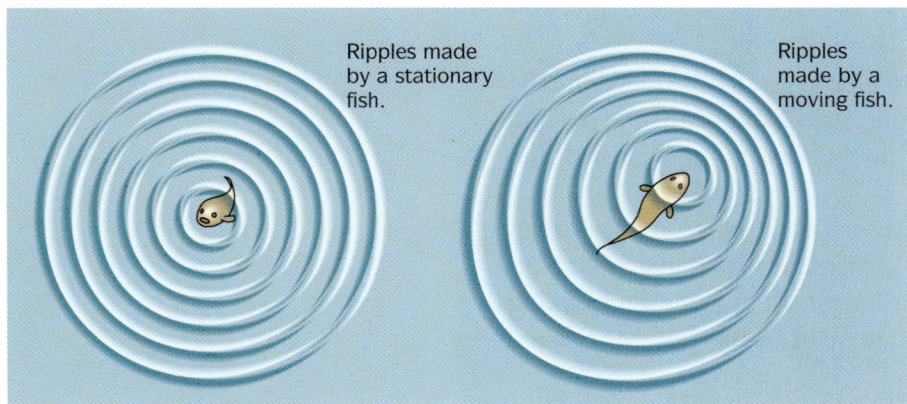

Ripples made by a stationary fish.

Ripples made by a moving fish.

A fish moving near the surface of the water creates ripples of different wave lengths.

PHYSICS

in different places. This means that in some places the ripples are close together, and in some places they are further apart. The wavelength of the ripples is now different in different places.

Light waves also spread out from a source. And, just as on water, if the source is moving then the wavelength is different in different places. Ahead of the source, the wavelengths are shorter. Behind the source, the wavelengths are longer.

So if a source of light is moving towards you then you see light that has shorter wavelength than light from an identical stationary source. The light is bluer. If the source is moving away from you then its wavelength is increased, and you see redder light. With stars we see redder light.

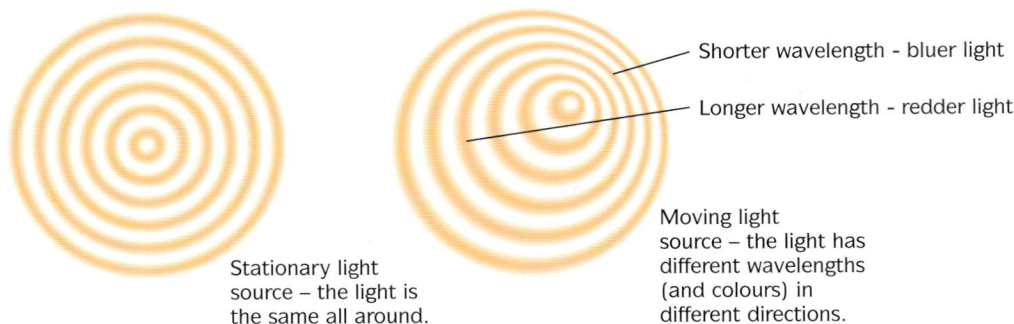

Shorter wavelength - bluer light

Longer wavelength - redder light

Stationary light source – the light is the same all around.

Moving light source – the light has different wavelengths (and colours) in different directions.

▲ Wavelengths from a stationary and a moving light source.

▶ *Sound waves spread out from the source of sound. If the source is moving, the waves are close together (short wavelength) in some places and further apart (long wavelength) in others. What would you expect to happen as a source of sound comes close to you, goes past, and moves away? What happens to the sound of a car as it goes past?*

Understanding what red shift means

A spectrum of light from a star is much like a spectrum of light from the Sun. The difference is that missing wavelengths, such as the pattern produced by helium, are all redder than they would be if the stars were stationary.

Red shift in the spectra of stars tells us that the stars are moving away from us. Everything seems to be moving away from everything else. It is as if the whole of the Universe is expanding.

Light from stars that are relatively close to us has just a little red shift. The further away the stars are, the more their light is shifted towards the red end of the spectrum. It seems that the further away from us the stars are, the faster they are moving away.

So it seems that a very long time ago there was no distance at all between different parts of the Universe. The whole Universe was just a single point, which burst apart. For 15 billion years the Universe has gone on bursting apart. The beginning of the process is called the **Big Bang**.

▶ *Imagine that you are stuck fast to a big balloon which is being blown up by a giant. Your friends are all there too. What do you notice about your friends as the balloon gets bigger?*

To imagine the Universe expanding you can think of yourself as a speck of dust in an explosion. It does not matter where the centre of the explosion is, or even if the explosion has a centre at all. If you can detect the other specks of dust they will all be moving away from you.

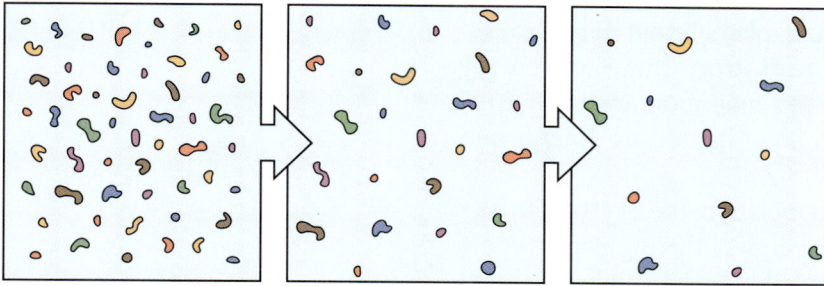

🔺 Specks in an explosion all move away from each other.

Alternative theories

People often think that science is about 'fact'. But it is impossible to prove that a theory is absolutely true. If a theory is a good one it fits all the evidence. And if new evidence comes along, then the theory should agree with it. If it doesn't, then the theory is wrong.

Scientists put their trust in the best theory that is available. We have a theory that all matter is made of atoms, and that the atoms themselves are made of still smaller particles. This has never been proved. But people have spent a lot of time and effort studying matter. Not a shred of evidence has yet turned up to show that our ideas about atoms are wrong. It makes a lot of sense to trust the atomic theory.

Sometimes there are alternative theories, and scientists have to think about which one is best. There may be a lot of talk. Some people will get very agitated. Eventually, one theory or another will become the favourite. That's how it is with theories of the beginning of the Universe.

One theory says that there was no beginning at all, but that the Universe has existed for ever. This is called the **Steady State** theory. It claims that the expansion that we can see has gone on for ever, and that matter is slowly but continuously created everywhere in the Universe. This theory has never been proved or disproved, but neither has the Big Bang theory. Scientists must continually ask themselves whether the Big Bang theory or the Steady State theory is better.

▶ *Can you think of alternative theories for the nature of matter, other than the theory of atoms? (If you can, you should skip your exams and go straight for a Nobel Prize! A Nobel Prize is like an 'Oscar' for science.)*

▶ *Do you believe that the Big Bang theory can be trusted as much as the atomic theory can?*

Evidence for the Big Bang theory

Human beings have temperatures of about 310 K (or 37 °C), and a density which is 3000 billion billion billion times bigger than the average density of the Universe. Compared with a human being, the Universe is very cold and very empty.

But the Universe is not completely cold nor completely empty. From everywhere in the sky comes **cosmic background radiation**. This is low-energy infra-red radiation, or thermal radiation. You can read more about thermal radiation in Chapter Two (A spectrum of light) and Chapter Six (Energy and resources).

Before people discovered cosmic background radiation, the Big Bang theory had predicted that it should exist, as left-over energy of the Big Bang. People said that if there was ever a Big Bang, the ultimate hot fireball, then it has had 15 billion years of expansion for its energy to spread out. But there should be faint traces of this energy everywhere in the Universe. So when people discovered the cosmic background radiation it seemed that the theory had provided a good prediction. After that, more people accepted the Big Bang theory.

▶ *Does cosmic background radiation* prove *the Big Bang theory?*

The lumpy Universe – more evidence

There was a problem with the Big Bang theory. The Universe is lumpy. In places it has incredibly low density – an average of about one atom in each cubic metre. In other places it has huge density – a teaspoonful of neutron star would have as much mass as the whole Earth. If the Universe is uneven now, then the unevenness must have been there from the beginning. But there was no evidence of any unevenness in the Universe in the first seconds of the theoretical Big Bang.

However, scientists took measurements from a satellite of the cosmic background radiation. They discovered that the radiation is not even all across the sky. There are ripples in it.

The radiation is left-over energy of the Big Bang. The ripples in cosmic background radiation show that the unevenness of the Universe has existed since the beginning. The discovery of the ripples defeated one of the main arguments against the Big Bang theory.

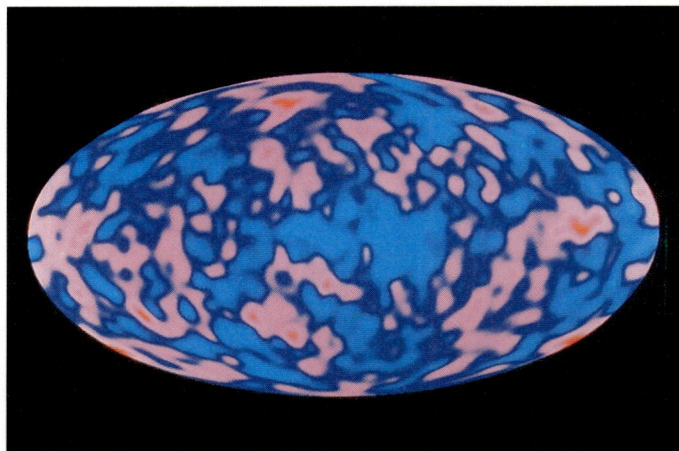
🔺 Ripples in space – evidence that the Universe has been lumpy ever since it began.

Possible futures for the Universe

Nobody knows whether the Universe will go on expanding for ever. It is possible that gravity acting between galaxies will be strong enough to pull them all back together again. That would put the Big Bang into reverse. Instead of expanding, the Universe would contract into a fireball and then into a single point. If that happens, scientists reckon that it will be in about another 15 billion years. Perhaps the Universe will then start all over again. Humans won't be around to find out.

Big Bang numbers

The age of the Universe has to be measured using some very big numbers. You may be given a worksheet to help you practice using these kinds of numbers.

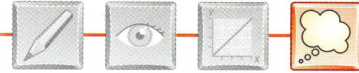

Some different kinds of stars

Stars do not last for ever. They have beginnings· and ends. We know this because there are so many stars in space, and they are not all the same. Scientists study the light from different stars. Some stars are large and cool. Their coolness makes them glow more red than blue. These are called the red giants. Then there are small cool stars – red dwarves. There are hot blue giants, and there are white dwarves.

Sometimes there are special events in space. In 1987 astronomers were amazed by their luck when their telescopes showed an exploding star. It was the first death of a star that anybody had seen since the age of telescopes began, 400 years ago. It gave scientists an opportunity to check out their theories of the life cycles of stars.

In some places in space there are huge dark clouds of hydrogen, where matter seems to be coming together. Gravity pulls the thin cloud of hydrogen in, faster and faster, until the nuclei have enough energy for dramatic changes to begin. That is how a star is born.

▶ *What does the colour, such as* red *or* blue, *in the description of a star tell you about the temperature of the star?*

▶ *How did the Sun begin?*

🔺 The exploding star, or supernova, that astronomers photographed in 1987.

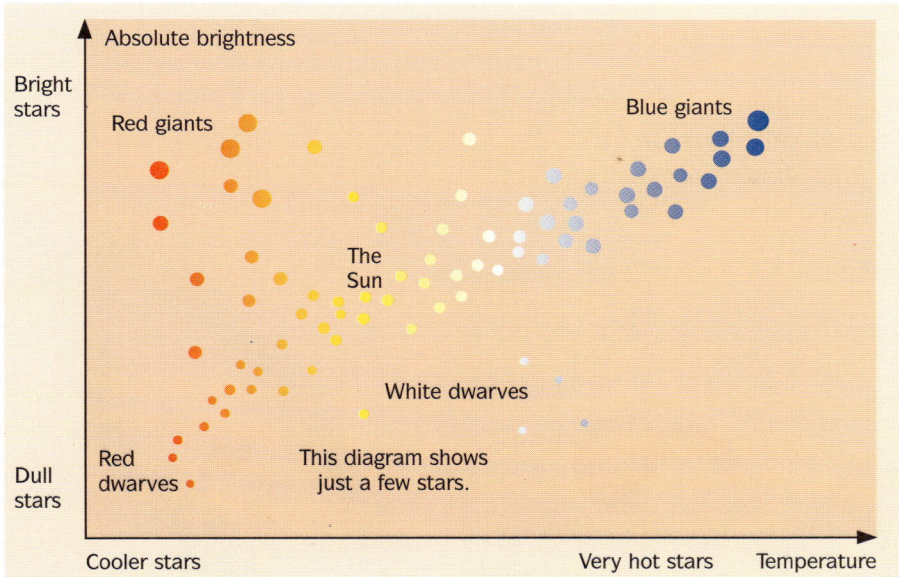

🔺 Scientists classify stars by their brightness and their temperature. On a plot of brightness against temperature, scientists can see at a glance the pattern of different types of star. Cool bright stars are red giants, and cool dull stars are red dwarves, for example. The Sun is near the middle of the pattern. (A plot of brightness against temperature is called a Hertzsprung-Russell diagram.)

The life of a star

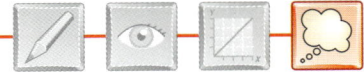

Stars form, change and die over a very long period of time. You may be given a worksheet to help you summarise the life of a star.

▶ *A newly formed star is made almost completely from one substance. What substance?*

ALIENS AND ASTRONOMERS

Jocelyn Bell Burnell is a down-to-Earth astronomer with some interesting ideas. She says that being an astronomer is a bit like being an alien visiting Earth. You can see people in houses, in factories and in hospitals, where you will see some being born and some who are dying. You could sort people according to their size and shape, whether they have grey hair, or no hair at all. In just a few days of looking around you will be able to work out the life history of a typical human being. That is how it is for astronomers. They cannot see stars going through billion-year life cycles. But they can study a lot of stars, and build a picture from that.

▲ Jocelyn Bell Burnell.

Nuclear fusion in stars

Hydrogen nuclei in stars join together and form helium nuclei, and helium nuclei join to make still bigger nuclei. The process, called **fusion**, releases a lot of energy. The atoms of oxygen, nitrogen, phosphorus, iron and so on in your body were all made in stars by fusion, starting with hydrogen.

▶ *What is the difference between a hydrogen atom and a hydrogen nucleus?*

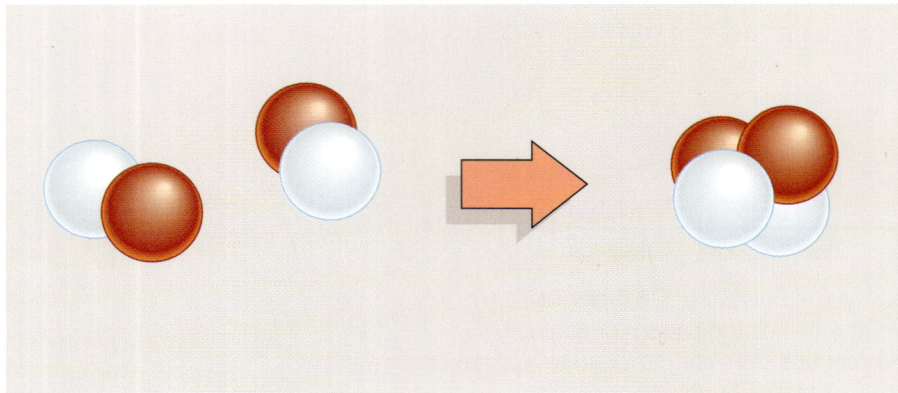

▲ An example of fusion of nuclei.

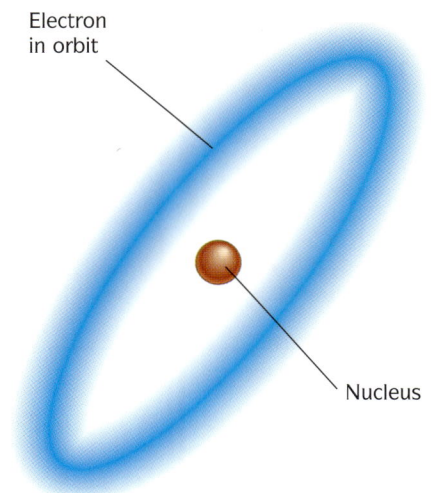

Electron in orbit

Nucleus

▲ A hydrogen atom.

The death of stars

Slowly and inevitably, the hydrogen in a star gets 'used up'. It gets turned into bigger nuclei. Eventually fusion slows down, and the star dies. Its death can be spectacular, like the explosion that people saw in 1987. Or the star cools more slowly and spreads outwards, becoming a red giant for a while before fading completely. That is what seems to happen to stars like the Sun.

Scientists estimate that the Sun will last another 5 billion years before becoming a red giant. Then as it spreads it will swallow up Mercury, Venus and then the Earth. The end of the world could be just 5 billion years away.

Turning hydrogen into iron

Stars work by nuclear fusion. Hydrogen nuclei join together to make larger nuclei of helium. But hydrogen nuclei are protons. They all have positive electric charge, and so they repel each other. At the temperatures that we are used to here on Earth, hydrogen nuclei do not naturally fuse together. They can only be made to join together if they are moving very fast.

In the Sun, hydrogen nuclei move fast because of the high temperature. Then they fuse together, and the process releases energy. The energy keeps up the temperature. So fusion keeps itself going, once started. Fusion in the Sun started because gravity caused a large cloud of gas to crash in on itself. It was the crash that first raised the temperature.

As the hydrogen becomes used up the star may start to cool and collapse in on itself a little. That produces a higher temperature at the centre of the star – high enough for helium nuclei to start to fuse together to make nuclei like carbon. Fusion of helium nuclei releases energy. When helium begins to run out the star tends to cool again, and collapse again. Once again the collapse pushes up the temperature, enough for carbon nuclei in the centre of the star to fuse together. Fusion of carbon nuclei releases energy.

Fusion of smaller nuclei eventually produces iron. The amount of iron in a star slowly grows, with most of the iron in the centre. Because of the high temperature in the star, some nuclei of iron fuse together. But fusion of iron is different. It does not release energy but takes it in. So the centre of the star loses energy and cools down. The hot material all around the centre no longer has hot material inside, holding it up. In a large star, these outer parts of the star can suddenly crash inwards, and then out again. That is a **supernova**, the death of a big star. It is what astronomers saw in 1987.

PHYSICS

Summary

- Rock contains radioactive material which acts as a source of energy inside the Earth.
- The amounts of different radioactive materials in a rock can show how long the rock has been solid.
- Stars form from clouds of hydrogen gas.
- The Sun formed in this way, with the Earth and other planets forming out of a spinning disc that developed around the new Sun.
- Stars pass through various stages until they exhaust their energy source and 'die'.
- Scientists have built up these ideas by studying light from different stars which seem to be at various stages of their life cycles.
- Red shift in the spectra of stars in distant galaxies leads to the idea that the Universe is expanding.
- The strongest theory of the Universe is the Big Bang theory.
- Scientists are continually looking for more evidence that supports or disproves this theory.
- Cosmic background radiation provides evidence to support the Big Bang theory.
- Scientists do not know whether the Universe will expand for ever, or whether gravity will make it collapse back again.

WYKE MANOR SCHOOL

Revision Questions

1 Suggest some possible reasons why dinosaur fossils are hard to find.

2 a Rivers carry mud out to sea. Where does all the mud come from? What happens to it after it goes into the sea?
   b How does Mississippi mud show that the Earth is very old?

3 Your body contains radioactive material. Where does it come from?

4 How does nuclear fusion keep you alive?

5 a How can you split up sunlight into a spectrum of different colours?
   b When can you see this happen naturally?

6 What can we tell about a star from its colour?

7 Draw a sketch to show the spectrum of light from the Sun compared with the spectrum of light from a distant star. Why are they different?

8 What is the Big Bang theory?

9 What causes a very large but very thin cloud of hydrogen to collapse into a much smaller ball? What happens next?

10 What does helium do to light?

11 Explain how we know that there is helium in distant stars.

12 Stars have colour but you cannot see it. Why not?

13 The diagram shows waves on a pond.

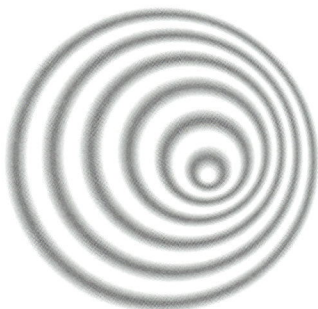

a What could have made a pattern of waves like this?
   b Explain why the wavelength is smaller in some places and bigger in others.
   c What has this got to do with the light of stars?

14 Imagine that you are an intelligent speck in a huge explosion. How would you know that there was an explosion going on?

15 What are the differences in temperature and brightness between a red dwarf and a blue giant?

16 Nearly all of the matter in the Universe is simple hydrogen.
   a Sketch a hydrogen atom.
   b Your body contains a lot of large atoms, such as carbon, oxygen and iron. How did the Universe make these atoms?

17 Why does the existence of layers of rock formed from sediment suggest that the Earth is very old?

18 How does the phenomenon of radioactivity help to explain that the Earth is hot and yet very old?

19 Why doesn't nuclear fusion normally happen on Earth? How does it become possible in stars?

20 What is the link between colour and wavelength of light?

21 a Use diagrams to explain why the pitch of a sound of a car changes as the car speeds past you.
   b Explain what this has got to with the expanding Universe.
   c If the car were going *very* fast, you would be able to see its colour change as it went past. What might you see for a yellow car?

22 Why does the build-up of iron in a large star cause it to collapse catastrophically and become a supernova?

23 A human being is about 10^{30} times denser than the average density of the Universe. A human being has a density of about $1000\,kg/m^3$.

a Write out 10^{30} in full – a 1 followed by 30 zeros.

b $\dfrac{\text{Density of}}{\text{human being}} = \dfrac{\text{Average density}}{\text{of Universe}} \times 10^{30}$.

What is the average density of the Universe?

c People and stars are concentrations of matter. What causes matter in the Universe originally to accumulate in relatively small spaces?

24 Measurement of red shift of many stars and galaxies has shown that the relationship between their distance from us and the speed with which they move away from us is

$$u = Hd$$

where u is the speed in km/s with which a light source is moving away, d is its distance from us in light years, and H is a constant of proportionality called the Hubble constant. $H = 0.000\,03\,km/s/light\ year$.

a Sketch a graph to show the relationship between u and d.

(You may read about graphs and relationships in Chapter Sixteen.)

b State the value of the gradient of the graph.

c A galaxy called M87 is $30\,000\,000$ light years away. How fast is it moving away from us, according to the above equation?

d Imagine that a galaxy is moving away from us at the speed of light, which is $300\,000\,km/s$. How far away is it? Using the figures given here, your answer will be in light years.

Use 1 light year = $9\,500\,000\,000\,000\,km$ to work out the distance in km.

e For how long has this galaxy been moving away from us?

f Why can we never see anything which is further away than this galaxy?

This activity is easier if you use powers of 10.

PHYSICS

Energy & resources

Keeping the baby warm

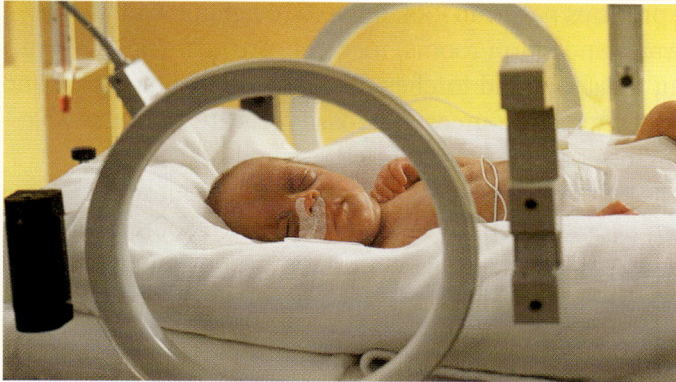
Electrical heaters keep up the temperature inside the incubator.

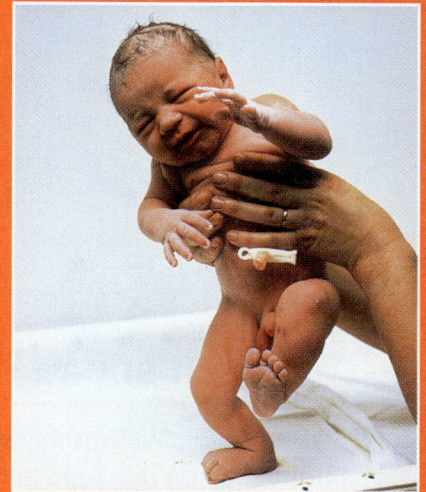
Before the baby was born he was in warm surroundings.

Warm clothes cut down the rate of energy transfer out from the baby's body into the cold air.

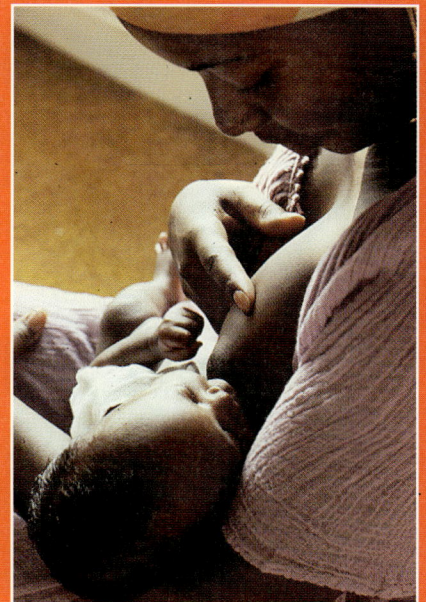
Food reacts with oxygen to provide the baby with a source of energy.

Power stations supply energy to run incubators and a lot more. But power stations need energy resources themselves.

Review

Before going any further, read this page and attempt the tasks. Write the answers in your notes.

The temperature inside a mother's womb is 37°C. That is the same as a baby's own body temperature, so keeping warm is not a problem. But when a baby is born, energy starts to flow from its body into the cold air. From then on, the baby will lose energy continuously into its surroundings, throughout its life.

Food has to replace the lost energy. Every mouthful of the mother's milk provides the baby with another few kilojoule (kJ) of energy. But without plants there would be no food at all for the baby. Plants can use sunlight as their energy resource, so that they can build complicated chemicals out of simple ones. Animals, including mothers and babies, get their energy by breaking down the complicated chemicals made by plants.

The babies on the previous page can look forward to light on winter nights. They will have hot water and warm rooms, rock concerts, cars and computers. Batteries will run their toys and torches. Fossil fuels – oil and coal and gas – may be their main energy resources. But fossil fuels are not renewable – once they are used up they are not replaced by the action of the Sun.

At some time in the future, fossil fuels will start to run out and become more expensive. Then people will have to turn to energy resources that are renewable, like biomass, wind and waves. Perhaps every house will have solar cells on its roof, to generate electricity directly from the energy of sunlight. The future will be different from the present.

CHECK SIX

1 Make a list of clues for the word puzzle. Use the information on this page to help you.

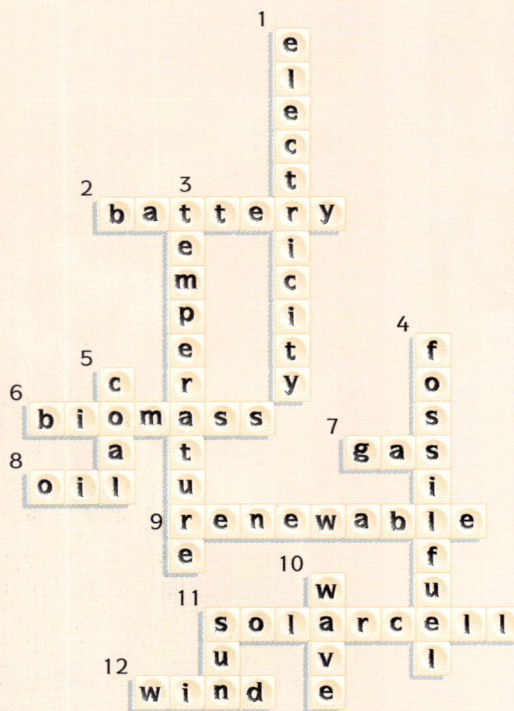

2 Copy and complete the table. Use it to classify these energy resources:
oil gas coal biomass wind waves solar

Renewable	Non-renewable

3 In what ways does the Sun keep you alive?

4 What is the temperature of your body? Find out the temperature of the air around your body. Which one changes most from one time to another?

5 What equipment inside an incubator transfers energy to a baby?

6 When does energy transfer most quickly away from a baby – on a cold day or a warm day?

7 'Food provides a baby with a store of energy.' Do you agree with this? Explain your answer.

Heating, cooling and equilibrium

The temperature of a stone statue goes up and down with the weather. As each new day warms up, energy transfers into the stone, and its temperature rises.

On a hot afternoon, the statue might still gain energy from the rays of the Sun. The statue is warm, and energy is also transferring away from it into the air. The two energy flows could cancel out, so that the statue just stays at the same warm temperature. That is **thermal equilibrium** – flow in equals flow out.

When the day cools down, so does the statue. As the air around it cools, energy flows away from the statue, and it spends another night stone cold.

▶ *A sculptor can make a statue by melting metal and pouring it into a mould. What energy transfers happen between the liquid metal and the mould?*

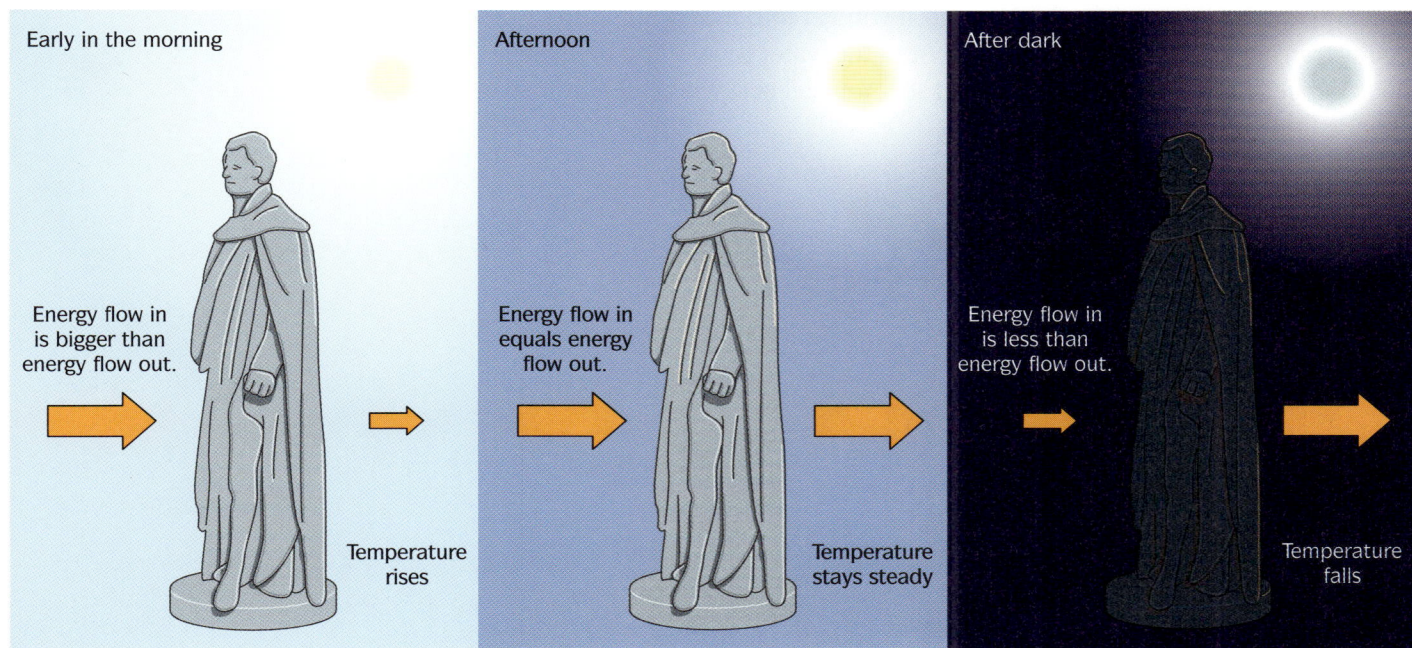

Early in the morning

Energy flow in is bigger than energy flow out.

Temperature rises

Afternoon

Energy flow in equals energy flow out.

Temperature stays steady

After dark

Energy flow in is less than energy flow out.

Temperature falls

🔺 Energy transfer throughout the day and night.

THE TEMPERATURE OF THE EARTH

The Earth is surrounded by very cold space. So energy is continuously transferring out from the warm Earth into its cold surroundings. Fortunately, energy arrives at the Earth from the Sun.

At a certain average temperature of the Earth, the rate of losing energy is big enough to exactly balance the rate of gaining it. The Earths' climate stays steady.

Burning fuels produces a lot of extra carbon dioxide. Carbon dioxide and certain other gases in the atmosphere make it harder for the Earth to lose energy. The average temperature of the Earth could rise. We call it **global warming**.

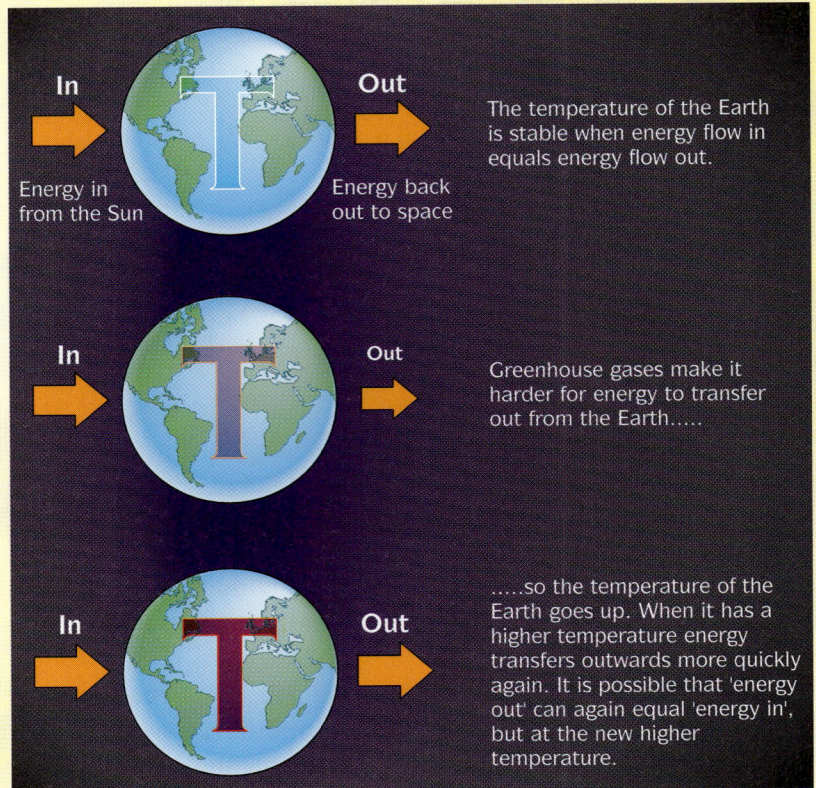

In — Energy in from the Sun
Out — Energy back out to space

The temperature of the Earth is stable when energy flow in equals energy flow out.

In   Out

Greenhouse gases make it harder for energy to transfer out from the Earth.....

In   Out

.....so the temperature of the Earth goes up. When it has a higher temperature energy transfers outwards more quickly again. It is possible that 'energy out' can again equal 'energy in', but at the new higher temperature.

🔺 Global warming happens because certain gases resist the rate of energy transfer away from the Earth.

Energy transfer and temperature

If you go into the sea around Britain it feels cold. You would not survive for many hours if you had to stay in the water. Your thermal energy flows away from you, and your temperature falls. But if you get into a very hot bath the energy transfer is the other way round – from the water to you. You are in as much danger as when you are in the cold sea. You feel best when there is just a gentle flow of energy away from you.

🔺 Energy flows quickly away from you when you are surrounded by cold water.

PHYSICS

⬆ Energy transfer between a person and their environment.

Energy flows between objects that have different temperatures. If you put a cold slice of butter onto a hot potato the potato loses energy to the butter. But if you put a cold slice of butter on to a cold potato nothing happens. When objects are at the same temperature then they do not gain or lose energy from each other.

▸ *When you run a bath you mix hot water with cold water. Which loses energy and which gains energy? When does the energy transfer between them stop?*

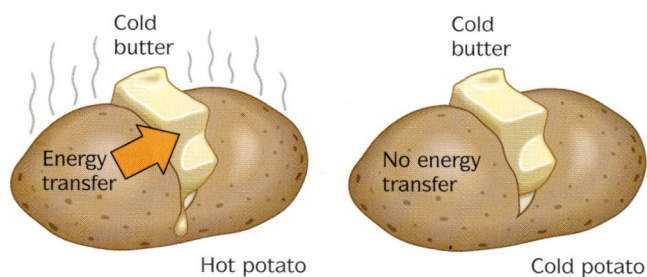

⬆ Energy transfer happens between a hot potato and cold butter.

Detecting energy transfer

A beaker with a small amount of hot water can be a model potato, and a test tube with a small amount of cold water can be model butter.

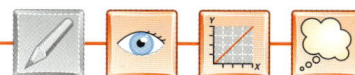

Thermometers in each container will show what is happening to the temperatures. Patterns of temperature change will be clear if the temperature is measured every 30 seconds.

After a minute or two the test tube 'butter' can be put into the beaker 'potato' to see if the temperature patterns change. A graph will show up the change.

▸ *What energy transfers are happening with the beaker of hot water (the potato) before the test tube (butter) is put in?*

▸ *What energy transfers happen involving the beaker of hot water and the test tube after the test tube is put into the beaker?*

▸ *What energy flows go on when you put a cold potato into a hot oven?*

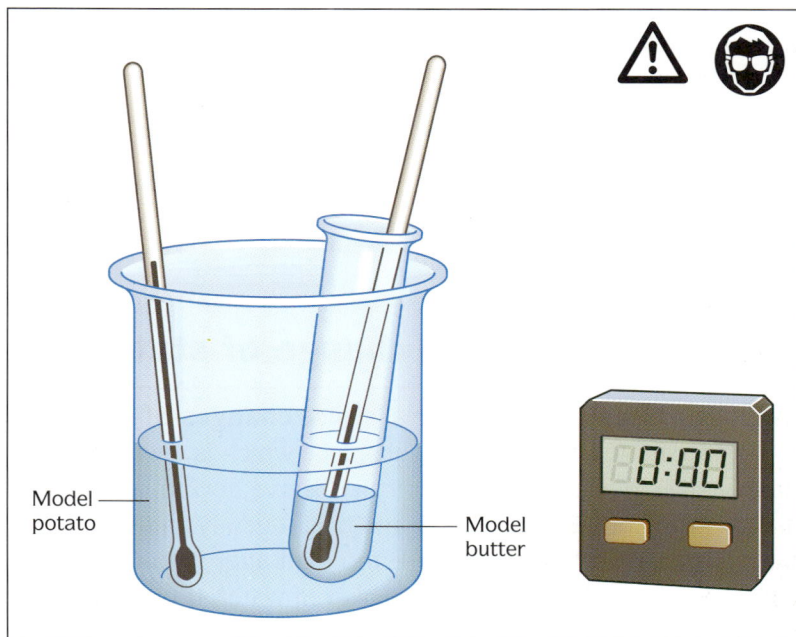

⬆ Making a model potato.

Energy and temperature

We measure energy in joule, or J for short. We measure temperature in kelvin, K, or in degrees Celsius, °C. The units are different because energy and temperature are not the same thing.

An object can gain energy but not go up in temperature. Think about the butter on the potato. At first, when you put it on the potato, the butter gets hotter. Its temperature goes up. But then it starts to melt. While it is melting it is still receiving energy from the potato, but its temperature does not necessarily go up at all. The energy is needed just to melt the butter.

Energy transfers and change of state

Melting ice, just like melting butter, takes energy away from its surroundings. You can feel that when you make snowballs. When an iceberg melts it first changes from ice at 0°C to water at 0°C. It has to take in a huge amount of energy just to do that, and it takes time for the energy to transfer into the ice. That is why icebergs can float for long distances into the oceans. The energy needed to melt ice, without changing its temperature, is called **latent heat** energy.

And just as ice needs to take in energy to melt, water gives out energy as it freezes. On a cold night, when the temperature falls to 0°C, quantities of water do not instantly freeze. It takes time. Even a tiny droplet of water must lose energy before it can freeze.

Boiling a substance – turning it from liquid to gas – also takes energy. Any boiling kettle demonstrates that. The kettle keeps providing energy and making steam, but the temperature in the kettle stays at 100°C.

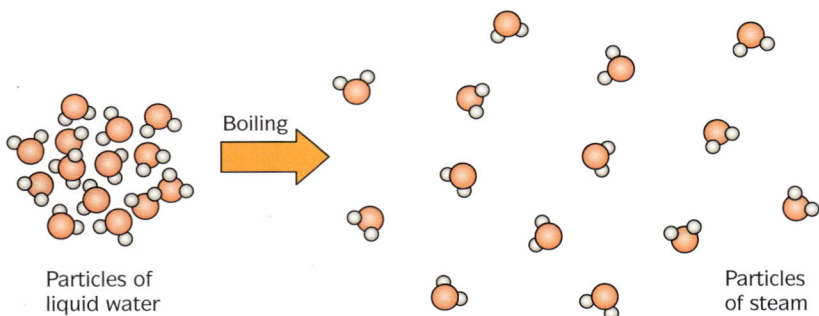

A freezing droplet of water

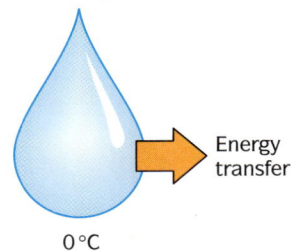

Energy transfer

0 °C

A melting crystal of ice

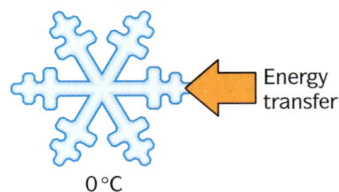

Energy transfer

0 °C

◢ Energy transfer during melting and freezing.

Boiling

Particles of liquid water

Particles of steam

◢ Particles of water spread out when energy turns the water into steam.

▶ *When snow is piled up it can take days to melt, even when the air temperature is well above freezing. What has that got to do with latent heat?*

▶ *A scalding by water at 100°C is bad enough, but steam at 100°C burns even more. Why?*

Energy transfer and change of state

Melting, freezing and boiling are all called **changes of state**.

Octadecanoic acid is a waxy substance which is useful for studying what happens when a solid melts. You can observe how its temperature changes as it melts if you use solid flakes and heat it gently and slowly. To make sure that its temperature does not rise too high after it has melted, the octadecanoic acid *must* be heated in a beaker of water. If you do this experiment, you should wear eye protection. You should also check your plan with your teacher.

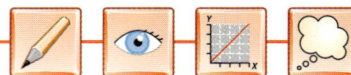

A graph of temperature against time clearly shows how the temperature changes at different times. In fact, the temperature does not change at all during the actual melting. But energy is going into the octadecanoic acid from the warm water around it. A substance which is changing state can gain or lose energy without its temperature changing.

Why evaporation causes cooling

We sweat to keep cool. The water on our skin turns into a gas. It **evaporates**. Water needs to gain energy (latent heat energy) to turn from liquid to gas. It takes energy away from our skin, cooling it down. The evaporation transfers energy from skin to air. The faster the evaporation, the faster the energy is transferred. You can read more about this in Biology, Chapter Eight.

A particle explanation of cooling by evaporation

Evaporation is the continuous escape of particles through the surface of a liquid, usually into the surrounding air.

In any amount of water, particles are moving randomly. The forces between particles make them jostle each other. So, at any one time, some particles are moving slowly and others are moving quickly. The ones that are moving quickly are the ones that have most chance of escaping through the liquid surface. So it is mostly the faster particles that escape.

The particles that are left behind have lower average speeds. Speed of particles affects temperature. The temperature of the liquid is reduced by the escape of faster particles.

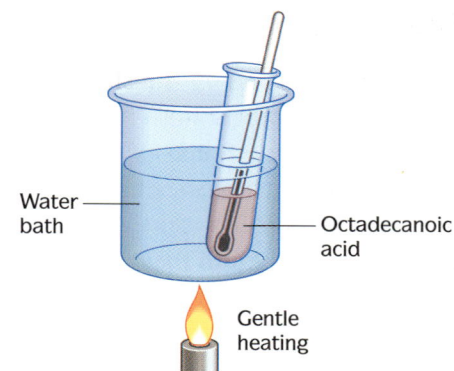
▲ Investigating changes of state with octadecanoic acid.

▲ Fast water particles carry away energy.

▶ *A flow of air makes evaporation of water happen more quickly. Why does your skin feel particularly cold when you sweat in windy weather?*

Energy transfers in refrigerators

Energy usually flows from a material that is at high temperature to a material that is at low temperature. But a fridge works hard to make the energy flow 'the wrong way', from the cold air inside the fridge to the warmer air outside.

The material circulating in pipes in a fridge turns from liquid to gas inside the fridge. It takes in energy (cools the fridge) as it does so. It turns from gas back to liquid in pipes outside the fridge. Then it gives out the energy.

▶ *Why should you never stand the back of a fridge right up against a wall?*

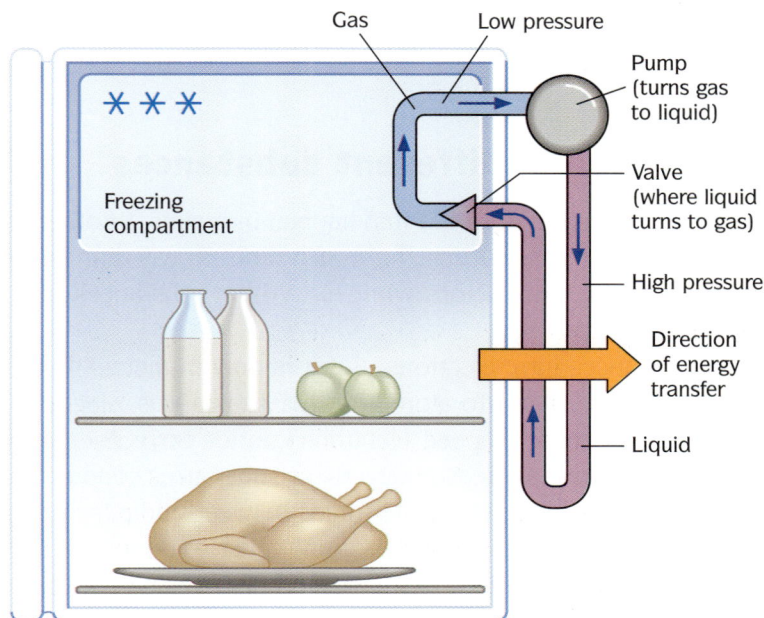

Gas   Low pressure
Pump (turns gas to liquid)
Freezing compartment
Valve (where liquid turns to gas)
High pressure
Direction of energy transfer
Liquid

Conduction of energy

Thermal (heat) energy transfer is often a very good thing. The inside of a motorbike engine is hot. The burning of the fuel provides a continuous supply of energy. Some of the energy pushes the pistons and turns the wheels. Some just pushes up the temperature. The engine would overheat if the energy could not flow safely away. It flows through the metal of the engine block, out into the air. Cooling fins provide a large surface where the cool air and hot metal meet. They increase the rate of the energy flow.

The metal must *conduct* the energy. To understand how that happens means understanding the structure of the metal – the particles it is made of. But it takes imagination.

As one part of a metal gets hotter, its particles move with more energy. Its atoms vibrate more and more violently, and some of its electrons move more energetically. Atoms set their neighbours vibrating more, and fast electrons race from atom to atom. So the energy spreads through the metal – the process is called **conduction**. (You can read more about atoms and electrons in the Chemistry book, and in Chapters 13 and 15 of this book.)

⬛ Energy transfers out from a motorbike engine through the metal. There are cooling fins to ensure rapid energy tansfer.

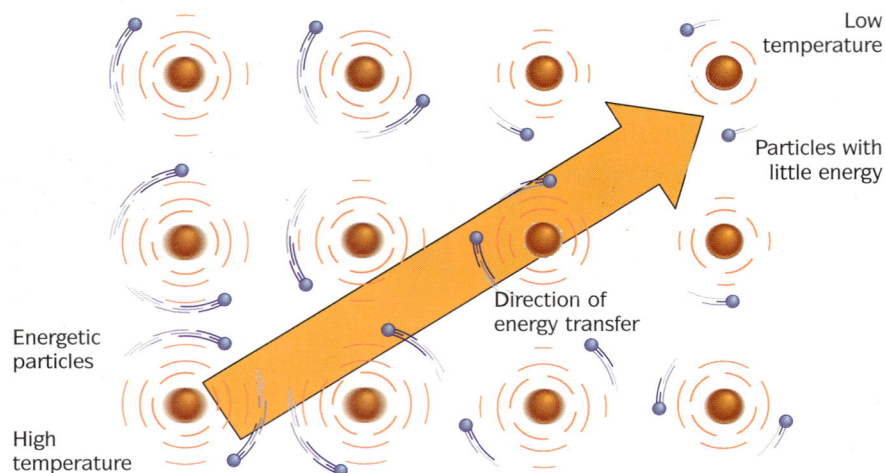

Low temperature

Particles with little energy

Direction of energy transfer

Energetic particles

High temperature

⬛ One artist's imagination provides a picture of the particles involved in conduction in metals.

▶ *Why is rapid energy transfer a good thing in the metal of a motorbike engine?*

▶ *Can you think of another situation in which rapid conduction is a good thing?*

Conduction in different substances

Thermal conduction does not just happen in metals. In other solids, energy flows from particle to particle, but much more slowly than in metals. Metals are good thermal conductors, while most other substances are good thermal insulators.

All substances have electrons. But it is only in metals that electrons can easily move from atom to atom. In other substances, electrons are trapped inside atoms. These trapped electrons cannot carry energy from atom to atom. That is the main reason why these substances conduct energy slowly.

Also, in liquids like water, the forces between the particles are generally weaker than in solids. So particles do not push and pull each other so much – they simply have less to do with each other. If one particle has more energy than its neighbours, it doesn't jostle them so much into moving faster. Liquids are usually not very good at thermal conduction.

Gases are very bad at conducting energy – there are hardly any forces between the particles. One speeding particle must crash right into another before it can give it any energy. And since the particles are small compared with the distances between them, collisions do not happen often enough for fast energy transfer.

▶ *Explain why aluminium is better than polythene as a thermal (heat) conductor.*

The conducting ability of different materials can be compared using their *thermal conductivities*.

Material	Thermal conductivity (in W/m/°C)
Copper	385
Gold	310
Iron	80
Water	0.6
Glass	1.5
Thermal building block	0.1

🔺 Materials that have high thermal conductivities are good conductors.

Convection in gases and liquids

If someone gave you the chance to climb into a big basket and go up into the sky, hanging from a ball of air, you might not like the idea. But that is what balloonists do. The 'ball of air' is enclosed in the fabric of the balloon. The air is the same as the air outside, only hotter.

A hot flame supplies energy to the air inside the balloon. That means that the particles of the air have more energy. They move around more quickly. They crash harder into the balloon fabric. They crash harder into each other. Each particle pushes its neighbours out of the way a little bit harder. So the particles move just a bit further apart. The whole of the gas expands.

Expansion of air inside a balloon makes some air escape through the opening at the bottom. The air inside becomes less dense – there is simply less air in the space than there would be if it was cold. When an object is less dense than its surroundings then it floats upwards.

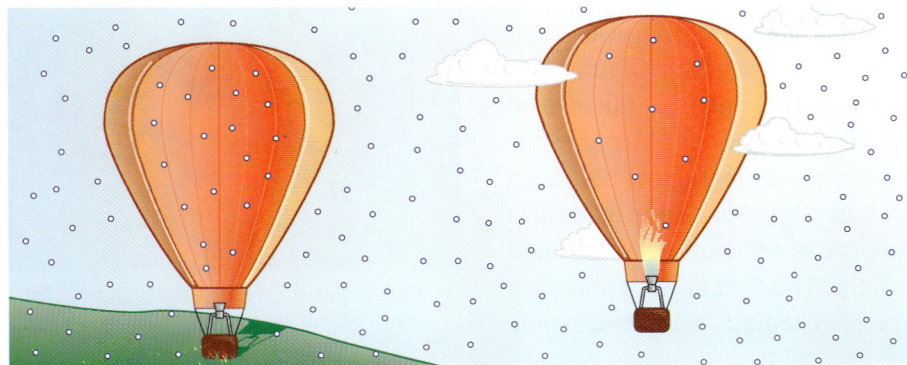

🔺 Hanging from a ball of hot air.

▶ *Chlorine gas sinks in air. What can you say about the relative densities of chlorine and air?*

PHYSICS

Hot water behaves in the same way as hot air. If one area of some tap water is heated, it expands. Its particles move apart. It becomes less dense than the cooler water around it, and it floats upwards. It takes its energy with it, transferring energy from place to place.

The process of energy transfer by movement of parts of a gas or liquid is called **convection**.

▸ *Why don't convection currents happen in:*
  a *solids*
  b *a bucket of water which is all at the same temperature?*

Examples of convection currents

- On a summer's day, some parts of the ground get more energy from the Sun than others. The air here gets warmer than air nearby, and it rises. Away from the warm ground, it starts to cool again. The air carries invisible water vapour with it. As the air cools, water molecules gather together into small droplets, and a cloud begins to form. If the droplets grow big enough then they fall, and we get wet.
- On the same summer's day, the strength of the Sun heats up the land much more than the sea. The warm air over the land rises. The cool air from above the sea rushes in across the coastline to take the place of the rising air. The weather on the beach is disappointingly chilly.

▲ Convection – the cause of summer showers.

Thermal radiation from the Sun

The Sun is hot – we can feel the heat through 140 million km of empty space. The Earth has little energy supply of its own, and it is much cooler than the Sun. As usual, energy flows from the hotter material to the cooler one.

The energy has to transfer through a vast distance of vacuum. There are no particles to conduct the energy. There are no hot liquids or gases to carry energy through space by convection. There is only one way in which the energy can travel – in the same way as light travels.

In fact, visible light itself carries a lot of the Sun's energy that reaches us. But other radiation, very similar to light but not detectable by our eyes, brings a lot of the Sun's warmth to us. Thermal radiation or infra-red, like visible radiation, is part of a range of waves called the electromagnetic spectrum. You can read about it in Chapter Two (A spectrum of light).

▲ Convection – sea breeze.

Thermal radiation from other objects

All objects emit (give out) infra-red or thermal radiation. You do. Your chair does. But the hotter an object is, the higher the energy of the radiation that it emits. The radiation not only gets stronger (more intense), but it also moves further along the electromagnetic spectrum. You emit more thermal radiation than your chair does. Objects that are hot enough glow red. Even hotter objects give out more of the other colours of the spectrum, as well as red light. A light bulb, for example, gives a mixture of red, orange, yellow and green light, but not so much blue or violet light. The Sun is hot enough to give out an even mix of all colours, and ultraviolet radiation and even some X-rays as well.

▲ Objects at different temperatures. The warmer objects emit more high energy radiation.

Energy transfers away from a black object more quickly than from a white or silver object which is at the same temperature. Dark objects also absorb (take in) thermal radiation more quickly.

▶ *Look at the photograph at the bottom of page 86 and identify four objects that are at different temperatures. Put them in order, according to the energy of the radiation they emit.*

▶ *Which would you expect to get hotter on a bright sunny day, the surface of a black car or the surface of a white car?*

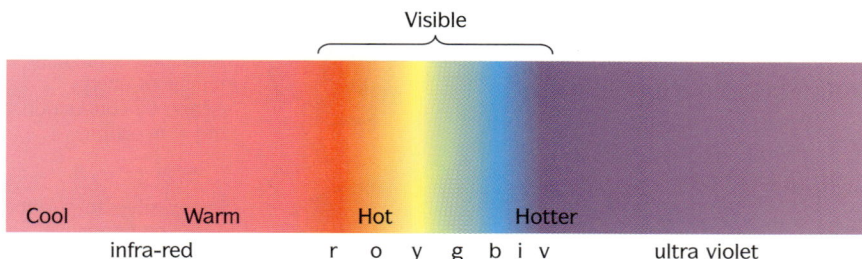

🔺 People are warmer than their surroundings. We give out higher energy radiation than the cooler things around us do. Radiation detecting equipment – thermal imaging cameras – can spot the difference. They can pick out a living person from a heap of cooler rubble.

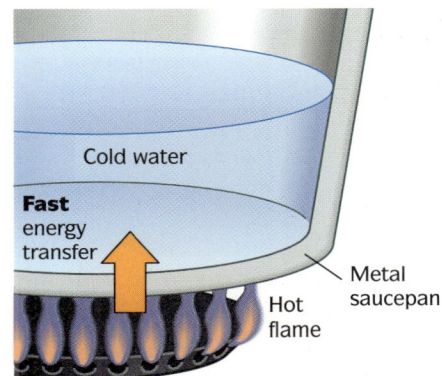

Visible

Cool — Warm — Hot — Hotter

infra-red   r o y g b i v   ultra violet

🔺 The kind of radiation that a body gives out depends on its temperature.

Examples of thermal insulation

Reindeer in the Arctic have to stand and face raging blizzards. Yet their bodies have temperatures similar to yours. Their thermal insulation keeps them alive. **Thermal insulators** are materials which cut down energy transfer.

Reindeer hairs themselves are quite good insulators. They are made of material with particles quite far apart, and no free electrons. Conduction of energy from particle to particle only happens quite slowly, compared to conduction in a material like a metal. But air is a much better insulator than the hair itself. It is the air inside a reindeer's coat that does most to keep it warm.

Double glazing uses the insulating property of air. The air is trapped between layers of glass.

🔺 Reindeer use a layer of trapped air as a thermal insulator.

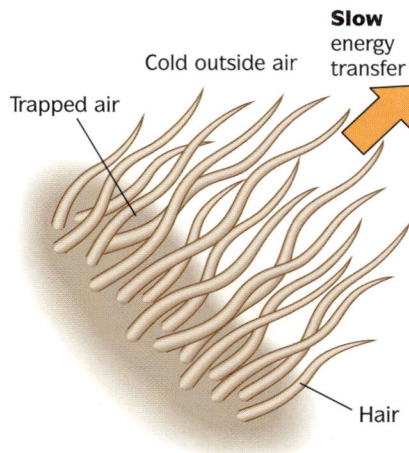

Slow energy transfer

Cold outside air

Trapped air

Hair

🔺 Slow and fast energy transfer.

Cold water

Fast energy transfer

Metal saucepan

Hot flame

▶ *Why is air such a good insulator? Look back a few pages, and read about conduction again.*

▶ *Write down another example of the use of trapped air for thermal insulation.*

A 'Thermos' flask will keep soup or tea hot for hours. It does it by cutting down energy transfer away from the liquid. It cuts down evaporation, convection, conduction and radiation.

Cutting down evaporation away from the liquid is quite easy. The stopper does that. A vacuum inside a glass 'jacket' reduces energy transfer by conduction or convection, because they only take place inside materials. To keep emission of radiation as low as possible, the surface of the glass has a coating of silver. Shiny surfaces emit radiation much more slowly than black surfaces.

▶ *Why does blowing on a cup of tea make it cool down more quickly?*

▶ *Why do conduction and convection only happen in materials, not in a vacuum?*

▶ *Why wouldn't it be sensible to make Thermos flasks with glass surfaces painted black?*

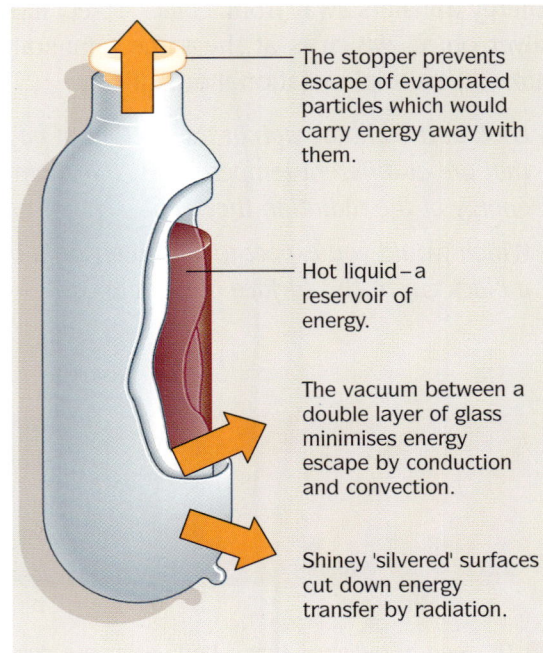

The stopper prevents escape of evaporated particles which would carry energy away with them.

Hot liquid – a reservoir of energy.

The vacuum between a double layer of glass minimises energy escape by conduction and convection.

Shiney 'silvered' surfaces cut down energy transfer by radiation.

🔺 A Thermos flask is designed to minimise energy transfers.

Testing insulating abilities of containers

There are many factors which can affect how quickly a liquid in a container will cool down. Shape, size, colour and material are four factors. Investigating the effect of one of these will need careful planning, meaningful measurements, clever recording of results, and a thoughtful conclusion. (See also 'An investigation of baby clothing' on page 89.)

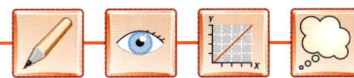

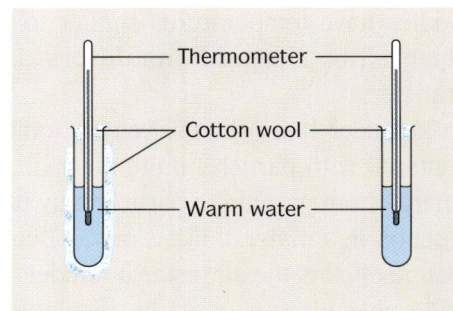

Energy flows and efficiency

Power stations consume energy resources and pollute the atmosphere. But we are all to blame, because we all use electricity. Electricity provides a very convenient way of transferring energy from one place to another.

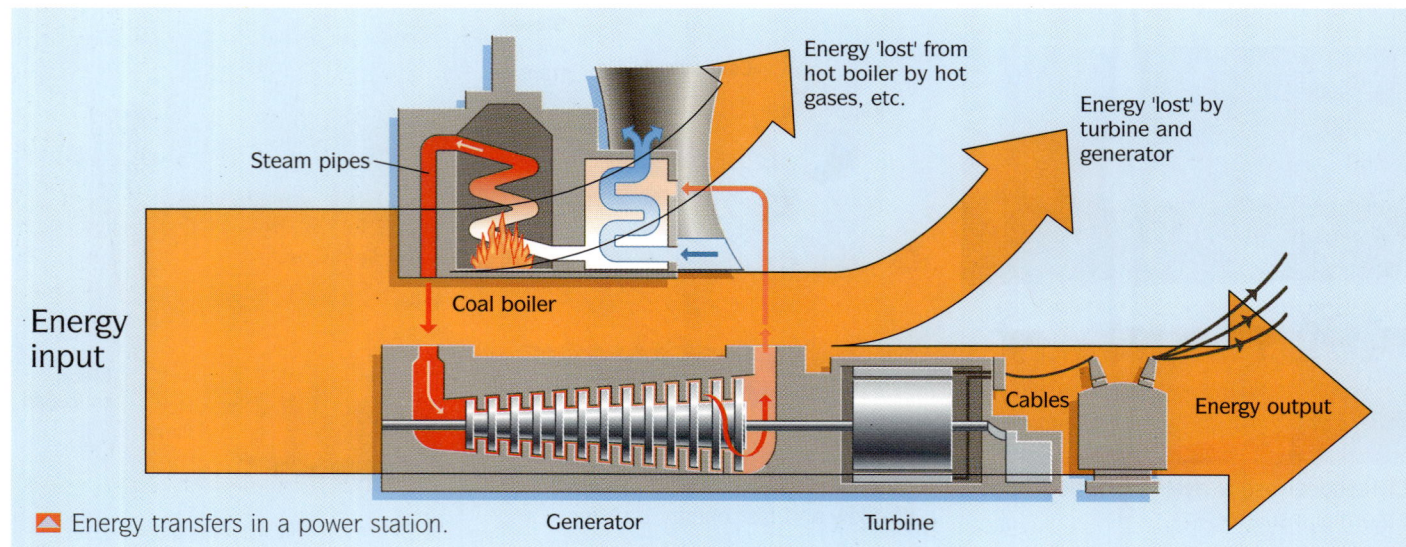

Thermometer

Cotton wool

Warm water

🔺 An idea to get you started.

Energy 'lost' from hot boiler by hot gases, etc.

Energy 'lost' by turbine and generator

Steam pipes

Coal boiler

Energy input

Cables

Energy output

🔺 Energy transfers in a power station.   Generator   Turbine

It is possible to cut down the amount of energy resources that power stations use. It is also possible to cut down their pollution. One way is to try to use as little electricity as possible. We can do that by switching off appliances that we are not using, by using efficient fridges and light bulbs, by not wasting hot water down the drain, and so on. Another way is to make power stations as **efficient** as possible.

Being efficient means making use of as big a proportion as possible of the energy from the original resource. A coal fire, for example, is *not* very efficient because most of the energy from the fuel is transferred straight up the chimney. Only a small proportion heats the room. You can find out how to work out efficiency in Chapter Seven (Energy measurements).

For a typical power station, only about 35 per cent of the energy available from burning fuel is actually transferred into the cables that connect the power station to users. The power station is 35 per cent efficient.

Engineers make sure that power stations run as efficiently as possible. If the efficiency of a power station drops, say, to 30 per cent then the furnaces will need more coal for the same rate of electricity generation. That would mean that there will be less coal for the future, and more pollution. It would also make our electricity more expensive.

🔺 An ordinary filament lamp has an efficiency of only about 3 per cent. Of all the electrical energy transferred into it, it only transfers 3 per cent back out as light. A modern compact fluorescent lamp is about 20 per-cent efficient. It wastes less energy, and less money.

Investigating baby clothing

You may be given a worksheet to help you investigate how a layer of insulator affects energy transfer and the rate of change of temperature.

Future energy resources for the world

Our biggest energy resource at the moment is fossil fuel. That is coal and oil and gas. But the fossil fuels that are in the ground took millions of years to form, and they cannot be quickly replaced. They are not **renewable**.

The burning of fossil fuels also causes smog and acid rain and the release of carbon dioxide, the main cause of global warming. You can read more about this earlier in this Chapter and in the Biology book.

Alternatives to fossil fuels

- Nuclear energy
  Nuclear power stations use tiny amounts of fuel, uranium. Uranium is radioactive and in the power station some of it changes into materials that are even more radioactive. This nuclear waste presents a problem.
- Wind energy
  The warming effect of the Sun on the atmosphere will always create wind. It is a renewable energy resource. The problem is that it takes many wind turbines to generate very much electricity and the turbines can look ugly.
- Solar energy
  Solar cells can take energy directly from sunlight to generate electricity. Solar cells have a big future, but they need sunshine.
- Biomass
  Trees, sugar-cane and algae can all be grown to provide fuel. But large land areas are needed for large-scale production.

🔺 Sunlight provides an energy resource that won't run out – it is a renewable resource.

▶ *Why do we say that solar cells provide a 'renewable' energy resource?*

CHAPTER SIX ■ ENERGY AND RESOURCES 89

World energy resources

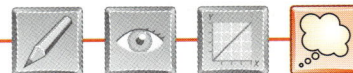

You may be given a worksheet to help you stage a group debate on the need for economical use of energy resources.

Saving the planet starts at home

Governments around the world have agreed to try to do something about reducing use of fossil fuels and carbon dioxide production. We can all help by cutting down on the energy transfers that we are responsible for.

We can start by looking after our homes. Draughtproofing doors and windows is the quickest way to make a difference. Loft insulation and double glazing also help.

Energy-efficient homes

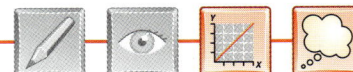

There are a number of ways to reduce energy transfers out of buildings. We can cut fuel bills by making our homes more energy efficient. You may be given a worksheet on energy efficiency.

Summary

- Heating an object means creating thermal energy transfer into the object.
- When an object cools, there is thermal energy transfer away from it.
- When an object is in thermal equilibrium with its surroundings there is no net energy transfer either into it or away from it.
- Conduction involves thermal energy transfer between particles of a material.
- During evaporation, particles of a material carry thermal energy away from it.
- Convection involves thermal energy transfer by movement of some or all of a gas or liquid.
- Radiation is transfer of thermal energy by electromagnetic waves.
- Insulation reduces thermal energy transfer.
- Most of our energy resources will not last for ever.
- Transfer of energy from energy resources can cause environmental damage.
- Efficient energy resources transfer as much as possible of the energy from resources to provide heating and other benefits.
- Inefficient energy transfers are expensive and use large amounts of energy resources.

Revision Questions

1 Make a rough copy of these two babies. Add arrows to your pictures to show the direction of the energy transfers. Use a different thickness of arrow to show fast and slow energy transfers.

2 A company which makes insulation systems uses these logos to represent conduction, convection and radiation.
  a Copy the logos and say which is which.
  b Design your own logo to represent evaporation.

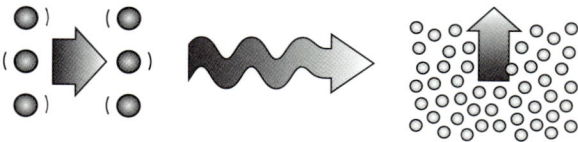

3 Draw a plan of your own home, or part of it. Show the walls, doors and windows. Show how and where you could improve the insulation.

4 Say what is wrong with each of these products:
  a

b

THE **NEW THERMOSTOP** SAUCEPAN MADE WITH THE LATEST INSULATING MATERIALS

c

AT LAST! A LIGHTWEIGHT FRIDGE WITH NO THICK DOORS OR WALLS. MADE OUT OF THIN SHEETS OF **ALUMINIUM** ☆☆☆

5 a Use this information to make a bar chart:

Type of heater	Efficiency [%]
Modern central heating boiler	80
Open fire	30
Gas fire	60
Electrical heater	100

  b Explain why an open fire, such as a coal or log fire, is so inefficient.

6 Filament lights are not very efficient. Compact fluorescent lights are much better.
  a Are there any compact fluorescent lamps:
    i in your home
    ii in your school?
  b Do you think that there should be? Why?

7 A statue has been gently warmed by some winter sunshine. When it goes dark the air temperature suddenly drops. Draw an energy flow diagram for the statue at this time. What happens to the temperature of the statue?

8 Televisions have an input of energy from their electricity supply. They have slots in the casing so that thermal energy can transfer away from them.

a What would happen if energy did not flow away from them while they were working?

b What kind of energy transfer do the slots encourage – conduction, convection, evaporation or radiation?

9

Explain how conduction, convection and radiation all help to keep this person warm.

10 A candle transfers 0.02 per cent of its energy from the burning process to provide the light energy that we want. Its efficiency is 0.02 per cent. The rest of the energy just heats the immediate surroundings.

a What percentage of the candle's energy heats the immediate surroundings?

b If the candle transfers 100 joule of energy, how much of this heats the immediate surroundings?

c How much provides light?

11 Saving energy is good for the environment. People might be more likely to save energy if it was more expensive. Some people suggest that tax on electricity, gas, coal, etc. should be increased to protect the environment. Do you agree with this? Explain your answer.

12 Imagine that you are a Government Minister responsible for future UK energy supplies. You are going to attend a world conference on reducing carbon dioxide emissions. Write a short speech on how the UK is going to tackle the problem.

13 What are the differences, in terms of temperature and energy flow, between a baby and a statue?

14 Do a beaker of hot water and a test tube of cold water make good models for demonstration of energy transfer between a potato and some butter, neither of which are initially liquids? Write down the benefits and the shortcomings of the models. Mention the change of state that is involved. Can you think of a better model?

15 Compare conduction in a metallic and non-metallic solid. Explain the role of the various particles.

16

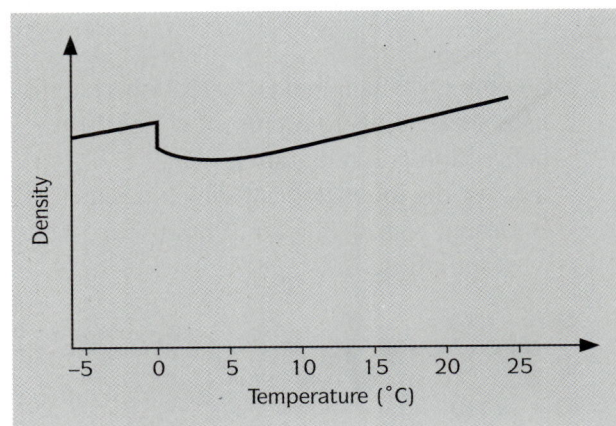

Water behaves uniquely. The graph shows how its density varies as its temperature changes. Refer to the graph.

a Explain why ice floats.

b Explain why water deep in the oceans remains at a near-constant temperature of about 4°C all year round.

c What is meant by the statement, 'For water between 0°C and 4°C, convection is upside down'?

17 Someone says to you, 'It stays cool in the cupboard under our stairs because that's where we keep our freezer.' Draw a sketch to point out the error in this statement.

Energy measurements

What people want

People want energy.

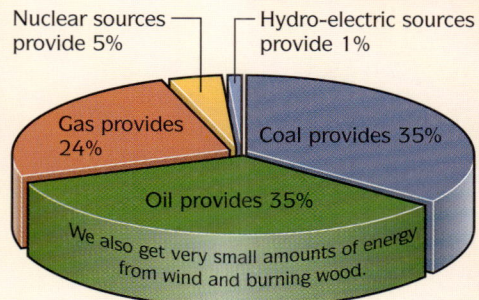

People want power.

Nuclear sources provide 5%

Hydro-electric sources provide 1%

Gas provides 24%

Coal provides 35%

Oil provides 35%

We also get very small amounts of energy from wind and burning wood.

UK energy resources

Daily electricity power in the UK

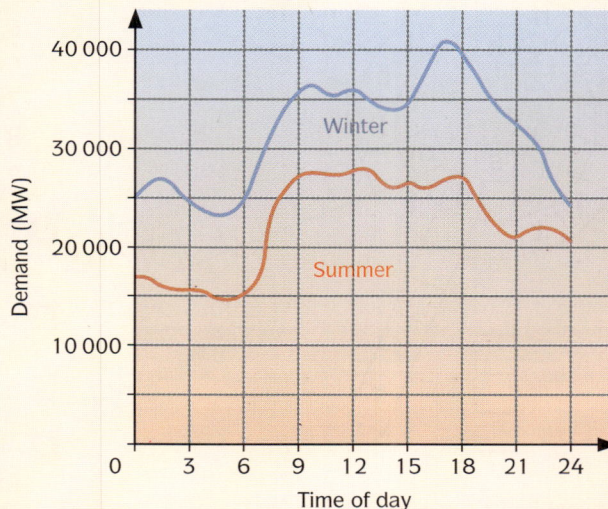

Demand (MW)

40 000

30 000

20 000

10 000

Winter

Summer

0   3   6   9   12   15   18   21   24

Time of day

CHAPTER SEVEN

Review

Energy can be transferred from place to place. In a power station, spinning machinery has energy. It is the energy of material in motion – called kinetic energy. Cables transfer energy to where people live and work. Light carries energy out from lamps. Heaters supply energy to the particles in a room. Motors in hair driers give energy to the air to make it move. Motors on giant cranes pass energy on to heavy loads.

Energy can be stored – transferred into some material and only transferred out again later, when it is wanted to do something useful. Plants transfer energy into their chemistry, by using sunlight to build bigger molecules out of smaller ones. They can store the energy for months or years. When the plant needs energy to live and grow it breaks the bigger molecules back down again. Water in a high reservoir stores energy, called potential energy. When the water is allowed to tumble through pipes it can do useful work, like turning electrical turbines.

In all energy transfers, the total amount of energy always stays the same. It is not possible to create energy out of nothing, or to destroy it. But energy does become less useful. In most energy transfers, energy passes to the molecules of material. It can make the molecules move more quickly. It can raise their temperature. Then it spreads from molecule to molecule, and it usually goes on spreading, until the energy is so spread out that it becomes undetectable.

CHECK SEVEN

1 Copy the word puzzle into your notebook.

Solve the clues and complete your grid.

Clues
1 energy of a moving object
2 energy stored by high-up material
3 it transfers energy to warm its surroundings
4 it transfers energy from a power station to your home
5 they have more energy when they are hot
6 you cannot do this to energy
7 plants' energy source
8 go from place to place, like energy
9 a name sometimes given to lamps

2 Where do you get your personal stored energy from?

3 Look around the room. Write down the names of three pieces of equipment which transfer energy.

4 Abseilers slide down ropes off cliffs. They lose potential energy. Why do they wear gloves? What happens to their energy?

Energy transfer and work

Stand next to the path of a big truck and you will feel a force from the moving air. The sudden gust might push back through a distance. The energy of the moving air does work on you. Energy is the ability to do work.

People all around the world study Science, and it is important that everybody agrees exactly what the key words mean. **Work** is the *force acting* multiplied by the *distance* over which it acts. So work is something that we can measure.

work = force × distance = $F \times d$

The force is measured in newton, the distance is measured in metres and the energy is measured in joule.

If the force of the air from the moving truck is 100 newton and, while the force is acting, it pushes you 0.1 m back, then:

$$\text{work done on you by the air} = \text{force} \times \text{distance} = F \times d$$
$$= 100\,\text{N} \times 0.1\,\text{m}$$
$$= 10\,\text{J}$$

Energy is the ability to do work, so when the air does 10 joule of work on you, it loses 10 joule of energy and transfers it to you. Energy, just like work, is measured in joule.

▶ *What does* energy *mean?*
▶ *What does* work *mean?*

N = newton
J = joule

🔺 A truck transfers energy to the air around it. The moving air can do work.

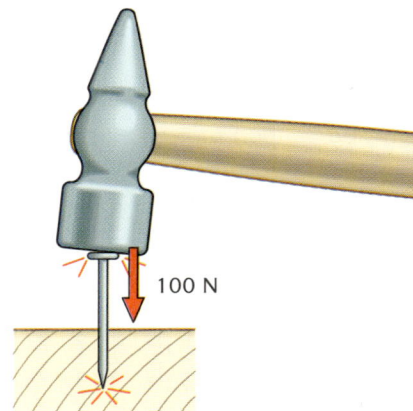

More examples of work

If a car pulls a caravan with a force of 2000 newton for a distance of 100 m, then

$$\text{work done by the car on the caravan} = \text{force} \times \text{distance}$$
$$= 2000\,\text{N} \times 100\,\text{m}$$
$$= 200\,000\,\text{J}$$

The car needs energy to be able to do work. The energy becomes available from burning fuel.

▶ *Imagine that a truck breaks down and has to be towed with a force of 1000 newton for a distance of 1000 m. How much work is done on the truck? Where does the energy come from?*

If a hammer exerts an average force of 100 newton and pushes a nail by a distance of 0.02 m, then:

$$\text{work done by the hammer on the nail} = \text{force} \times \text{distance}$$
$$= 100\,\text{N} \times 0.02\,\text{m}$$
$$= 2\,\text{J}$$

The hammer needs energy to be able to do work on the nail. The hammer has energy because it is moving before it hits the nail. The energy transfers away from the hammer when it hits the nail.

100 N

PHYSICS

▲ Force and distance together – work being done.

▲ Force on the lamp-post but no distance – no work being done.

▲ Distance but little force – little work being done.

Notice that work only gets done if a force acts over a distance. A shelf holding heavy pots of paint does no work because there is force but no distance. A skater does no (or very little) work because there is distance but no (or very little) force.

▶ *How much work is done by a gust of wind on a temporary road sign if it exerts a force of 200 newton while pushing the sign through a distance of 0.4 m?*

▶ *What is the work done by an identical gust of wind on a permanent road sign if it exerts a force of 200 newton but the sign does not move?*

Heating and work

Air from the tube in the picture is pushing water out of the way. It is exerting a force over a distance. It is doing work. But doing work needs a supply of energy.

The hands are warmer than the air in the flask. So energy transfers from the hands to the air. After a few minutes, so much energy could transfer from the hands to the air that the hands cool down and the air warms up, until they have the same temperature. Then there is no more energy transfer. The air no longer has an energy supply, so it cannot do any more work to push water out of the way.

Heating the air allows it to do work. Energy transferred into the air makes its particles move faster. They crash into the glass of the flask harder. At the end of the tube, they crash into the water faster and push it out of the way.

▶ *Why is a balloon more likely to burst if you put it next to a heater?*

▲ Letting the air do the work – but you supply the energy.

Engines

Steam engines use a burning fuel to supply energy to water. The water turns to hot steam, and particles of the steam push on a piston. The particles do work. But not all of the energy is transferred to the piston. A lot of the energy from the burning fuel just heats up the engine and its surroundings. You could say that this energy is wasted.

In car engines, the burning takes place inside a cylinder. The mixture of burned fuel and heated air pushes a piston. The energy of the piston transfers to the wheels, which do work by pushing on the road beneath them. Just as in a steam engine, a lot of energy is wasted in merely heating up the engine and the air around it.

▶ *A car engine and a steam engine both depend on burning fuel, or 'combustion'. Why is a car engine called an* internal *combustion engine?*

Efficiency

An explosion of gunpowder inside the barrel of a cannon provides energy. Some of the energy transfers to the cannonball, which flies out of the gun at high speed. That is what the gunners want. But some energy also makes the gun recoil backwards. And some energy just makes the barrel of the gun very hot. These effects are not what the gunners want. A recoiling cannon can injure or kill a careless gunner who gets in the way. The barrel could become too hot to touch. There is even a danger that a fresh load of gunpowder inside the hot barrel will explode while the gunners are still loading the gun.

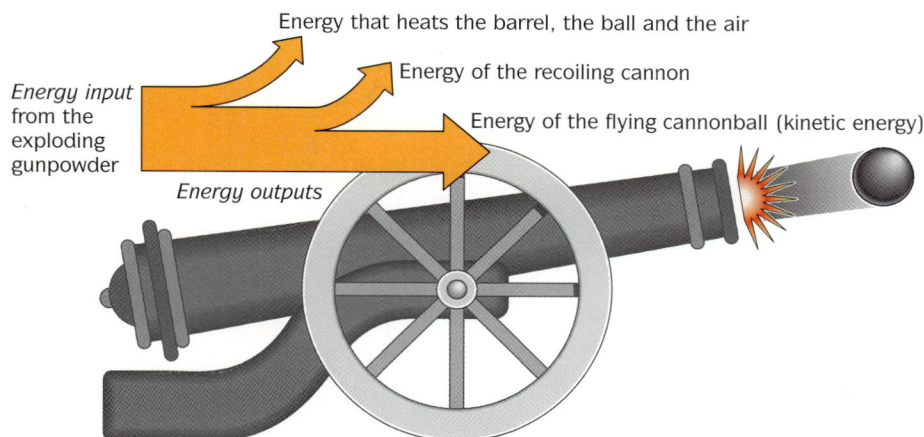

Energy that heats the barrel, the ball and the air

Energy of the recoiling cannon

Energy input from the exploding gunpowder

Energy of the flying cannonball (kinetic energy)

Energy outputs

▶ *In what ways is the process inside a cannon barrel similar to the process inside a car cylinder?*

▶ *Sketch an energy flow diagram for a car engine (see page 88 if you need help).*

The energy input for a cannon is the energy from the explosion of gunpowder, which is a rapid burning process. The useful energy output is the energy that is transferred to the motion of the cannonball.

Efficiency gives us a way of measuring the proportion of the energy from the burning explosive that successfully transfers to where it is wanted. It is expressed as a percentage.

$$\text{efficiency} = \frac{\text{useful energy output in a certain time}}{\text{energy input during the same time}} \times 100\%$$

▶ *For the cannon, why is the useful energy output less than the energy input?*

PHYSICS

An efficiency example

An electric motor transfers energy. Its energy input comes from the electricity supply. The story of transfer of energy to a motor is a long one, and at each stage of the story energy is 'wasted' in heating up the surroundings.

The useful energy output of a motor is the work that it does when it exerts a force on some material while making it move through some distance.

Suppose that somebody cleans a bedroom carpet with a vacuum cleaner. In the time that it takes, the energy transferred to the motor from the electricity supply could be 50 000 joule. The useful work that the motor does, moving air so that it picks up dirt, is 20 000 joule.

$$\text{efficiency} = \frac{\text{useful energy output while the motor is running}}{\text{energy input to the motor during the same time}} \times 100\%$$

useful energy output is 20 000 J

$$= \frac{20\,000\,\text{J}}{50\,000\,\text{J}} \times 100\%$$

energy input is 50 000 J

$$= 0.4 \times 100\%$$

$$= 40\%$$

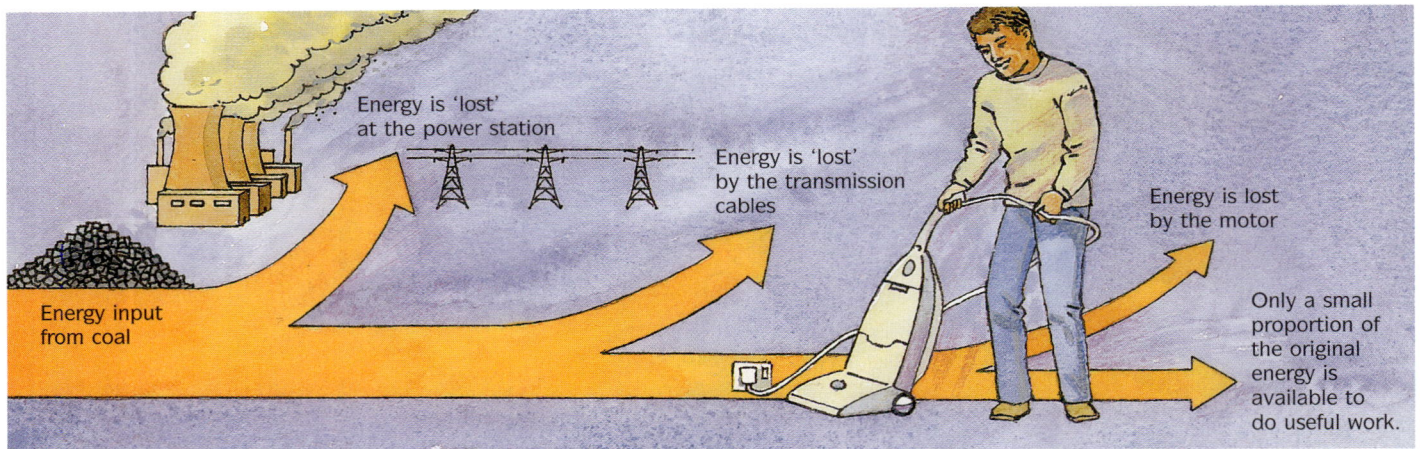

▲ Energy transfer from a power station to the home.

▶ *Why is it important to the environment to make the efficiency of a power station as high as possible?*

Efficiency and streamlining

A modern car has an efficiency of about 30 per cent – its useful energy output is 30 per cent of the energy input from the fuel. But 70 per cent of the energy potentially available from the fuel simply heats the engine, or other moving parts, and creates turbulence in the air.

Car manufacturers try to improve the fuel consumption figures of their vehicles. They can make sure that air flows out of the way in a smoother, less turbulent way by 'streamlining' their cars.

▲ Lower drag gives higher efficiency.

Comparing efficiency of transport

A bike is the most efficient form of transport that exists. But it is not easy to measure the efficiency of transport. You need to know the energy input and the useful energy output during the same time.

Measuring the energy input is not too difficult. It is a matter of measuring the amount of fuel or oxygen taken in, and working it out from that. Measuring the energy output is more difficult, because energy transferred to the air ends up creating a chaos of swirling air and finally doing nothing more than slightly warming the air. What you can do is measure how much energy input the different forms of transport need to do the same useful job. The graph shows the energy inputs needed to move each kg of load through a distance of 1 km.

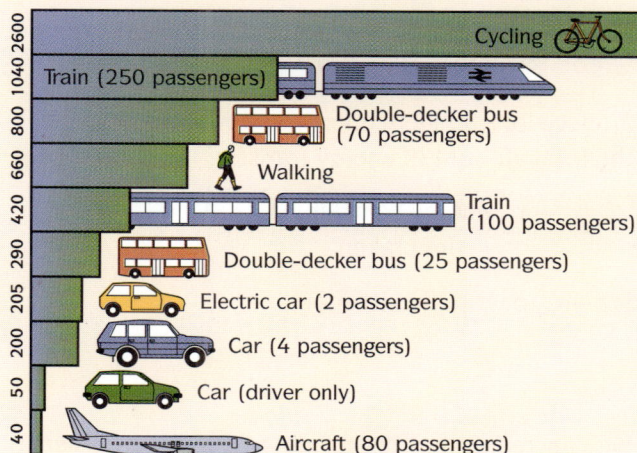

Passenger Transport Energy Consumption

How far can one passenger go on 5 litres of petrol or the equivalent amount of energy? Distances are in kilometres.

Power

Doing work and transferring energy can be very useful. And the rate of doing the work is important. A horse and a human might both be able to pull a boat along a canal, but the horse can do it faster. The horse is more powerful.

Before steam engines came along, horses provided the most powerful way of doing work. James Watt was a Scottish engineer who built steam engines. He was also good at selling. To sell steam engines to owners of mills and mines he compared them with horses. He measured his engines by their *horsepower*.

Now the watt, not the horsepower, is the international unit, but **power** is still the rate of doing work.

$$\text{power} = \text{rate of doing work} = \frac{\text{work done}}{\text{time taken}} = \frac{E}{t}$$

Very often, energy is transferred without any physical work being done. For example, on a cold day energy is continuously transferring from a warm building to the air outside. We still use power to measure the rate of the energy transfer.

$$\text{power} = \text{rate of energy transfer} = \frac{\text{amount of energy transferred}}{\text{time taken}} = \frac{E}{t}$$

▶ *Which transfers energy faster, a 100 watt light bulb or a 60 watt light bulb?*

▶ *How could you use a horse to light up a light bulb?*

W = watt. 1 watt is 1 joule per second.

Here, we have used E for work as well as for energy.

🔺 Pulling power. A horse can work at a higher rate than a human.

A power example

An electric fire transfers 1000 joule of energy in 1 s. To work out its power:

energy transferred is 1000 J

$$\text{power} = \frac{\text{energy transferred}}{\text{time taken}} = \frac{1000\,\text{J}}{1\,\text{s}} = 1000\,\text{W}$$

time taken is 1 s

PHYSICS

Harder power examples

A horse pulling a barge exerts a steady force of 2000 newton for 1 minute, and moves the barge 300 m. To work out its power:

$$\text{power} = \frac{\text{work done}}{\text{time taken}} = \frac{\text{force} \times \text{distance}}{\text{time taken}} = \frac{2000\,\text{N} \times 300\,\text{m}}{60\,\text{s}} = 10\,000\,\text{W}$$

Note that 10 000 W can also be written as 10 kW. This cuts out the need to write down so many noughts.

A television transfers energy at a rate of 500 watt for 3 hours. To work out the total amount of energy transfer:

$$\text{power} = \frac{\text{energy transfer}}{\text{time taken}}$$

It helps to write this in short:

$$P = \frac{E}{t}$$

We can rearrange this formula to make it easier to work out E. (You can read more about this in *Rearranging formulae* in Chapter Sixteen – Physics help).

$E = P \times t$ power   time

$= 500\,\text{W} \times 3\ \text{hours}$

$= 500\,\text{W} \times 3 \times 3600\,\text{s}$

$= 5\,400\,000\,\text{J}$

Note that 5 400 000 J is the same as 5 400 kJ or 5.4 MJ.

k (kilo) always means 'thousand' and M (mega) always means 'million'.

Personal power

You may be given a worksheet to help you practise measuring your own power in some different situations.

Car safety – kinetic energy

Every passenger in a car has kinetic energy. In fact, every moving object is capable of doing work on anything with which it collides. A problem arises when the passenger or driver loses this kinetic energy too quickly. Then she does work, at high power, on other objects such as a steering wheel, a windscreen or a seatbelt.

The purpose of safety devices like seatbelts and airbags is to increase the distance travelled by the passenger while the energy loss takes place. For a given amount of energy, a bigger distance results in a smaller force, since:

energy loss = force × distance

▶ *The front of most cars is built as a 'crumple zone'. It gradually buckles and bends in a head-on accident. Why does it make a car safer to have a section that is designed to crumple in this way?*

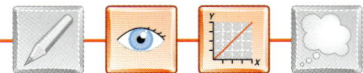

A car windscreen only gives a little. The force on the head is big.

A seatbelt is designed to stretch. The person is stopped more gradually and more gently over a longer distance.

Gaining kinetic energy

A tennis player, serving the ball, throws the ball up. Then she hits it when it is roughly at the top of its motion. At that point, just for an instant, the ball is not moving. Kinetic energy is the energy carried by a moving object. A ball that is not moving has no kinetic energy.

But the moving racket transfers some of its energy to the ball. It does work on the ball, exerting a force over a distance. The ball gains kinetic energy.

kinetic energy gained by ball = energy transferred to it from the racket

= work done on the ball by the racket

▶ *A person gives a ball 100 joule of energy. How much work do they have to do on the ball to achieve this?*

Losing kinetic energy

To slow down, an object must lose kinetic energy. It must transfer its energy to something else. In fairground bumpercars, for example, one car can transfer kinetic energy to another. One car does work on another. If the cars are perfectly bouncy, and a moving car bumps into a stationary car, then:

kinetic energy lost by first car = work done by first car on the second car

= kinetic energy gained by the second car

However, in reality the cars are not perfectly bouncy, and some of the original energy heats up the material of the cars by a small amount.

▶ *A bumper car with 3000 joule of kinetic energy crashes into a stationary car. What is the maximum kinetic energy that the second car could gain? Why will the actual energy gained be less than this?*

▲ Losing and gaining kinetic energy.

Kinetic energy – speed and mass

Energy is the ability to do work. So kinetic energy is the ability of a moving body to do work on other objects when it collides with them. A snooker ball does work on other snooker balls, and transfers energy to them.

A fast snooker ball can do more work, and transfer more energy, than a slow one. The fast ball has more kinetic energy.

Suppose that a snooker player uses a steel cue ball. The steel ball is heavier – it has more mass. The player will have to hit it hard to give it a good speed – it takes more work to accelerate the steel ball than a standard snooker ball. The player must transfer more energy to the steel ball.

Then when the steel ball hits other balls, it has more energy to transfer to them. The heavy ball has more kinetic energy than an ordinary one going at the same speed.

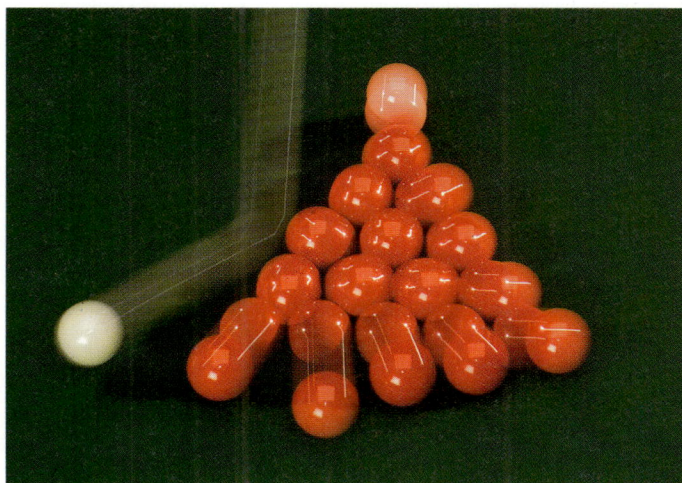

PHYSICS

So kinetic energy of a moving body depends on two things, its speed and its mass. The formula that relates total kinetic energy to mass and speed is:

$$\text{kinetic energy} = \frac{1}{2} \times \text{mass} \times \text{speed}^2$$

$$= \frac{1}{2}mv^2$$

> If two objects collide and the total amount of kinetic energy stays the same, it is an **elastic** collision.
>
> If some energy is transferred into the objects to heat them up, it is an **inelastic** collision.

STOPPING DISTANCES

Two factors that influence the distance travelled by a car in an emergency stop are the reaction time of the driver and the time it takes for the brakes to bring the car to a halt.

The time taken for the driver to see a hazard and to apply pressure to the brake pedal is fixed. For an alert driver this could be 0.7 s, regardless of speed. In this 0.7 s the car will travel further at higher speed. The relationship between speed and distance travelled during reaction time is relatively simple.

The car loses kinetic energy during braking. Kinetic energy does not increase by the same proportion as speed, but by the same proportion as the *square* of the speed.

$$\text{kinetic energy} = \frac{1}{2}mv^2$$

So, for example, doubling the speed quadruples the kinetic energy of the car that must be lost in an accident. It quadruples the necessary braking distance for a given braking force.

You can read more about stopping distances in Chapter Nine (Measuring motion)

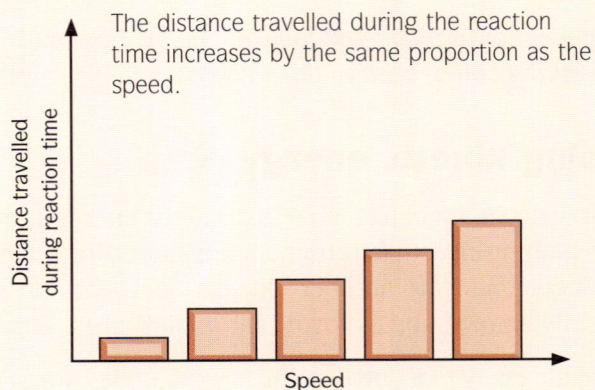

The distance travelled during the reaction time increases by the same proportion as the speed.

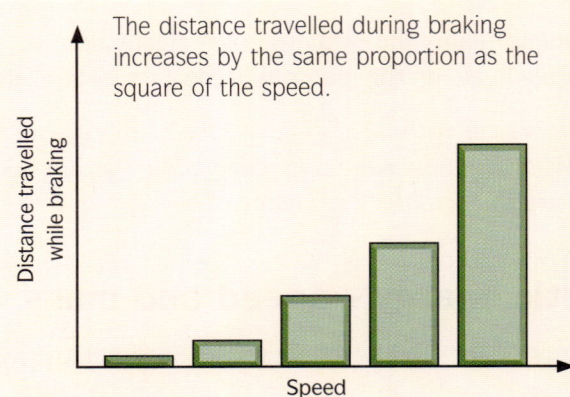

The distance travelled during braking increases by the same proportion as the square of the speed.

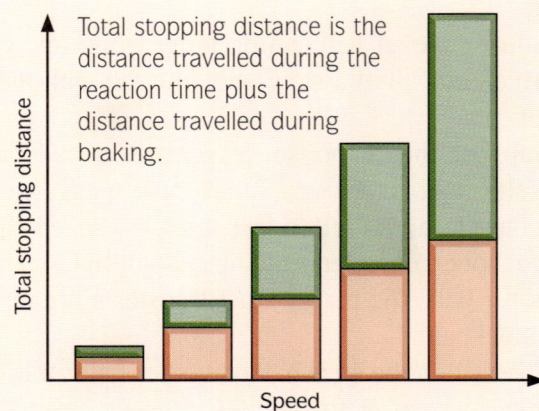

Total stopping distance is the distance travelled during the reaction time plus the distance travelled during braking.

Gaining potential energy

To lift an object up, you have to do work on it. You have to transfer energy to it. Then when the object falls back down it loses the energy. This energy is called the **potential energy** of the object.

For example, for a lift,

potential energy gained by a lift

> = work done on the lift in giving it potential energy

> = the work that the lift can do if it falls back down

You can work out the potential energy gained by the lift and its passengers:

potential energy gained

> = work done

> = force × distance

> = weight of lift × height gained

> $= W \times h$

▶ *When does a lift have more work to do – when it is lifting a pair of twins through 4 floors or just one twin through 10 floors?*

Using water to store potential energy

Electricity companies need to supply energy to match the energy transfers going on in homes and factories. But people's demand for energy can change very rapidly. For example, during a commercial break in a popular television programme kettles go on all over the country.

It is not possible for coal-fired power stations and nuclear power stations to increase their power quickly enough to cope with sudden changes in electrical demand. But hydro-electric systems can be turned on and off very quickly.

At Dinorwic in North Wales, there is a huge underground reservoir system. At night, when most people are sleeping, motors pump water up into a high-level storage reservoir. Then when there are bursts of high demand for electricity, the water is allowed to fall back down again. The falling water drives generators.

The process is quite efficient. Little energy is lost in causing unwanted heating.

work done by motors pushing water into storage reservoir

> = potential energy gained by the water

> = work the water can do to turn generators when it falls back down

▶ *What is most likely to be happening to water at Dinorwic,*
a *at two minutes to eight on a Monday evening*
b *at two o'clock in the morning?*

🔺 High-level storage of water means that there is potential energy which can be made available very quickly.

Weightlifting

A competing weightlifter must do work, exerting a force on the weight and moving it through a vertical distance. The hoisted weight then possesses energy – it has the potential to do work itself when it falls back down. This energy is potential energy.

The power output of the lifter varies considerably during the lift. There are times when she is manoeuvring her body and the weight is not rising. At these times she is doing no work on the weight and her effective power output is zero. At other times she uses leg muscles, which are much stronger than her arm muscles, to provide maximum power and rapid lift.

Some typical values:

height through which weight is lifted = 2.0 m

mass = 120 kg

time taken for the lift = 6 s

The average force needed to lift this mass is its weight, found by multiplying the mass by the strength of the Earth's gravitational field, 10 N/kg (see box):

force = weight = 120 kg × 10 N/kg = 1200 N

Note that there is a distinction between mass, in kg, and weight, in newton. Mass is the quantity of material of a body, which is the same wherever the body might possibly go, and that could include the surface of the Moon, or somewhere outside the Galaxy. Weight is the force of gravity on a body, which is very nearly the same at all points on the Earth's surface, but would be less on the Moon and less again in far space. Everyday life goes on on the surface of one planet, so often there is no need to trouble with the distinction. Physics deals with universal behaviour, and so the distinction matters here.

work done by the lifter on the weight = average force × distance

= 1200 N × 2.0 m

= 2400 J

This is equal to the gravitational potential energy gained by the weight. Note that any change in gravitational potential energy can be calculated by:

change in gravitational potential energy
    = mass × gravitational field strength (10 N/kg) × change in height

The power of the lifter varies considerably during the lift, but,

$$\text{average power} = \frac{\text{total energy transfer}}{\text{total time taken}} = \frac{2400\,\text{J}}{6\,\text{s}} = 400\,\text{W}$$

This is similar to the power of four ordinary electric lamps.

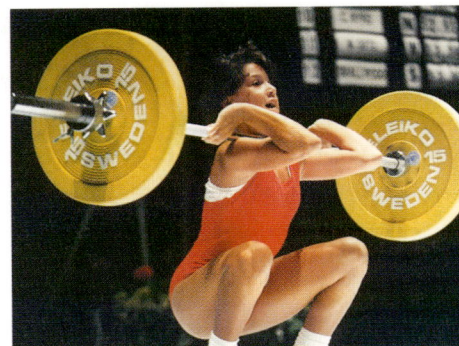
Weightlifting involves work, power, and gravitational potential energy.

A more precise measurement of the Earth's gravitational field strength is 9.81 N/kg. In most calculations it is precise enough to use a value of 10 N/kg. See also page 146.

Transfer and conservation of energy

An engine burning fuel transfers energy to a pile-driver, raising it up so that its gravitational potential energy increases. The pile-driver then falls, its kinetic energy increasing as its potential energy decreases. It hits the pile, exerting a force and moving the pile a short distance further into the ground. But, this is not the end of the energy. The engine, the air, the pile-driver, the pile and the ground beneath them, all become a bit warmer. Energy has gone to the molecules of the materials. The energy still exists, in a useless form, inside the various materials.

The fuel of the pile-driver engine is not the start of the story. If it is a fossil fuel (oil or gas or coal) then the energy is available now as a result of photosynthesis by plants, hundreds of millions of years ago. The plants used sunlight to create their original carbohydrate fuel stores. It was the Sun that supplied the energy.

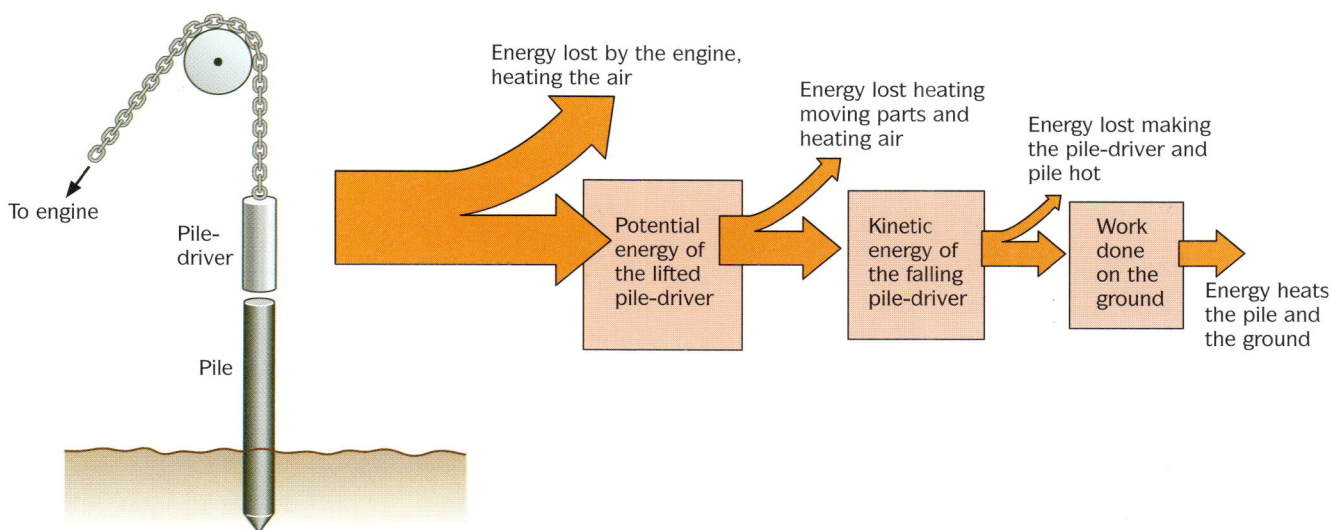

Energy input equals total energy output.

To make the pile-driver work, energy has been transferred from place to place. During photosynthesis it was transferred from sunlight into chemical bonds in the plants. In the burning of the fuel some of it was transferred into the kinetic energy of the engine, though much of it simply heated the engine and its surroundings. The gravitational potential energy of the pile-driver increased as it lifted up. As it fell the potential energy became kinetic energy. Then useful work was done on the pile, pushing it into the ground. Finally, the ground and the pile became a little bit warmer, and energy transferred out from them by conduction into the surrounding materials.

At the end of the process the energy has not been destroyed, but has spread uselessly into the surroundings. The total energy output of any process, whether useful or not, is identical to its input – this is the principle of **conservation of energy**.

▶ *You have to burn food in your body to run up a hill. What happens to the energy that is made available by the burning food?*

Bouncing balls

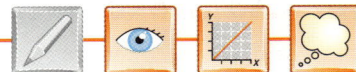

Ball manufacturers need as much information as they can get about their products. People who make the rules of sport also need full and reliable information. You could carry out an investigation to compare the bounce of different types of ball. You may be given a worksheet to help you with this investigation.

Summary

- Work is done when a force makes an object move through a distance.
- The amount of work is the force multiplied by the distance.
- Energy is the ability to do work.
- Work and energy are measured in joule, J.
- Efficiency can be worked out using:

$$\text{efficiency} = \frac{\text{useful energy output}}{\text{energy input in the same time}} \times 100\%.$$

- Power is the rate of doing work, or the rate of transferring energy.
- Power can be worked out using:

$$\text{power} = \frac{\text{work done}}{\text{time taken}}$$

or

$$\text{power} = \frac{\text{energy transferred}}{\text{time taken}}$$

- Power is measured in watt, W.
- A moving object has kinetic energy.
- An object gains kinetic energy when work is done on it. The amount of kinetic energy it gains is equal to the work done on it.
- An object with kinetic energy can do work on other objects. Then it loses kinetic energy.
- The kinetic energy of an object depends on its mass and its speed.
- When an object is lifted up it gains potential energy.
- The amount of potential energy it gains is equal to the work done on it to lift it.
- The potential energy gained by an object depends upon its weight and the height that it gains.

Revision Questions

1 How can a skater glide along without doing any work?

2 Why is it hard to do work on a lamp-post, even if you push very hard?

3 How does a car engine 'waste' energy?

4 An old car engine is 5 per-cent efficient. A modern electrical car is 90 per-cent efficient. Which one wastes more energy for a particular journey?

5 One horsepower is the same as about 750 watt. Estimate the maximum power (in watt) that you could manage.

6 A baseball player does 100 joule of work with a bat on a ball. How much kinetic energy does the ball gain?

7 What is the difference between energy and work?

8 You lift a pile of plates onto a shelf. You have to exert a force and do work. The shelf also exerts a force. Why doesn't it have to do any work?

9 Why do you have to do more work to push a car for 100 m than to push a truck for 1 m?

10 A footballer's boot is in contact with a ball, and the average force on the ball is 80 newton. During this time the ball moves 0.2 m.
   a How much work is done on the ball?
   b Where does the energy come from?
   c What type of energy does the ball gain?

11 An electric winch is attached to a boat by a cable. It exerts a steady force of 800 newton on the boat, and pulls it 6 m up a slipway. How much work does the winch do on the boat?

12 A street light transfers energy outwards at a rate of 400 joule of energy every second. The energy input is 2000 joule every second. What is the efficiency of the street light?

13 'A long-distance runner uses more energy, but a sprinter has more power.' Do you agree with this? Explain your ideas.

14 Calculate the power of a person who runs upstairs, gaining 10 000 joule of potential energy every 5 s.

15 A force of 5000 newton acts on a spacecraft for a distance of 400 m. How much kinetic energy does the spacecraft gain?

16 When a hockey ball bounces, is it an elastic or inelastic collision?

17 Mount Everest is about 8000 m above sea level. The weight (force of gravity) of an average adult is about 800 newton.
   a Estimate your own weight in newton.
   b How much potential energy would you gain if you climbed Everest?

18 What is the principle of conservation of energy?

19 Your voice does work when you speak. Energy transfers to your surroundings. What happens to the energy?

20 A hammer exerts a force of 40 newton and does 0.60 joule of work on a nail. How far does the nail move?

21 Explain why engines are not 100 per-cent efficient.

22 A steam turbine in a power station has an efficiency of 45 per cent.
   a What energy input per second is needed if the turbine is to supply an energy output at a rate of 100 megajoule every second?
   b Where does the turbine get energy from?
   c Where does the energy go to?
   d What is the power output of the turbine?

23 A car engine has a power output of 75 kilowatt.
  a How much useful work can it do in 10 s?
  b What is the maximum amount of kinetic energy that it could gain in the 10 s?
  c If it has a mass of 1000 kg, what speed would it then reach?
  d Why does a car have to keep on using fuel, after it has stopped gaining speed?

24 Explain why the graph of car stopping distances against speed is not a straight line.

25 The diagram shows an adventure park ride.
  a What energy transfers go on as the truck moves along the ride?
  b How does the principle of conservation of energy help the ride designers to build a ride that is both effective and safe?

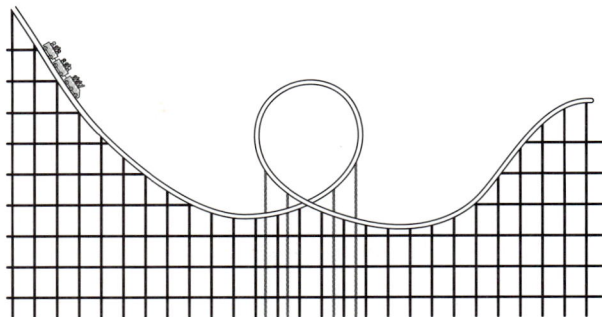

Moving, falling & stretching

■ Gravity games

Getting the Physics right is a matter of life and death in more than just bungee jumping. People who design buildings, aircraft and cars all need to understand about motion and the effects of forces on materials.

Some people like to be scared. They like the feeling of surviving their own fear. Bungee jumping provides an excellent way to get very, very scared. Yet the Physics is all worked out – the force of the stretching cord eventually matches gravitational force. The jumper bounces to a stop, safely hanging above the ground.

Review

Before going any further, read this page and attempt the tasks. Write the answers in your notes.

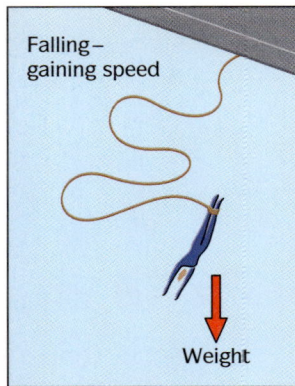

Falling – gaining speed

Weight

▲ The speed of the bungee jumper changes as she falls. When she takes to the air, there is no other force to balance the force of gravity – she accelerates towards the Earth. She could fall nearly 5 m, the height of a two-storey building, in the first second. That is an average speed of 5 m/s.

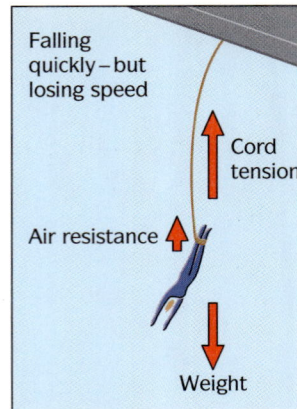

Falling quickly – but losing speed

Cord tension

Air resistance

Weight

▲ The jumper feels the wind in her face as air resistance begins to play a part, acting on her in the opposite direction to the gravitational pull. And as the cord stretches its tension provides an upwards force that gets bigger and bigger. So her speed increases, but then decreases. She might take 4 s to complete a 16 m fall. That is an average speed of 4 m/s.

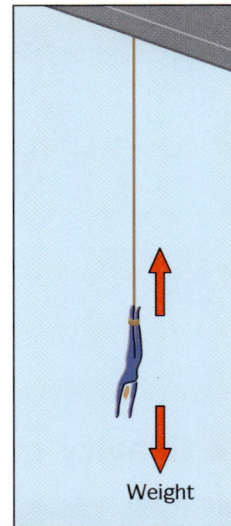

Weight

▲ Eventually, after several up and down bounces, the bungee jumper comes to a halt at the place where the upwards force of the cord and the downwards force of her weight are balanced.

CHECK EIGHT

1 Solve the anagrams:
cofer – it changes motion
ari – it produces resistance to the motion of a bungee jumper
clear notice – it happens when your speed changes
ned is cat – at high speed you cover a lot in a short time
deeps – a measurement of motion
it gravy – it gives you your weight
emit – it's measured in seconds

2 Which force grows to be bigger (some of the time) than the gravitational force (weight) acting on the jumper?

3 What is another name for the force of gravity acting on you?

4 Why is the average speed of the bungee jumper less for the whole jump than it is for the first second?

Steady speed

High speed means covering a large distance in a short time. High-speed trains manage 250 km/h – 250 kilometres per hour. A formula shows how speed, distance and time are related together:

for anything moving at a steady speed,

$$\text{speed} = \frac{\text{distance covered}}{\text{time taken}}$$

or, in short,

$$s = \frac{d}{t}$$

You could use a table to work out how far a high-speed train will travel in different lengths of time, if it keeps up a steady speed:

Speed (km/h)	250	250	250	250	250
Time (h)	0.5	1.0	1.5	2.0	2.5
Distance (km)	125	250	375	500	625

▶ *Use a calculator to check the table. Divide the distances by the times.*

▶ *How far would the train travel in 3 hours at a steady speed of 250 km/h?*

▶ *Do you think that a real train could keep going at exactly 250 km/h for 3 hours?*

High speed, low speed and units

The usual unit of distance is the metre, or m for short. The usual unit for time is the second, s. Using these units in calculations gives answers in metres per second, or m/s. For the motion of some objects, it is sometimes easier to use other units, such as millimetres, mm, for distance, and hours, h, for time.

Some calculations of speed and average speed

A cyclist on a clear stretch of road keeps up a steady speed and travels 180 m in 12 s. To work out the cyclist's speed:

the speed formula $d = 180\,\text{m}$ $180 \div 12 = 15$

$$s = \frac{d}{t} = \frac{180\,\text{m}}{12\,\text{s}} = 15\,\text{m/s}$$ unit

$t = 12\,\text{s}$

▲ High-speed trains like this one in France, can manage speeds of up to 250 km/h – that's about 70 m/s.

▲ Snails only travel short distances in one second. So millimetres are sensible units for measuring snail distance. A snail which travels 4 mm in every second has a speed of 4 mm/s.

▲ For really high speed you have to start thinking about the motion of objects in space. A television satellite in orbit needs a speed of about 500 m/s to keep up with the spinning Earth. That's 1800 km in an hour.

PHYSICS

Suppose that the cyclist travels a short journey through traffic, and takes 100 s for the 750 m journey. This time the cyclist's speed is not steady. Some of the time, such as at traffic lights, speed is zero. At other times the speed is fast. A speedometer on the bike would tell the cyclist the speed, instant by instant. But for the whole journey we can only work out the *average* speed. The calculation is exactly the same as for a steady speed journey:

the formula in letters   the formula in numbers   the answer with the unit for speed

$$s = \frac{d}{t} = \frac{750\,m}{100\,s} = 7.5\,m/s$$

▶ *Work out the speed of a snail which covers 40 mm in 20 s.*
▶ *Work out the average speed of a car which travels 1000 m in 50 s.*

Useful calculations

If you know your speed and how long you have been travelling at that speed, you can work out how far you have travelled. But the formula has to be rearranged to work out distance.

$$s = \frac{d}{t} \text{ becomes } d = s \times t$$

You can find out more about the mathematical rules of rearranging formulae in Chapter Sixteen (Physics help).

For example, to find the distance travelled by a ship in 3 hours, at a steady speed of 35 km/h:

$$d = s \times t = 35\,km/h \times 3h = 105\,km$$

That information could help a submarine's navigator to work out the submarine's exact position.

Alternatively, if you know how far you want to travel, and you know what average speed you can manage, then you can estimate how long it will take. That requires a third version of the formula:

$$s = \frac{d}{t} \text{ becomes } t = \frac{d}{s}$$

Then to find out how long it will take you to do a 60 km journey at an average speed of 40 km/h:

$$t = \frac{d}{s} = \frac{60\,km}{40\,km/h} = 1.5 \text{ hours}$$

Before setting off, the calculation provides an estimate of the time of arrival at the end of the journey.

▲ Speed varies. Average speed is total distance divided by total time taken.

Distance–time graphs

Safety regulations on the UK rail network say that a gang of workers on a track must have 25 seconds' warning of an approaching train. That gives them time to make sure that they are well out of the way.

It means that trains have to be seen from a long way away. The gang needs a lookout on constant duty. Distance–time graphs are useful for working out just how far the lookout needs to be able to see. Of course, that depends on the speed of the train.

The steepness or gradient of the graphs provides an instant way of seeing which train is faster. Looking more closely, the gradient provides more information.

The gradient of a graph is a number, worked out by first drawing a right-angled triangle, using the line of the graph as the longest side (hypotenuse). The length of the vertical side of the triangle is a measurement of a particular distance travelled. The length of the horizontal side is a measurement of the time taken to travel the distance. You divide the vertical length by the horizontal length to work out the gradient.

So the gradient of a distance–time graph is a measurement of distance divided by the matching time. That means that it is a measurement of speed.

$$\text{gradient of a distance–time graph} = \frac{\text{distance}}{\text{time}} = \text{speed}$$

▶ *What is the distance travelled by a 90 km/h train in the 25 s warning time?*

▶ *What is the gradient of the graph for the fastest train? If you need help with graphs and graph gradients, you can read more about them in Chapter Sixteen (Physics help).*

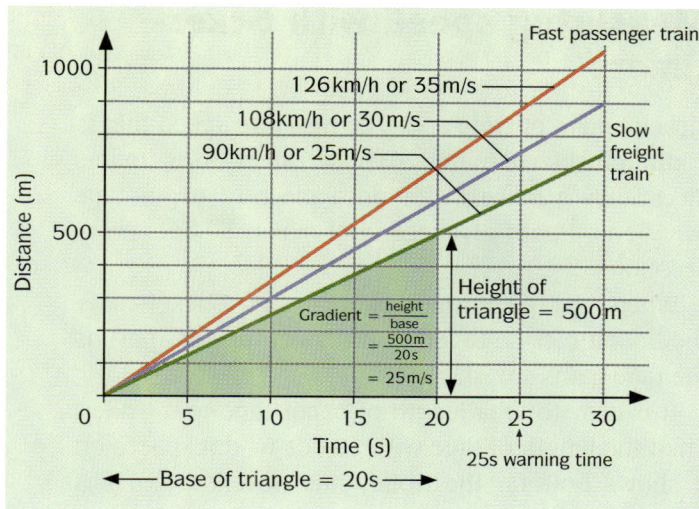

Distance and time on the tracks

You will probably need practice before you can be confident about using graphs. You may be given a worksheet to give you some practice.

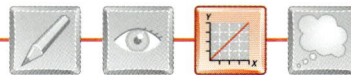

Measuring speed, instant by instant

A driver wanting to stay inside the speed limit in a town does not want to know the average speed for the last half hour or the last half minute. The car speedometer must give an instant-by-instant measurement of speed.

A car speedometer is an electromagnetic device. The faster the wheels go around, the bigger the current in the circuit. The speedometer on the car instrument panel is a lot like an ammeter – it gives a reading that depends on the current flowing through it.

▶ *Roughly how far had Car A gone when it had its highest speed?*

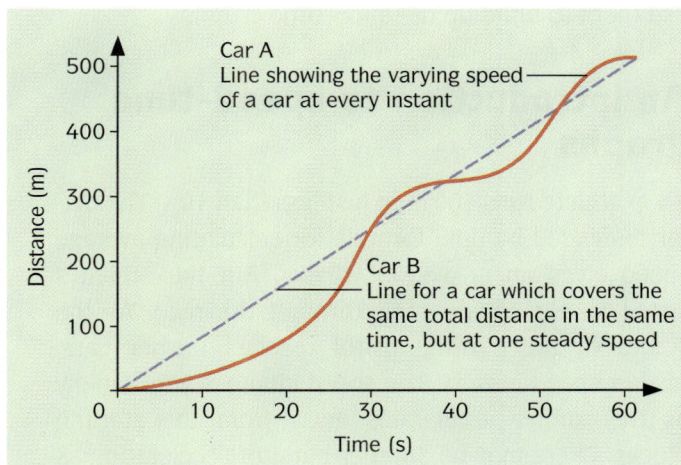

▲ In this distance–time graph, both lines show the same average speed.

Measuring speed with ticker-timers

Ticker-timers provide a way to measure speed that is continuously changing. A ticker-timer uses mains electricity to make a dot on a piece of paper tape every one-fiftieth of a second. It makes 50 dots every second.

When the tape moves slowly through a ticker-timer the dots are close together. They get further apart as the tape gains speed.

It is easy to fix a length of paper tape to a trolley. Then the length of tape with 50 dot-to-dot spaces on it shows how far the trolley has travelled in 1 s. A piece of tape with 10 dot-to-dot spaces is as long as the distance the trolley has travelled in one-fifth of a second (0.2 s). To find the distance travelled in 0.2 s is a matter of measuring spaces between dots.

The usual speed formula gives the speed of the trolley:

$$s = \frac{d}{t} = \frac{\text{length of tape for 10 dot-to-dot spaces}}{0.2 \, \text{s}}$$

▶ *What happens to the pattern of dots on a ticker-tape attached to a trolley that is slowing down?*

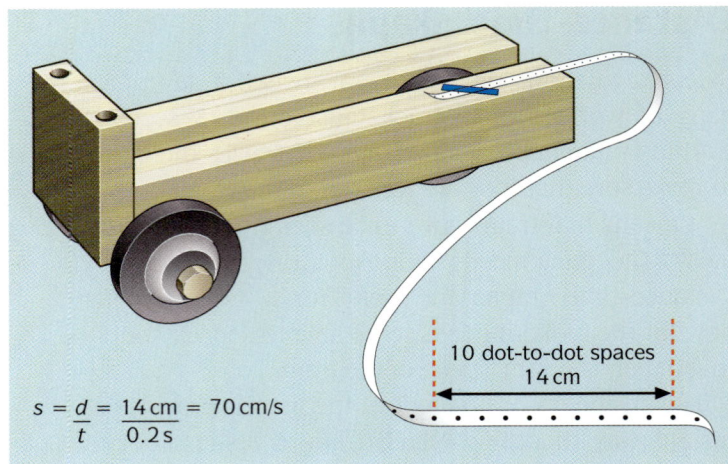

$$s = \frac{d}{t} = \frac{14 \, \text{cm}}{0.2 \, \text{s}} = 70 \, \text{cm/s}$$

10 dot-to-dot spaces
14 cm

Using ticker-timers to investigate motion

You can use ticker-timers and tape to make measurements for different types of trolley motion – such as constant speed motion, acceleration, and deceleration.

By sticking the tapes to a sheet of paper you can use them to build up distance–time graphs.

An introduction to speed–time graphs

A top athlete runs 100 m in just less than 10 s. The distance divided by time formula for calculating average speed gives an answer of 10 m/s. But the athlete's speed is not constant all through the race. As the sound of the starting pistol reaches his/her ears, his/her speed is zero. The speed changes very rapidly as the runner accelerates away from the starting blocks. There may be another burst of acceleration as the athlete makes a final lunge for the finish tape.

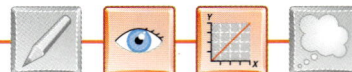

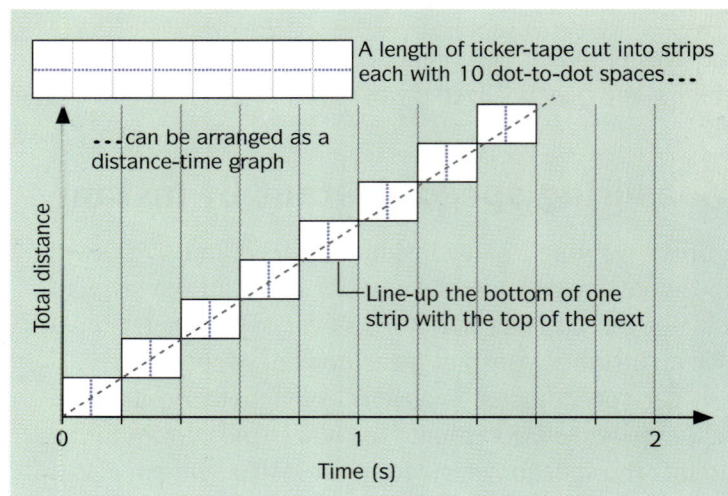

A length of ticker-tape cut into strips each with 10 dot-to-dot spaces...

...can be arranged as a distance-time graph

Line-up the bottom of one strip with the top of the next

Total distance

Time (s)

🔺 In this case the graph is a straight line, so the trolley was moving at constant speed.

A sport scientist helping the athlete to improve his/her performance will be interested to see exactly how speed changed during the race. Then the athlete will be able to look for ways to improve.

△ 100 m in 9.98 s.

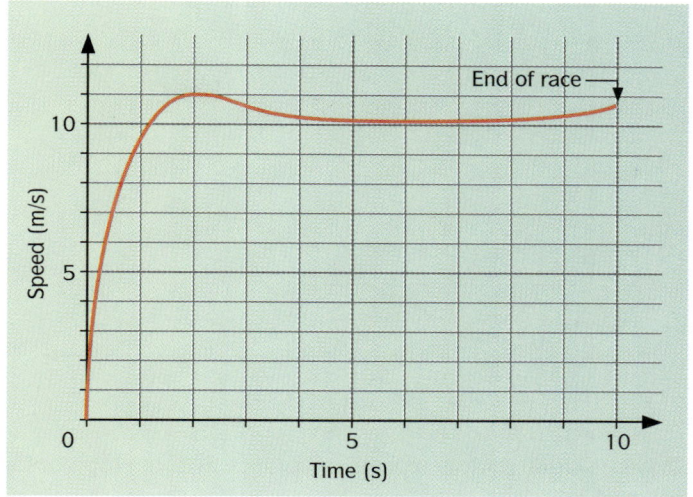

△ An athlete's speed-time graph.

▶ *At what time did the athlete have the highest speed?*

Two graphs for the same motion

There is no faster motion, on two legs, than skiing down a mountain. Top skiers can reach speeds of more than 100 km/h, which is about 28 m/s. Like all motion, a ski-run starts with acceleration. But on the way down there will be bumps and turns. While the *distance* travelled by the skier goes on increasing, *speed* fluctuates up and down.

△ No faster motion on two legs. Distance and speed both change as time goes by.

A big difference shows up when two graphs are side by side. One graph can show how distance varies as time passes, and one graph can show how the speed varies with time.

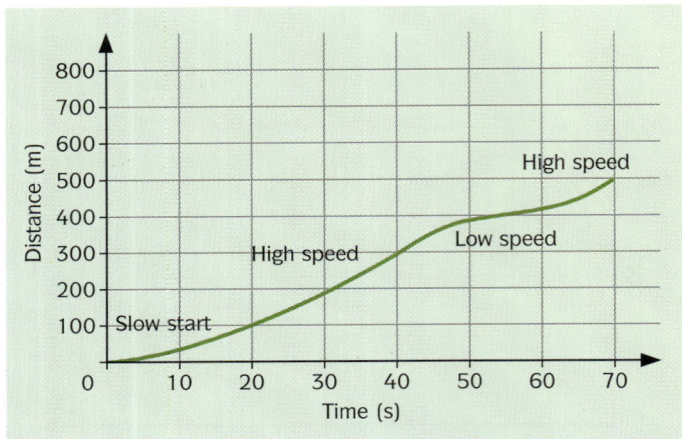

▲ On a ski-run down a mountain, distance from the top goes on increasing.

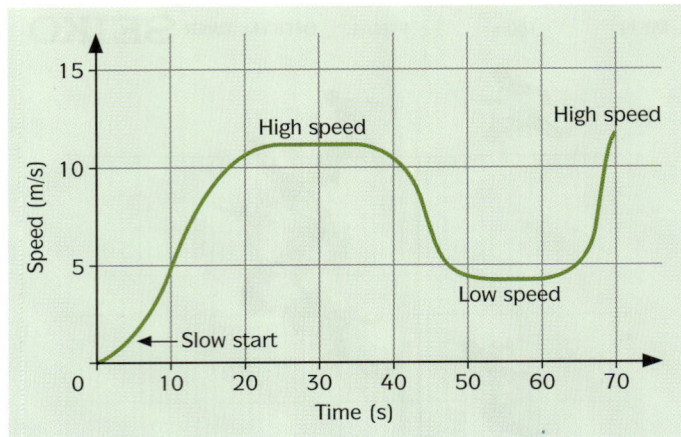

▲ For the same journey, speed fluctuates.

▶ *Describe what is going on, 50 s after the start of the motion.*

Showing force

Force can change motion. The direction and the size of the force are important to what happens. We can use arrows to show the direction and size of different forces. You can find out more about this in Chapter Nine (Measuring motion).

▲ Arrows show the size and direction of different forces.

The effect of air on falling objects

The Moon has no atmosphere. It is not big enough to have a gravitational pull strong enough to hold on to a layer of gas like air. So when astronauts visited the Moon they took some time out to play with the Moon's gravity. They gave a demonstration of what gravity can do when there is no air to get in the way. They dropped a hammer and a feather at the same time.

'Common sense' tells us that a hammer hits the ground before a feather. But on the Moon, they fall perfectly together – side by side all the way down to the surface.

▲ No atmosphere. On the Moon, objects fall without air resistance.

It is the Earth's air resistance which reduces the downwards acceleration of the feather. Without air resistance, the feather and the hammer react only to the force of gravity.

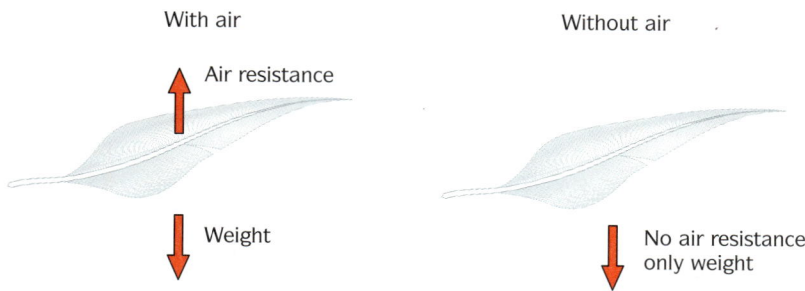

With air

Air resistance

Weight

Without air

No air resistance only weight

Motion of a falling body

A diver falls with a straight body and outstretched arms, to cut down forces of air resistance. That way s/he falls more like a hammer than a feather. Gravitational force dominates his/her motion.

To analyse the diver's fall, it is easier to start with something simple like a ball. It is possible to use regular flashes of light to produce a picture of the ball at the different stages of its motion. The time taken for the ball to fall from one position to the next is always the same. The faster the ball falls, the further it travels between flashes of the light.

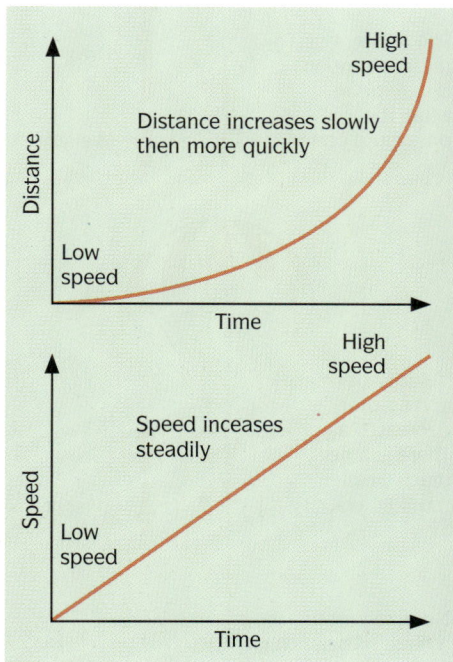

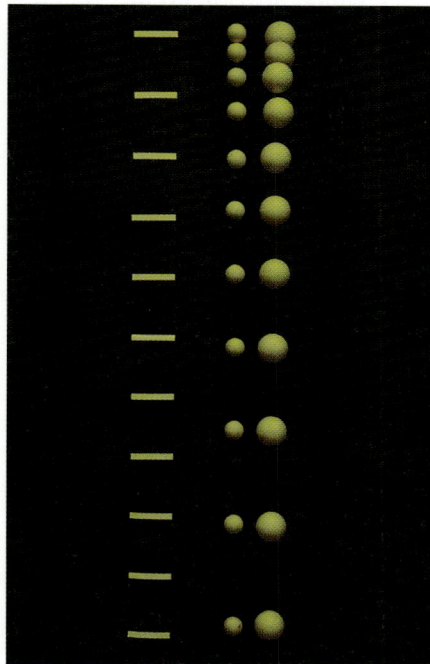

High speed

Distance increases slowly then more quickly

Distance

Low speed

Time

High speed

Speed inceases steadily

Speed

Low speed

Time

🔺 The diver can reduce his air resistance by diving headfirst towards the water.

🔺 Graphs to show the motion of a diver or a falling ball. For these graphs, air resistance is not big enough to make a detectable difference to the motion.

🔺 Falling and accelerating. The distance between flashes gets bigger.

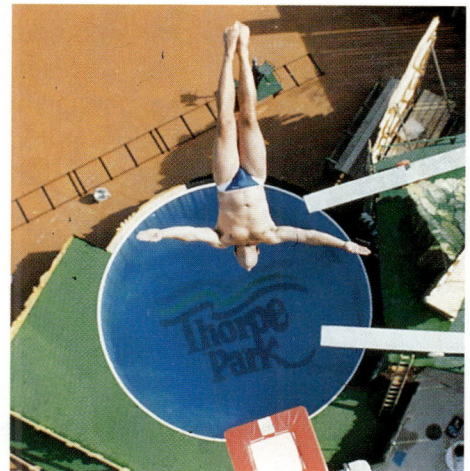

▶ *Why are graphs for a diver the same shape as graphs for a ball?*

Air resistance and high-speed motion

🔺 Different forces of air resistance.

You take up space. You push air out of the way every time you move. It is not difficult, because air is not very dense and its particles are not strongly bonded together. Moving through water is more difficult, and moving through something solid is impossible.

Even moving in air is not always so easy. The faster you move, the faster the air has to move out of your way, and the more you become aware of it. Riding a bike is enough to demonstrate that air resists your motion. On a motorbike, visors and leathers are needed to protect a person from continuous impact with air.

Designers try to reduce air resistance forces, which are sometimes called drag forces. They make sure that bikes and cars are shaped to help air to slip more easily out of the way. It is called streamlining.

▶ *Why does a racing motorcyclist duck down as low as possible?*

Parachutists and terminal velocity

Free-fall jumpers use parachutes, but they don't open them until they have to. They enjoy the exhilaration of falling into the wind, as fast as they can go.

🔺 Forces in balance, and a steady speed.

Accelerating downwards — Weight

As speed increases so does drag... — Drag / Weight

...until drag equals weight... — Drag / Weight

...and the forces are balanced so there is no acceleration. You fall at terminal velocity. — Drag / Weight

Still falling, but there is sudden deceleration when the parachute opens — Drag / Weight

Velocity decreases and so drag decreases again. There is a new, much smaller, terminal velocity — Drag / Weight

No acceleration, the ground exerts a force to balance gravity. — Weight

Accelerating · Steady speed · Decreasing · Steady speed

🔺 Skydiving forces.

PHYSICS

118   LONGMAN CO-ORDINATED SCIENCE

As jumpers step out of the aircraft door, the only vertical force acting on them is the force of gravity, or weight. Not surprisingly, they accelerate downwards. As they get faster, they can feel the air resistance pushing on them harder and harder. They gain speed more and more slowly as this upwards drag force takes effect.

After about 14 s the drag force becomes as big as the downwards pull of gravity. Drag and weight are balanced. Then they stop accelerating and just keep on falling at a steady speed. This steady speed is called **terminal velocity**. For a human-sized object, terminal velocity is about 60 m/s.

▶ *Why does drag force start off small and get bigger?*

At terminal velocity the jumper can count 5 s for every 300 m they fall. Then, when they are about 15 s away from the hard ground, they pull the handle which opens their parachute. That creates a sudden increase in drag, because of the large area of fabric that is now pushing air out of the way.

The new drag force is much bigger than weight, and the jumper slows down. As they slow down the drag force reduces back to the same size as their weight. Once again, weight balances drag. But now the jumper has a much smaller terminal velocity – only about 3 m/s. That is slow enough for contact with the ground to be fairly gentle. A few hundred grams of fabric make a big difference.

Graphs for a parachute jump

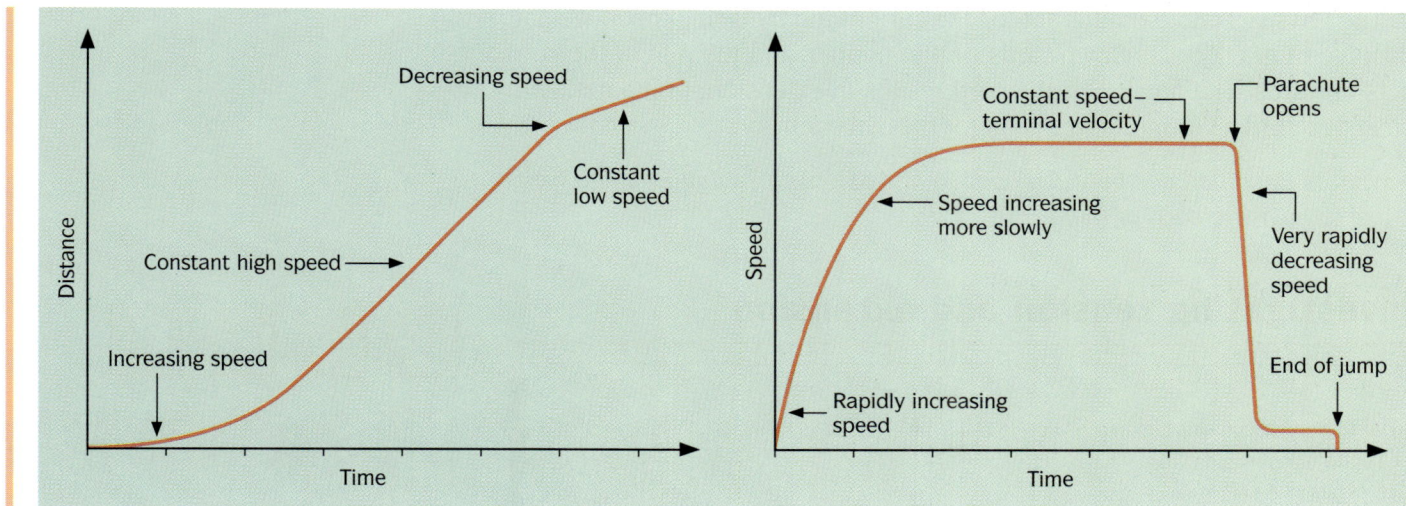

▲ Distance-time and speed-time graphs provide two different ways to study the same motion.

Weight, tension and extension

You may have stepped into a lift, and felt the floor ease downwards as you put your weight onto it. That is caused by the cables above you stretching a little, in response to the extra force of gravity. The force of the cables on the lift is called **tension**.

While the lift is still, the tension in the cables holds up the lift by exactly balancing the total force of gravity. The more people that get into the lift, the more the cables have to balance the weight. There is more tension in the cables. And the more they stretch. The lift cables are built to take the tension, and the engineers who designed the lift system took the stretch, or **extension**, of the cables into account.

Bungee tension

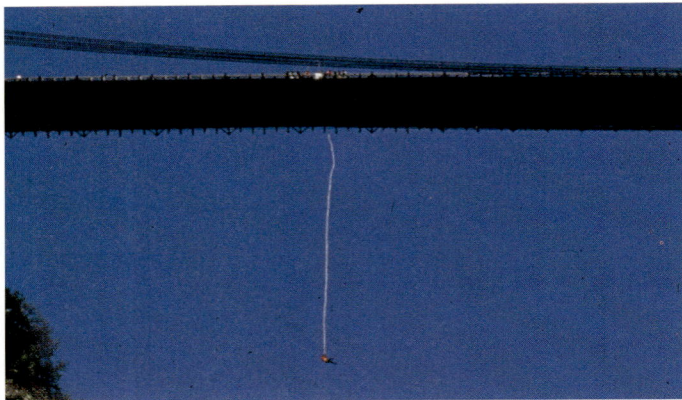

▲ Stretch upon stretch. The weight of the bridge roadway extends the cables that hold it up. The bungee jumper uses material that extends a lot more.

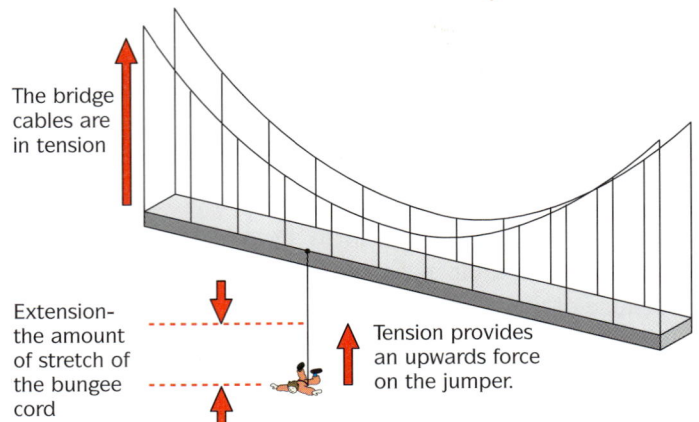

The bridge cables are in tension

Extension- the amount of stretch of the bungee cord

Tension provides an upwards force on the jumper.

▲ Tension is a force which can cause an object to stretch. Extension is a measurement of the increase in length.

A suspension bridge is basically a roadway hanging by cables. The cables are continuously stretched, applying an upwards force to the roadway to balance its weight.

The Physics is not so different for the cord of the bungee jumper. Weight, or force of gravity, acts downwards on the jumper, and the pull of the cord acts upwards. The tension in the cord results in extension. Compared with steel, the cord gives more extension for the same tension.

▶ *What is the difference between tension and extension? What units do we use to measure each of them?*

Investigating tension and extension

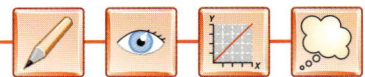

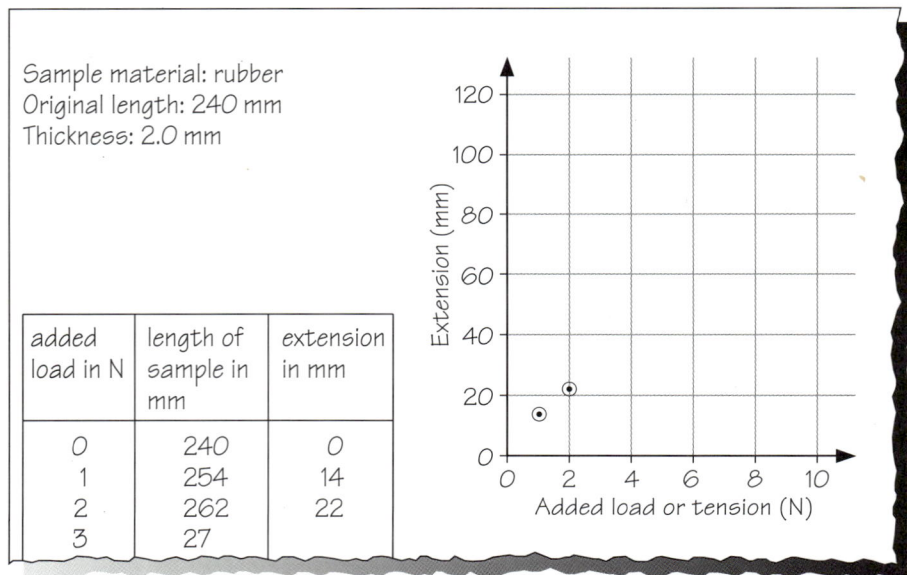

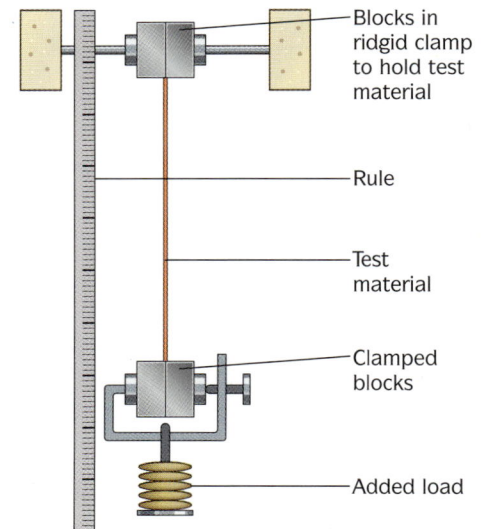

Sample material: rubber
Original length: 240 mm
Thickness: 2.0 mm

added load in N	length of sample in mm	extension in mm
0	240	0
1	254	14
2	262	22
3	27	

Blocks in ridgid clamp to hold test material

Rule

Test material

Clamped blocks

Added load

Different materials behave differently. Even samples of the same material behave differently, depending on their sizes. By taking lengths of materials it is possible to collect evidence to make useful comparisons.

Different weights hung from materials can provide a way of varying the tension in the materials. The bigger the weight, the bigger the tension. Then extension can be measured using a rule.

The best way to record the data is in a table, and then on a graph. Graphs for different samples provide quick ways of seeing the different types of behaviour.

Comparing springs and rubber cord

Bungee cords are made mostly of rubber and springs are made of metal. You may be given a worksheet to help you to practise making measurements, and using graphs.

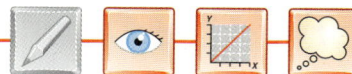

More about extension-tension graphs

The extension–tension graph for a steel cable looks very different from the graph for a bungee cord plotted on the same scale. The obvious difference is that the bungee graph is much steeper – it has a bigger gradient.

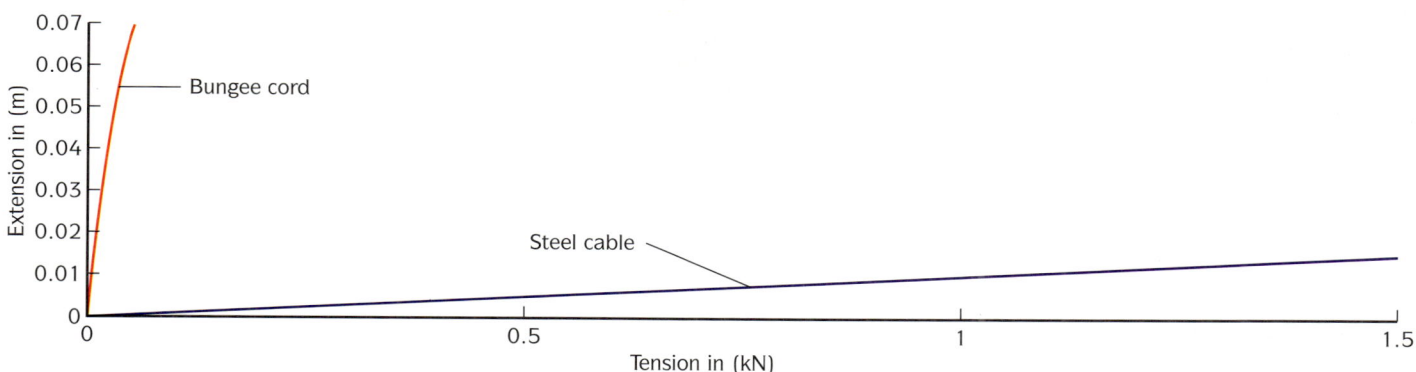

🔺 Graphs provide a quick way to see differences between materials.

Engineers can use the gradients of such graphs in their calculations. First they must measure the gradients.

You can read more about measuring gradients in Chapter Sixteen (Physics help).

In these graphs, the gradient for the steel cable is 0.01 m/kN. That means that it stretches by 0.01 m for every 1 kilonewton of force. That particular cable can be stretched over and over again, always stretching by 0.01 m for each kilonewton.

The cable stretches in a fairly simple way. A 1 kilonewton force stretches it by 0.01 m. And 2 kilonewton of tension produces twice the extension – 2 × 0.02 m. Trebling the tension produces treble the extension, and so on. In fact, however the tension changes, the amount of extension changes by the same proportion, provided that the cable is not overstretched. We say that the extension is **proportional to** the tension.

kN is short for kilonewton. A kilonewton is a force of 1000 newton.

▶ *What will happen to the total extension of the cable if the tension is:*
  a *halved*
  b *quadrupled?*

The bungee cord is not so simple. Doubling the tension does not exactly double the extension. The extension does not change by the same proportion as the tension does. It shows on the graph – the line does not have a constant gradient, but is steeper in some places than in others. A bungee jumper has to take account of this. A jumper might not live to check out where they got their calculations wrong.

Summary

- Speed = $\dfrac{\text{distance}}{\text{time}}$.
- Speed is equal to the gradient of a distance–time graph.
- Ticker-timers measure speed, using

$$\text{speed} = \frac{\text{length of tape with 10 dot-to-dot spaces}}{0.2\,\text{s}}$$

- Motion can be shown on distance–time graphs and on speed–time graphs.
- Arrow diagrams can represent the size and direction of forces acting on an object.
- Gravitational force on an object like a parachutist does not change during the fall.
- The force of air resistance changes during a parachutist's fall.
- Gravitational forces and air resistance forces are unbalanced during the first part of a fall.
- Air resistance force can grow during a fall, until it balances gravitational force.
- A falling object can eventually reach terminal velocity.
- The extension of materials depends on the tension or stretching force.
- Extension–tension graphs provide useful comparisons of materials.

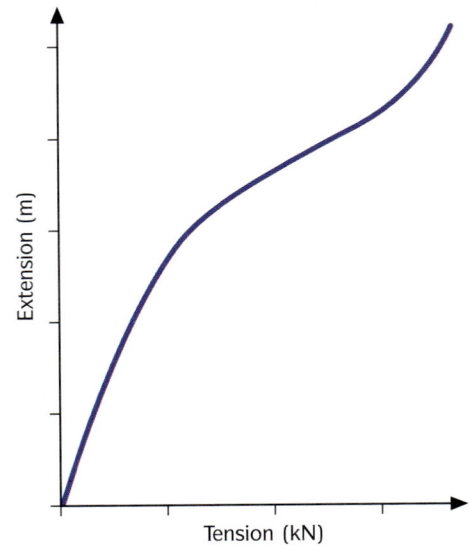

🔺 The extension-tension relationship is more complicated for a bungee cord than for a steel cable. The graph is not a simple straight line.

Revision Questions

1 In the formula, $s = \dfrac{d}{t}$, what do s, d and t stand for?

2 A car has a speed of 20 m/s. Copy and complete this table:

Time in s	0	1	2	3	4	5
Distance in m	0	20		60		

3 Look at the distance–time graph.
   a How far has the train travelled after 10 s?
   b How long did it take to go 900 m?

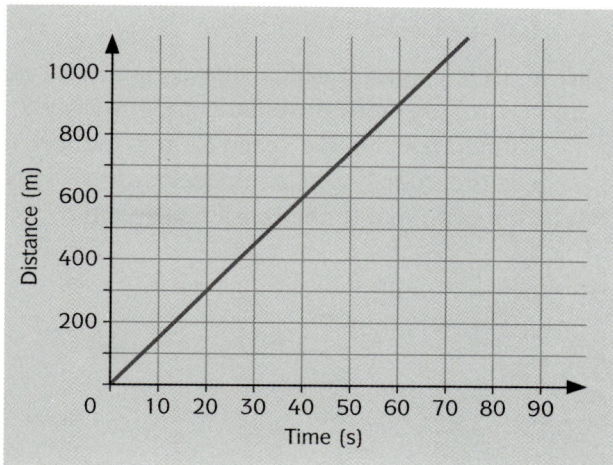

4 A sprinter runs a 100 m race in 10 s. Estimate the speed of the sprinter half-way through the race. Why is it impossible for you to work out the sprinter's exact speed at that time?

5 Why does a feather fall faster on the Moon than it does on Earth?

6 What happens to air resistance force on a biker as the bike gains speed?

7 On page 119 it says, 'Drag and weight are balanced'. Draw a diagram with force arrows to show what this means.

8

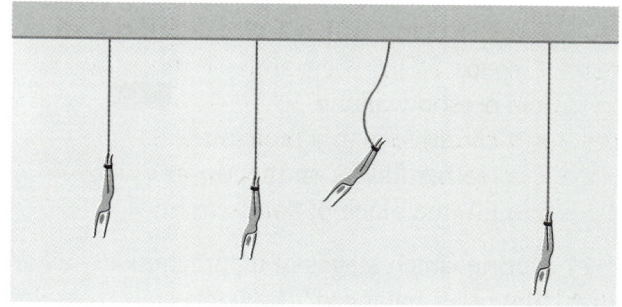

The diagram shows identical bungee cords. Which sketch shows,
   a a bungee cord with the most tension
   b a bungee cord with no tension?

9 What is the speed, in km/h, of a spacecraft which travels 56 000 km in 2 hours?

10 What is the average speed, in m/s, of a car which covers 180 m in 10 s?

11 Look back at the table in question 2. How far will the car get in 10 s?

12 Give an example of a situation in which the value of average speed is more useful information than the value of instant-by-instant speed.

13 Use the distance–time graph in question 3 to find out the speed of the train.

14 What is the speed shown by this length of ticker-tape? (Tape is actual size.)

15 Compare air resistance on a motorbike to water resistance on a boat. What similarities are there in design to help to cope with the problem?

16 These are some examples of motion. Put them in order, starting with the motion in which air resistance is most important:
- a spacecraft with a speed of 10 km/s in space
- a person walking
- a car driving on a motorway
- a feather falling on the Moon
- a lift in a block of flats.

17 During which stages of a parachutist's fall are the forces balanced? Draw sketches to explain your answer.

18

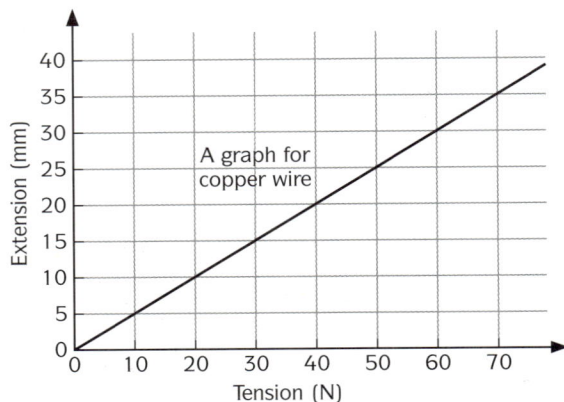

a How much does the copper wire stretch when the tension is 5 N?
b What is the gradient of the extension-tension graph for the copper wire?

19 How far will a train travel in 4 s at a speed of 50 m/s?

20 How long would it take a spacecraft to travel 12 000 km at a speed of 4 000 km/h?

21 The 100 m race is timed to the nearest one-hundredth of a second (0.01 s).
a A sprinter completes the race in 10.01 s. Roughly what distance does the sprinter cover in 0.01 s?
b What is the distance, at the finishing line, between two athletes who take 10.01 s and 10.04 s for the race?

22 Sound travels at about 300 m/s. Estimate how long it takes to travel across the width of an athletics track. Does that make the race unfair?

23 Look back at the distance–time graph in question 3. Sketch a speed–time graph for the motion of the train.

24 Explain why a bomb dropped from an aircraft reaches a terminal velocity provided that it falls for more than about 14 s.

25 What is the direction of the total force on a bungee jumper at the bottom of their motion? Draw a sketch to show this.

26 a Sketch a graph which shows motion for which distance travelled is proportional to time. Describe the speed for this motion.
b Is the extension of a bungee cord proportional to the tension? Explain.

Measuring motion

■ **Wheel life**

The new coupé
On sale June
Standard features include front and rear crumple zones and side impact bars.

PETROL UP AGAIN
The Chancellor of the Exchequer yesterday added another 5p per litre to the price of leaded and unleaded petrol.

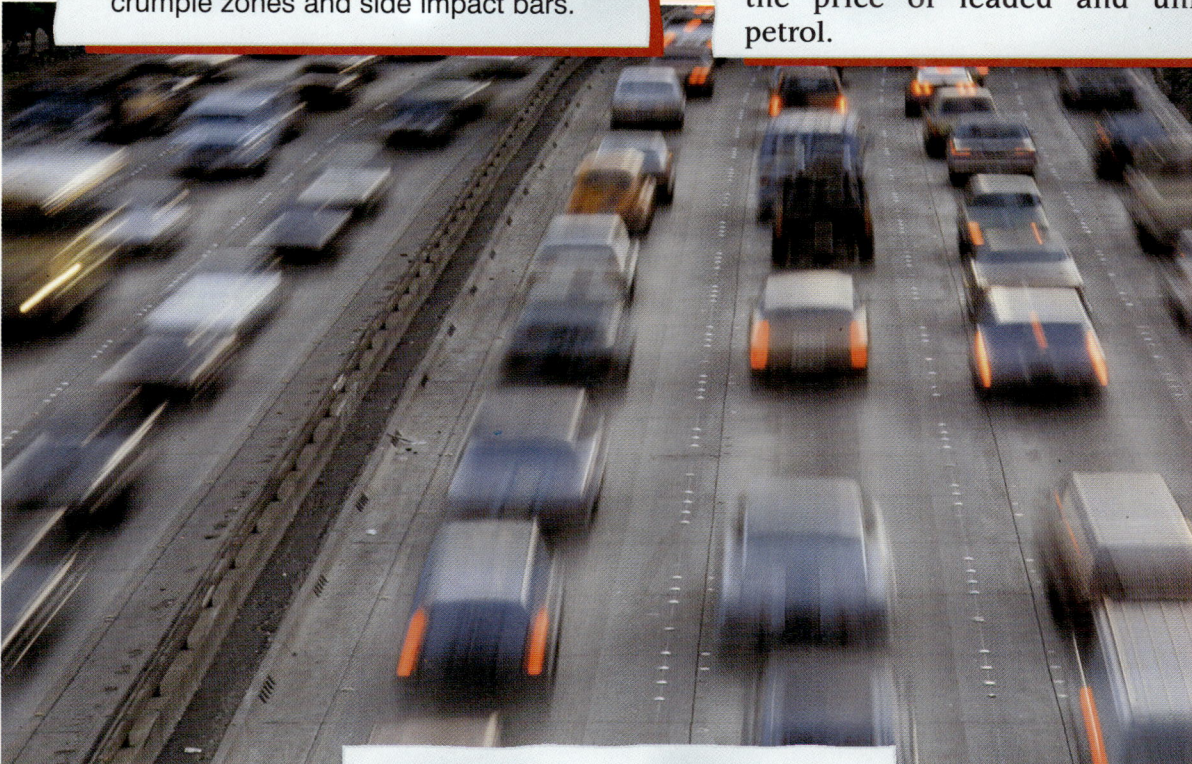

City car ban
From next year, only drivers with permits will be allowed to bring cars into the city centre.

Three more victims at death corner
Three more young people lost their lives when their car collided with the railway bridge at the notorious Bunker's Corner on the A699.

The fuel economy is unbelievable – 28 km per litre at a constant 90 km/h

Motion is always in the news.

Review

Before going any further, read this page and attempt the tasks. Write the answers in your notes.

The Tour de France is a race that lasts for nearly a month. The riders have to go out day after day for high-speed sprints and gruelling mountain climbs. Their bikes and their bodies have to cruise, accelerate and decelerate, climb and fall, around nearly every part of France.

Cycle makers want their bikes to be winners, and they spend a lot of money developing cycle technology. Air resistance is the first problem in building fast bikes. The position of the cyclist has to present a low profile to the air.

Friction between moving parts is the next problem to be reckoned with. Manufacturers invest a lot in research into finding the best materials to use in the bearings where the wheels are attached to the bikes. Friction between the turning wheels and their axles causes unwanted energy transfer. The surfaces become hot, and the energy is wasted.

Between the tyres and the road, however, there has to be some friction. If the surfaces were slippery the cyclist would never get anywhere at all. The wheels would just spin around and around. Tyres have to provide a good backwards push on the road, good stability on corners, but as little as possible heating effect. Tyre design is a whole world of technology in its own right.

▲ Technology in motion.

CHECK NINE

1 Solve the anagrams:
   No car ate lice – it happens when speed changes
   Rotini FC – it produces force which opposes motion

2 Where on a bike is friction a nuisance?

3 How can bike designers reduce air resistance?

4 Why is friction important for brakes?

5 What happens to air resistance as a cyclist gets faster?

6 Why does a cycle reach a top speed, even though the rider keeps pedalling hard?

What force can do

Left to themselves, objects keep on doing what they are already doing. If they are still, they stay still. If they are moving steadily, they stay moving steadily. Objects resist change in their motion.

Force is what causes change in motion. It can accelerate objects – and that includes speeding them up, slowing them down, and changing the direction of their motion. Force can also change the motion of just one part of an object, and change its shape.

▲ An object that is moving steadily keeps its motion until a force makes it change.

▲ As the apple accelerates towards the ground its motion is changing. There is a force acting.

▲ Effortless motion. It is possible to have motion without force. Force is only needed to *change* motion.

Isaac Newton recognised that change in motion could be predicted by using the notion of force. He wrote this idea down in his First Law about 300 years ago. He wrote in Latin, but a translation is:

'Objects keep moving with steady speed in a straight line unless a force acts.'

The steady speed can include no speed at all. An object standing still has a steady speed which happens to be zero.

▶ *Name four effects that force can have on an object.*

▶ *How does a skater stop?*

▶ *How can a spacecraft travel at high speed with its rockets turned off? When would the spacecraft need to use its rockets?*

Force and direction

Force is called a **vector** quantity – a quantity which has a definite direction as well as size. Arrows are useful for representing vectors like force. An arrow can point in the right direction and its length can show how big the force is.

Other quantities, like volume and energy, do not have a particular direction. These are **scalar** quantities.

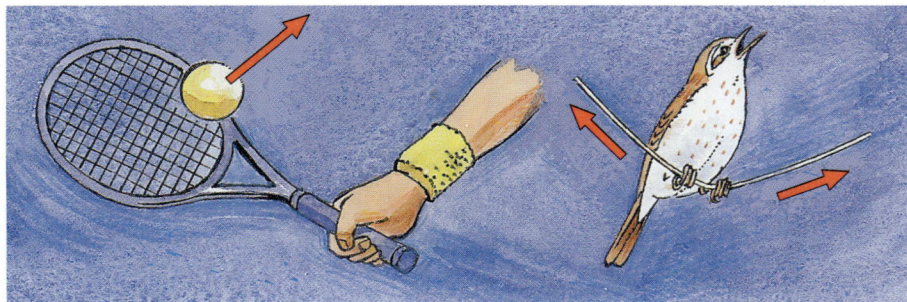
▲ Arrows can show forces.

▲ In tennis, how hard you hit the ball is important. But where you hit it is even more important. You must apply force of the right size and direction.

▶ *Does temperature have a particular direction? Is it a vector or a scalar quantity?*

PHYSICS

Balanced vectors

One and one makes two, for scalar quantities. The amount of money you have is a scalar quantity. One pound coin and another pound coin makes two pounds.

But it is not so simple for vector quantities. Two tug-of-war teams can pull in opposite directions, both with total forces of 1 kilonewton. But for the middle of the rope the forces are balanced. Balanced forces do not affect motion. They have the same effect on the motion of the rope as no force at all. The two 1 kilonewton forces effectively add up to zero.

▲ Equal and opposite forces balance each other, and there is no change in motion.

▶ *When does 1 + 1 = 0?*

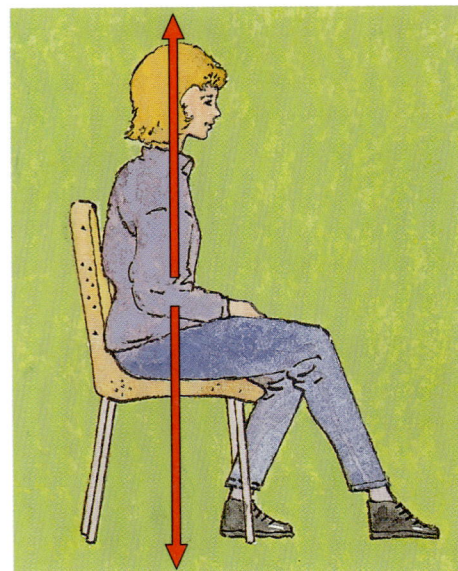

▲ Balanced forces act on a sitting person. One force is weight, the force due to gravity. The chair pushes upwards with a force that is exactly equal. The combined force is zero.

Examples of balanced and unbalanced forces

▲ Unchanging motion and balanced forces.

▲ No acceleration.

When a goose flies at steady speed the total effect of all the forces is zero. The goose has motion, but the motion is not changing. The forwards thrust of the wings balances the backwards drag of air resistance. The downwards weight is balanced by the aerodynamic lift created by the bird's wings.

The wings of a diving gannet are positioned to provide little lift. The weight is bigger than the upwards force. The forces are not balanced, so motion changes. The gannet accelerates downwards.

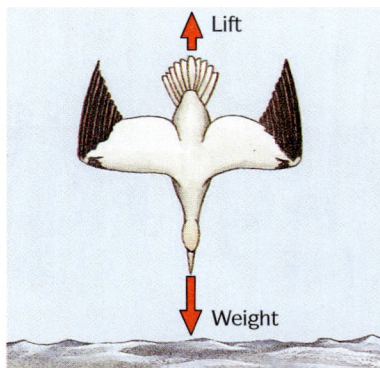

▲ Downwards acceleration.

▲ Changing motion and unbalanced forces.

PHYSICS

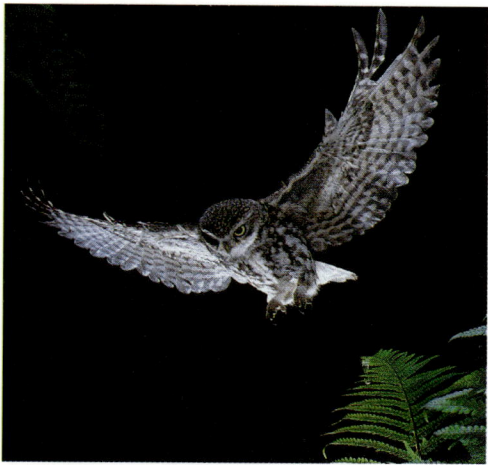
△ Changing motion and unbalanced forces.

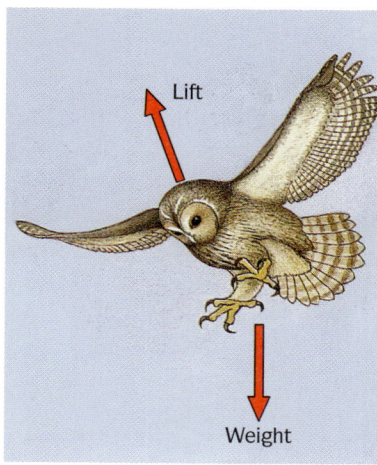
△ Sideways acceleration.

If an owl tilts its wings then the lift force acts partially upwards and partially sideways. The sideways force changes the direction of the owl's motion.

▶ *What does unbalanced force do to the gannet?*

▶ *A car travels along a motorway at steady speed. Are the forces balanced or unbalanced? How do you decide?*

Velocity vectors

Force is not the only quantity which has a particular direction. When you are riding a bike, ice skating or pushing a supermarket trolley, the direction of actual motion is also important. **Velocity** is the special name given to speed in a particular direction. Velocity is a vector quantity.

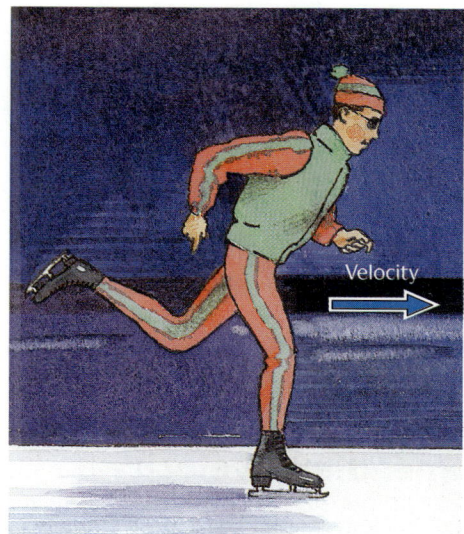
△ Arrows can show size and direction of velocity. Direction of motion matters.

Adding velocities

The motion of a beaver in a river is made up of two velocities. There is the velocity of the beaver swimming through the water, and there is the velocity of the water itself. A beaver wanting to go from one place to another has to take account of both velocities.

Moving walkways can carry people and their baggage through busy places. If the walkway moves at 1 m/s, then that is the velocity of a person standing on it. But if the person walks along at 1 m/s, then they get to the end in half the time. Their combined velocity is 2 m/s. If, for some reason, the person turns and walks in the opposite direction, the combined velocity can be zero.

▶ *In a canoe, can you go faster up a river or down a river? Why?*

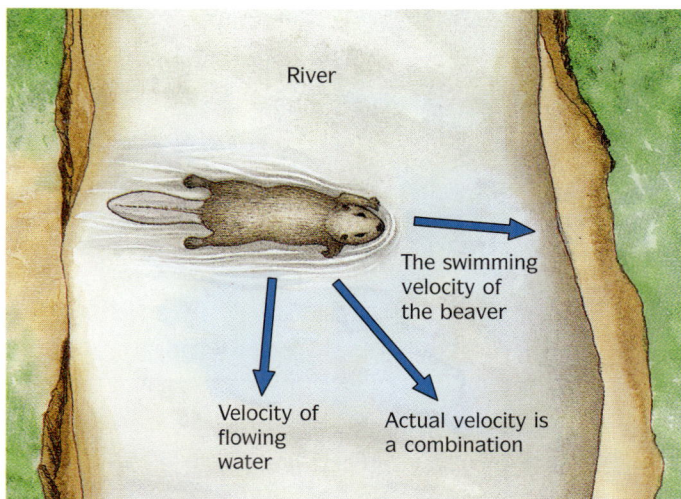

River

The swimming velocity of the beaver

Velocity of flowing water

Actual velocity is a combination

Person's walking velocity   Person's walking velocity

Actual velocity is   Actual velocity is
a combination   a combination –
                                    zero

velocity of the walkway

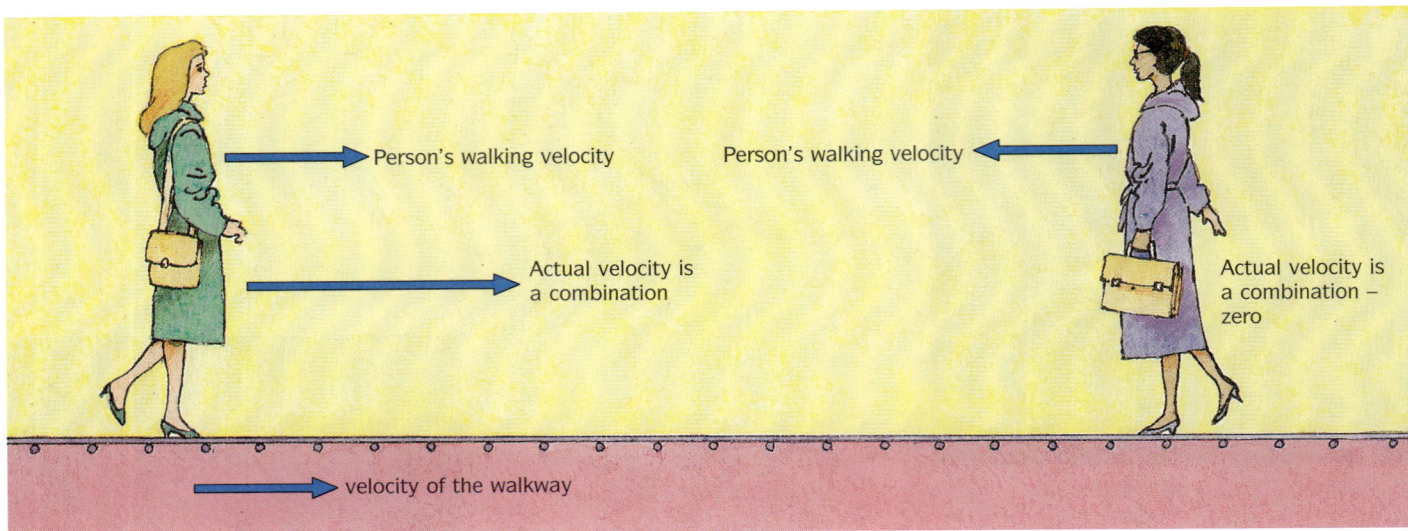

Investigating vectors

Velocity and force are vector quantities. You may be given a worksheet to help you practice working with vectors.

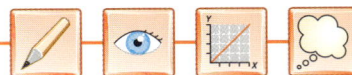

Speed and velocity

Speed and velocity are both measurements of motion. They have the same units – metres per second, m/s. But speed has no direction. It is a scalar quantity. A car speedometer measures speed. It does not tell the driver anything about the *direction* the car is going in. It does not measure velocity, which is a vector quantity with a clear direction.

If the size of speed changes, then size of velocity also changes. If the direction of the motion changes, velocity changes even if speed stays the same.

▲ Velocity can change, even if speed stays constant. Athletes on a bend can have steady speeds, but the direction is changing, so the velocity is changing.

▲ Speed is the same all of the time. Velocity changes on the bend, when direction is changing.

▲ Velocity and speed can change together. For athletes on the straight track, the size of speed *and* velocity changes. The direction stays the same.

Changing velocity

A spacewalking astronaut can use a backpack rocket to manoeuvre around. A burst of the rocket provides the force, and the astronaut's velocity changes. The bigger the force, the more quickly the velocity changes. Rate of change of velocity is called **acceleration**.

Acceleration is change in velocity in each second. So if the astronaut speeds up by 2 m/s every second, then acceleration is 2 m/s per second. That is normally written as 2 m/s^2.

▶ *A car goes faster by 3 m/s every second. What is its acceleration?*

Acceleration

$$\text{acceleration} = \frac{\text{change in velocity}}{\text{time taken to change}}$$

If the velocity changes steadily then the change in velocity is the final velocity minus the velocity at the start of the change.

change in velocity = final velocity – starting velocity

So,

$$\text{acceleration} = \frac{\text{final velocity – starting velocity}}{\text{time taken to change}}$$

By using letter v for final velocity and letter u for starting velocity, and t for time, we can write this in short:

$$a = \frac{v - u}{t}$$

▲ Change of motion – measured by acceleration.

Acceleration is a vector quantity

Acceleration is a measurement of change of motion. Change in velocity is a vector quantity – it has direction. So acceleration itself is a vector quantity, with direction as well as size.

▲ Acceleration has to be in the right direction to keep the wagons on the rail.

Change in motion does not have to be in the same direction as the motion itself. Acceleration arrows can point in different directions from velocity arrows. A person on the Corkscrew at Alton Towers, for example, has velocity and acceleration. If the change in velocity had the same direction as the velocity itself, the person would keep going in a straight line instead of following the curve of the rail. That is not what happens.

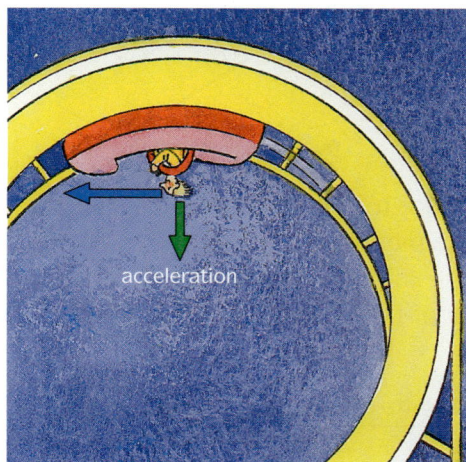

acceleration

▲ The direction of the acceleration decides which way the velocity changes.

Velocity–time graphs

In Chapter Eight we were not concerned about direction, and we used the word *speed*. In this chapter we are using the word *velocity*, because this chapter goes further into the study of the effect of force on motion. However, for objects moving in straight lines, a velocity–time graph is the same as a speed–time graph.

Think about the astronaut again, with a steady acceleration of 2 m/s^2. A velocity–time graph shows an increase in velocity of 2 m/s every second.

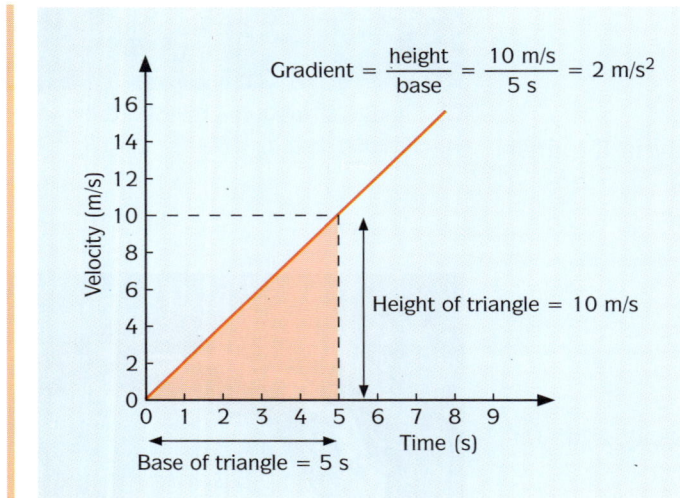

Gradient = $\dfrac{\text{height}}{\text{base}}$ = $\dfrac{10 \text{ m/s}}{5 \text{ s}}$ = 2 m/s^2

Height of triangle = 10 m/s

Base of triangle = 5 s

🔺 The gradient of a velocity–time graph is equal to the acceleration.

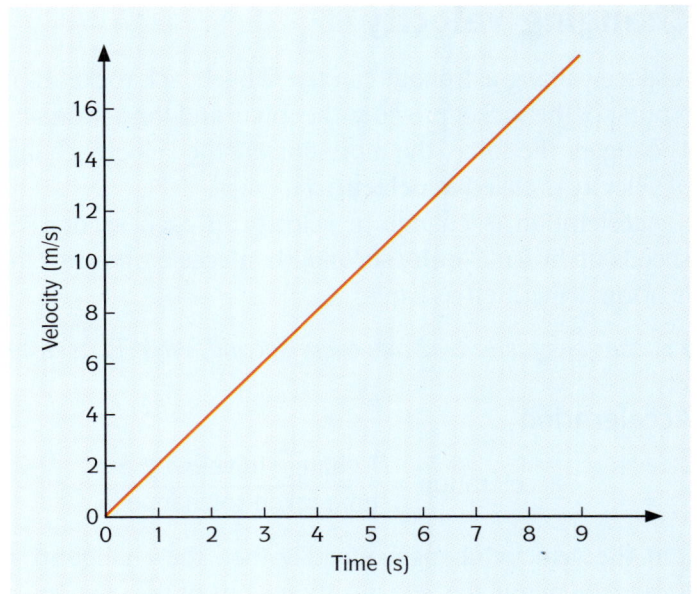

🔺 Velocity–time graph for an astronaut with a steady acceleration. Note that the velocity increases by 2 m/s in every second.

▶ *From the graph, what is the astronaut's velocity after 5 s?*

Investigating acceleration

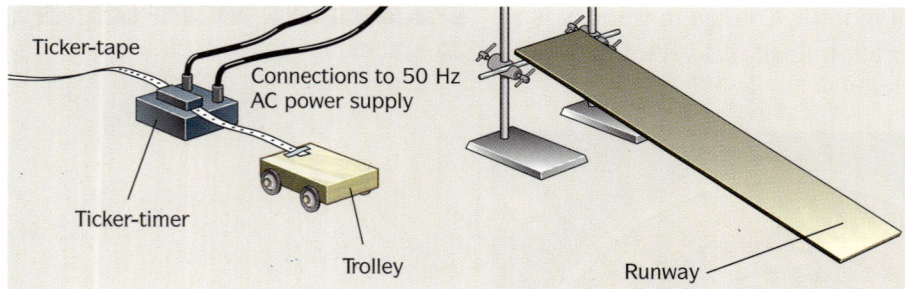

Ticker-tape

Connections to 50 Hz AC power supply

Ticker-timer

Trolley

Runway

The length of a piece of ticker-tape with 10 dot-to-dot spaces is the distance travelled by the tape in 0.2 s. The faster the motion, the longer the piece of tape.

You can work out the speed or velocity of the motion by measuring the length of the tape and dividing by 0.2 s.

velocity, $v = \dfrac{d}{t} = \dfrac{\text{length of tape for 10 dot-to-dot spaces}}{0.2 \text{ s}}$

Sticking a set of tapes side by side shows how the velocity changes from one time to another. It forms a kind of velocity–time graph.

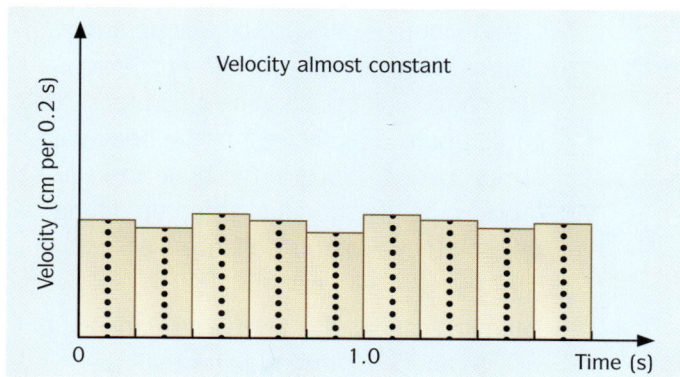

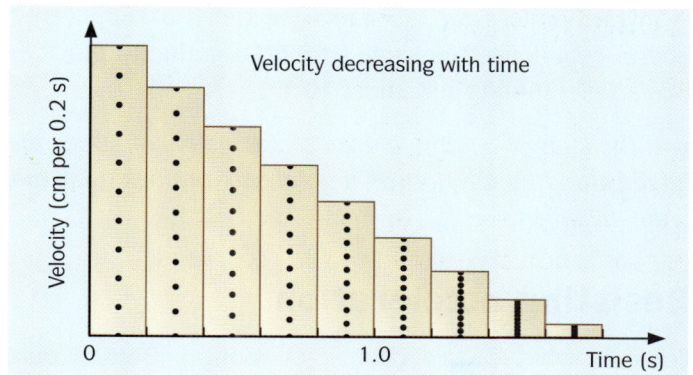

Examples of ticker-tape velocity–time graphs. Each piece of tape shows the distance travelled in 0.2 s.

This method can be used to analyse the motion of trolleys and other moving objects in different circumstances.

You may be given a worksheet on using a ticker timer to investigate acceleration and mass.

Velocity–time graphs for journeys

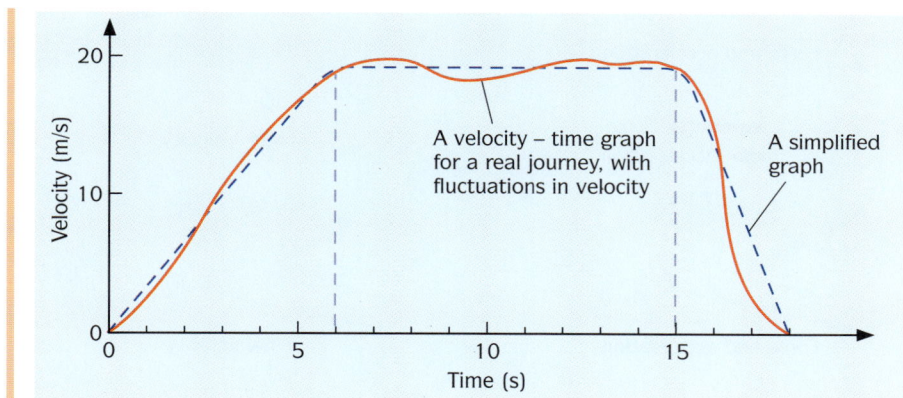

Using the simplified graph it is possible to estimate:

- the average acceleration during the first 6 s (from the gradient)
- the average velocity during the next 9 s, and the distance travelled using $d = s \times t$
- the average deceleration (negative acceleration) during the last 3 s (from the gradient).

▶ *Estimate each of these quantities.*

Acceleration due to gravity

When a diver stands on a diving board, the board exerts an upwards force which balances the diver's weight. Once the diving board is out of the way, weight takes over. The diver accelerates towards the water below.

Synchronised diving has not been introduced as an Olympic sport yet, but it could provide some interesting spectacles. Two divers, no matter how big or small, could fall side by side. Their velocities would increase identically, and they would hit the water together. Even though their weights might be different, they experience the same acceleration due to gravity.

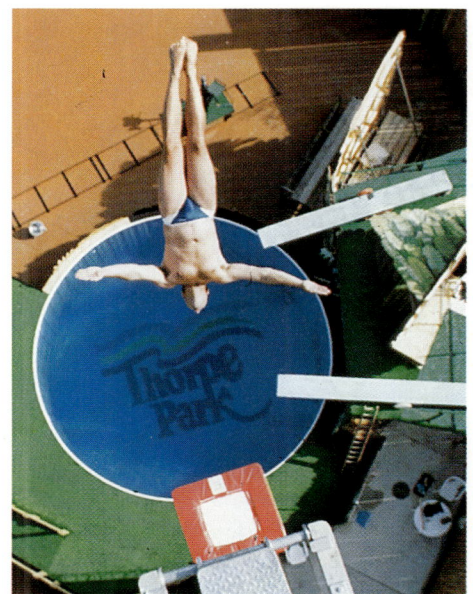

Unbalanced force of gravity causes acceleration.

In fact, unless air resistance becomes a significant factor, all bodies experience the same acceleration due to gravity. On Earth, this acceleration is just under 10 m/s².

▶ *At the start of a jump, a diver's watch slips off. Does the watch fall behind the diver, does it go ahead, or does it fall alongside the diver?*

Resisting acceleration

Force is what causes change of motion. But all objects resist changes to their motion – they resist acceleration. A small object like a pin has just a little resistance to acceleration. Just a flick makes its velocity change very quickly. A plane needs a much bigger force to reach the same acceleration. Acceleration depends on mass as well as force.

Astronauts experience big accelerations during a rocket launch. High accelerations are dangerous because the blood tends to get left behind as the rest of the body gains speed. Lack of blood in the brain can cause blackouts. If astronauts stood up during take-off they would experience blackouts or worse.

Humans can survive brief accelerations up to about 12 times bigger than the acceleration due to gravity – 120 m/s². Astronauts call this '12 g'.

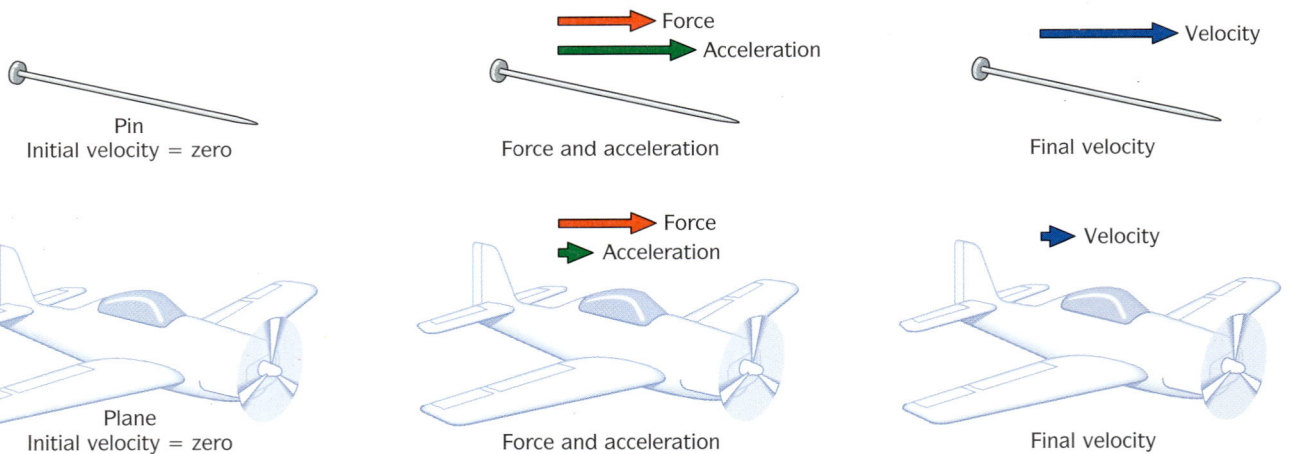

Pin
Initial velocity = zero

Force
Acceleration

Force and acceleration

Velocity

Final velocity

Plane
Initial velocity = zero

Force
Acceleration

Force and acceleration

Velocity

Final velocity

🔺 The same force produces different results.

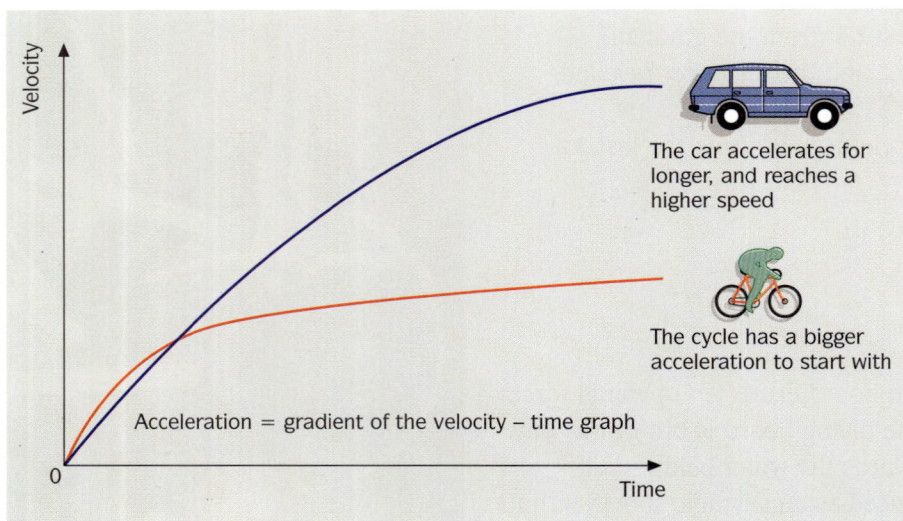

The car accelerates for longer, and reaches a higher speed

The cycle has a bigger acceleration to start with

Acceleration = gradient of the velocity – time graph

🔺 When the traffic lights turn green, a cycle can get ahead of a car for a short while, even if they set off at exactly the same moment. The cycle can have a bigger acceleration. The car has more mass and more resistance to acceleration. (The car can accelerate for longer, and soon catches up with the cyclist.)

▶ *A truck is more powerful than a car, but it cannot accelerate as quickly. Why?*

Relating acceleration to force

The harder an archer pulls back the string of the bow, the bigger the force on the arrow when the archer lets go. In fact, doubling the force produces double the acceleration of the arrow. Trebling the force produces treble the acceleration, and so on. Any change in the force will change the acceleration by the same proportion. For the arrow, acceleration is **proportional** to force.

When the arrow reaches its target, it decelerates. Deceleration is a negative acceleration. Just like positive acceleration, it takes force. A fast arrow requires a high value of deceleration and a lot of force to stop it quickly.

🔺 Acceleration is proportional to force.

▶ *Why does an arrow fly faster from a crossbow than from an ordinary bow?*

Relating acceleration to mass

Car advertisments boast about the acceleration of their vehicles. For the car in the picture the makers claim that it can go from standstill to 80 km/h in 8 s – that is an acceleration of 10 km/h/s.

Of course, the makers test their cars when the total mass is low. They put the car onto a test road with only the driver inside, and with the petrol tank nearly empty. But with a car full of five large adults, a boot full of luggage, and a fuel tank full of petrol, the mass of the car is a lot bigger. Then the car will not manage such a big acceleration.

Doubling the mass of an object halves the acceleration that it can achieve without changing the force. Trebling the mass makes the acceleration three times smaller. We say that, if force does not change, acceleration is **inversely proportional** to mass.

🔺 0 to 80 km/h in 8 s.

▶ *Why does a loaded airliner need a longer take-off than an unloaded one?*

Acceleration, mass and force

In Physics, we predict the future. We cannot predict everything, but there are some things which we can predict very precisely. We can, for example, say that if a mass of 4 kg is going to have an acceleration of 2 m/s^2, then the force that will be needed is 8 newton.

We can use a formula for this prediction:

force = mass × acceleration

or, in short,

$F = ma$

This formula can provide reliable predictions, time after time, provided that all of the forces are taken into account.

▶ *How much force will be needed to give an acceleration of 5 m/s^2 to a ball of mass 2 kg? What unit should you use for this answer?*

PHYSICS

Investigating *F = ma*

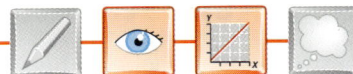

An 'air track' gets rid of the complication of the effect of friction. A small vehicle glides on a bed of air. A falling mass can provide a constant force on the vehicle. Light sensors connected to a computer can detect the vehicle as it goes by, and work out the acceleration.

An investigation can test the relationship between force and acceleration. For a fair test, the mass of the vehicle must not be allowed to change. Another investigation can test the relationship between mass and acceleration, keeping the force the same. See 'Investigating acceleration' on page 132 for more details of this.

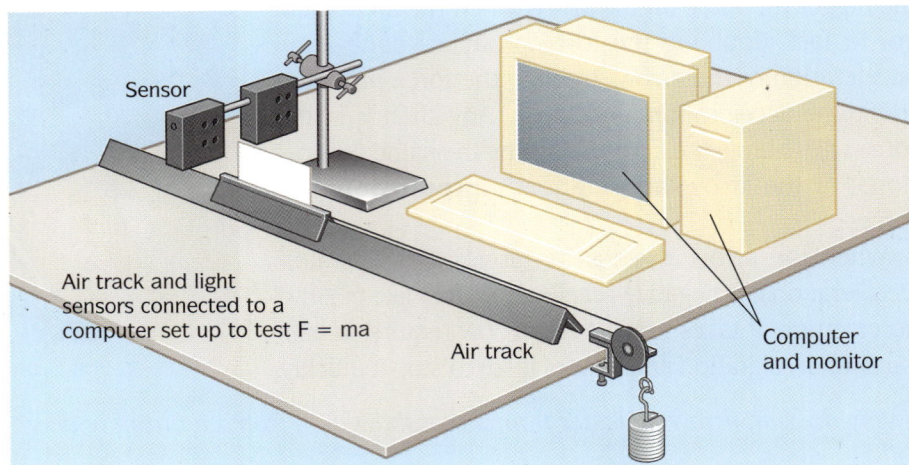

Air track and light sensors connected to a computer set up to test F = ma

Sensor

Air track

Computer and monitor

Vehicle stopping distances

If you were riding a bike and someone stepped in front of you, you would not be able to put the brakes on straight away. All humans take time to react. A signal has to pass along your nerves from your eyes to your brain. Then your brain has to send signals out to your hands on the brakes. The reaction time is usually just a fraction of a second, but in that time you can travel several metres.

The Highway Code contains tables of figures for the distances that a car needs for stopping. The stopping distance is divided into two parts – the thinking distance and the braking distance. The car travels through the thinking distance during the driver's reaction time, before the brakes go on. Deceleration happens while the car travels through its braking distance.

▶ *What happens to the speed of a bike during the rider's reaction time?*

Force [No. of masses pulling the vehicle]	0	1	2	3
Acceleration [cm/s^2]	0	45	95	

🔺 Force and acceleration – recording the results.

Speed		Thinking distance in m	Braking distance in m	Stopping distance in m
in mph	in m/s			
20	9	6	6	12
30	13	9	14	23
40	17	12	24	36
50	21	15	38	53
60	26	18	55	73
70	30	21	75	96

🔺 Car stopping distances.

Analysing stopping distances

You can use a computer spreadsheet to analyse stopping distances. You may be given a sheet to help you to use a computer to analyse physical information.

Forces in collisions

In snooker, a moving ball collides with a ball that is still. Both of the balls experience a force. The forces are the same size, but in opposite directions. Whenever one object exerts a force on another, it experiences a force of the same size.

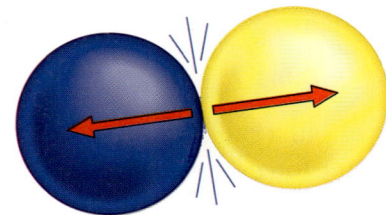

🔺 Colliding objects experience equal and opposite forces.

The force on the moving ball changes its velocity – usually both its direction and its size change. The force on the static ball makes it accelerate for as long as the force acts.

▶ *When a cannonball hits a pirate ship, which one experiences a bigger force, or are the forces the same size?*

Equal and opposite forces in skating

If you try pushing on a large object, you can feel it pushing back. A push on the table is just as likely to make you move backwards as to make the table move forwards. Friction usually stops you or the table moving very far.

But ice dancers move on a low-friction surface. A pair of skaters can create impressive dancing effects by exerting forces on each other.

One skater can provide a force on both partners. If the woman pushes on the man, or the other way round, they accelerate away from each other. There are two equal and opposite forces.

▶ *What happens to* both *rock-and-roll dancers on the dance floor when one pulls on the other?*

Equal and opposite forces in walking

When you walk you push backwards on the ground. You make use of friction. Without friction, on a very slippery surface, your foot would just slide backwards and you would not go anywhere.

The ground exerts an equal force on you, but in the opposite direction. This is the force that pushes you forwards.

▶ *What happens to a boat as you step out of it? Why?*

Rockets

A rocket, large or small, burns fuel which expands. There is only one direction for it to expand – out of the back of the rocket. The force that accelerates the gas out of the rocket results in an exactly equal and opposite force acting on the spacecraft. The spacecraft accelerates.

▶ *Name an animal that moves by pushing backwards on other material. Now (if you can) name an animal that doesn't.*

🔺 Exerting forces on each other to create changes in motion.

🔺 It does not matter which partner starts to push – they both experience the same size of force, but in opposite directions.

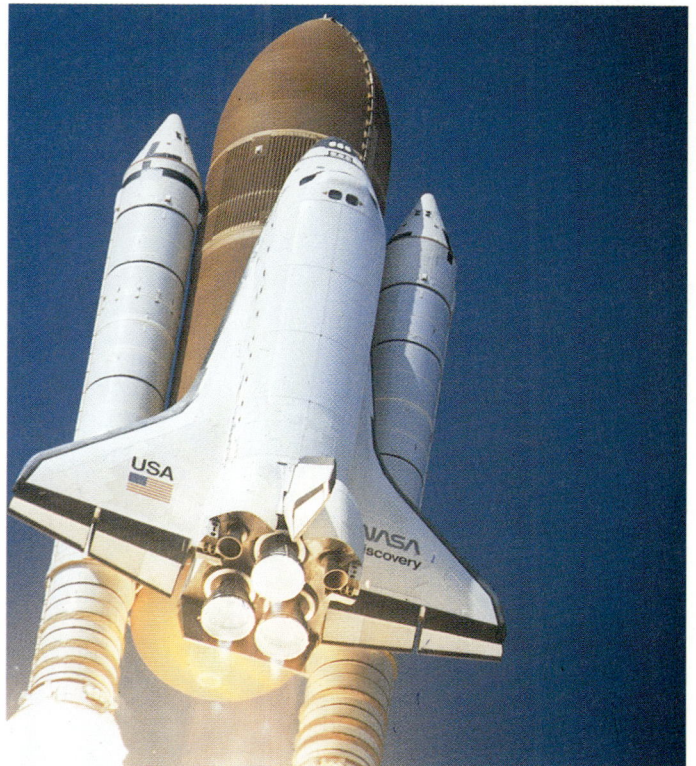
🔺 There is a downwards force on the burning gases, and an equal upwards force on the rocket.

Summary

- A force has direction as well as size. Force is an example of a vector quantity. Arrows can show the size and direction of forces.
- If forces act in the same direction, they must be added to find the total force.
- If forces act in opposite directions, they must be subtracted to find the total force.
- Velocity is speed with a particular direction. Velocity is a vector quantity. Arrows can show the size and the direction of velocities.
- Balanced forces have the same effect on motion as no force at all.
- Balanced forces do not change the velocity of an object.
- Unbalanced forces cause acceleration.
- Acceleration is change in velocity per second.
- Acceleration can be worked out by dividing the change in velocity by the time taken for the change.

$$a = \frac{v - u}{t}$$

- Acceleration due to the Earth's gravity is about $10\,\text{m/s}^2$.
- The acceleration of an object depends on its mass and on the force acting on it.

$$a = \frac{F}{m} \text{ and } F = ma$$

- Car stopping distances increase as the car's speed increases.
- Total stopping distance is 'thinking distance' added to 'braking distance'.
- Stopping distances also depend on the state of the road surface, tyres, brakes and the driver's concentration.
- When one object exerts a force on another object, it experiences an equal and opposite force.

Revision Questions

1 What causes change in motion?

2 How do skaters change their motion?

3

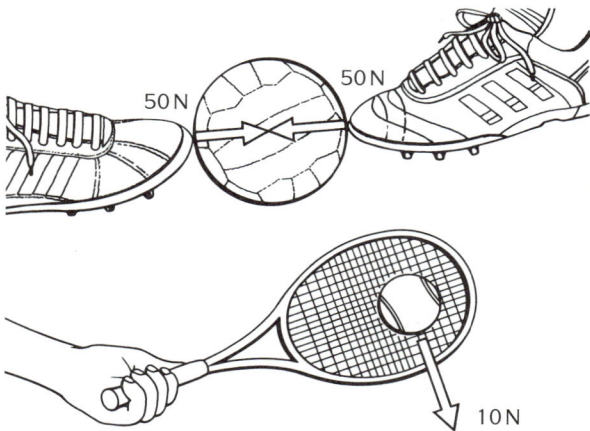

Which ball experiences the biggest total force?

4 What happens to a tennis ball when you hit it? What happens to the racket?

5 How fast would you have to walk to stay in the same place on a walkway moving at 2 m/s? Make a sketch with arrows to show the walkway velocity and your own walking velocity.

6 What force acts on a diver after the diver jumps off the diving board?
How big is the diver's acceleration?

7 A space station with a mass of 5000 kg has to have an acceleration of 2 m/s^2. Copy and complete the calculation to predict the force that will be needed.

$$F = ma$$
$$= \_\_ kg \times 2\,m/s$$
$$= \_\_ N$$

8 For a car travelling at 21 m/s, what is:
   a the thinking distance
   b the braking distance
   c the stopping distance?

9 Why is friction needed for walking?

10 a Which of these are examples of changing motion:
   i a skater gliding in a straight line
   ii a falling apple
   iii a train slowing down
   iv a train at a steady 100 km/h?
   b In which of the motions are the forces balanced?

11 Write down an example of motion without force.

12 Describe an example of motion at constant velocity which changes when a force acts. What causes the force to act?

13 One tug-of-war team pulls with a force of 1.2 kilonewton. The other team pulls with a force of 1.0 kilonewton.
   a Sketch a diagram to show the forces acting on the middle of the rope. Sketch the arrows so that it is possible to see which force is bigger.
   b What is the *total* force acting on the centre of the rope?
   c What happens next?

14 a How does an owl turn as it flies?
   b How does a spacecraft turn as it flies?

15 A mouse in a biscuit factory crosses a conveyor belt, running at right angles to the edge of the belt. The running speed of the mouse is 1 m/s. The belt also moves at 1 m/s. Draw a sketch and use arrows to show the velocities. Show roughly where the mouse ends up.

16 'The velocity of an object provides more information than its speed.' Do you agree with this? Explain your answer.

17 A car increases its velocity by 3 m/s in every second. It keeps this up for 10 s.
   a What is the car's acceleration?
   b Sketch a velocity–time graph to show the car's motion during the 10 s.

18

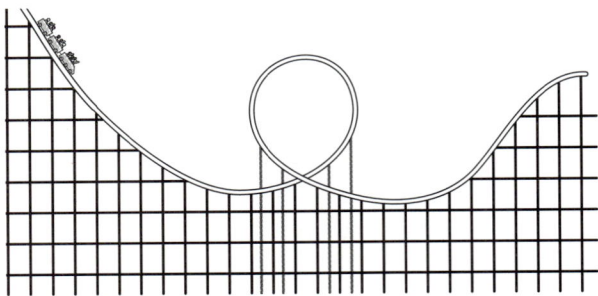

The diagram is a design for an adventure park ride. Copy the sketch and show:

a where you think the cars will have most acceleration

b where you think the cars will have most velocity.

19 Explain how it is possible for a cycle to have a bigger acceleration than a car.

20 Two arrows, one heavier than the other, are fired side by side from a bow. What happens next?

21 Predict the total force needed to accelerate a 500 kg boat by 2.5 m/s^2.

22 How does a fish move forwards?

23 At what speed does thinking distance equal braking distance according to the Highway Code?

24 What is the value of your velocity relative to the rest of the room that you are in?

25 If you travel in a train with no windows, and on smooth track, can you tell whether you are moving:

a as the train starts

b at steady speed in a straight line (constant velocity)

c when going around a bend

d when slowing down?

26 Is time a vector or a scalar quantity?

27 Sketch a diagram of the forces acting on a rocket as it accelerates upwards from its launch pad.

28 Aircraft pilots talk about 'air speed' and 'ground speed'. Air speed is the speed with which they move through the air. Ground speed is the speed with which they fly over the land below. Why are they different?

29 a Calculate the acceleration of a car which goes from 5 m/s to 35 m/s in 6 s.

b Sketch a velocity–time graph for this motion.

c How does this acceleration compare with the acceleration due to gravity on Earth?

d What do you think it would feel like?

30 Sketch velocity–time graphs for:

a a car which has an acceleration of 3 m/s^2.

b a stone falling from a cliff

c a person bouncing on a trampoline

d on the same axes, a loaded oil tanker and an unloaded oil tanker of the same size as they accelerate away from a port

e a car stopping in an emergency, starting from the time when it has a steady speed of 20 m/s.

31 Would you expect acceleration due to gravity on the Moon to be the same as on Earth, less than on Earth, or nothing at all? Explain your answer.

32 A locomotive pushes on a 4000 kg railway truck with a force of 5 kilonewton. Why is the acceleration of the truck less than 0.8 m/s^2?

33 On a flat calm day, two pirate ships exchange fire with their cannon. Why do they move apart?

34 You live alone at an Antarctic base. You go skating on some very slippery ice. You fall over, and every time you try to stand up you fall over again. There is no friction at all. How do you get back to the edge of the ice?

Pressure

We can use knowledge of pressure to help us to explore under the sea and out in space.

We can store gases, or empty the gas completely out of glass flasks to make TVs and X-ray machines. But, first we need the knowledge.

Imagine climbing into a metal vessel like this, and sinking yourself to the bottom of some deep ocean. The pressure on the surface of your submersible craft gets bigger and bigger as you go down, thanks to the weight of water above you. You can hear the metal bending. That is just your first worry. The second one is just as scary, if you don't know much about pressure – how will you get back up again? It is a matter of controlling the pressure on some gas, making it fit into bigger or smaller volumes, so that you can take it in and out of your submarine's chambers. Knowledge gives you confidence. Ignorance leaves you scared.

Review

Before going any further, read this page and attempt the tasks. Write the answers in your notes.

The area of a pair of skis is big enough to allow the skier to travel over the top of the snow without sinking. The large surface area reduces the effect of the weight of the skier on the snow. It reduces the pressure.

Bigger area, smaller pressure

Pressure is a useful way of measuring the possible effect of a force on a surface. You work out pressure from the size of the force and the size of the area. The bigger the force, the bigger the pressure. But the bigger the area, the smaller the pressure.

$$\text{pressure} = \frac{\text{force}}{\text{area}}$$

Force is measured in newton, area in square metres and pressure in pascal, or Pa for short.

The skier and skis, on the left, together have a weight of 600 newton. The total area of both skis is $0.3\,\text{m}^2$.

When wearing the skis the skier exerts a pressure on the surface of the snow of:

$$\text{pressure} = \frac{\text{force}}{\text{area}}$$

$$= \frac{600\,\text{N}}{0.3\,\text{m}^2} = 2000\,\text{Pa}$$

This is a good example of how to do a Physics calculation. Start with the formula. Then write out the same pattern, but with the numbers in place of the words. Do the arithmetic and write down the answer, not forgetting the correct unit at the end.

The skater's weight is concentrated onto a small area of ice. The pressure is high enough to melt a thin layer of ice to make it slippery.

N = newton
Pa = pascal

CHECK TEN

1 Copy the word grid into your notebook. Solve the clues and complete your grid.

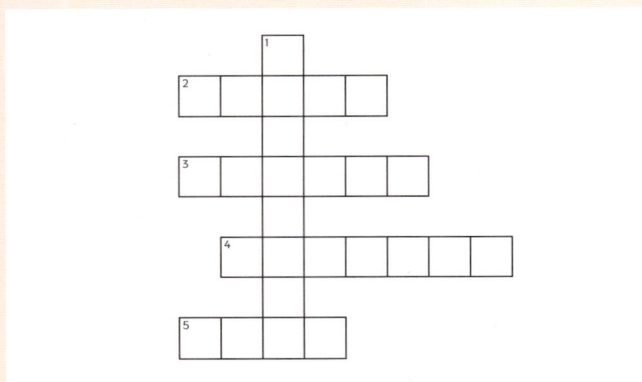

Clues

1 a measure of the possible effect of a force on a surface
2 your weight is one of these
3 a unit for measurements of pressure
4 what pressure acts on
5 when it gets bigger, pressure gets smaller

2 Use the word *pressure* to explain the following:
  a A sharp knife cuts cheese more easily than a blunt one does.
  b Some earth-moving vehicles have tracks and not wheels.

3 If the skier takes off the skis and stands on the snow, will the pressure on the snow be more or less than 2000 pascal?

4 The skier finds a large board, with an area of $1\,\text{m}^2$, and uses it to slide on the snow. What pressure does the skier exert on the snow? (Remember to use the usual steps for getting the answers in Physics – write down the formula, put in the numbers, and then do the arithmetic. Do not forget to include the unit with your answer.)

You exert pressure on the floor

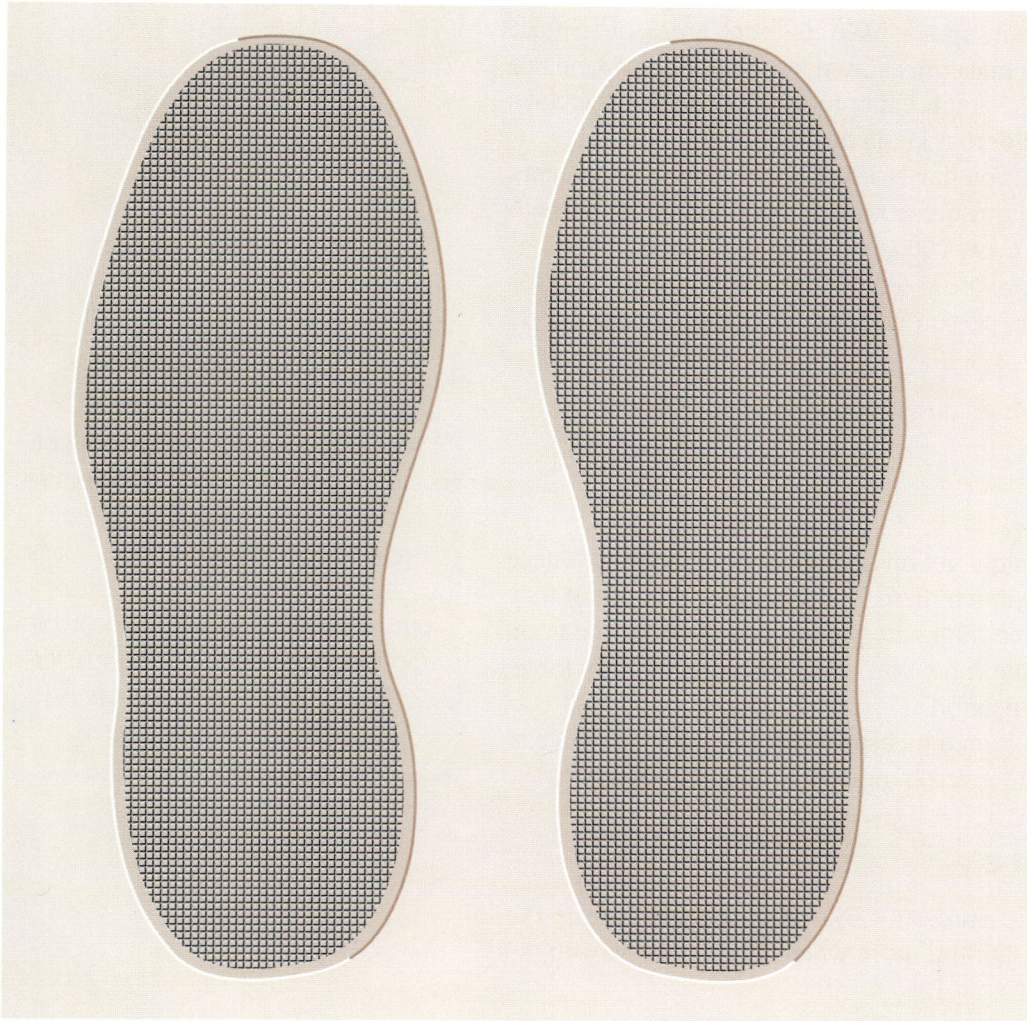

⬥ If you counted all the millimetre squares that make up the area of these toddler's footprints, you would find that the total area was 10 000 mm². That is the same as 0.01 m².

The force that you exert on the floor is the same thing as your weight measured in newton.

Pressure is worked out by dividing force by area. Suppose a 200 newton child wears the shoes that made the footprints. The usual pressure formula will tell us how much the pressure on the floor will be:

$$\text{pressure} = \frac{\text{force}}{\text{area}}$$

$$= \frac{200\,\text{N}}{0.01\,\text{m}^2}$$

$$= 20\,000\,\text{Pa}$$

▶ *Why doesn't a big person always exert more pressure on the ground than a small person?*

▶ *How could you write down a pressure measurement of 100 000 Pa without using so many noughts?*

⬥ You can change the pressure you exert on the floor by changing your shoes.

To save writing out a lot of noughts, we sometimes use kilopascal, kPa, as units. A kilopascal is 1000 pascal. So, 20 000 Pa = 20 kPa.

Investigating sports shoes

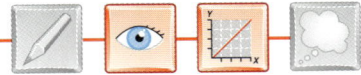

Sports shoes designed for different sports have different areas of contact with the ground. It is possible to make measurements on different kinds of shoes, and then to compare them. Graph paper footprints can provide ways to measure areas of contact for different kinds of shoe.

To work out pressure in pascal, you have to start with area measurements in square metres. There are a million square millimetres in a square metre. A more useful practical hint is that every $1000\,mm^2$ is $0.001\,m^2$.

The usual pressure formula, pressure = force ÷ area, will give answers for the pressure exerted by the same person wearing different types of sports shoe.

▶ *Can you explain why different shoes are designed to exert different pressures?*

Mass and weight

When you 'weigh' yourself you might get an answer in pounds or kg. These are useful measurements of how much there is of you (your mass), but they are not measurements of the force of gravity pulling you down to the floor. They are not measurements of the force you exert on the floor. This force, your true weight, is measured in newton.

To find your weight in newton from a measurement (mass) in kg, you can multiply by 9.81. Multiplying by 10 gives an answer that is very close.

Liquids exert pressure

Water and other liquids exert pressure. The source of the pressure is the weight of water. The deeper you go, the more water there is above you, so the bigger the pressure is.

Some fish that live deep in the sea could be sources of food for hungry people. Unfortunately these deep sea fish are usually very ugly, and people are not keen to eat them once they see them. There is another snag. The fishes' bodies are suitable for a life in an environment where the pressure is much bigger than the pressure that we are used to here in the Earth's atmosphere. The fishes' bodies have high pressure on the inside, to match the high pressure of water on the outside. When the fish are brought up to the surface, their body pressure can be just too much, and they explode.

> Pressure melts ice. That is why squashing a snowball makes it firm. The pressure melts some of the ice, but when you release the pressure it re-freezes. It also explains how a glacier 'flows'. It is heavy and so there is a lot of pressure acting on the ice near the bottom of the glacier. The glacier 'floats' on a thin film of water between it and the ground.

▶ *What happens to human bodies when the pressure is very low?*

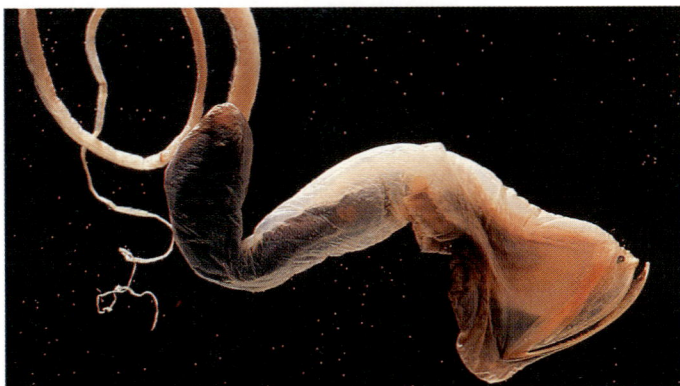

▲ A body built for a high pressure environment.

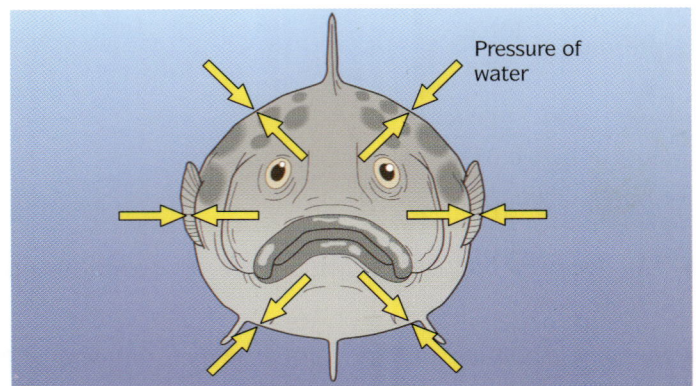

▲ The pressure inside a fish balances the pressure outside.

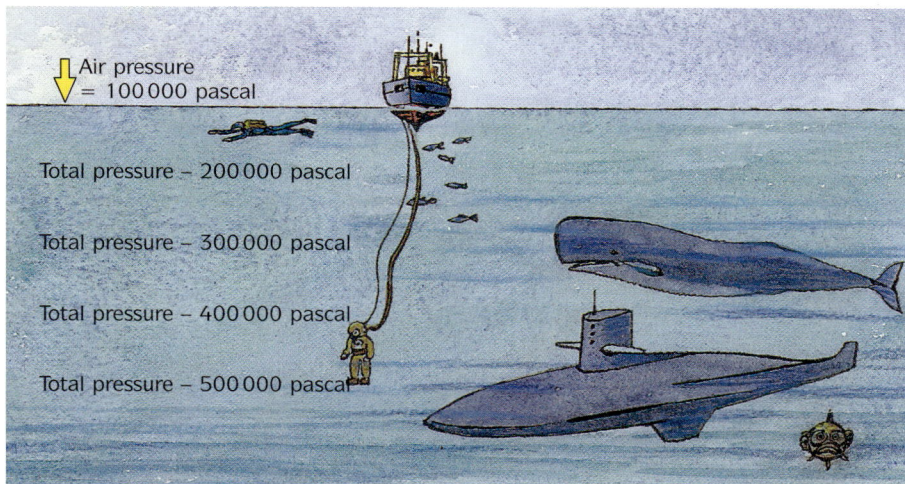

△ Pressure increases with depth in the sea.

Liquid pressure acts in all directions

Liquids can flow. They not only exert a force on the base of the container but also on the sides and they need to be supported there. A drink exerts pressure on the sides of the container as well as on the base.

Liquid pressure depends on density

Salmon are creatures which can live in both sea water and fresh water. When they swim from the sea into a river, they have to allow for the change in the water density. Salty sea water is denser and easier to float in, and if they did not make adjustments they would sink.

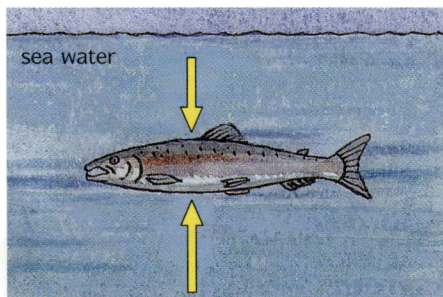

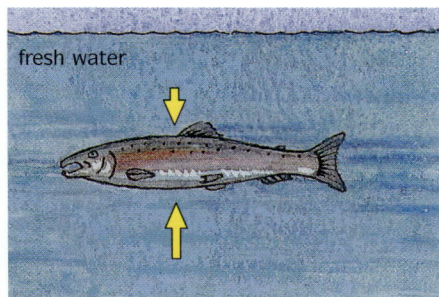

△ The density of water makes a difference to the pressure it exerts at any particular depth.

Mercury is a very dense liquid. Quite a small volume has a comparatively large weight. So a small amount of mercury exerts a large pressure.

▶ *Why is the pressure at the bottom of a 50 m deep lake not as big as the pressure 50 m down in the sea?*

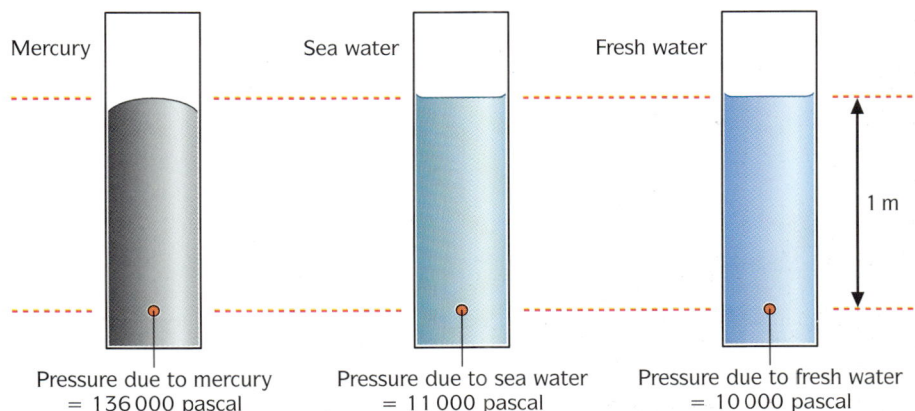

△ To dive to great depths divers must wear protective suits. The pressure inside the suit can be kept close to the pressure on the surface of the sea. The pressure at the bottom of an ocean trench can be as high as 100 MPa (or about a thousand times bigger than the air pressure at the surface).

△ A liquid exerts pressure on the sides and bottom of a glass.

Mercury	Sea water	Fresh water
Pressure due to mercury = 136 000 pascal	Pressure due to sea water = 11 000 pascal	Pressure due to fresh water = 10 000 pascal

△ The pressure 1 m down is different in different liquids.

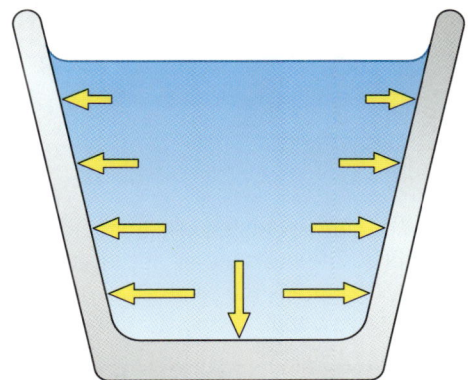

Remember that the density of a substance, whether it is solid, liquid or gas, is worked out from the formula:

$$\text{density} = \frac{\text{mass}}{\text{volume}}$$

Density is measured in kg per cubic metre, or kg/m^3

The pressure that a liquid exerts on the base of its container does not depend on the area of the base but only on the depth and density. This pressure can be calculated by using the formula:

pressure due to liquid = depth × density × g

g is the conversion factor for turning measurements in kg into measurements in newton. It is the weight on Earth of each kg of mass.

On Earth, every kg of mass has a weight of 9.81 newton. So g is 9.81 newton per kg. For a lot of practical purposes, it is accurate enough to say that g is 10 newton per kg.

$$g = 10\,\text{N/kg (approximately)}$$

Explaining water spouts

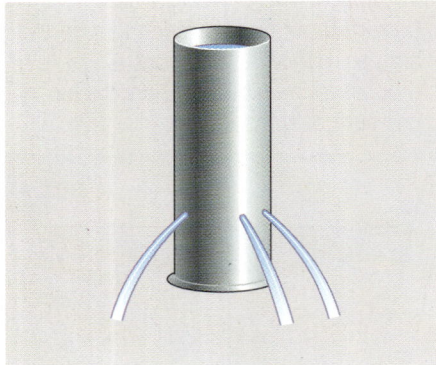

△ The water spouts equally from all of the holes. The holes are all at the same depth. Pressure is the same at all points at the same depth.

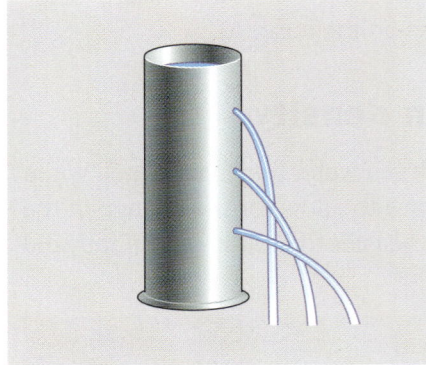

△ The pressure is bigger at greater depth, so some spouts are longer than others.

▶ Why is the pressure of the water from the hot water tap greater in the kitchen than in an upstairs bathroom?

▶ If you had to choose the site of a reservoir to serve your school where would it be?

△ This fountain is at Chatsworth House in Derbyshire. It works without any kind of pump, but just with pipes that come from the nearby hillside.

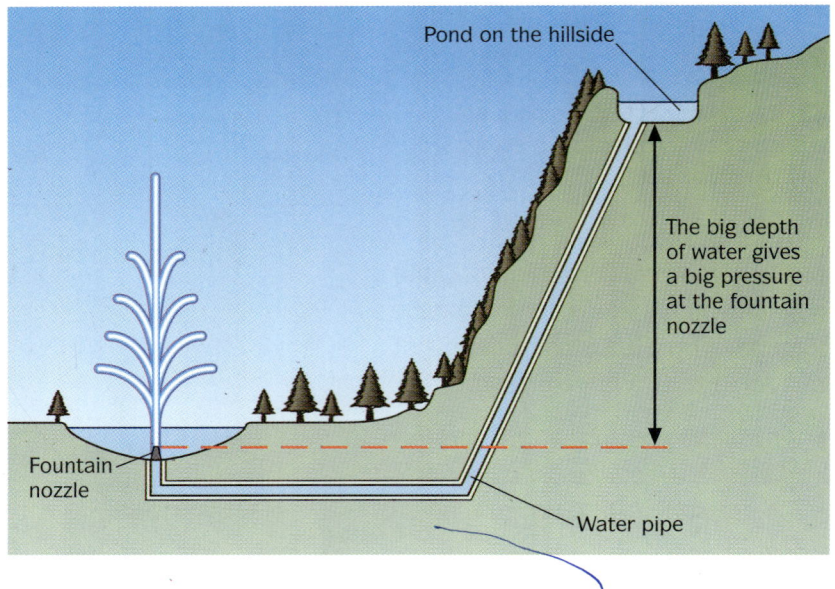

Pond on the hillside

The big depth of water gives a big pressure at the fountain nozzle

Fountain nozzle

Water pipe

PHYSICS

Investigating the relationship between liquid pressure and depth

You may be given a worksheet to help you investigate how pressure in a liquid varies with depth.

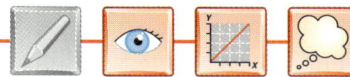

Testing dams

You can build a model dam with thin 'bricks' of Plasticine so that it divides a small tank or bowl. The model can be used for investigations to find the minimum amount of material needed to build a dam that stays up and holds back the water.

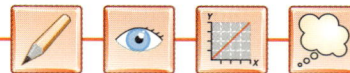

Pressure acting on liquids

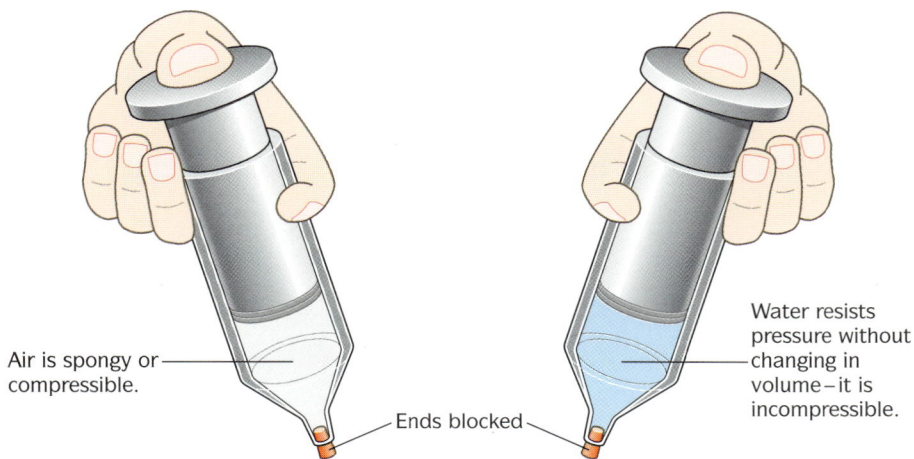

Air is spongy or compressible.

Ends blocked

Water resists pressure without changing in volume – it is incompressible.

🔺 If you tried to press the plunger on the two syringes one would be easy but the other would be impossible. Gases like air can be compressed into a smaller volume, but liquids like water cannot.

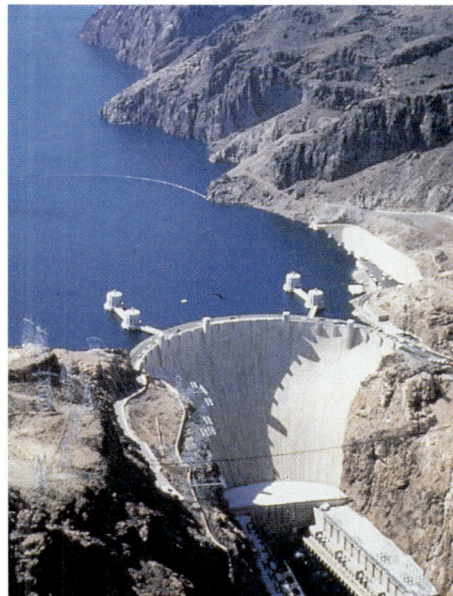

🔺 Holding back a great depth of water requires clever engineering.

🔺 Pressure acting on liquid does not change the volume of the liquid. In a water pistol, the liquid escapes.

🔺 This is a water bed. The mattress is a container of water. Lying on the bed does not change the volume of the liquid, it just makes it move around inside the container.

▶ *Which is easier to squash: a plastic bottle full of air or a plastic bottle full of water?*

Hydraulics

Pressure on a gas can squash the gas into a smaller space. But a liquid cannot be compressed into a smaller space. In the water pistol and the water bed, pressure applied to a liquid in one place makes the liquid try to push out everywhere straight away. Liquids are excellent transmitters of pressure.

Hydraulic equipment (like the hydraulics of the earth-mover in the picture) takes advantage of transmission of pressure in liquids. In the earth-mover, pressure is applied to the liquid in one place, and the liquid pushes on the different moving parts of the arm and shovel.

▲ In hydraulic machines, liquid in pipes transmits pressure from one place to another.

Observing hydraulic pressure

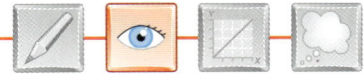

▲ Pushing on one piston makes it move down until it reaches the bottom of the syringe. The second piston moves up to the 40 cm³ mark.

The same pressure but different force

The use of hydraulic pressure in a car jack allows a small force to generate a much larger one.

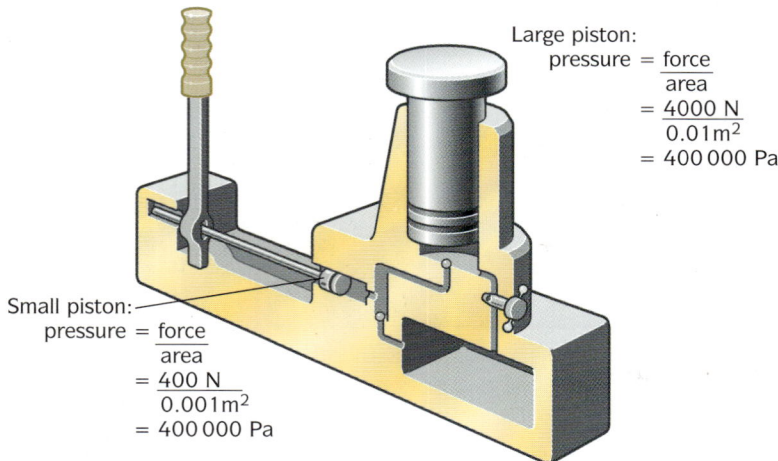

Large piston:
$$\text{pressure} = \frac{\text{force}}{\text{area}}$$
$$= \frac{4000\ \text{N}}{0.01\ \text{m}^2}$$
$$= 400\,000\ \text{Pa}$$

Small piston:
$$\text{pressure} = \frac{\text{force}}{\text{area}}$$
$$= \frac{400\ \text{N}}{0.001\ \text{m}^2}$$
$$= 400\,000\ \text{Pa}$$

▲ The pressure is the same on both pistons. But the push of the small cylinder on the liquid is smaller than the push of the liquid on the large piston.

▲ Using a car jack to convert a small force into a bigger one.

▶ *What would happen if someone tried to make a car jack filled with air?*

Drums and discs

In a car the brake pads are forced against the brake disc. Friction between the two causes the car to slow down. The first force is the push of the driver's foot on the pedal. The brake fluid transmits the pressure to exert a much bigger force on the brake pads.

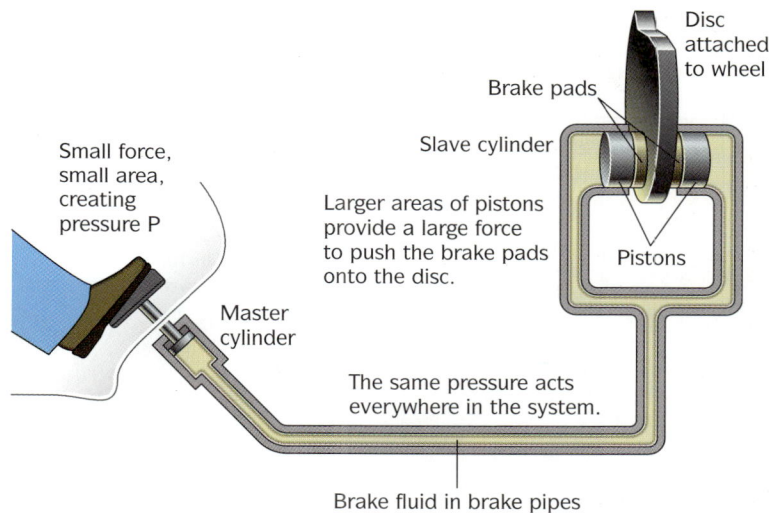

Disc attached to wheel

Brake pads

Small force, small area, creating pressure P

Slave cylinder

Larger areas of pistons provide a large force to push the brake pads onto the disc.

Pistons

Master cylinder

The same pressure acts everywhere in the system.

Brake fluid in brake pipes

Calculations for a brake system

Pressure on the master cylinder piston:

$$\text{pressure} = \frac{\text{force}}{\text{area}}$$

$$= \frac{500 \text{ N}}{0.01 \text{ m}^2}$$

$$= 50\,000 \text{ Pa} = 50 \text{ kPa}$$

Force on the slave cylinder piston:

$$\text{force} = \text{pressure} \times \text{area}$$

$$\text{force} = 50\,000 \text{ Pa} \times 0.05 \text{ m}^2$$

$$= 2500 \text{ N}$$

Notice that the brake system turns a 500 newton force into a 2500 newton force.

This is a rearrangement of the basic pressure formula. You can read more about rearranging formulae in Chapter Sixteen (Physics help).

Vacuum and atmosphere

We cannot see the air, but we can feel it. Air is a material that surrounds us. The idea of a space with no air (or any material at all) inside it is a difficult idea. People used to believe that a space like that, called a **vacuum**, was impossible. That was 400 years ago. But engineers trying to pump water from wells and mines kept coming across the same problem. None of their pumps could lift the water much more than 10 m.

Early experiments with water

To try to find out more, some Italian scientists made a lead pipe which was more than 10 m tall, and they filled it up with water. Then they closed the pipe at the top and opened it at the bottom. The water didn't all drain out. Only a bit went into the tub at the bottom, leaving a space in the flask at the top.

🔺 There was an 'empty' space at the top of the flask.

There was a lot of discussion about what was in the space.

Evidence that there is material all around us.

Early experiments with mercury

One of the scientists, called Torricelli, thought about the idea that the space was a vacuum, and that the sea of air around the tub could press down on the water and held it in place up to a height of 10 m. He reckoned that if this was right then the air would not be able to hold up so much mercury, because mercury is much denser than water.

To try out his idea Torricelli took a glass tube, like a very long test tube, and filled it with mercury. Then he turned it upside down with its open end dipping into a bowl of mercury. Mercury stayed in the tube up to a height of about 75 cm, with a space above, just like the space in the experiment with water. That seemed to support the idea of the vacuum and the sea of air, or atmosphere.

▶ *In the experiments with water and mercury, what are the similarities and the differences?*

Mercury in the mountains

Some French scientists then came up with the idea that the atmosphere or sea of air is not so deep at the top of a mountain as at the bottom. To try out their idea they set up two mercury tubes, one at a mountain top and one on low level ground.

The height of mercury was smaller in the tube up the mountain. This showed that the atmosphere really does exert less pressure higher up, on the mountain. That provided more support for the idea that we live in an atmosphere that does not go on for ever. The air goes on for many km upwards. But above that there is no air, just vacuum.

▶ *Why do some people get nose bleeds in very high mountains?*

Now we can shoot electrons through a vacuum in a glass tube, to light up a screen, so that we can find out about the changing patterns of air pressure in the atmosphere.

The Earth has a layer of air. Above that, space is a vacuum.

Pressure of the atmosphere

The Earth is surrounded by a layer of gas. The atmosphere, like all gases, exerts a pressure. The pressure of the atmosphere varies with altitude and temperature. Typical values are in the table.

Altitude	Pressure (pascal)
Sea level	100 000
Summit of Ben Nevis (1000 m high)	90 000
Summit of Mount Everest (9000 m high)	40 000
Flight path of an airliner (12 000 m)	35 000

🔺 Variation of atmospheric pressure with altitude

▶ *A column of mercury at sea level is about 75 cm high. Roughly how high would you expect it to be at the top of Mount Everest?*

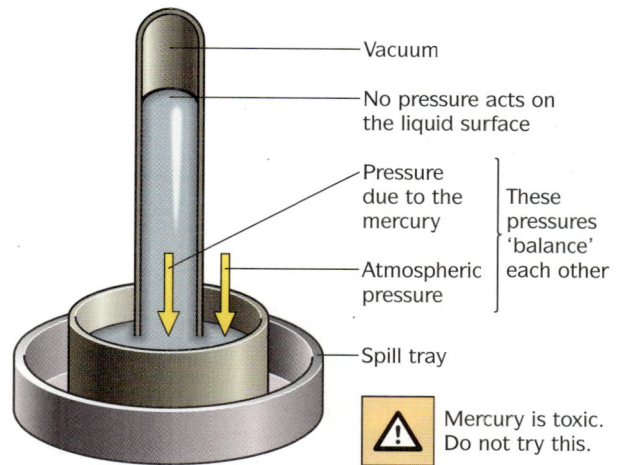

Looking for pressure trends

🔺 A data logger with a pressure sensor can be used to record the atmospheric pressure over a 24-hour period, repeated on several days. Any daily trends show up.

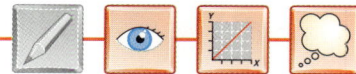

Vacuum

No pressure acts on the liquid surface

Pressure due to the mercury

Atmospheric pressure

These pressures 'balance' each other

Spill tray

⚠ Mercury is toxic. Do not try this.

🔺 The apparatus that Torricelli used. The pressure of the air can support a column of mercury. The bigger the air pressure, the higher it pushes the mercury.

Observing atmospheric pressure

🔺 With most of the air removed from the inside of these spheres there is little pressure on the inner surfaces. The pressure of air on the outside is much bigger and the force pushing the two hemispheres together is very large.

Increasing the pressure on the inside

Atmospheric pressure

Very low pressure

Decreasing the pressure on the outside

Pressure pump extracting air

SAFETY

⚠ Use a safety screen and wear eye protection.

🔺 There are two ways to blow up a balloon. One is to increase the pressure on the inside, the other is to reduce the pressure on the outside. When the pressure outside the balloon is reduced the pressure inside becomes enough to make it inflate.

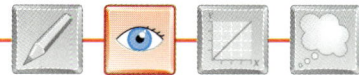

PHYSICS

Pressure and the gas supply

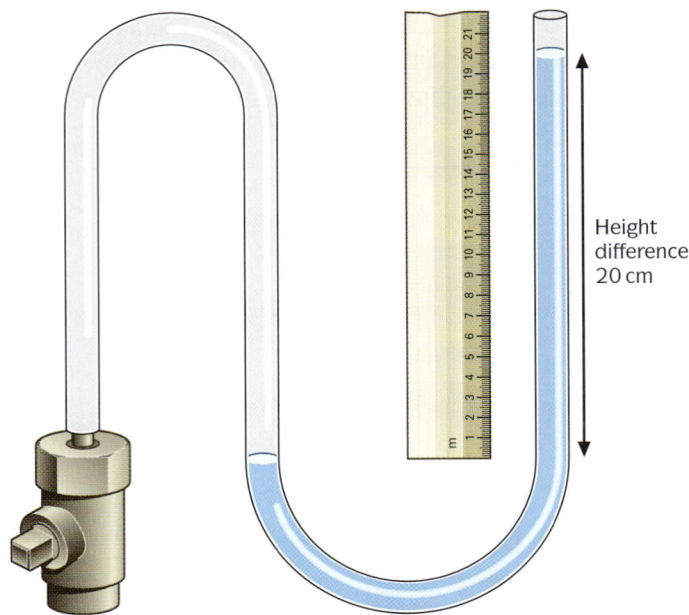

Height difference 20 cm

🔺 When a new gas appliance is fitted in a home the fitter might use a manometer to check the pressure of the gas before and after the work is done. If there are any leaks then the pressure of the gas at the meter will be less than normal.

🔺 The pressure of the gas supply is bigger than atmospheric pressure. If it wasn't, then the gas would not be able to escape. The difference in pressures makes the water in a manometer settle at different levels. The bigger the difference in pressure, the bigger the height difference between the two water surfaces.

▶ *Apart from health reasons, why is water rather than mercury used in the manometer?*

A manometer makes use of the fact that in a static liquid, pressure is equal at all points on the same horizontal level. The pressure acting on the water in the gas arm of the manometer that is connected to the gas supply is, of course, the pressure of the gas. The pressure acting on the water surface in the arm that is open to the air is the pressure of the atmosphere. It takes the extra pressure of the column of water to balance the pressure of the gas supply.

The difference between the gas pressure and the atmospheric pressure is called the excess gas pressure. It is equal to the pressure due to the column of water. We can work out that pressure:

excess gas pressure = pressure due to the column of water

$$= \text{depth} \times \text{density} \times g$$

The density of water is 1000 kg/m³. If the height of the water column is 0.2 m, then,

excess gas pressure = depth × density × g

$$= 0.2\,\text{m} \times 1000\,\text{kg/m}^3 \times 10\,\text{N/kg}$$

$$= 2000\,\text{Pa (or 2 kPa)}$$

Pressure and bicycle pumps

To put air in the tyre, the pressure in the pump must be bigger than the pressure inside the tyre. The cyclist applies pressure to the air in the pump. Notice that increasing the pressure on the air also reduces its volume. For a gas, when pressure goes up then (if nothing else changes enough to make any difference) volume goes down. We say that there is an inverse relationship between pressure and volume.

▶ What happens to the pressure acting on a gas, and its volume, when:
  a you stand on a tennis ball
  b a bubble of air rises from deep in the sea to the surface?

▲ The cyclist applies pressure to the air in the pump.

Investigating pressure and volume of a gas

A gas syringe with the end sealed traps some air which can then be studied.

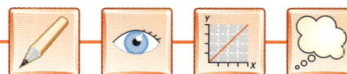

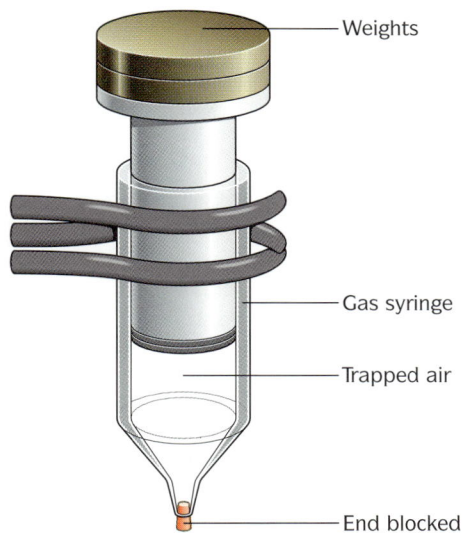

▲ The apparatus used for the investigation. You should carry out a risk assessment before starting this investigation.

Number of weights	1	2	3	4	5
Volume of gas in cm³	75	40	27	22	16

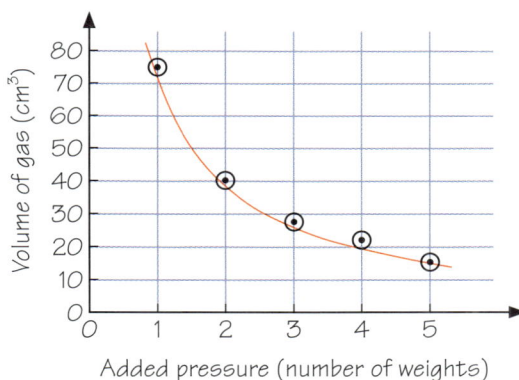

The number of weights controls the pressure on the gas. I can use the number of weights as my measurement of pressure. I can read the volume from the scale on the syringe.

Pressure and particles

We can think about changes in pressure and volume of a gas by thinking about molecules. A gas exerts a pressure on the walls of its container because the molecules are constantly hitting the walls. When a molecule hits a wall it rebounds and travels until it hits either another molecule or another wall. If the volume is reduced the molecules have less distance to travel between collisions and so they hit the walls more often. That means that the gas exerts more pressure.

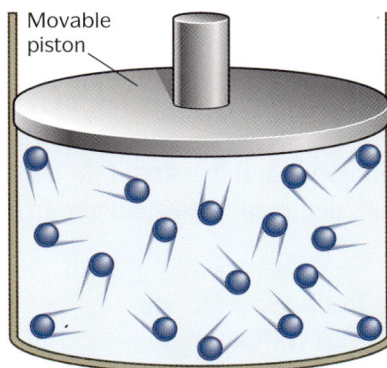

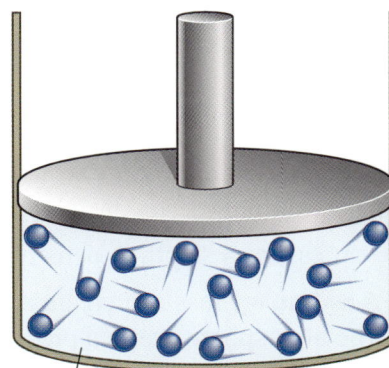

• Same number of molecules
• Same speed
• Smaller volume and more pressure

▲ An artist's impression of molecules striking the walls of a container and what happens when the volume gets smaller.

Four variables

Pressure affects the volume of a gas. Pressure and volume are variables. But there are other variables which can affect the volume of a gas – the mass of the gas and its temperature. So we have to be careful. We have to say that increasing the pressure of a gas always reduces its volume *provided that* the temperature and mass of gas do not change. We can only say something definite about the relationship between two variables when other variables are not allowed to change.

▶ *What is a 'fair test'?*

A graph of pressure against volume clearly shows that volume goes down as pressure goes up. But a graph of $\frac{1}{\text{volume}}$ (sometimes called the *inverse* of the volume) gives a very simple kind of graph – a straight line that passes through the origin.

A simple graph means that there is a simple mathematical relationship between pressure and the inverse of volume. They are *proportional.* You may read more about proportionality in Chapter Sixteen (Physics help). Since all gases generally obey this pattern it is called a law, and it is named after an Irish scientist of the 17th century, Robert Boyle. **Boyle's law** is:

The volume of a fixed mass of gas at constant temperature is inversely proportional to the pressure.

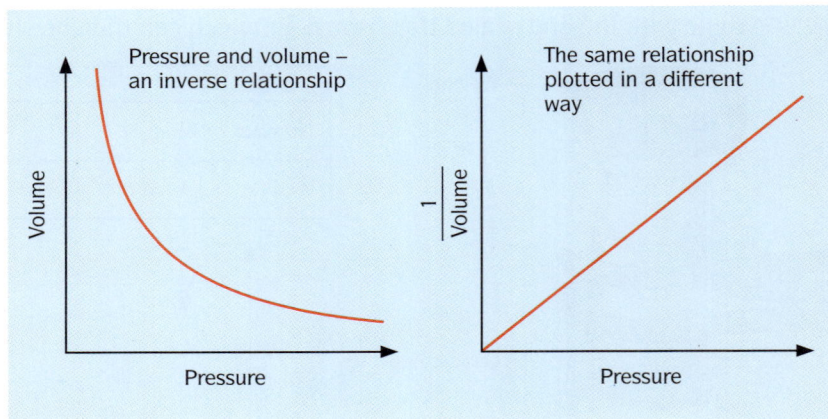

▲ Volume goes down as pressure goes up; $\frac{1}{\text{volume}}$ is proportional to pressure.

Pressure units

You may be given a worksheet to help you learn about units of pressure.

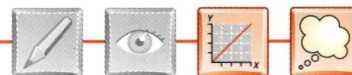

Summary

- Pressure is the force acting on a unit (usually 1 m^2) of area.
- The pressure exerted on a surface can be calculated using the equation:

$$\text{pressure} = \frac{\text{force}}{\text{area}}$$

- Liquids exert a pressure which depends on depth and density of the liquid.
- The pressure exerted by a liquid at a certain depth can be calculated using the equation:

$$\text{pressure} = \text{depth} \times \text{density} \times g$$

- A hydraulic press can create a larger force from a smaller one.
- The atmosphere exerts a pressure which varies with altitude.
- The pressure of a gas supply must be greater than atmospheric pressure.
- Measuring the gas pressure leads to a safer use of gas appliances.
- The volume of a gas is inversely proportional to the pressure acting on it. This is called Boyle's law.
- Gases exert pressure because their molecules collide with surfaces.

Revision Questions

1 Copy and complete the following passage using words from the list:

air   pascal   atmosphere   surface   pressure

The _____ is a layer of _____ that surrounds the Earth. The air exerts a _____ of about 100 000 _____ on the _____ of the Earth.

2 Snow shoes look a bit like tennis rackets. Explain why snow shoes make it easier to walk on snow.

3

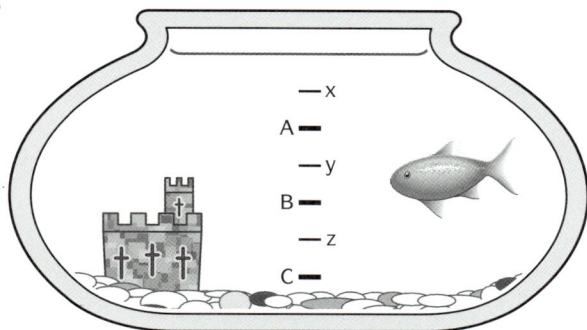

If the pressures due to the water at A, B and C are 400 Pa, 800 Pa and 1200 Pa, what are the pressures at x, y and z?

4 Explain why dams have to be much thicker at the bottom than the top.

5 a Why do firefighters need high-pressure water?
  b Why do airliners need pressurised cabins that are sealed from the air outside?

6 A man of weight 750 newton is wearing shoes that each have an area 0.03 m². What pressure does he exert on the ground:
  a when standing with both feet on the ground
  b when he stands on one foot?

7

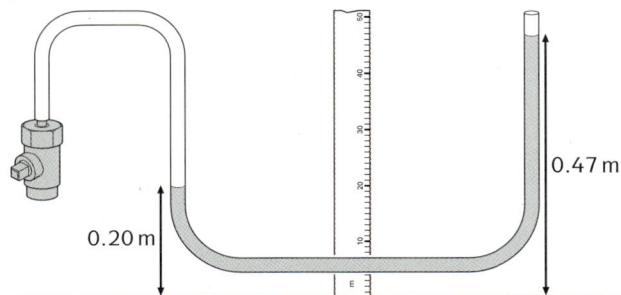

0.47 m
0.20 m

▲ A manometer.

The manometer contains water of density 1000 kg/m³. What is the excess pressure of the gas supply?

8 Use the data on page 151 to plot a graph with pressure on the y-axis and height above sea level on the x-axis.
  a Use your graph to predict typical pressures at 5000 m and 15 000 m above sea level.
  b Why does atmospheric pressure decrease with altitude?

9 Explain why the output force from a hydraulic car jack is bigger than the input force.

10 One way to stop a bicycle is to let your foot scrape along the ground. But that is not very practical as a way to stop a car. Explain the importance of hydraulics in safe braking of a car.

11 a Do you believe that a vacuum can exist? What evidence have you got? Why do you think that this was once a controversial issue among scientists?
  b If space is a vacuum, why doesn't air in the atmosphere spread out into space?
  c Would a vacuum cleaner work in space?

12 Some divers want to lift a heavy treasure chest from the bottom of the sea. They take down a nearly empty balloon and a pressurised gas cylinder.
  a What happens to the volume of the balloon as they swim deeper?
  b They connect the gas cylinder to the balloon. What happens to the total volume of gas when they open the valve?
  c How does the balloon help them to lift the treasure chest?
  d What happens to the volume of the balloon as it rises back to the surface?

13 The glass in a shop window measures 2.5 m × 3.0 m. If atmospheric pressure is 104 000 pascal, what force acts on the window due to the atmosphere? Why doesn't the window break?

14 Estimate the pressure at the nozzle of the Chatsworth fountain if the water supply is a pond on the hillside 50 m above the nozzle.

15 A hydraulic car jack has pistons of areas $5\,cm^2$ and $250\,cm^2$. A mechanic can manage an input force on the small piston of 100 newton. What is the output force?

16 Write a letter to Giuseppe Vivaldi, an engineer working in the year 1610, to explain why his pumps will never raise water by more than 10 m.

17

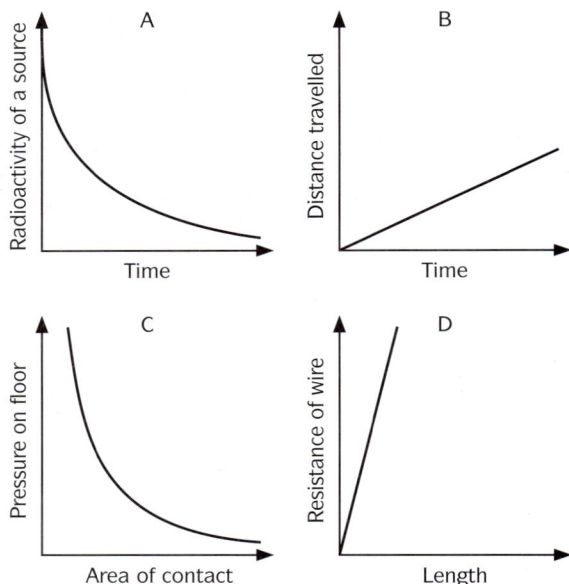

a Which graphs show clear proportionality between the two variables?

b These are the data from which graph C was drawn. Use the data to find out whether the pressure a person exerts on the floor is inversely proportional to the area of their shoes in contact with the floor.

Area of contact (cm^2)	25	50	75	100	125	150	175	200
Pressure (newton/cm^2)	40	20	13	10	8	7	6	5

18 a In the case of the relationship between pressure and volume of a gas:
  i What pressure acting on a gas will produce zero volume? Do you think that this can happen in practice?
  ii What pressure will produce infinite volume of gas?
 b Explain why Boyle's law has to be so carefully worded.

Circuits & components

■ Working together

A stereo system with remote control – a lot of components working together.

Electricity works. Components like resistors, diodes and light-dependent resistors, joined together by metal, provide light and sound, warmth and motion. But components are useless when they are on their own. What matters is how they are connected together.

Review

Before going any further, read this page and attempt the tasks. Write the answers in your notes.

▲ Using head torches.

Inside a torch is a simple circuit – a loop of electrical conductors. There are also batteries with their positive and negative ends, or terminals. They provide the push that drives the current around the loop. There are metal springs in contact with the battery terminals, and other metal strips to carry the current. Even the filament in the bulb is made of metal. From positive to negative, there is a continuous trail of metal whenever the torch is switched on.

Switching off the torch is just a matter of breaking the circuit of metal. Air is an electrical insulator. When there is an air gap, no current can flow. The plastic switch moves a springy strip of metal backwards and forwards to make and break the circuit.

A picture that shows what the batteries, lamp and switch look like is all very well, but we are not all brilliant artists. Circuit diagrams use simple standard symbols for components like these, joined together in a simple rectangle. They are much easier to draw. When you get used to them they are also much easier to use.

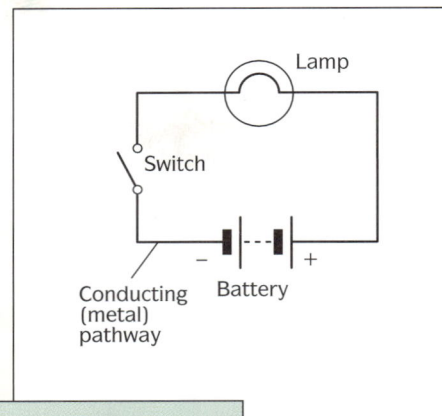
▲ A circuit diagram for the torch – easier to draw.

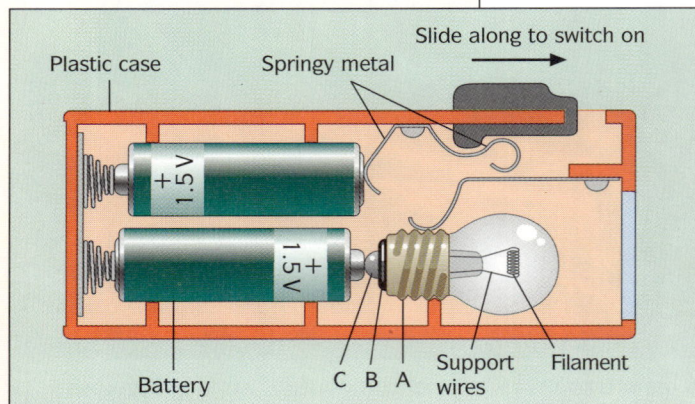
▲ A diagram to show how a torch works.

CHECK ELEVEN

1 Copy the 'circuit' grid into your notebook. Unravel the letters to make the names of components in a torch circuit, and complete your grid.
  1 try beat
  2 hits w.c.
  3 palm
  4 let ma

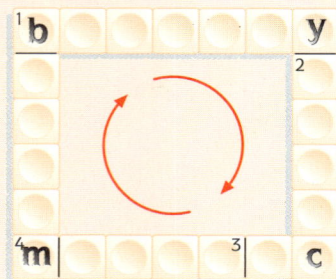
▲ Circuit grid.

2 Why can't the filament in a lamp be made of plastic?

3 Why are the battery terminals made of metal?

4 Does the picture of the torch show it when it is on or off? How can you tell?

5 Explain how the switch works.

6 Would the torch work if both batteries were put in the same way up? Explain your answer.

7 What kinds of material, conductors or insulators, must parts A, B and C in the picture be made of?

Circulation and circuits

An athletics track is one kind of circuit. The flow, or current, is stronger if the athletes run faster. There is also more flow of people if there are more athletes. In an electric circuit it is obviously not people that flow, but something much, much smaller. An electric current is a mass movement of tiny charged particles called **electrons**. You can read more about electrons and electric charge in Chapter Thirteen (Particles, charge and current).

In a central heating system, water circulates in a loop, driven by a pump. The pipes must not be too narrow, or there would be too much resistance to the flow, and the pump might not cope.

We cannot see electrons carrying their charge around a circuit, but they circulate like the water in the heating system or athletes around a track. They travel from the negative terminal of the battery towards the positive. They travel quite easily in thick metal wires, but they need a good supply of energy from the battery to keep them going through resistors.

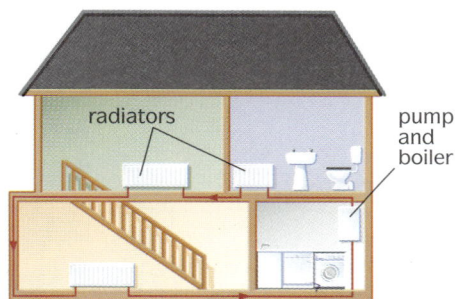

▲ A flow of people around a circuit.

▸ *Which part of your body's circulation system does a similar job to a battery in an electrical circuit?*

▸ *Where in a heating system does water meet resistance?*

▲ Flow of water around a heating system.

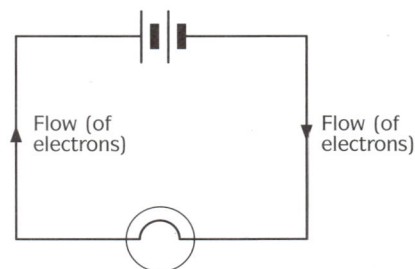

Flow (of electrons)

Flow (of electrons)

▲ Flow of electrons around an electrical circuit.

radiators

pump and boiler

Setting up circuits

A circuit diagram might be a simple way of drawing, but real wires bend and you can easily end up with a mess a bit like spaghetti. The answer is to work slowly and carefully, one step at a time. You may be given a worksheet to help you practice building circuits.

The best idea is to lay out the components in the same arrangement as in the circuit diagram. Then join them up, one by one. If things go wrong, it is usually best to disconnect your wires and start again from the beginning.

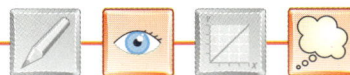

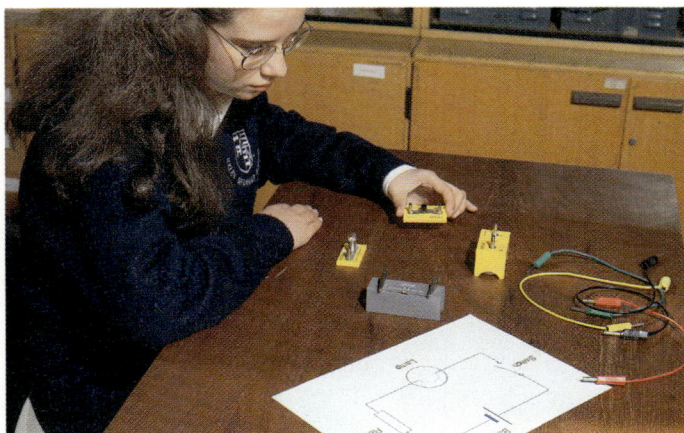

▲ Follow the pattern of the circuit diagram.

▲ The finished circuit is a loop of wires and components.

Current and resistance

Current is a measurement of electrical flow. It is rate of flow of charge.

The comparison between electrical current and water currents is useful. Flowing water is easier to imagine than flowing charge or electrons. Think about a river. The current of water is a measure of the amount of water passing, say, under a bridge every second.

Where the river becomes narrow or shallow, the water must squeeze through. There is a lot of resistance to the flow. The water may become turbulent – white with froth and roaring endlessly. The current in an electrical circuit also meets more resistance in some places than in others. In places of high resistance the flow is not so easy. These places may become hot. They are called **resistors**.

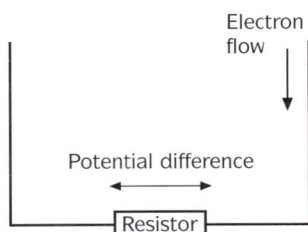

🔺 Water can become turbulent when it meets high resistance.

A resistor in an electric circuit. It takes a 'potential difference' to drive the current through the resistor.

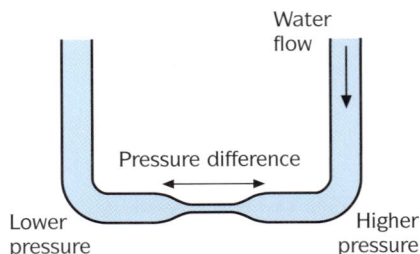

A narrow pipe in a water circuit 'resists' the current. It takes a pressure difference to drive the water current through the pipe.

🔺 Electron flow can be compared to water flow.

▶ *Where does a water current get its energy from to flow through a narrow rocky channel?*

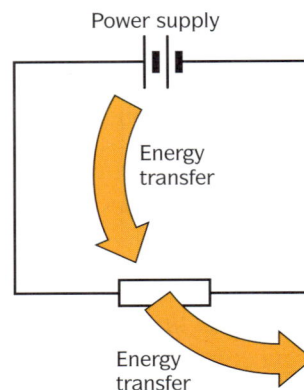

🔺 A power supply can transfer energy to a resistor. The resistor transfers energy to the surroundings.

Energy transfer in electric circuits

A very thin wire with a lot of resistance can get very hot when a current flows through it. The temperature of a filament lamp, for example, rises until the lamp radiates the energy away at the same rate as it arrives.

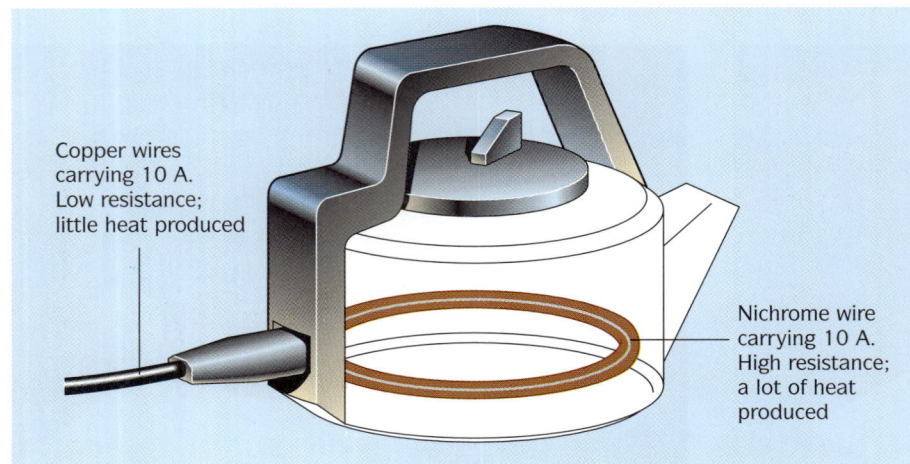

Copper wires carrying 10 A. Low resistance; little heat produced

Nichrome wire carrying 10 A. High resistance; a lot of heat produced

🔺 We use electrical heating for more than just keeping warm.

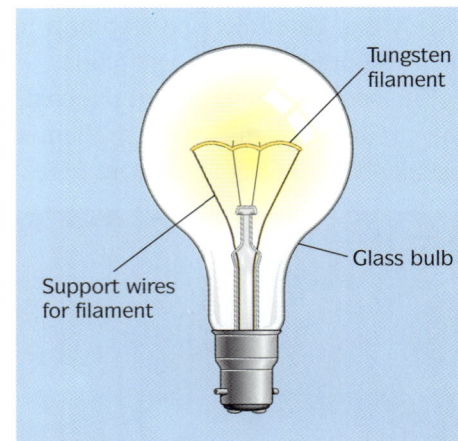

Tungsten filament

Glass bulb

Support wires for filament

🔺 The filament of a lamp is made from tungsten, a metal with a high melting point. The tungsten filament would burn in air at this temperature. It would react with oxygen. So it is kept in a glass bulb full of argon and nitrogen, which are unreactive gases.

The wire in the heating element in a kettle is made of a material with a high resistance so that it gets hot and transfers energy to the water. The kettle element can carry a current of 10 amp. The copper wires in the kettle lead that connect it to the plug also carry this current, but they do not get anywhere near as hot as the element. Copper wires have less resistance. High resistance wires get hotter than low resistance wires when the same current flows through them.

▶ *Where does an electric current get energy from to flow through resistors?*

▶ *How many electrical heaters have you got at home?*

Current creates magnetism

There is a strong link between electric charge and magnetism. You can read more about this in Chapter Fourteen (Electromagnetism). Magnetic forces exist between charged particles that are moving or spinning.

So a flow of charged particles exerts a force on magnetic materials around it. Current creates a magnetic field in its surroundings.

▶ *How could you check whether there is a magnetic field around a wire in a circuit?*

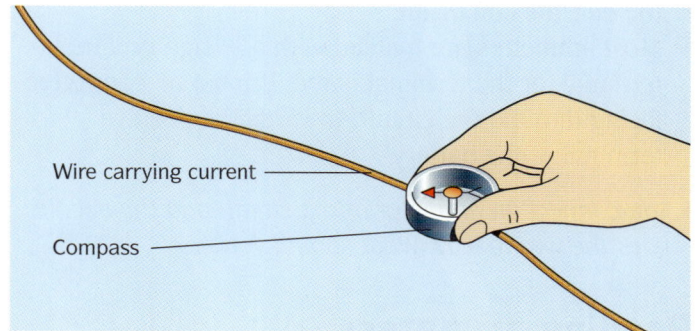

Wire carrying current

Compass

🔺 A wire carrying a current can move a compass needle. The wire has a magnetic field around it.

Measuring current with magnetism

Electrons are far too small to see and far too many to count. It is impossible to get inside a wire and measure the flow of the charge that the electrons carry. So we measure the size of a current by measuring the strength of its magnetic effect. For this we use an **ammeter**.

In an ammeter, the current flows around a coil that is surrounded by a magnet. The force between the coil and the magnet makes the coil turn, and it takes the ammeter needle with it.

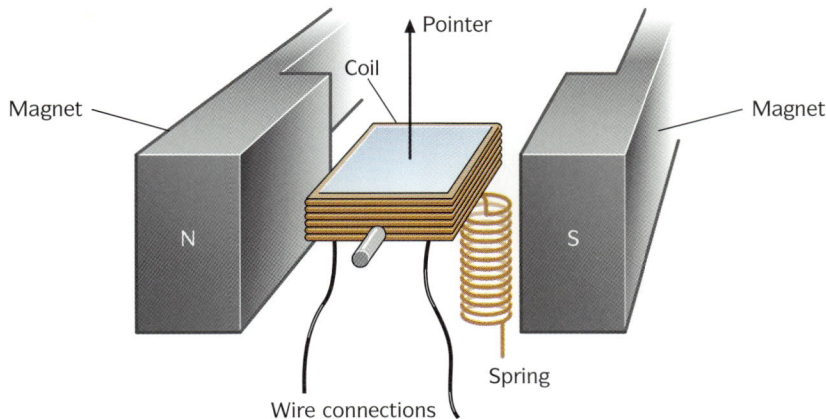

🔺 Some people claim that the magnetic field around power lines is bad for health.

Pointer

Coil

Magnet

Magnet

N

S

Spring

Wire connections

🔺 Inside an ammeter. The bigger the current, the more the coil tries to turn, and the more it stretches or squashes the spring.

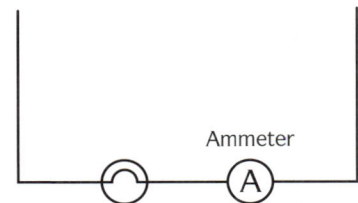

Ammeter

🔺 A lamp and an ammeter connected in series – one after the other.

▶ *In what ways is an ammeter really a kind of force meter?*

Connecting ammeters in circuits

An ammeter measures the current as it flows through. It needs two terminals, or connecting points, for the current to flow in and out.

Rights and wrongs

- If an ammeter is connected to a battery without an energy transfer component such as a lamp in the circuit then a large current could flow. If it is too much for the ammeter it will overheat and damage the delicate coil inside.
- Most ammeters are marked with a + sign on one terminal, or the terminal is red. It must be connected facing (around the circuit) towards the positive terminal of the battery.

▶ *You connect an ammeter into a circuit and the needle goes the wrong way. What should you do?*

Reading ammeters

Electric current is measured in units called **amp**, or A for short. Some ammeters are very sensitive, and measure small currents. These meters detect changes in current that are as small as a milliamp, mA, or even a microamp, μA.

Other ammeters are not so sensitive, but they are more useful for measuring big currents.

If you need more help with reading ammeter scales you can find it in Chapter Sixteen (Physics help).

▶ *How many milliamp make one amp?*

Big and small currents

▲ The lightning conductor on the Empire State Building in New York has been known to carry currents as big as 10 000 amp.

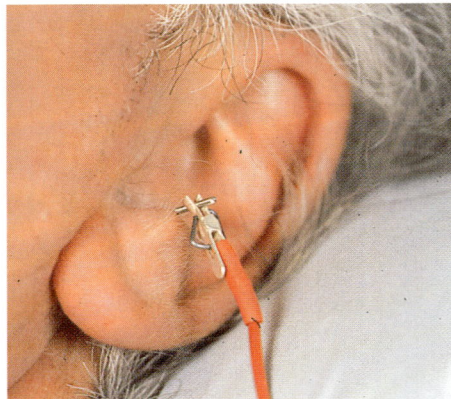

▲ Electroacupuncture involves passing a small current, about 10 milliamp, through a person's body, between two pins. The current has to be very small, or it could kill. Electroacupuncture is meant to relieve pain.

Wrong   Right

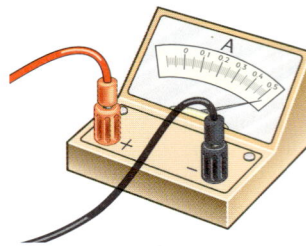 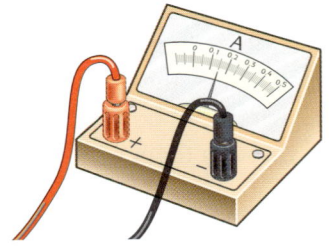

▲ If the needle goes off the end of the scale, the current is too large.

Wrong   Right

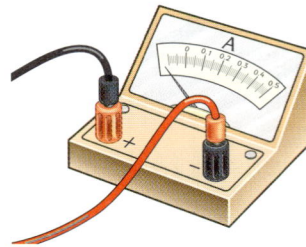 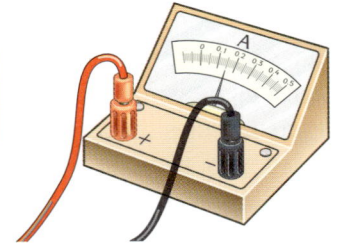

▲ If the needle goes the wrong way, the current is flowing in the wrong direction.

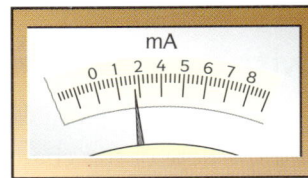 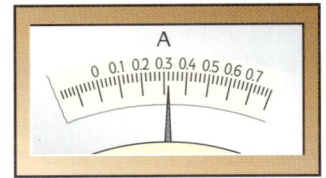

Current = 1.8 mA
(1.8 mA = 0.0018 A)

Current = 0.32 A
(0.32 A = 320 mA)

▲ Different ammeters measure different ranges of current.

A milliamp is one thousandth of an amp. A microamp is one millionth of an amp.

Conventional current and electron flow

People worked with electrical circuits long before electrons were discovered. They knew that there was a flow in the wires, but they did not know exactly what it was that was flowing. So, for the sake of being able to talk about the direction of the flow, they guessed that it was always from positive to negative.

This flow from positive to negative is called **conventional current**. Then, in 1897, electrons were discovered. People quickly realised that electrons are the mobile particles inside a metal. It is electrons that carry charge around circuits. But electrons have negative charge. They are repelled by the negative terminal of a battery and attracted to the positive terminal. They flow in the *opposite* direction to conventional current.

A flow of negatively charged particles in one direction has much the same effects (like heating and magnetism), in our human-sized world, as a flow of positive charge the other way. So many textbooks still show current flowing from positive to negative.

You may read more about particles and charge in Chapter Thirteen (Particles, charge and current).

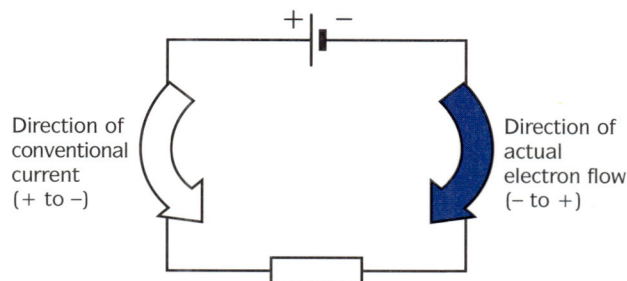

Direction of conventional current (+ to −)

Direction of actual electron flow (− to +)

🔺 Electron flow and conventional current.

Useful components

Switches and lamps in series and parallel

A **series** circuit is a single loop. All of the components follow on, one after the other, around the loop. A **parallel** circuit is slightly more complicated – it has branches which run side by side. Lamps and switches can be connected in series and in parallel.

Two different parallel arrangements

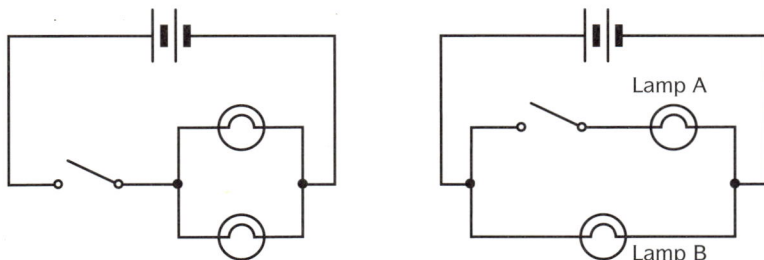

Lamp A

Lamp B

🔺 One switch, two identical lamps. Both lamps come on and glow equally brightly when the switch is closed.

🔺 One switch, two identical lamps. Lamp B is on all of the time. Lamp A comes on when the switch is closed.

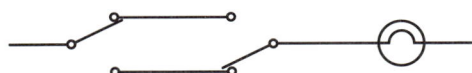

The lamp is off with switches in these positions

🔺 Two-way switching. Whichever switch is switched it changes the state (on or off) of the lamp. Systems like this are useful for stairways.

Switch and lamps in series

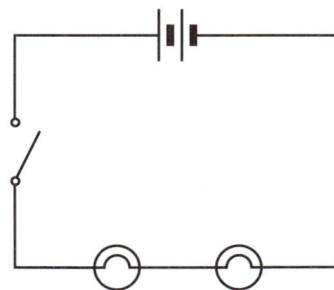

🔺 One switch, two identical lamps. Closing the switch turns on both lamps, and they glow equally brightly.

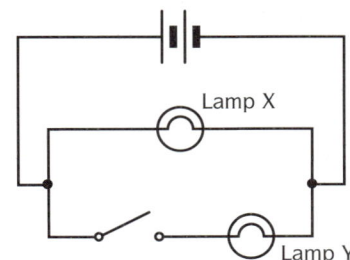

Lamp X

Lamp Y

▶ *Explain what happens in this circuit.*

Variable resistors

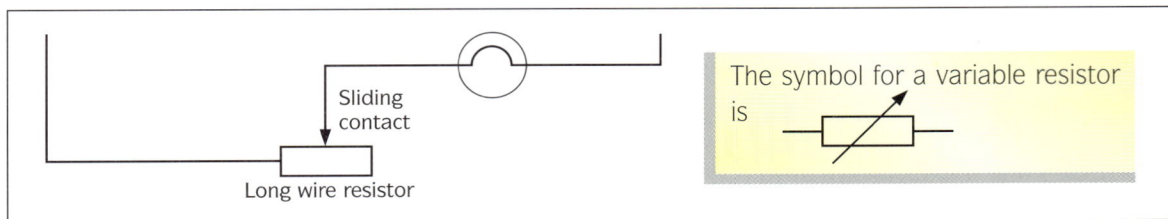

Sliding contact

Long wire resistor

The symbol for a variable resistor is

🔺 When the sliding contact is at one end of the resistor wire, the current has to flow through the whole wire. It meets a lot of resistance. When the contact moves to the other end, the resistance is left out of the circuit. The current has an easier path.

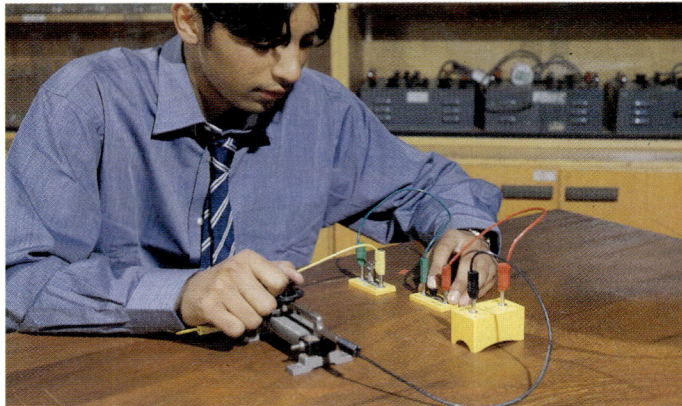

🔺 What you get is what you set. A variable resistor can control the size of the current in a circuit.

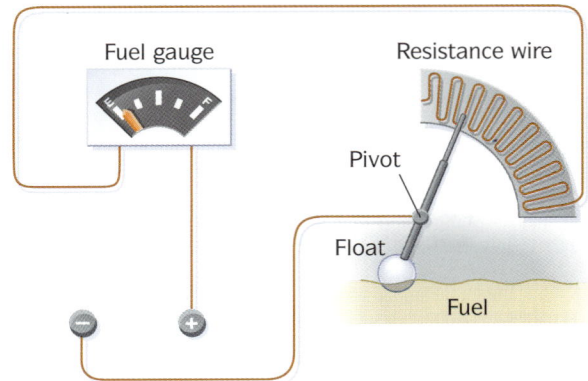

Fuel gauge

Resistance wire

Pivot

Float

Fuel

🔺 Inside a fuel tank, a float rides on the surface of the fuel. As it moves up and down, it moves a contact on a variable resistor. The reading on the meter in the car depends on how much current flows through the resistor.

▶ *Which has more resistance – a long wire or a short length of the same wire?*

Diodes for one-way flow

Batteries provide a one-way current. Many other power sources provide a current that not only gets bigger and smaller, but can change direction completely. A diode allows the current to flow one way only.

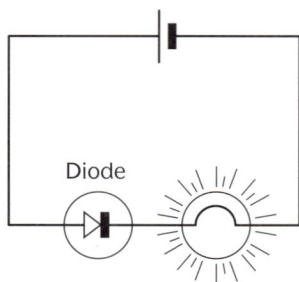

Diode

Current flows in this circuit...

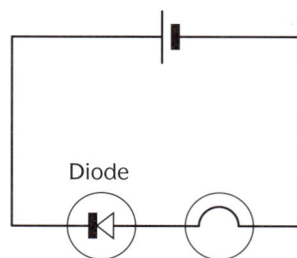

Diode

...but not in this circuit

🔺 Current can only flow in one direction when a diode is in place.

LDRs respond to light

In some homes you don't have to get out of your seat to close the curtains. An LDR reacts to the level of light outside. In bright light the LDR has low resistance and the current flows quite easily. In dull light the resistance goes up and the current goes down. A circuit which includes an LDR and a motor can automatically close or open the curtains.

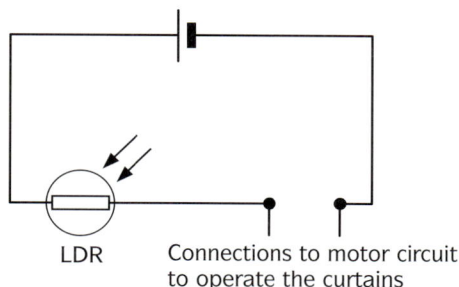

LDR   Connections to motor circuit
         to operate the curtains

🔺 More current flows in this circuit when the light shining on the LDR is brighter.

▶ *Describe what happens to the current in an LDR as the light gets brighter.*

Thermistors respond to temperature

In large commercial greenhouses, it is expensive to leave heaters on when they are not needed. It is even more expensive if cold weather ruins your crop. The resistance of a thermistor changes rapidly as the temperature changes. A thermistor circuit can sense the temperature change and operate the heaters.

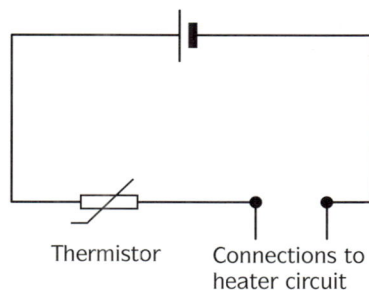

Thermistor   Connections to
                heater circuit

🔺 More current flows in this circuit when the thermistor is warmer.

Investigating variable resistance

You can use a circuit like this to find out how much current flows with different lengths of resistance wire in the circuit. The results can be plotted as a graph.

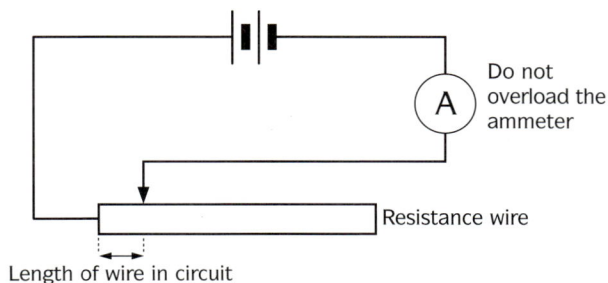

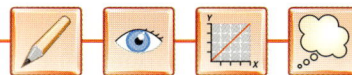

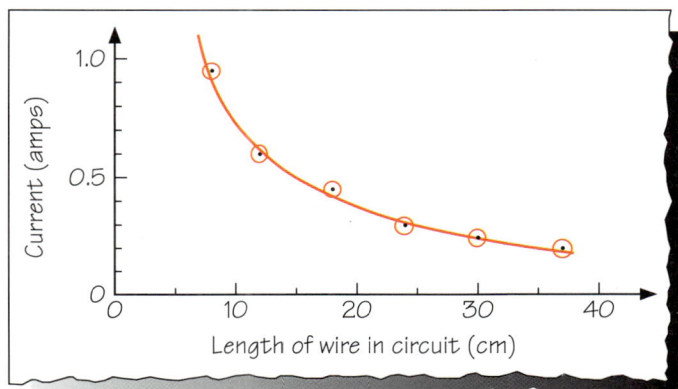

Do not overload the ammeter

Resistance wire

Length of wire in circuit

🔺 Less current flows when the length is increased.

Investigating current in a thermistor

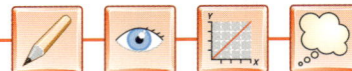

You can use a circuit like this to measure the current in the circuit when the thermistor is at different temperatures. You should carry out a risk assessment before starting this experiment.

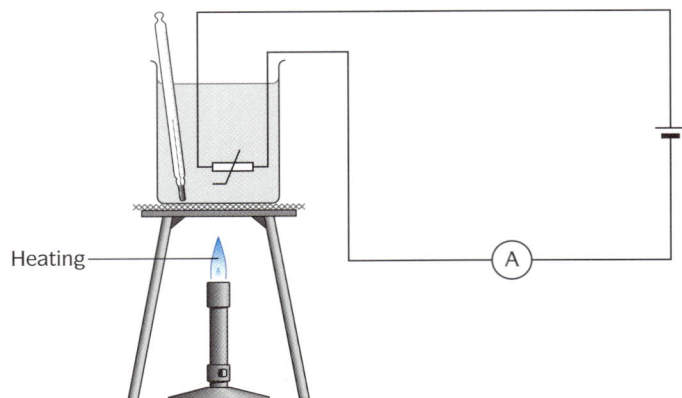

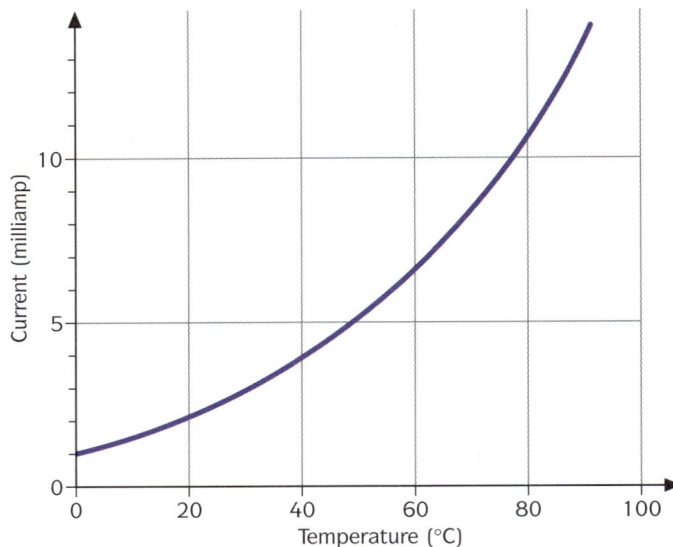

Heating

▲ More current flows when the temperature of the thermistor is increased.

The temperature of the thermistor can be controlled and measured by putting it into a beaker of liquid. A problem occurs with water if current can flow straight across between the thermistor's metal connections. Then you are not measuring the current that is flowing through the thermistor but the current that is flowing through the water. The water 'short circuits' the thermistor. One answer is to use a thermistor which has insulated connections.

The results of the experiment can be recorded in a table and shown on a graph.

Current in series and parallel circuits

In a series circuit there is only one path that the current can take.

▶ *Which is bigger, the current leaving a battery or the current returning to it, or are they the same?*

Current has a 'choice' of routes in a parallel circuit. At a junction in the circuit the current splits.

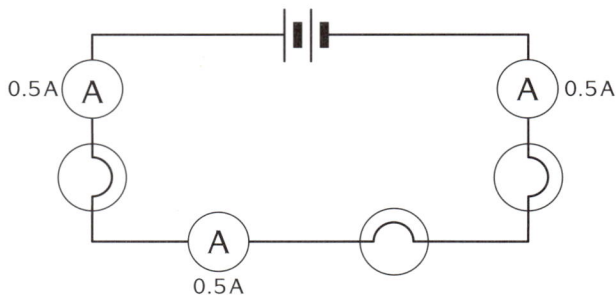

▲ The current is the same size all the way round a series circuit.

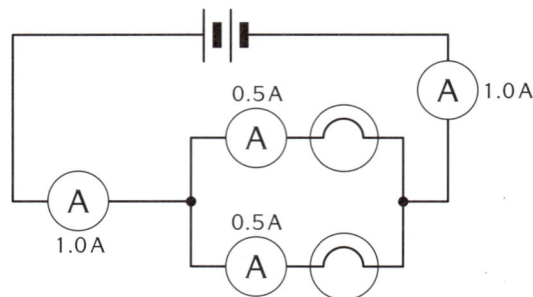

▲ The total current arriving at a junction in a parallel circuit is always the same as the total current which leaves the junction.

Batteries and potential difference

The two ends or terminals of a battery are not the same. One is positive and one is negative. When they are in circuits we say that they have a **potential difference,** or pd. People use the word *voltage* for potential difference, because we measure it in volt, V. The bigger the voltage of a working battery, the better it is at making current flow.

Using voltmeters

A voltmeter measures a difference between two points in a circuit. So it is connected to the two points. That means that it is in parallel with some part of the circuit.

A voltmeter can look a lot like an ammeter. So it is easy to confuse voltage and current readings. Look out for the A and V on the scales of meters.

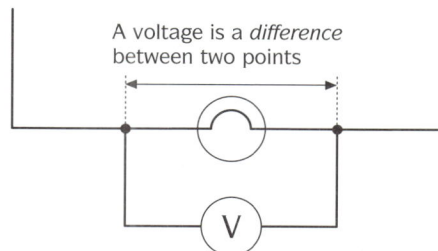

> One millivolt (1 mV) is one thousandth of a volt.

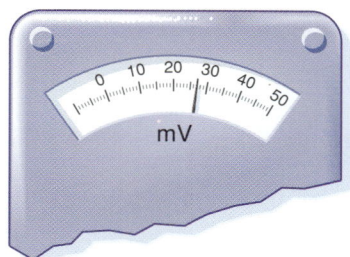

A voltage is a *difference* between two points

Voltage = 27 mV
(27 mV = 0.027 V)

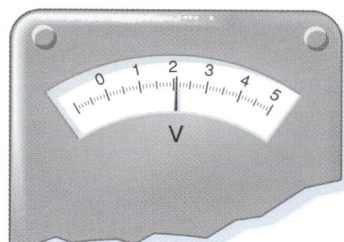

Voltage = 2.1 V
(2.1 V = 2100 mV)

🔺 Different voltmeters have different scales.

▶ *How can you tell the difference between a voltmeter and an ammeter?*

Big and small voltages

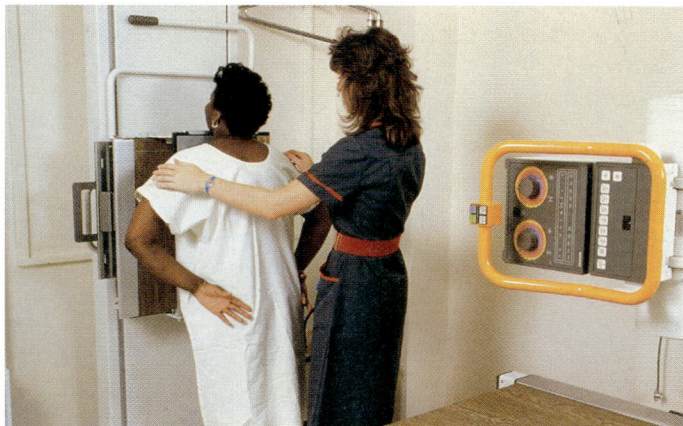

🔺 There is a voltage of a few hundred thousand volt in an X-ray tube. The voltage gives electrons very high speeds so that they generate X-rays when they crash into a metal target.

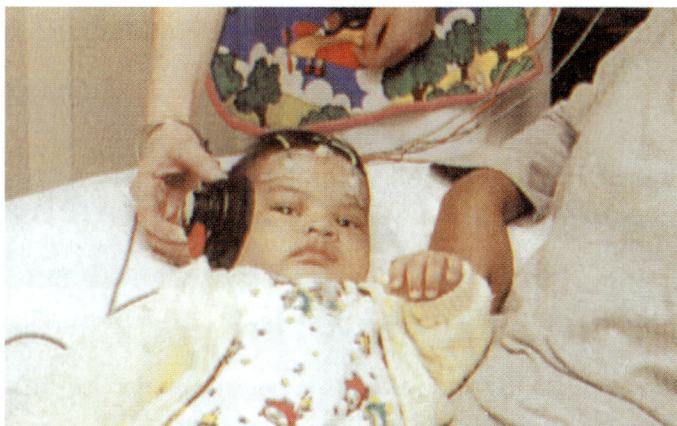

🔺 This baby is having a hearing test. Electrodes on the baby's skin pick up tiny voltages – just a few millivolt – caused by nerve impulses between his ear and his brain.

Voltage in series and parallel circuits

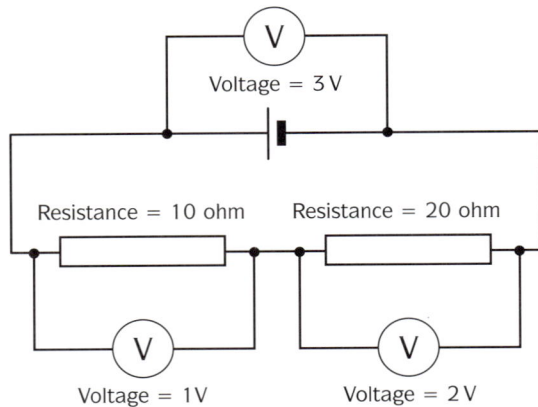

Voltage = 3 V

Resistance = 10 ohm   Resistance = 20 ohm

Voltage = 1 V   Voltage = 2 V

🔺 The voltages across resistors in series add up to the same as the voltage between the battery terminals. The resistor with the bigger resistance takes the bigger share of the voltage.

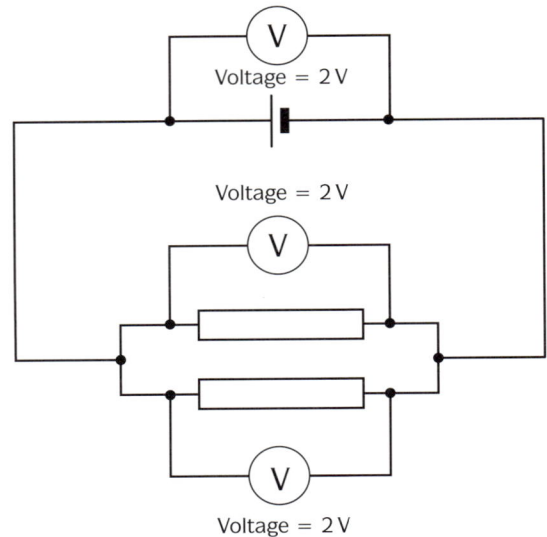

Voltage = 2 V

Voltage = 2 V

Voltage = 2 V

Voltage = 2 V

🔺 In a circuit with a battery and resistors in parallel, the voltage across each of the resistors is the same.

Measuring resistance

We can measure current with ammeters and voltage with voltmeters. Voltage pushes, current flows. The more resistance there is, the more voltage is needed to make a certain size of current flow.

▶ *If voltage stays the same, what happens to current when resistance gets bigger?*

We can measure resistance by comparing voltage and current. A good way of comparing two numbers is to see how many times one goes into the other. We divide voltage by current.

$$\text{resistance} = \frac{\text{voltage}}{\text{current}}$$

If a lot of voltage is needed to drive a small current, the division gives a big answer. The resistance is big. But if small voltage gives a lot of current then dividing produces a small answer – resistance is low.

Dividing voltage by current gives an answer in volt per amp. Because resistance is an important and common quantity, a volt per amp has its own name. It is called an **ohm**, or Ω for short.

$1 \text{ V/A} = 1 \text{ Ω}$

▶ *Why can't we use 'O' as short for ohms?*

🔺 Resistance: 1000 ohm.

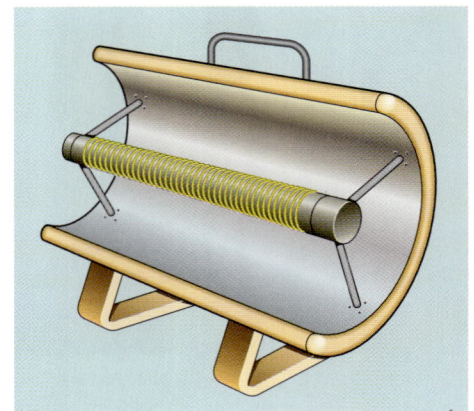

Big and small resistance

Current flows more easily through the coils of an electric heater than through the filament of a lamp. The lamp has more resistance.

▶ *If a light bulb and a heater are connected to the same power supply, which one has the bigger current?*

🔺 Resistance: 60 ohm.

A resistance example

Imagine that you work for a company which makes shower heaters. You need to know how much resistance the heating element should have. A shower heater runs on 230 volt, and a current of 10 amp. So to work out its resistance:

$$\text{resistance} = \frac{\text{voltage}}{\text{current}} = \frac{230\,\text{V}}{10\,\text{A}} = 23\text{ ohm}$$

▶ *What would the resistance need to be if you decided that the current should be only 5 amp?*

Electrical connections

Resistance wire   Ceramic powder

🔺 Part of a shower heating element.

Investigating voltage and current

Voltage provides the 'push' that drives current. So you would expect more voltage to produce more current. That usually happens, but different components do behave in different ways. You may be given a worksheet to help you to study this. Graphs make the different types of behaviour easier to see.

The graphs have the independent variable, voltage, on the x-axis (along the bottom) and the dependent variable, current, on the y-axis (up the side).

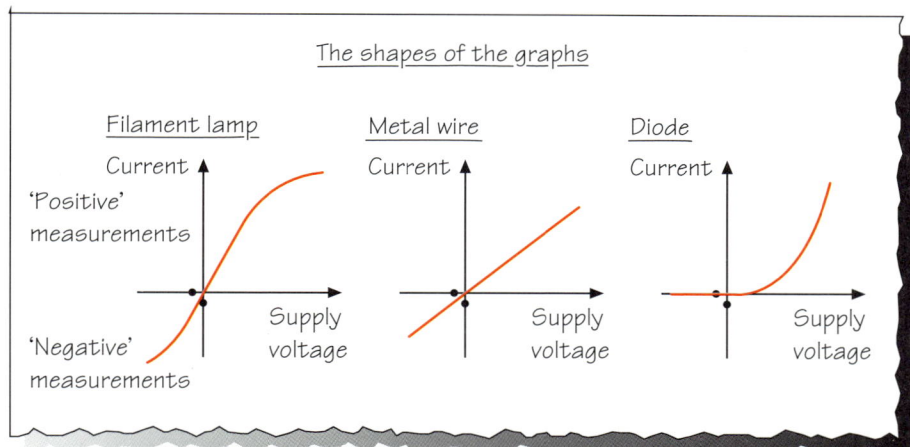

The shapes of the graphs

Filament lamp   Metal wire   Diode

Current   Current   Current

'Positive' measurements

Supply voltage   Supply voltage   Supply voltage

'Negative' measurements

🔺 Different components have different effects on current. Turning the component around in the circuit 'reverses' the voltage. If any current flows, it is now flowing 'in reverse' through the component. Measurements of voltage and current taken with the component turned around are negative measurements.

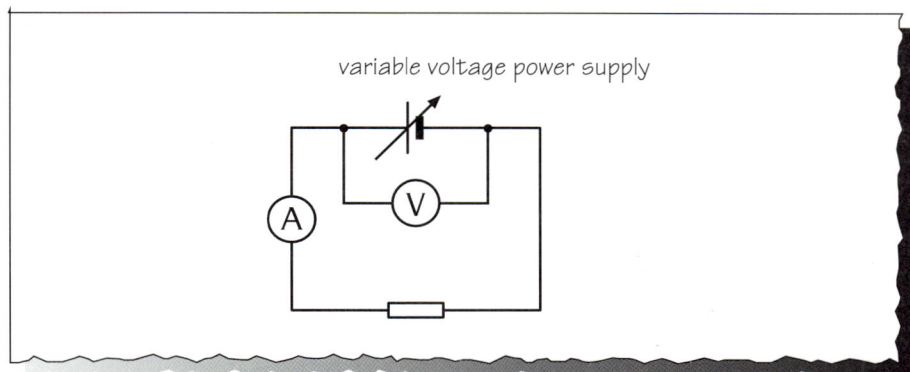

variable voltage power supply

🔺 Circuit for investigating the effect of voltage on the current in a wire.

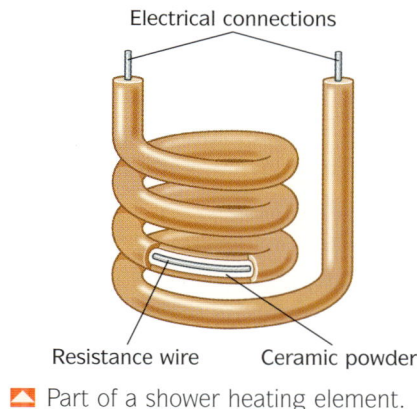

▶ *What happens to the resistance of the wire as the voltage increases? What happens to the resistance of the diode as the voltage increases? How does a diode behave when the voltage is 'negative'?*

PHYSICS

Summary

- Current is measured in amp, A, using ammeters.
- Current is the same at all points in a series circuit.
- Current splits or joins together at junctions in circuits.
- The current arriving at a junction is always the same as the current leaving it.
- Batteries transfer energy to components in a circuit. Most components then transfer energy to their surroundings.
- Most components resist the flow of current through them. They are resistors.
- Transfer of energy by resistors results in heating of their surroundings.
- Current has magnetic as well as heating effects.
- Current is a measure of flow of charge. In metals, the charge is carried by tiny particles called electrons.
- Voltage is a measure of potential difference, and it drives current through resistors. It is measured in volt.
- Resistance is measured in ohm.
- Resistance of a component is the voltage between its ends divided by the current that flows through it:

$$\text{resistance} = \frac{\text{voltage}}{\text{current}}$$

- The resistance of a metal wire, provided that it does not get too hot, does not change when voltage and current changes. A graph of current against voltage is a straight line through the origin. Current is proportional to voltage. This is Ohm's law.
- Resistance of a wire that gets hot, such as a filament of a lamp, and of other components such as diodes, LDRs and thermistors is not constant. These components do not obey Ohm's law.

Revision Questions

1 Athletes, hot water and electrons all flow around circuits.
 a Where does the energy come from for each type of flow?
 b How could you increase the rate of flow in each case?

2 Electrical resistors transfer energy. What do they do to their surroundings? Where does the energy come from?

3 Copy and complete the table:

Quantity	Measuring instrument	Unit
current		amp
	voltmeter	

🔺 Electrical quantities and their measurement.

4 What is the reading on each of these ammeters?

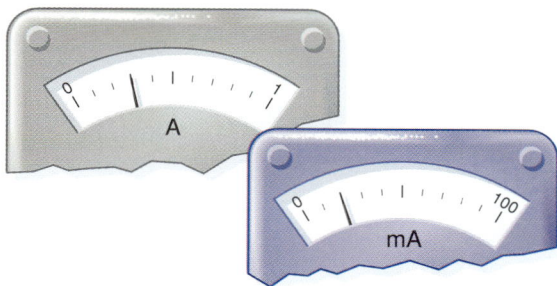

5 What will happen when the switch in this circuit is closed?

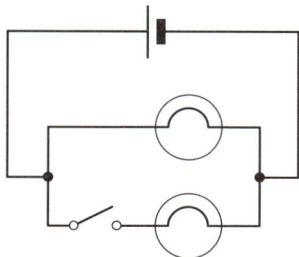

6 How much current flows at points X, Y and Z?

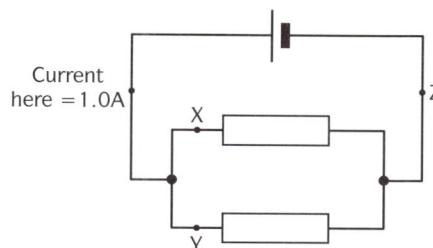

Current here = 1.0A

7 A steeplechase is a race around a track, but with jumps to provide obstacles to the athletes.
 a What effect do the jumps have on the flow of athletes around the circuit?
 b How are the jumps like electrical resistors? Think about the effect resistors have on flow (current) and on energy transfer.

8 Look at the diagram of a refrigerator on page 83 of Chapter Six.
 a Which part of the circuit does a similar job to a battery?
 b Which part of the circuit helps to make sure that the liquid flows one way only? What electrical component does a similar job?

9 One light bulb has a resistance of 600 ohm and another has a resistance of 1200 ohm. Imagine that you connect the 600 ohm resistor in a circuit, and the current is 0.2 amp. What would you expect to happen to the current if you replaced the light bulb with the one with 1200 ohm of resistance?

10 What should you do if an ammeter needle:
 a goes beyond the end of the scale
 b goes the wrong way?

11 Copy and complete the table relating switch states to lamp states in this circuit.

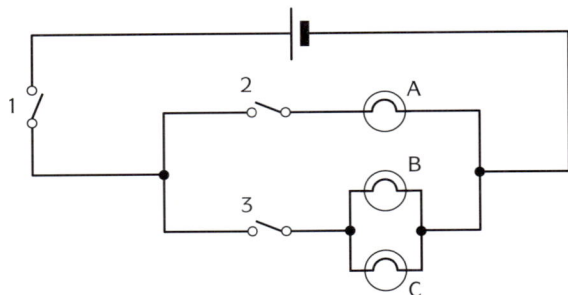

Switches closed	Lamps on
1 only	none
2 only	
3 only	
1 + 2	
1 + 3	
2 + 3	
1 + 2 + 3	

12 What will happen in this circuit when
a the surroundings become brighter
b the surroundings become warmer?

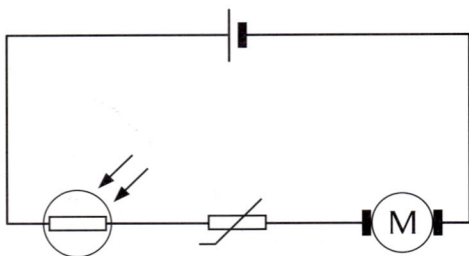

13 A fish tank heater runs at 12 volt and has a current of 2 amp. What is its resistance?

14 When water flows down a river, is it part of a circuit? Where does the energy come from?

15 Why is it necessary to measure current in terms of its magnetic effect? Why is a spring an essential part of an ammeter? What would happen if the spring in an ammeter were replaced by a stronger one?

16 What is the difference between electron flow and conventional current? Why do many textbooks show current in the 'conventional' direction? Explain which, to you, makes more sense.

17 What will happen to voltage V when it goes dark?

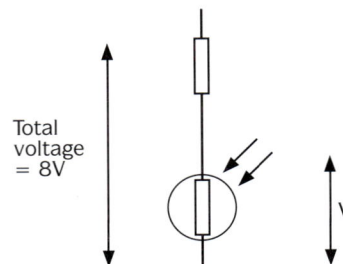

Total voltage = 8V

V

18 What voltage will you need to make a current of 2.3 amp flow through a 100 ohm resistor?

Mains electricity

■ Fairground energy

The colour of a fairground is driven by electricity, and so is the light and entertaiment that we can enjoy at home.

There are hundreds of things that work by electricity – lights, music players, heaters, food machines, telephones, telescreens and more. These are all electrical appliances. They all transfer energy.

Review

Before going any further, read this page and attempt the tasks. Write the answers in your notes.

Electricity provides a clean and convenient source of energy for homes and other places. Power stations generate most of this electricity by burning coal, gas or oil. This produces high-pressure steam which turns a turbine and a generator.

But not everybody is connected to power stations and the mains electricity supply. In a remote house, people might use wind or sun as their energy resources. Travelling fairs cannot rely on having connections to a mains supply wherever they go, and their fuel bills would be enormous. They use their own generators.

▲ In a fairground, large diesel engines generate electricity. They transfer energy from burning the fuel to the electric circuits. The smell of the 'diesel fumes' is part of the fairground experience, though the fumes are a form of pollution.

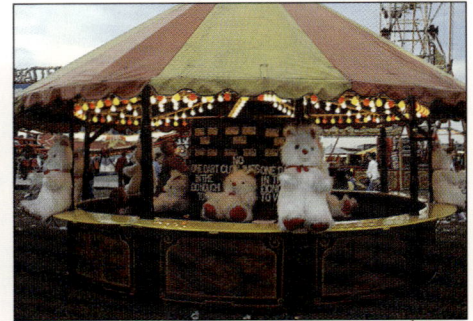
▲ A light bulb in a games booth and the huge motor that drives the Twister ride need different amounts of power to make them work. In the fairground the voltage of the supply is the same for all the appliances. Energy must be delivered to the Twister motor more quickly by having a much thicker cable and more current.

▲ A microphone and a loudspeaker transfer energy. Energy transfer devices like these are sometimes called transducers. A light bulb also transfers energy into its surroundings. The filament in the light bulb is a thin piece of wire with a high resistance to electric current. It heats up when the current flows through it.

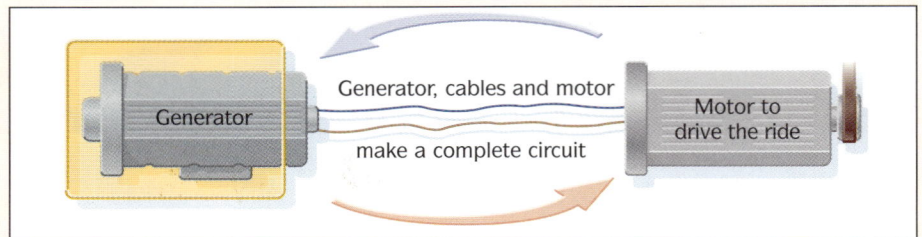

Generator

Generator, cables and motor

make a complete circuit

Motor to drive the ride

▲ The electric current flows along cables to the appliances and back to the generator. This is a power supply circuit for a fairground ride.

CHECK TWELVE

1 Solve the anagrams:

u elf – a material which makes energy available when it burns with oxygen

greeny – the ability to do work

under carts – energy transfer device

u critic – an electrical network that has to be complete

truncer – electrical flow or rate of flow of charge

nicer seats – opposition to current

2 How many different uses of electricity in the fairground can you list?

3 Would it be possible to generate the fairground electricity supply using
  a solar energy resources (solar cells)
  b wind energy resources (wind turbines)?

4 Are the fairground appliances and transducers connected in series or parallel?

Electricity comes home

Thick cables run under the ground to houses and schools. Every house and every school has a meter, which is owned by the electricity company. The meter is like a laboratory joulemeter. It measures the quantity of electrical energy that passes into the house.

The fuse box is next to the electricity supply meter. It splits the supply into several circuits and connects it to different parts of the house. The fuses protect the wiring from overload and help prevent electrocution. Sometimes re-settable contact breakers are used instead of fuses. There are different circuits for the house lights, the three-pin plugs and the electric central heating. There will be a heavy-duty circuit with thick cables specially for the kitchen cooker on its own.

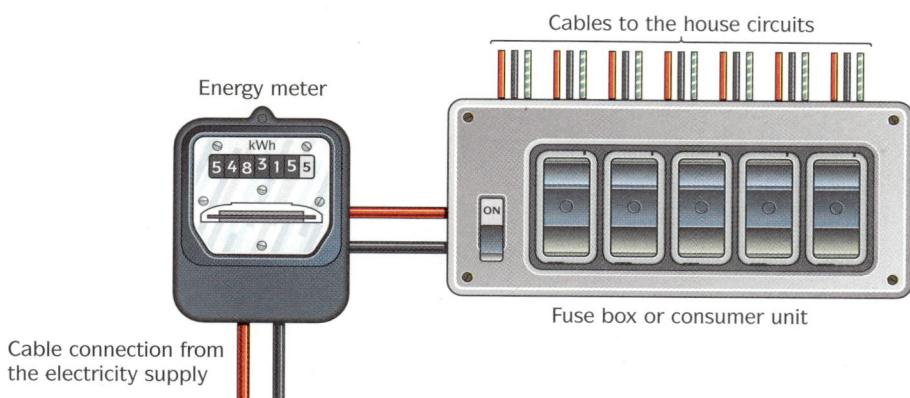

▲ The meter belongs to the electricity company

▶ *Does the electricity meter in your home measure current, voltage or energy?*

Live to neutral

A current will flow through any conductor that is connected between the live wire and the neutral wire. If the conductor has a low resistance then the current will be big. If the conductor has a high resistance or if it is in a spinning motor then only a small current will flow.

▶ *What size of current will flow between the live and the neutral wires if they are connected together with a thick piece of metal that has very little resistance?*

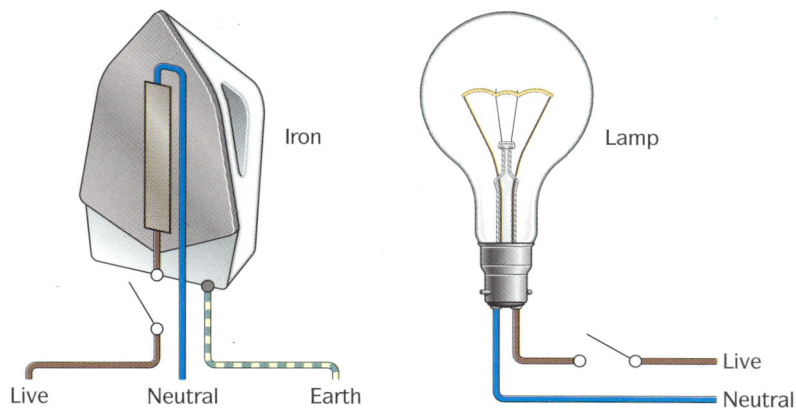

▲ Hilary Lewis works on the wiring of new houses and on rewiring old ones. 'Lights and sockets in houses have separate circuits. The lights need less current, so the wires can be thinner' she says.

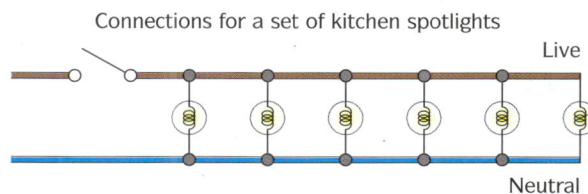

▲ The high resistance wires in these appliances are connected between the live and neutral wires.

PHYSICS

Live to earth

The ground or earth is electrically neutral. Any conductor which connects a live wire to the earth will have a current flowing through it. A human body can act as the conductor. If part of your body is connected to the earth, and you touch a live wire, the current could kill you.

Direct and alternating currents

A battery circuit has two wires to carry the current. One is connected to the battery's positive terminal. The other is connected to the negative terminal. The current flows around the circuit, always in the same direction. It is a **direct current**, or DC circuit.

Mains electricity also has two wires which are needed to carry the supply to an appliance. These two wires are called live and neutral. The live wire carries the energy input and the neutral wire effectively completes the circuit back to the generator. Every hundredth of a second the live wire changes from positive to negative. That makes the current change direction. We say that the current **alternates** – one way and then the other. It is AC.

▶ *What is the difference between AC and DC?*

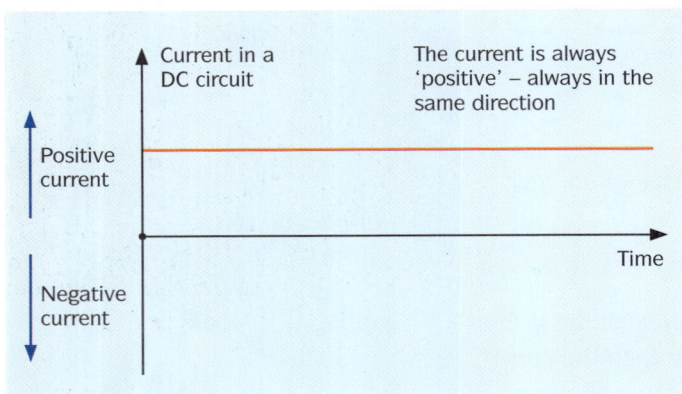

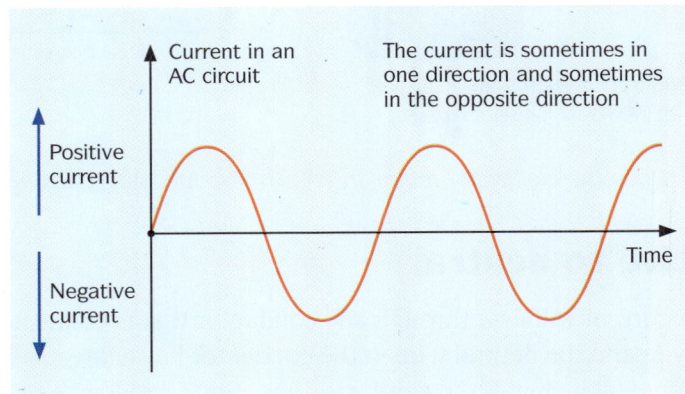

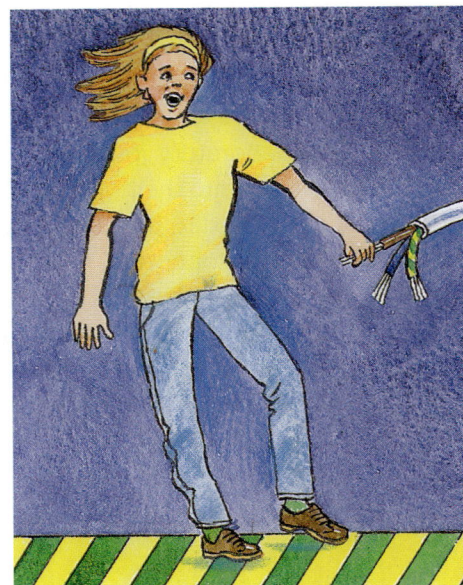

▲ A human body can provide a pathway for electric current between live and earth.

Current in a DC circuit — The current is always 'positive' – always in the same direction

Positive current

Negative current

Time

Current in an AC circuit — The current is sometimes in one direction and sometimes in the opposite direction

Positive current

Negative current

Time

Cables and insulators

Electric cables on pylons are made from metal with no outer covering. But they are high above us and insulated from the metal pylons by big ceramic hangers. They are also insulated from us by the air around them. All other mains electric cables must be kept safe inside an insulating covering. The covering used is plastic or rubber.

Switches and fuses

Switches are always put in the live wire. If they were in the neutral wire the wires inside an appliance would still be live even when the switch was off.

Fuses are also always put in the live wire. Fuses are placed in electric circuits to act as weak points. When the current is too high, the fuse heats up and melts. This breaks the connection from the appliance to the live wire before any serious damage is done.

▲ 'If I get this wrong someone could get killed. If I connected the neutral wire to the switch, an appliance could still be connected to the live supply but people will think that it is switched off.'

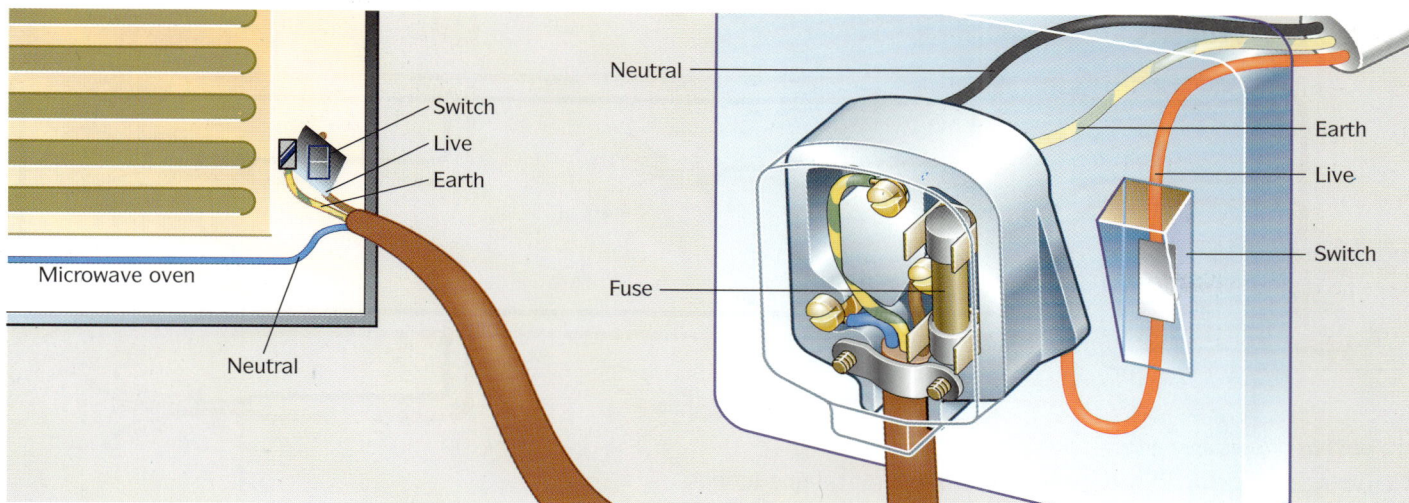

Switch
Live
Earth
Microwave oven
Neutral

Neutral
Earth
Live
Switch
Fuse

The switches and fuse are connected in the live wire. This diagram shows the inside of a plug, but a plug must never be connected to the mains without its cover.

How the earth wire protects

The wire in the yellow-green stripey plastic does not normally carry any current. It is only there as a safety device. It protects people from electric shock.

The live wire inside a metal case of an electrical device, such as a microwave oven, can come away from its proper connection. When this happens it could make contact with the metal case. When the user touches the metal case, they will be electrocuted.

The earth wire is bolted onto the metal case, so if the live wire comes in contact with the casing then the current will flow straight to the earth wire. There is then little or no resistance between live and earth, so the current is big. It is much bigger than the normal current that flows through the appliance, and it blows the fuse. That cuts off the appliance from the live supply.

▶ *Why will the fuse blow quickly when a live wire touches the casing of a washing machine?*

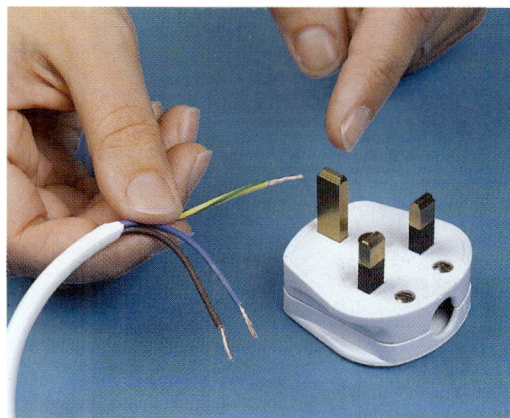

The large pin on a three-pin plug connects the earth wire inside an appliance to a house's earth circuit. Every house has its own separate earth circuit.

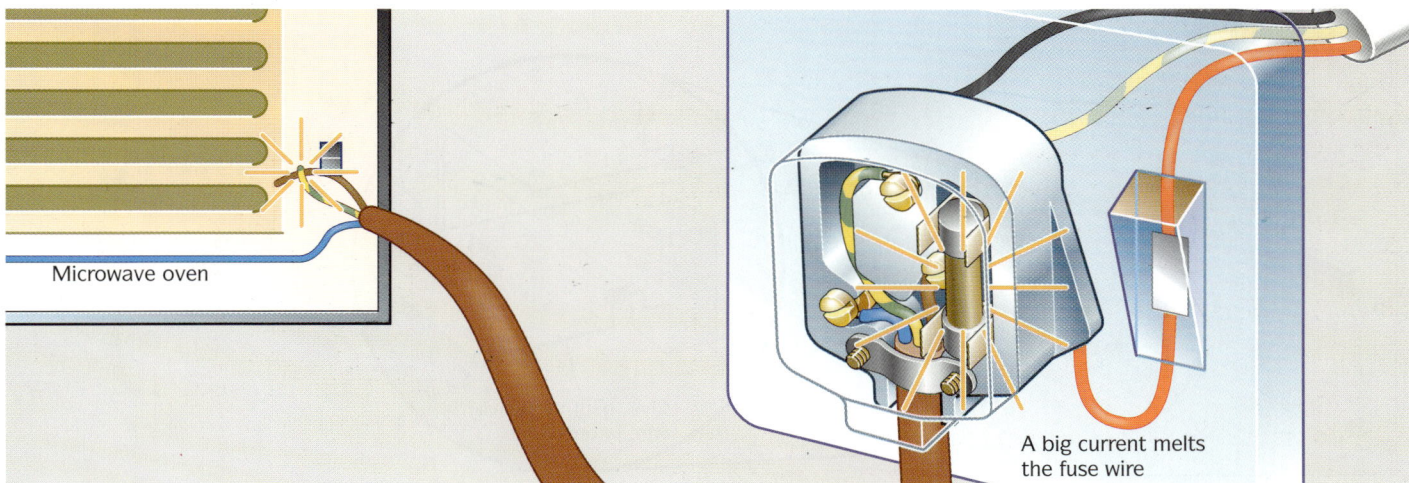

Microwave oven

A big current melts the fuse wire

If there is a metal pathway between the live wire and earth then resistance is small and a big current flows. This diagram shows the inside of a plug, but a plug must never be connected to the mains without its cover.

Lighting circuit

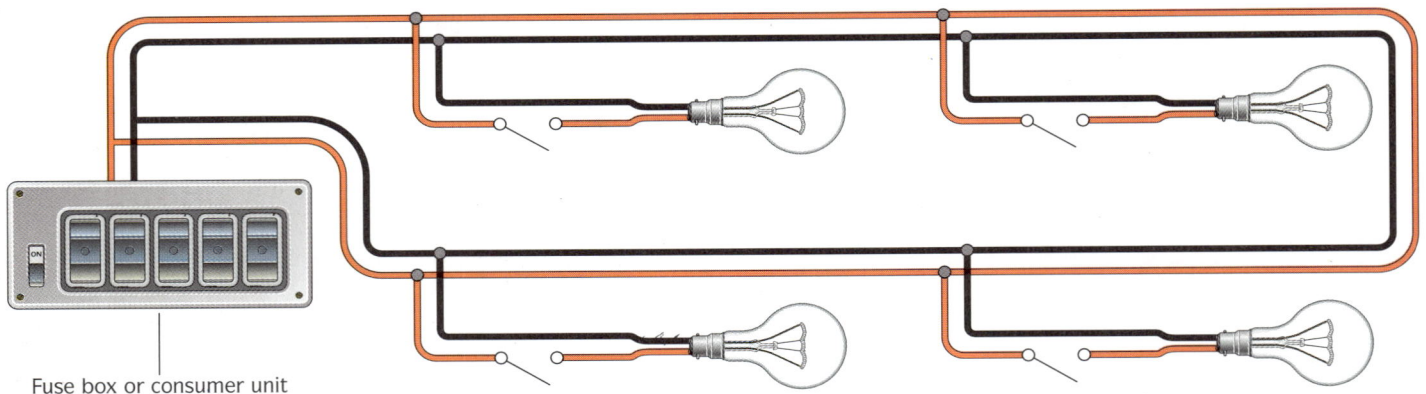

Fuse box or consumer unit

🔺 The lighting circuit links the fuse box to a loop of lighting fittings.

Ring main

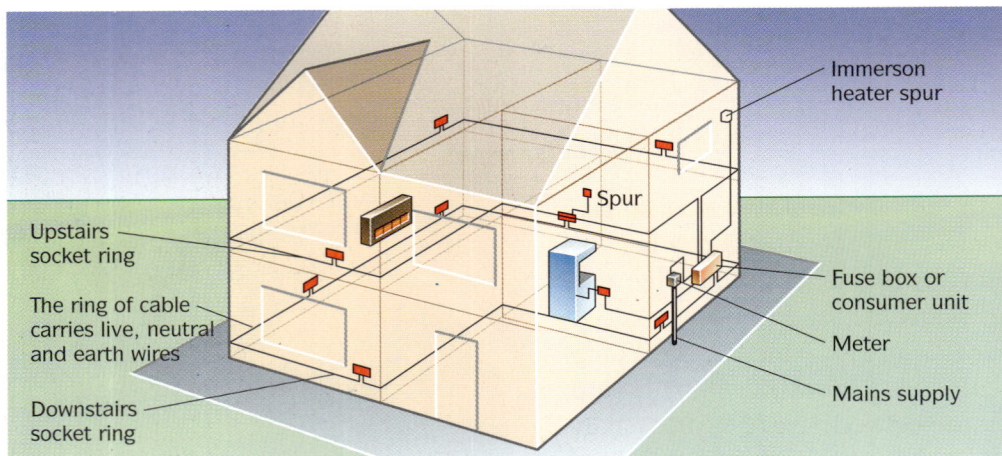

Immerson heater spur

Spur

Upstairs socket ring

The ring of cable carries live, neutral and earth wires

Downstairs socket ring

Fuse box or consumer unit

Meter

Mains supply

🔺 A ring main is basically a loop of cable and sockets. It starts from the fuse box and returns to it. At the sockets the live, neutral and earth wires are connected to screw terminals. In normal use, the only current that flows is between live and neutral through the appliances that are plugged in.

▶ A ring main consists of three continuous loops of metal. What are the three loops called?

Cooker circuit

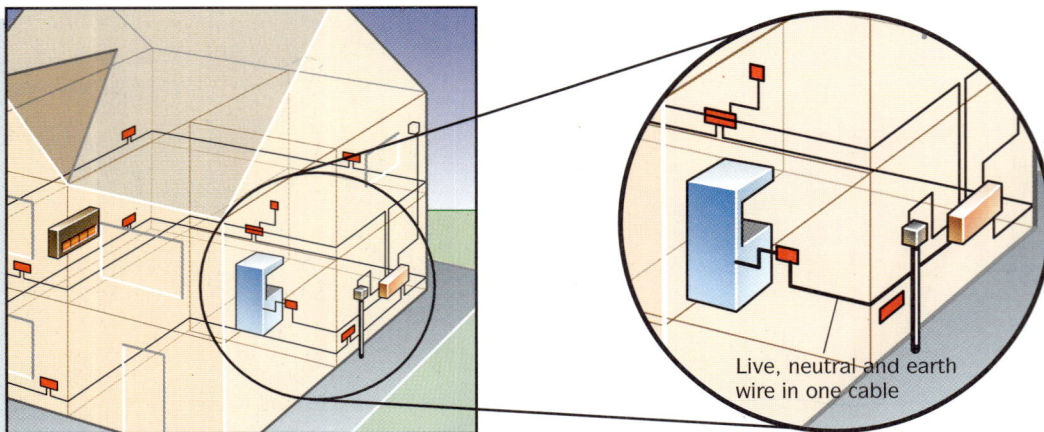

Live, neutral and earth wire in one cable

🔺 An electric cooker needs a big current to supply it with energy. It has its own circuit running from the fuse box.

Wiring a plug

Step 1 Remove the cover.

Step 2 Loosen the cable clamp by undoing the small screws. Take the fuse out of the plug. This will make wiring the plug easier.

Step 3 Using wire strippers, remove about 5 cm of the outer covering of the cable. Taking great care not to damage the insulation of the wires inside.

Step 4 Cut off about 2 cm of the insulation from each of the wires. Twist the strands together.

Step 5 Connect each wire to its correct terminal. Check that the correct wires are in the right place:
- brown = live (L)
- blue = neutral (N)
- yellow/green = earth (E or ⏚).

Make sure that the terminal screws are tightened onto the bare wires. Do not have stray strands inside the plug.

Step 6 Do up the clamp so that it grips the cable firmly.

Step 7 Check:
- Have you tightened the cable grip?
- Have you connected the wires correctly according to the colour code?
- Have you tightened the terminal screws?
- Have you made sure that no bare wires are touching?

Step 8 Check that the fuse is the correct rating. Push the fuse into the holder. Screw on the cover of the plug.
Test the appliance by plugging it in and switching on.
For some appliances there is no earth wire and the larger pin is left unconnected, but whenever there is an earth wire it *must* be connected.

▸ *How many appliances with plugs are there in your home? Make a list of them.*

▸ *The earth pin is longer than the others. Give one reason for this.*

▸ *Look at the pictures of other plugs from elsewhere in Europe.*

▸ *Make a list of*
  a *the common features*
  b *advantages and disadvantages of the different types of plug.*

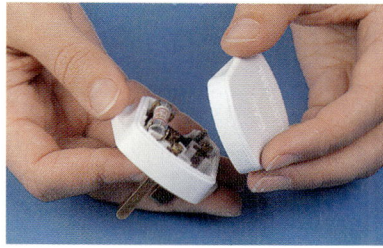
🔺 Step 1.

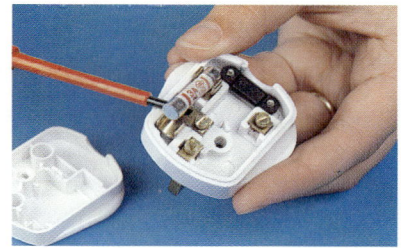
🔺 Step 2.

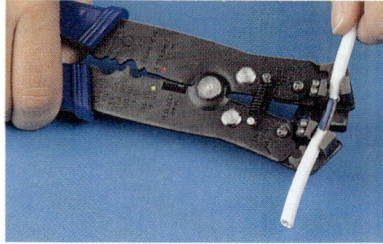
🔺 Step 3.

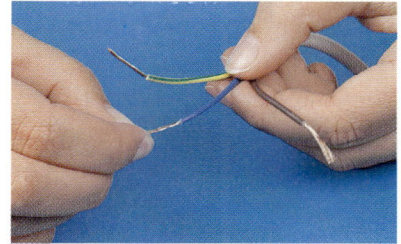
🔺 Step 4.

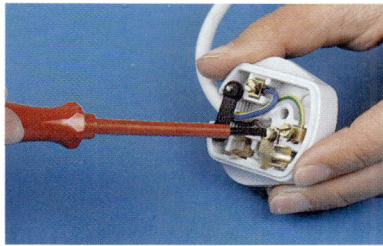
🔺 Step 5.

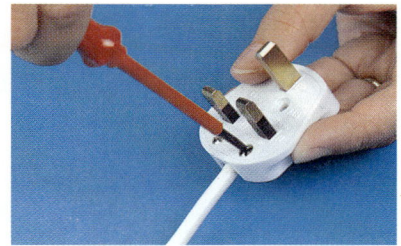
🔺 Step 6.

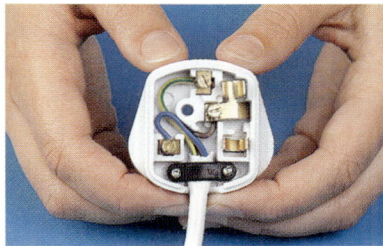
🔺 Step 7.

🔺 Step 8.

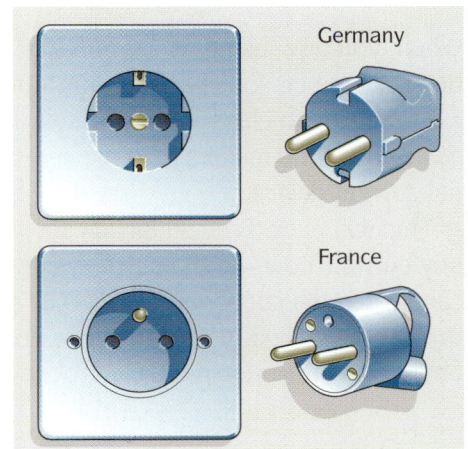
🔺 Plugs and sockets from Germany and France.

Germany

France

More about fuses

High-power appliances such as kettles need 13 amp fuses. A 3 amp fuse is suitable for lower power appliances such as lights and computers.

If you fit a 13 amp fuse to the plug of a low-power appliance you give little or no protection to the connecting cable or the appliance. If the appliance becomes faulty and the current becomes bigger than it should be, the fuse will not melt. The appliance, or its connecting cable, will overheat and may catch fire. A 3 amp fuse will blow when the current goes over 3 amp.

Fuses are found in fuse boxes or consumer units (next to the electric meter), in three-pin plugs, and inside sensitive equipment (such as hi-fi amplifiers). You find lots of fuses in car electrical circuits. Car electrics carry quite high currents – 5 amp through a headlamp bulb, for example. Nearly all car fires are started by electrical problems – fuses help to prevent this.

▶ *Why would a 3 amp fuse be no good for a car headlamp circuit?*

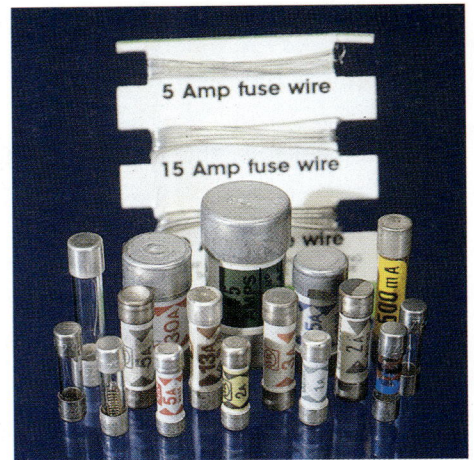

⬛ All 13 amp fuses are brown, and 3 amp fuses are red. Colour coding makes it quick and easy to spot the right fuse.

Investigating fuses

You can investigate the effect of changing the length of the fuse wire on the current at which it blows. You may be given a worksheet to help with your investigations.

Miniature circuit breakers

Replacing a fuse or a piece of fuse wire is not easy, particularly if all the lights have gone out. Some houses have their circuits protected by small automatic switches called miniature circuit breakers.

Miniature circuit breakers, just like fuses, have to cut the supply at different values of current. A 5 amp circuit breaker is used to protect the lighting circuit and a 30 amp circuit breaker protects the socket or ring main circuit.

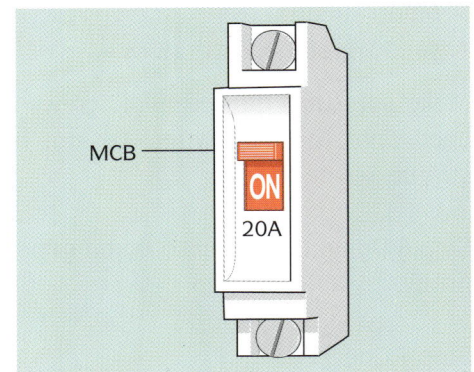

⬛ A miniature circuit breaker (MCB) automatically switches to 'off' if the current in the circuit is too high.

Residual current devices

When you are using a lawnmower or hedge trimmer, for example, you could cut the flex and electrocute yourself. The advice from the makers is to use a residual current device.

This will cut off the supply as soon as any current flows in the earth circuit. It can switch the supply off within 0.03 s of the cable being damaged. That is quick enough to prevent serious electrocution.

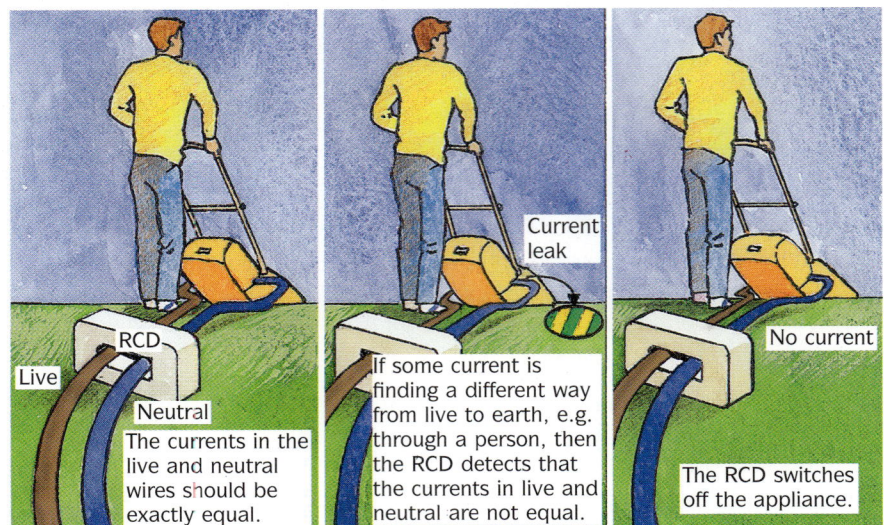

Live / **Neutral**
The currents in the live and neutral wires should be exactly equal.

Current leak
If some current is finding a different way from live to earth, e.g. through a person, then the RCD detects that the currents in live and neutral are not equal.

No current
The RCD switches off the appliance.

⬛ A residual current device (RCD).

Some questions answered

Why don't small batteries harm you?

▲ The resistance of your skin is so big that a voltage of 6 volt can only drive a very small current through your body or across the surface of your skin. The very small current that flows is too small to feel.

Which way does the current flow?

▲ Your body has very little resistance inside. Your flesh is wet and salty, and current can easily flow through it. Adult skin has high resistance, because you are covered in layers of dry, dead cells. A child's skin may be softer and have much less resistance. Electrical current finds the route with the least resistance.

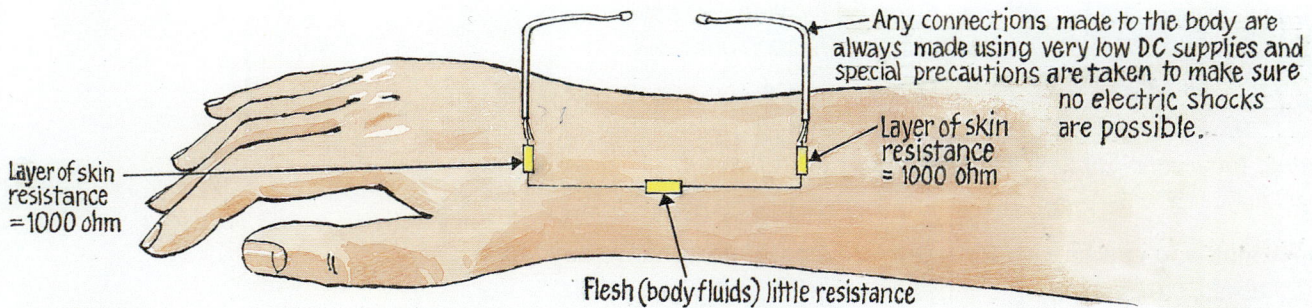

Layer of skin resistance = 1000 ohm

Any connections made to the body are always made using very low DC supplies and special precautions are taken to make sure no electric shocks are possible.

Layer of skin resistance = 1000 ohm

Flesh (body fluids) little resistance

▲ When two electrical contacts touch a body a tiny current flows through one thickness of skin (resistance = 1000 ohm), through your flesh (little resistance) and back through a second thickness of skin (resistance = 1000 ohm). So the resistance between any two parts of your body is about 2000 ohm.

Does a lie detector really work?

▲ Skin is not a good conductor of electricity, but sweat is basically salty water. Sweat conducts.
So if two terminals are connected to your body with a voltage applied to them, then the current will be bigger when your skin is sweaty. The current has an easier route to follow through the layer of sweat. The idea behind lie detectors is that you sweat a little every time you tell a lie. But results of a lie detector test cannot be accepted as evidence in a British court.

Where is it most dangerous to get an electric shock?

▲ A shock in the chest area will make your heart fibrillate. You are in trouble if it does not restart quickly.

Damp surfaces, where there are salts dissolved in the water provide pathways for electric current. Dampness can also provide pathways for currents in switches and plugs. This makes it more likely that you will get an electric shock. That is why bathroom light switches are pull switches.

Electric shock data

In all electric circuits voltage drives the current. A current of a small fraction of 1 amp can cause heart fibrillation that kills. Here is a table which shows some approximate levels of danger:

Time connected to mains supply (s)	Current that flows through the body (amp)		
	Small chance of fibrillation (dangerous)	Moderate chance of fibrillation (very dangerous)	Fibrillation very likely (extremely dangerous)
5.0	0.03	0.1	0.2
1.0	0.05	0.2	0.4
0.5	0.1	0.3	0.5
0.1	0.2	0.5	1.0
0.05	0.3	1.0	2.0
0.01	1.0	3.0	4.0

▶ *How much current will be caused to flow through your body by mains 230 volt? (Assume that the resistance of your body is 2000 ohm and use*

$$current = \frac{voltage}{resistance} .)$$

▶ *Estimate the level of danger from this current if it flows for*
  a *5s*　　　**b** *0.5s.*

You may think you can survive for a few seconds. Unfortunatly, very small currents, about 0.01A, make the muscles contract and you can't let go of whatever is giving you the electric shock. So, dangerous fibrillation can't be stopped.

Paying for electricity

The standard international unit of energy is the joule, or J for short. A joule is quite a small amount of energy, so we often measure in kilojoule, kJ.

Electricity companies use a unit of their own for measuring the amount of energy that the appliances in our homes transfer. The unit is the kilowatt-hour. It is sometimes abbreviated to kWh, and sometimes it just called a 'unit' of electrical energy. It is equal to the amount of energy transferred by a 1 kilowatt appliance if it is on for one hour.

To work out the cost of using an electrical appliance you need to know these numbers:

- the power of the appliance in kilowatt (divide watt by 1000 to find kilowatt)
- the number of hours for which it was used
- the cost per kWh or cost per 'unit' of electricity.

$$\frac{total\ cost}{(in\ pence)} = \frac{power}{(in\ kW)} \times \frac{time}{(in\ hours)} \times \frac{cost\ per\ kWh}{(in\ pence)}$$

▶ *What is the total cost of using a 1 kW heater for 1 hour, if electrical energy costs 8p per kWh?*

A kilojoule is a thousand joule
A megajoule is a million joule.

Electricity bill

METER READINGS Present	Previous	Units Used	Unit Price (pence)	VAT Code	Amount £
04792	04292	500	7.590	1	37.95
04497	02997	1500	2.760	1	41.40
STANDING CHARGE				1	14.10
TOTAL CHARGES (EXCLUDING VAT)					93.45
VAT 1　£93.45	@　8.0% DOMESTIC				7.47
			TOTAL		100.92
VAT CHARGE THIS BILL					7.47

E = Estimated reading. If you are not happy with this reading, please phone us now.
C = Your own reading.

🔺 Electricity bills show energy measured in 'units' of kilowatt-hour, kWh.

Gran's all-electric flat

You may be given a worksheet to investigate the cost of running some electrical appliances.

Electrical quantities

Tiny particles like electrons and protons have electrical charge. What that means is that they can exert and experience electrical forces. Neutrons do not exert or experience electrical force – they have no electrical charge.

The standard international unit of charge is the **coulomb**, C.

When a large number of particles which have charge flow together they make up an electrical current. Current is a measure of rate of flow of charge. A current of 1 amp is a flow of 1 coulomb past a point in a circuit every 1 second.

$$\text{current} = \frac{\text{charge}}{\text{time}}$$

or, in symbols $I = \frac{C}{t}$

Potential difference or voltage is a measure of how much energy is transferred into and out of a part of an electric circuit for each unit of charge that flows. A potential difference of 1 volt means that 1 joule of energy is transferred every time 1 coulomb of charge flows.

$$\text{potential difference} = \frac{\text{energy}}{\text{charge}}$$

or, in symbols: $V = \frac{E}{C}$

Multiplying potential difference by current turns out to be useful:

$$I \times V = \frac{C}{t} \times \frac{E}{C}$$

The right-hand side of this equation can be written more simply:

$$I \times V = \frac{E}{t}$$

Energy transferred divided by time taken is a measure of how quickly the energy is transferred. That means that it is a measure of power, P:

$$P = \frac{E}{t}$$

Power is measured in watt, W. You can read about power in Chapter 7 (Energy measurements). Note that power, P, and current × voltage, $I \times V$, are both equal to energy divided by time, E/t. So they must be equal to each other.

$$P = I \times V$$

In words,   power = current × voltage

Since $E/t = P$, then also $E = P \times t$

In words,   energy = power × time

Note that   energy = current × voltage × time or $E = I \times V \times t$

Example 1

How much energy is transferred when a 5 watt motorcycle bulb is turned on for 10 minutes?

Answer

Energy transferred = power × time

$\qquad = 5\,W \times (10 \times 60)\,s$

$\qquad = 3000\,J$

Example 2

If a current of 5 amps flows through a 12 volt heater, how much energy will it transfer in 3 minutes?

Answer

Energy transferred = current × voltage × time

$\qquad = 5\,A \times 12\,V \times (3 \times 60)\,s$

$\qquad = 10\,800\,J$

Generating current in circuits

To generate electric current some energy has to be transferred to the circuit. There are two main ways of doing this – batteries and generators. There are also some less common but interesting ways, for example photocells and piezoelectric spark makers.

▸ *Which type of electrical power supply is most useful for*
a *a mobile phone,*
b *a satellite?*

Bicycle dynamos

A current in a wire produces a magnetic field. It works the other way around as well. A changing magnetic field around a wire generates current if the wire is part of a circuit. Generators work by taking advantage of this. You can read more about the principles involved, in Chapter Fourteen (Electromagnetism).

The size of the current produced by a bicycle dynamo depends on the speed of the spinning magnet. As it spins faster the current in the circuit increases so the bicycle lights get brighter. When the bicycle stops, the dynamo does not generate any electricity and the lights go out.

▸ *How do generators work? Write one sentence.*

Generating in power stations

At power stations, fuel heats water and turns it into steam. The steam then turns turbines connected to generators. They work on the same basic principle as the bicycle dynamo. The current in the circuit is induced. Dynamos use permanent magnets to provide the magnetic field, but power station generators use electromagnets. The electromagnets have much stronger magnetic fields.

The current from a power station generator is produced by spinning motion. The result of that is that the current does not flow in one direction, but goes one way and then the other. It is alternating current.

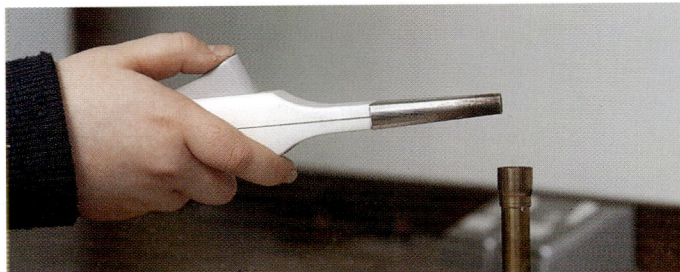

🔺 In a gas flame lighter, sparks are made by twisting a crystal of quartz. This produces high enough voltage to make a spark. A spark involves an electric current through air, but the current is small.

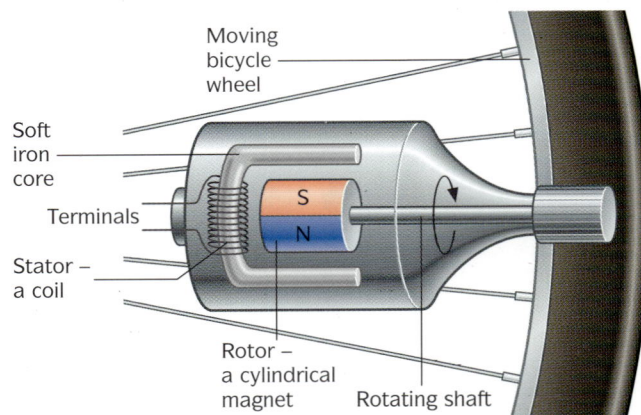

Moving bicycle wheel

Soft iron core

Terminals

Stator – a coil

S
N

Rotor – a cylindrical magnet

Rotating shaft

🔺 In a bicycle dynamo, a permanent magnet spins near a coil of wires, to make a current flow in a circuit. The energy to generate electricity in a bicycle dynamo comes from the rider.

▶ *Write down two similarities and two differences between a bicycle dynamo and a power station generator.*

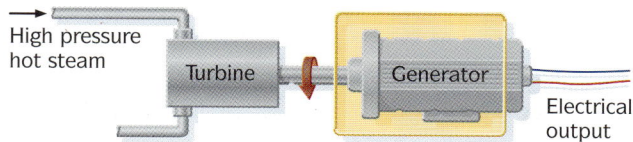

High pressure hot steam

Turbine

Generator

Electrical output

Spinning shaft connecting turbine to generator

🔺 The generator has two sets of coils, one inside the other. The inner coil spins, and it provides a magnetic field. Current is induced in the outer coil which does not move.

Principles of a simple AC generator

Field lines show the direction of magnetic force. Where the lines are closest together, the force is strongest. Magnetic field lines are useful in understanding how the size of the current produced in a generator circuit can vary.

The simplest AC generator is made from a rectangular coil put in between magnetic poles. More turns of wire in the coil means more wires cutting the magnetic field lines. So more current is generated.

A stronger magnetic field from the magnet can result in a bigger current. And turning the coil faster means that it cuts the lines of magnetic field more often. That also gives more current.

▶ *Write down three changes that you could make to a generator to make it provide bigger current in a circuit.*

▶ *Look at the graphs on page 176. Sketch a graph of current against time for an AC generator.*

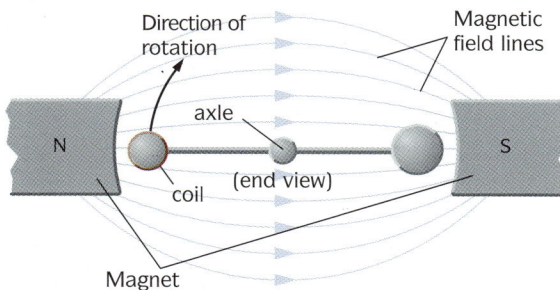

Direction of rotation

Magnetic field lines

axle

N

coil

(end view)

S

Magnet

🔺 **1** As one side of the coil moves upwards through the magnetic field it cuts vertically through the field lines. That produces the maximum current in the circuit.

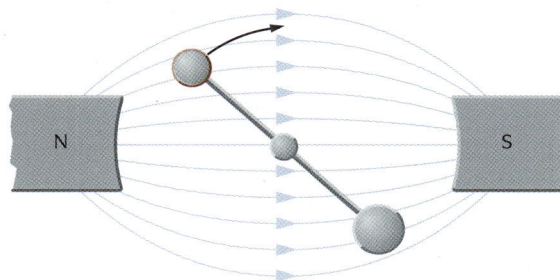

N

S

🔺 **2** Now the coil is moving diagonally through the lines of magnetic field. So they are being cut less frequently. The current has fallen from its maximum value.

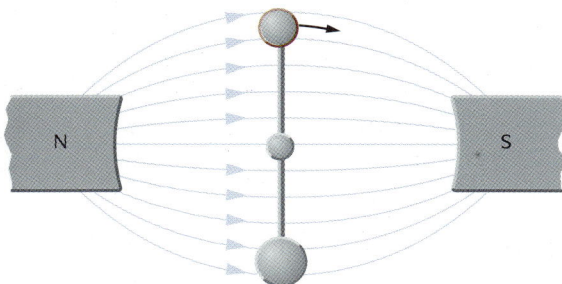

N

S

🔺 **3** The coil is moving horizontally through the magnetic field. Then no field lines are being cut, and no current is generated.

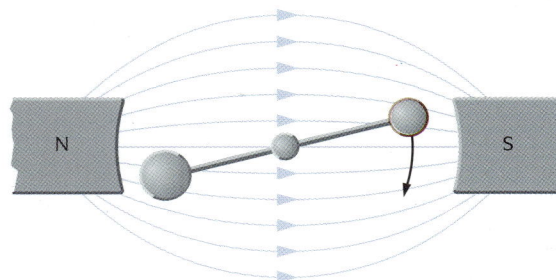

N

S

🔺 **4** The coil is now moving in the opposite direction through the magnetic field. The field lines are being cut at nearly maximum rate again. Current is high, but it has changed direction.

Summary

- Batteries provide direct current, DC, while power station generators usually provide alternating current, AC.
- Direct current flows in just one direction. Alternating current flows one way and then the other.
- In house wiring, the live wire provides the energy input to appliances. The neutral wire makes a complete circuit for current to follow. Earth wire provides a pathway for current to prevent the outsides of appliances becoming live.
- Fuses are weak points in circuits. They are thin lengths of wire which melt when the current gets too big.
- Circuit breakers are devices which cut off connection to a live supply, just as fuses do.
- Voltage is energy transferred per unit charge that flows.
- Electrical power is the rate at which a component or circuit transfers energy:

$$power = \frac{energy}{time}$$

and is measured in watt, W, or kilowatt, kW.
- Electrical power can be worked out from voltage and current:

$$power = voltage \times current$$

- Electricity company bills are based on energy transferred. The energy is measured in 'units' or kilowatt-hours (kWh).
- Energy transferred = power × time. To work out energy transferred in kWh, power must be in kilowatt and time must be in hours.
- The cost of running an electrical appliance can be worked out using:

$$cost = power\ in\ kWh \times time\ in\ hours \times price\ per\ kWh\ of\ electrical\ energy$$

- A voltage is induced when the magnetic field around a coil or wire changes. The change can be caused by movement of the wire through the magnetic field.
- An AC generator works by the spinning of a coil relative to a magnetic field.

Revision Questions

1 When does a current flow between the live and neutral wires?

2 What do DC and AC stand for? What is the difference?

3 Why don't National Grid cables, supported by pylons, need any plastic coating?

4 How does a fuse cut off the current in a circuit? When is that likely to happen? What could happen if an amateur electrician uses fuse wire that is:
   a too thin?
   b too thick?

5 An electrician designing house wiring must take account of safety and cost.
   a Which do you think is more important?
   b Make a list of safety devices that the electrician might use.
   c How does the electrician try to keep the cost as low as possible?

6 Copy and complete the table to show the correct colours for wiring a plug.

Wire	Colour
earth	
live	
neutral	

7 What is the main cause of car fires?

8 Describe two ways in which an electric shock can kill.
   What other harm can an electric shock do?

9 Why are torch batteries not as dangerous as mains electricity?

10 A bicycle has a dynamo. Why do the lights go out when the cyclist stops at traffic lights?

11 Are appliances connected to a socket circuit in series or in parallel with each other? Sketch a circuit to show what you mean.

12 What quantity is measured by the meter in the electricity supply of a house?

13 Why does a kitchen cooker need thick cables?

14 Describe a sequence of events that could cause a fuse to blow. Present your sequence either as a list of sentences or as a pictorial storyboard.

15 Why is it fair to describe a ring main as a triple loop?

16 The electrical resistance between two parts of your body is normally about 2000 ohm. Why is it much less when you are wet?

17 Calculate the cost of running these appliances for the times shown.

Appliance	Power (kW)	Time (hours)	Price per unit (pence)
Heater	2	2	8
TV	0.250	6	8
Spotlight	0.100	10	8
Games console	0.012	24 (all day)	8

Which one is most expensive?

18 a A length of wire is placed next to a spinning magnet. Why does no current flow along the wire?

Spinning magnet   Wire

   b A loop of wire is placed next to a stationary magnet. Why does no current flow around the loop?

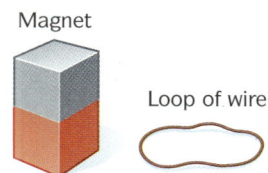

Magnet

Loop of wire

19 In what ways are live and neutral wires,
   a like
   b unlike
   the terminals of a battery?

20 The graph shows the potential difference between live and neutral wires.

Potential difference (volt)

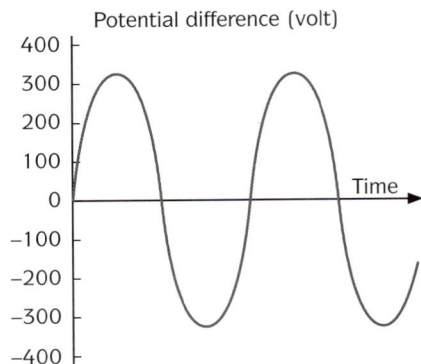

Relate to the graph to explain the following:
a The current sometimes flows one way and sometimes flows the other way.
b The mains voltage of 230 volt is a 'mean' value.
c The voltage between neutral and earth wires is always zero.
d Fuses and switches are connected into the live wire and never into the neutral wire.

21 On building sites people often work in damp conditions. They use electrical power tools that work off a supply which is only 55 volt.
a Explain why these are much safer in such conditions.
b Why does a 55 volt power drill generally need a higher current than a 230 volt power drill to do the same job?

22 In a 230 volt mains circuit, a charge of 1 coulomb passes through a lamp in 4 s. What is:
a The current in the lamp
b The power of the lamp
c The energy transferred by the lamp in the 4 s?

23 Explain why a simple loop generator provides AC and not DC.

CHAPTER THIRTEEN

Particles, charge & current

If you pass smoky air, non-stop, in and out of a sponge then the sponge will get pretty dirty. That is what happens in your lungs. Your body contains a lot of poison that got in through your lungs. One way to have cleaner air is to burn less fossil fuel – less oil and coal in particular. Another way is to remove smoke from the air while it is still in the chimney. And the way to do that is to take advantage of the electric charge that lies inside all matter.

Review

Before going any further, read this page and attempt the tasks. Write the answers in your notes.

We experience gravitational force all of the time. But electrical force is usually hidden. It becomes noticeable when friction disturbs the normal state of balance of charge of an object. That happens when you take off a sweatshirt, and the sparking effect of electricity can be heard as crackles. Sometimes it happens when you comb your hair, and then you can see a very special difference between gravitational force and electrical force. Gravity always results in attractive force, never repulsion. Electrical forces can be either attractive or repulsive. It is repulsion between hairs on your head that can cause them to move away from each other, and to stand up.

▲ Becoming charged by a Van de Graaff generator.
Charge causes repulsive force between the different parts of the body. Hair, and sometimes shoelaces, stand on end.

Only some objects are affected by electrical force. Only these objects can exert electrical forces. We say that these objects have electric charge.

To explain attraction and repulsion we have to suppose that there are two types of charge. The names for the two types could be just about anything – when people first did experiments with static electricity they called them 'vitreous' and 'resinous'. But the names *positive* and *negative* are the ones that have stuck. Objects with positive charge repel each other. So do objects with negative charge. It is only objects with opposite charges that attract.

Most everyday objects are electrically *neutral* – with a balance of positive and negative charge. That is why we don't notice electrical forces, most of the time.

CHECK THIRTEEN

1 Solve the anagrams:
I vet cat rat – pulling things together, like a force
in for it, c – it rubs away electrical balance
ant rule – electrical balance
O, I've spit – a kind of charge

2 Write down one difference between gravitational force and electrical force.

3 Describe an event that you have seen that was caused by an imbalance of electrical charge in some materials.

4 Explain why electrical force is sometimes attractive and sometimes positive.

The start of the electronic age

Spare a thought for the ghost of J J Thomson. He was curious about electricity. In a quiet laboratory in Cambridge he tried to find out more. He used a glass tube with metal parts, called **electrodes**, sealed into it. Inside the tube was a vacuum – no air.

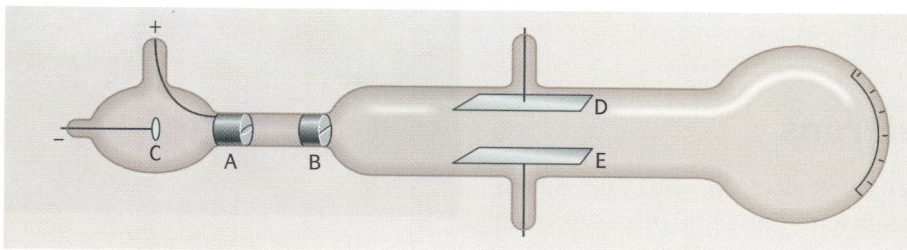

When Thomson connected the electrodes to his power supply the end of the tube would glow, as if there were 'rays' coming from one of the electrodes. He worked on the 'rays', and discovered that they were really streams of very, very tiny particles coming out of the metal. Their paths could be bent by electric and magnetic forces. He used the name **electrons** for these particles.

It was 1897 when J J Thomson told people about what he had found. There have been few discoveries with so much impact. Electrons help us to explain what is going on inside materials. They are the starting point for entertainment and communication systems, for computers and control. We live in the age of the electron.

▶ *What kind of material were Thomson's electrodes made from?*

Televisions and electrons

Imagine life without television. There would be no comic hero crazes, no 'sitcoms' or soaps, no weather forecast, no charity appeals. If all the televisions in all the world suddenly stopped working, the world would become a very different place. Television technology has grown from the discovery of the electron.

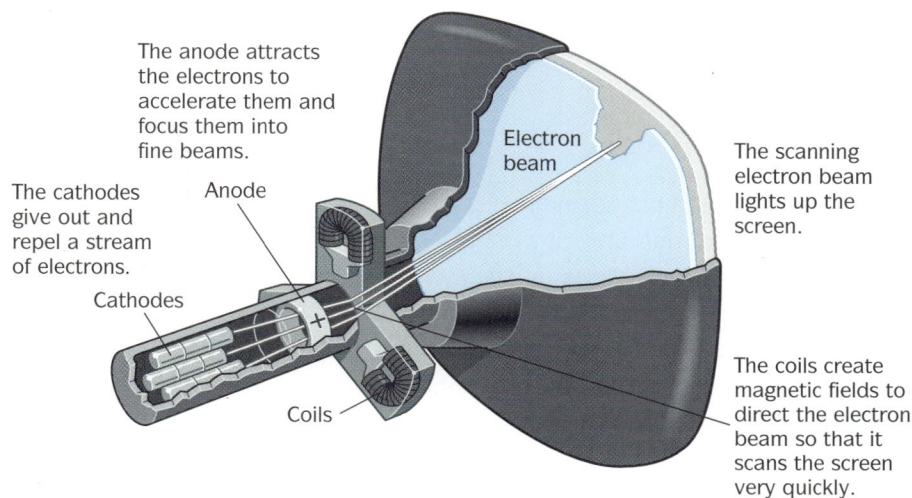

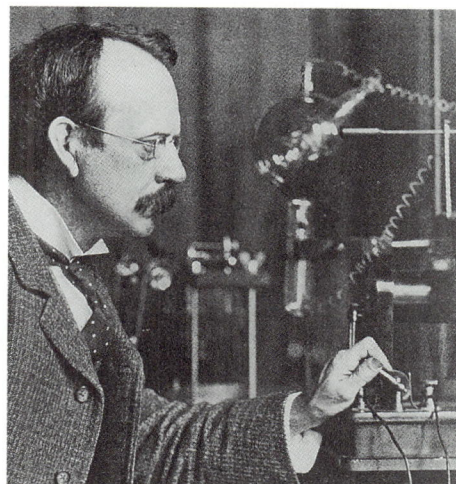

🔺 J J Thomson could never have dreamed of how knowledge of electrons affects our present-day lives.

'The experiments . . . were undertaken in the hope of gaining some information as to the nature of the Cathode Rays. According to the almost unanimous opinion of German physicists they are due to some process in the ether. Another view of these rays is that they mark the paths of particles of matter charged with negative electricity.'

🔺 Extracts from the beginning of J J Thomson's write-up of his experiments, October 1897. Some physicists believed that all of space was filled with 'ether'. The results of Thomson's experiments supported the particle idea.

The anode attracts the electrons to accelerate them and focus them into fine beams.

The cathodes give out and repel a stream of electrons.

Cathodes

Anode

Coils

Electron beam

The scanning electron beam lights up the screen.

The coils create magnetic fields to direct the electron beam so that it scans the screen very quickly.

🔺 Electron technology.

In a television set the electrons come from metal right at the back of the tube. The metal is called a *cathode*, and we sometimes call the tube a *cathode ray tube*. But a metal is made of atoms. Electrons come out from among the atoms.

Electrons escape most easily from a metal, through its surface, when the metal is hot. We call the process **thermionic emission**.

▶ *Explain how the working of a television set provides evidence that materials like metals contain electrons.*

Using charge to control electrons

Inside a television tube, electric force accelerates electrons into high-speed beams. Then magnetism can steer the beams to the right places on the screen. The signal arriving from the television station through the aerial provides the instructions for where the electrons must hit the screen.

Electrons can be accelerated and steered because they have electric charge. For example, the electrical supply to the television gives the cathode a negative charge. Negative charge repels negative charge – the cathode repels electrons. The repulsive force begins to accelerate electrons towards the screen.

▶ *What kind of charge do electrons have?*

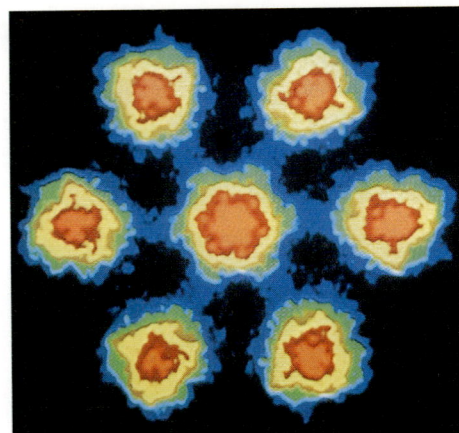

🔺 We have come a long way since J J Thomson's experiments. In electron microscopes we can use the electrical behaviour of electrons, jumping between atoms, to build up pictures of individual atoms.

Electrons and atoms

All atoms contain electrons, which have negative electric charge. But many atoms are neutral. So atoms must contain positive charge to balance the negative charge of their electrons.

▶ *Write a sentence to explain what thermionic emission is.*

▶ *Do you believe in atoms? What evidence have you got?*

You can read more about atoms and their balance of positive and negative electric charge, and electrons and protons, in Chemistry, Chapter Nine.

A neat and tidy picture of a flourine atom.

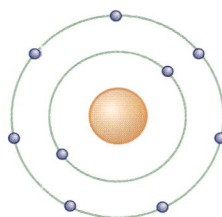

The blue dots are electrons (negative charge). The nine electrons are balanced by positive charge in the nucleus.

Is this more like what a flourine atom is really like? Or is it just another picture, with a bit more detail? It shows the neutrons and protons in the nucleus. (There will be nine protons but you can't see them all here.) It shows the electrons (there are still nine of them) in cloudy orbits.

2 in 1st orbit

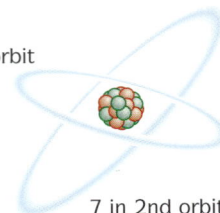

7 in 2nd orbit

🔺 Two ways of looking at an atom.

Electrons explain electrostatic effects

Balloons on the wall

A lot of everyday objects can be 'charged' by friction. A balloon is normally electrically neutral. It has a balance of negatively charged electrons and of positively charged particles (protons) in its atoms. Rubbing the balloon on your sweater scrapes electrons off one surface and onto the other. There is transfer of electrons. Some electrons are loosely held on the outside of atoms, and they are easy to remove. Positively charged particles (protons) do not transfer across because they are stuck deep inside atoms and they can only move when whole atoms move.

The transfer of electrons between the surfaces destroys the electrical balance of the balloon and sweater. Suppose that electrons are rubbed off the balloon and

Neutral balloon ...
Positive and negative charges cancel out.

Some negative electrons are rubbed off the surface of the balloon. The balloon has less negative than positive charge.

Direction of electron transfer

Electrons in the wall are attracted by the positive charge on the balloon.

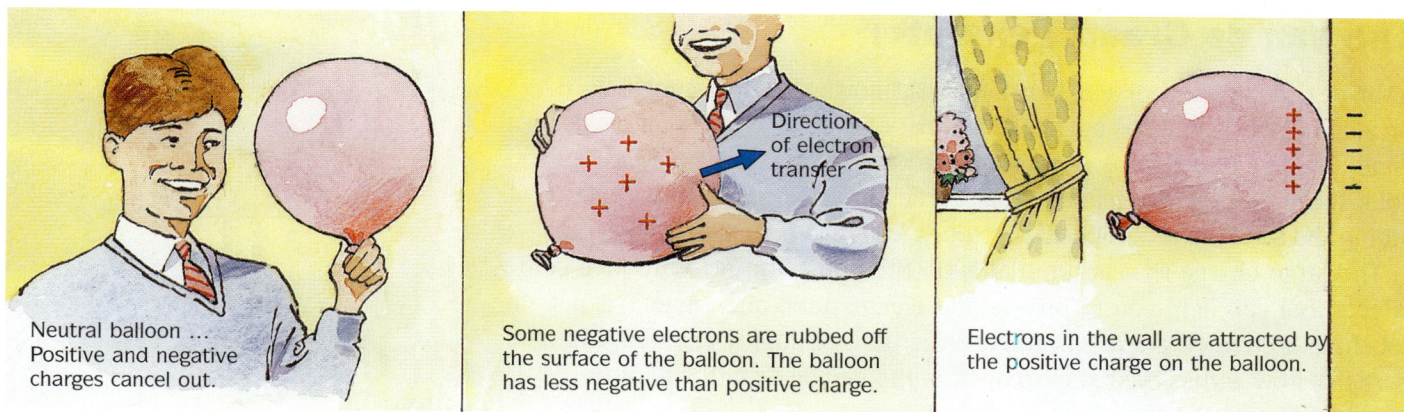

onto the sweater. The sweater gains the negative charge of the electrons. The balloon loses negative charge, and that leaves it with more positive than negative charge. The balloon and the sweater now have opposite charge, and they attract each other weakly.

▶ *Why does friction cause a transfer of electrons but not of positively charged particles?*

▶ *What is the name of the positively charged particles inside atoms?*

▶ *The person sitting next to you is (near enough) electrically neutral. What does that tell you about the number of electrons and the number of positively charged particles inside them?*

If you hold the positively charged balloon against a wall, it will attract electrons that are in the wall. The wall, close to the balloon, becomes negatively charged. The result is that there is an attractive force between the wall and the balloon.

Shuffle and shock

A carpet is an electrical insulator. That means that there are no charged particles such as electrons which are free to move around inside it. One part of a carpet can become charged, and electrons cannot easily flow to or from that area to neutralise it. Metals, on the other hand, are good conductors of electricity. They have electrons that are not stuck fast to individual atoms. These electrons can move around inside the metal, and carry their charge with them.

If you shuffle your feet on a carpet, electrons can transfer between you and the carpet. You lose your electrical balance, and you become either positively or negatively charged.

Then if you touch something like a metal handrail you regain your electrical balance. You may feel an electric shock, as electrons flow between you and the handrail to neutralise you.

▶ *How can a charged object (like you) be neutralised?*

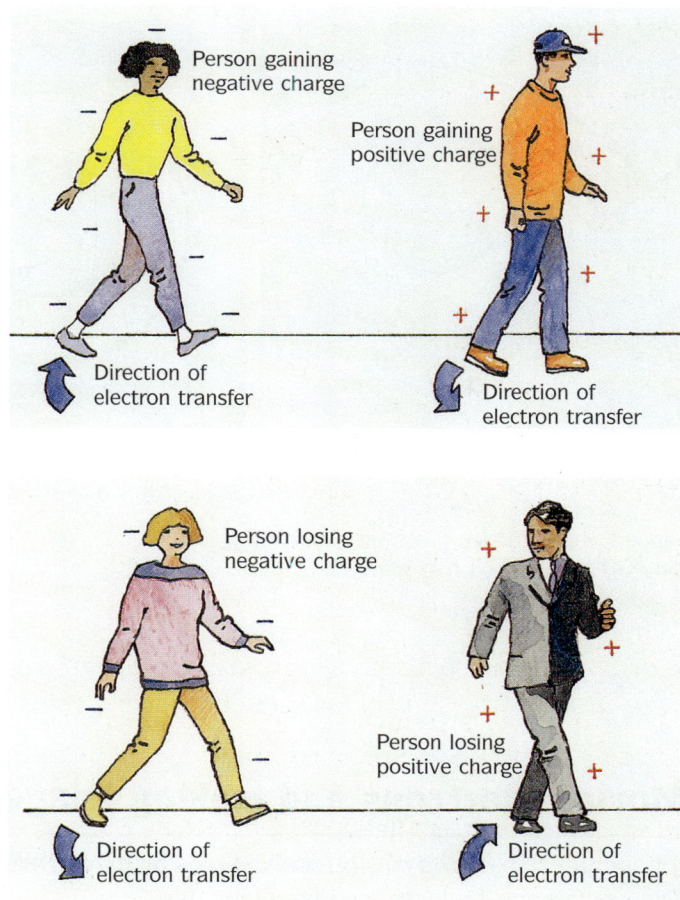

Person gaining negative charge

Person gaining positive charge

Direction of electron transfer

Direction of electron transfer

Person losing negative charge

Person losing positive charge

Direction of electron transfer

Direction of electron transfer

The Van de Graaff generator

A Van de Graaff generator uses a continuously moving belt to accumulate charge on a dome. It either builds up a large number of extra electrons or it builds up a large shortage of electrons. That creates a very high voltage – several million volts. It can be used to accelerate small particles to change the deep structure of atoms and so to create radioactive isotopes for use in hospitals.

The large charge that accumulates on the dome can also produce some effects that can help you to understand electrostatic phenomena. A person touching a charged dome can themselves become highly charged. Charged particles flow across their skin to or from the Van de Graaff generator.

▶ *Explain why a person being charged by a Van de Graaff generator must stand on an insulator.*

🔺 A negatively charged dome – an excess of electrons means that the total negative charge on the dome is bigger that the total positive charge.

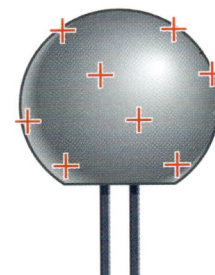

Electrons, ions and ionisation

Neutral atoms contain equal amounts of positive and negative charge.

It is the protons in the nuclei of atoms that provide the positive charge. It is not normally possible to change the number of protons in an atom.

Electrons contribute negative charge to atoms. Electrons are held quite loosely onto the outer layers of atoms. It is comparatively easy to change the number of electrons in an atom. When that happens to a neutral atom it loses its electrical balance, or neutrality. Then we say that the atom has become an **ion.** The process is called **ionisation**.

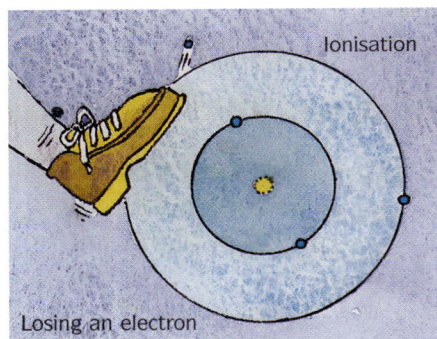

🔺 A positively charged dome – a shortage of electrons means that positively charged particles outnumber the negative ones.

🔺 Ionisation – removing an electron from an atom destroys its electrical balance. The atom then has a shortage of negative charge. It becomes a positive ion. This process takes energy. It can happen when atoms are heated, when they are hit hard by other particles or radiation, and in chemical reactions.

🔺 Some atoms gain electrons more easily than they lose them. The extra electrons turn them into negative ions.

🔺 Many chemical reactions involve turning neutral atoms into ions.

▶ *An oxygen atom contains eight protons. How many electrons will it have if it is neutral? What kind of ion will it become if it gains two electrons?*

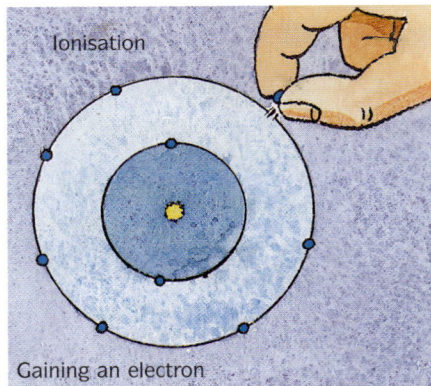

Moving electrons and making images

You can make patterns of electrical charges by moving electrons. You may be given a worksheet to help you investigate this.

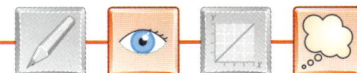

Explaining sparks

Air normally acts as an insulator. But imagine you are in a department store which has a metal handrail near the escalators. If the handrail isn't earthed, charge can accumulate on it. You reach out to touch the handrail.

Just before your finger touches it there may be some flow of charged particles through the air. That happens when there is a very high voltage between you and the handrail. There are a small number of free charged particles in the air, and the electric force can be strong enough to make these move quickly between hand and handrail. They crash into molecules, knocking electrons out of them. That creates a supply of free electrons and of molecules which are not neutral. A molecule, or an atom, which does not have electrical balance is called an ion.

Electric current is a flow of charged particles. If there are large numbers of ions and electrons which are free to move around in the air, they turn it into a good conductor of electric current. In a spark, air conducts.

When an electron moves closer to the nucleus inside an atom it loses energy, just as an object falling to the ground loses energy. In an atom, the energy emerges in the form of light. Sparks give out light because electrons get knocked out of atoms and then fall back in again.

🔺 A flash of lightning is a large-scale spark. Huge voltages mean that there are strong electric forces. A few charged particles in the air accelerate and collide with molecules, 'ionising' them. Soon there are large numbers of free ions and electrons.

Ions and attraction

Farmers can use aircraft to spray pesticides onto their crops. But a lot of spray can drift away on the wind. That means that the farmers have to use a lot of pesticide to make up for what gets lost. That is expensive, and too much pesticide can be harmful to wildlife and people.

An electrostatic crop-spraying gun cuts down waste and pollution. The spraying gun has a needle with a high voltage. The needle has a strong positive charge. That creates strong electrical force on the air. The small number of free ions – positively charged particles – that are in the air accelerate away from the needle. They make energetic collisions with neutral air molecules. The collisions thump electrons out of the molecules. The molecules become ions.

The droplets of spray pick up some of the ions as they travel out of the gun. So the droplets become charged. Since the ions are positive, the charge on the droplets is positive.

The mist of positively charged droplets of pesticide above the field attracts electrons inside the soil and plants. The upper surfaces of soil and plants become negatively charged. So there is attraction between these surfaces and the droplets. The droplets are pulled downwards, and are less likely to drift away with the wind.

▶ *In a spraying gun, what makes molecules become ions?*

▶ *Why is there a force of attraction between droplets and leaves?*

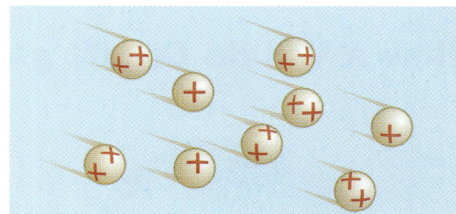

🔺 Droplets of spray pick up positive ions.

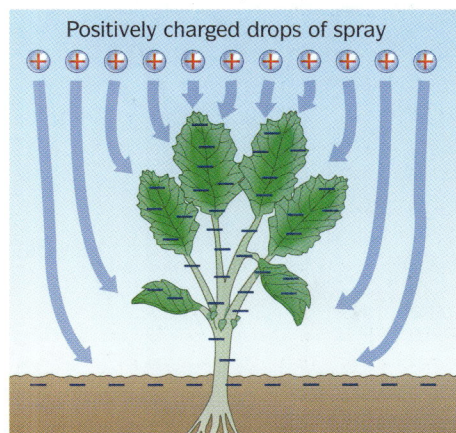

Positively charged drops of spray

🔺 The presence of the positively charged spray attracts negative charge to the surfaces of the ground and leaves.

PHYSICS

Smoke precipitators

A smoke precipitator removes a lot of the small grains of smoke before they can escape through the top of a chimney. The material collects as dust and falls to the bottom of the chimney. It often contains metal oxides which are quite valuable. But more importantly it stops the material polluting the air.

A high voltage inside the chimney results in large forces on any free charged particles in the air or in the smoke. These particles accelerate to high speeds, crashing into other particles and ionising them. That creates more free charged particles, which also accelerate.

Smoke grains become charged by collisions with the fast-moving ions. Some ions knock electrons out of the atoms in the smoke. Other ions stick to the smoke grains. The result is that the smoke grains become positively charged.

A negative wire in the middle of the chimney attracts the positively charged smoke grains. When they touch the wire, electrons flow from the wire to neutralise them. The grains collect on the wire. They build up until they fall off under gravity, or until they are shaken or scraped to the bottom of the chimney. Eventually the dust can be buried, after any valuable materials have been removed.

▶ *Air contains very few free charged particles. How does a smoke precipitator increase the number of charged particles in the air in the chimney?*

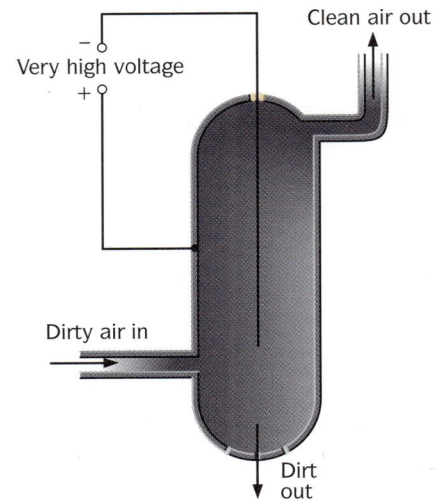

🔺 A smoke precipitator.

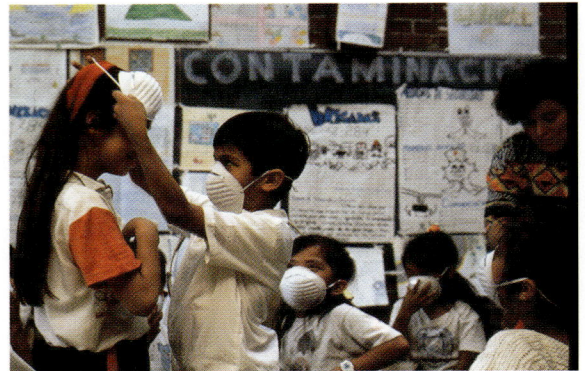

🔺 Smoke chokes.

How a Van de Graaff generator works

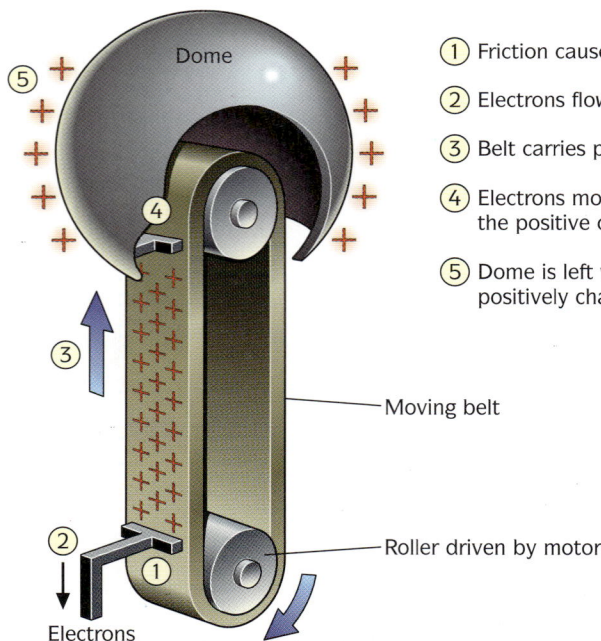

Dome

Moving belt

Roller driven by motor

Electrons

① Friction causes belt to lose electrons.

② Electrons flow away along conducting path.

③ Belt carries positive charge upwards.

④ Electrons move off the dome to neutralise the positive charge.

⑤ Dome is left with a shortage of electrons – positively charged.

Gold leaf electroscopes

If you charge a plastic rod and hold it near the top disc of a gold leaf electroscope, then the gold leaf rises. It moves away from the central metal bar that it is fixed to. That happens because the metals repel each other. They both have the same type of charge on them.

Suppose that the plastic rod is negatively charged. It has an excess of electrons. It repels the electrons in the metal of the gold leaf electroscope. A large proportion of the electrons in a metal are free to move around inside the metal. So electrons in the metal move away from the plastic rod – downwards. They collect on the gold leaf and the metal that it is fixed to.

When you move the rod away the electrons, which all repel each other, spread as far away from each other as they can. They spread back out, evenly through all of the metal. The bottom of the metal loses its negative charge and the disc at the top loses its positive charge. The leaf falls back down.

▶ *Explain what happens to electrons in the gold leaf electroscope when a positively charged plastic rod is brought near the top disc.*

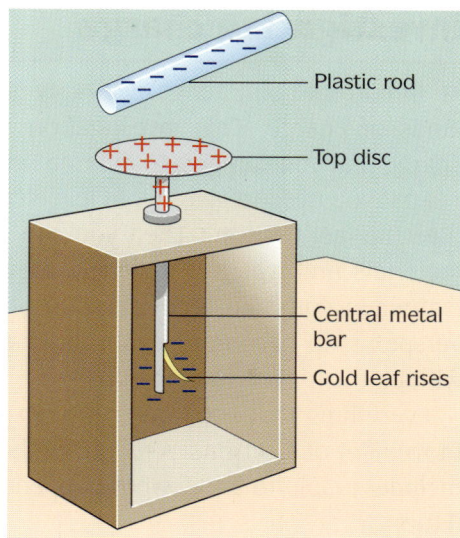

▲ A charged object causes redistribution of electrons in a gold leaf electroscope.

Charging an electroscope

It is possible to charge the gold leaf electroscope so that the leaf stays repelled when you move the plastic rod away.

If you hold the rod in place and touch the disc with a finger for a moment, electrons can flow from you onto the disc. You are not a very good conductor, but you are good enough for the 'missing' electrons on the disc to be replaced. You neutralise the disc, but there is still an excess of electrons at the bottom of the gold leaf electroscope.

If you remove the plastic rod, the excess electrons are still on the gold leaf electroscope. They spread through the metal, but there is still an excess. The gold leaf is still repelled.

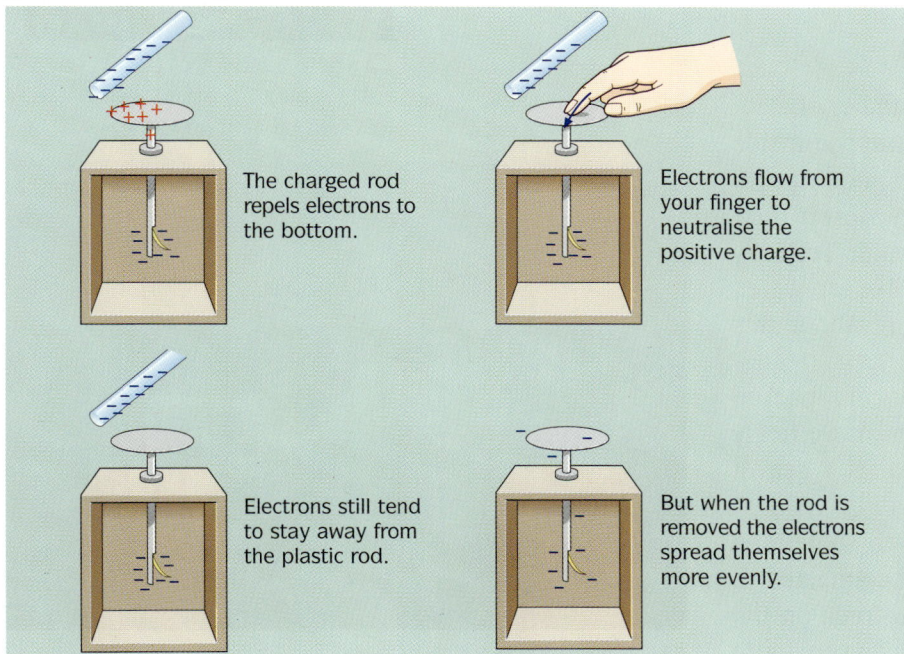

The charged rod repels electrons to the bottom.

Electrons flow from your finger to neutralise the positive charge.

Electrons still tend to stay away from the plastic rod.

But when the rod is removed the electrons spread themselves more evenly.

▲ 'Permanent' repulsion in a gold leaf electroscope.

▶ *Suppose a gold leaf electroscope is neutral to start with, and you make it negatively charged. Where do the extra electrons come from?*

Investigating charge

An important point about electricity is that there are two kinds of charge. This investigation shows the type of charge that you can give to different materials by friction.

First you need to give a gold leaf electroscope a charge. (See the last section.) Then you can simply rub various materials and watch what effect they have on the gold leaf when you hold them close. Try different plastics. A Perspex strip becomes negatively charged when rubbed with cloth. Try glass and metals.

Everything that happens can be explained in terms of movement of electrons. A record of the experiment might include a table to show what happens and a brief explanation.

Action	Effect	Explanation
Charged perspex rod held close to electroscope	Leaf rises more	The perspex has negative charge which repels electrons. The build up of electrons increases the repulsion between the gold leaf and the central metal bar

▲ Investigating positive and negative charge using a gold leaf electroscope.

Measuring charge

You cannot count electrons. They are too small, and there are too many of them. Your work in Chemistry may tell you roughly how many molecules there are in, say, a cup of water. The number is bigger than the number of blades of grass that there are on Earth.

So we cannot measure charge simply by the number of electrons. Instead we measure charge in coulombs. A coulomb is the charge on about 6 million million million electrons.

▶ *How many protons would you need for a total positive charge of 1 coulomb?*

UNIMAGINABLE NUMBERS

Six million million million (6 followed by 18 noughts) electrons have a negative charge of about 1 coulomb. That number is the same as the number of people in a billion worlds just like Earth.

▲ There are a lot of people on Earth – about 6 billion, which is 6 followed by nine noughts.

Flow of electrons in metals

A cup of water contains an unbelievable number of electrons. Nearly every single one of them is trapped inside water molecules. They cannot jump from molecule to molecule. The electrons are not free to move on their own. So electron flow is not possible in water. Perfectly pure water is an insulator. (Impure water, like tap water, can conduct electricity. You can read more about this later in the chapter.)

Metals are very different. Their atoms are packed closely together. Some of the electrons can move freely from atom to atom. The inside of a metal is a sea of mobile electrons.

If one end of any material is connected to something with positive charge, and the other end is connected to something with negative charge, there is a force on the electrons in the material. In insulators like very pure water and plastic, nothing much happens. But inside

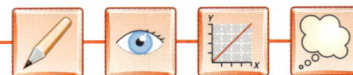

▲ Creating a metal link between Britain and France. Flowing electrons can transfer energy from one country to the other.

metals, the free electrons move in huge numbers – in an electric current.

▶ *Why does nothing much happen in a plastic when it is connected to a high-voltage power supply?*

Relating current to charge

Current is rate of flow of charge, just like the current in a river is the rate of flow of water.

In a wire, it is electrons which carry the charge. It would be impossible to get inside a wire in a circuit and count electrons flowing past you. So current is measured in ampere, or amp for short. If you could be inside the wire, and there were 6 million million million electrons flowing past you every second, then the current would be 1 amp.

current = rate of flow of charge = amount of charge flowing per second

1 amp is the same as 1 coulomb per second.

If charge flows for some time, then to find the amount flowing in each second we divide by the time:

$$\text{current} = \frac{\text{total charge flowing}}{\text{total time taken}}$$

▶ *Explain the difference between an amp and a coulomb.*

▶ *If a charge of 2 coulomb flows around a circuit every 2 s, what is the current?*

Preventing static build-up

When tanker arrives at a petrol station to fill the underground tank there is a major fire hazard. There is some petrol vapour in the space in the tank, along with air. That is an explosive mixture.

The tanker lorry or the petrol tank could have charge. Either of them, or both, could have an excess or a shortage of electrons. So when the driver connects the hose from the lorry to the tanks, there could be a spark which could set off an explosive fire.

The answer is to make a connection with a cable from the lorry to the tanks, before opening the tanks. The cable provides an easy route for electrons to flow along. Electrons repel each other, and they will use the cable to spread out evenly through the tanks and the lorry. That gets rid of any charge difference between the lorry and the tanks so that there is no spark.

▶ *Why do electrons spread out in a metal as much as possible?*

Some electrons can flow freely through an array of closely packed metal atoms.

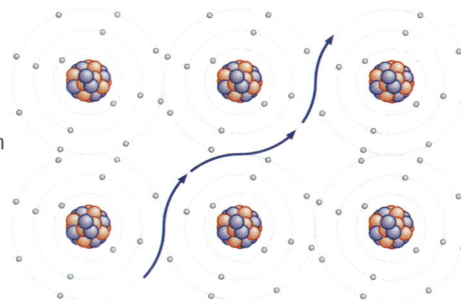

A spark could set off a huge explosion.

Movement of ions in nerve impulses

Your nervous system picks up information from your surroundings, and turns it around so you can react. Nerves are long cells, that radiate like fibres to all the extremities of your body. Impulses travel along them from one end to the other, so one part of your body can quickly respond to what is happening somewhere else.

Nerve cells carry electrical impulses, but no particles flow from one end to the other. The movement of charged particles, ions of sodium, is *in and out* of the nerve.

Sodium ions each have an electron missing (11 protons but only 10 electrons – neutral sodium atoms have 11 of each). They are positive ions. They are dissolved in the water of your body, and there are far more outside your nerve cells than inside. The sodium ions normally cannot get through the outer skin or membrane of a nerve cell. But as an impulse passes along the nerve then, section by section, it lets sodium ions in. Almost straight away, it pumps them back out again. Then sodium ions in the next section of the nerve move in and out, and the impulse moves along.

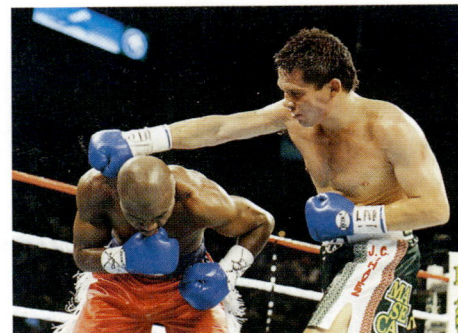

▲ Reacting fast.

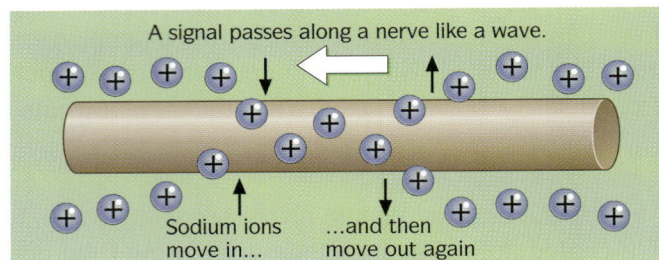

▲ Movement of sodium ions in a nerve impulse.

Flow of ions in liquids

In metals, it is electrons which flow. But electrons are not the only kind of charged particle. In a salt solution, for example, there are not only water molecules but there are ions of sodium and chlorine as well.

In salt crystals the ions attract each other because they have opposite charge. Sodium ions have positive charge and chlorine ions have negative charge. The attraction makes the ions line themselves up in very orderly rows, so crystals have flat faces and sharp straight-line edges.

When salt dissolves in water, the crystals crumble away into the liquid. The liquid is no longer pure water, but is a mixture of water molecules and of ions of sodium and chlorine which can wander around in the liquid.

If one part of the liquid is connected to a metal plate with a negative charge, and the other end is connected to a metal plate with a positive charge then the ions experience force. The sodium ions tend to go one way and the chlorine ions tend to go the other way. Ions can begin to collect on the metal plates.

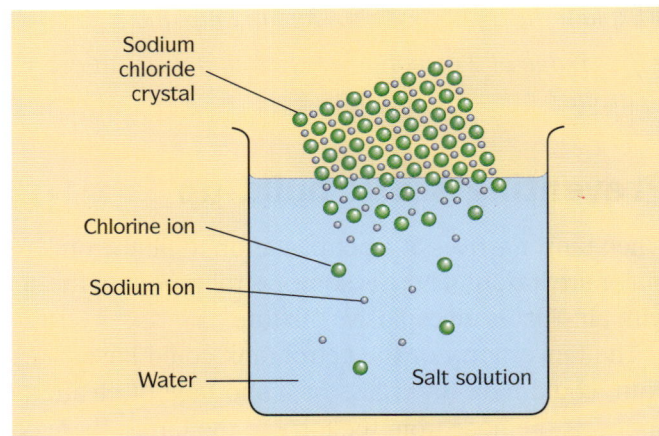

▲ Ions in a salt solution.

‣ *What charged particles are free to move in some liquids?*

‣ *Very pure water is an insulator but tap water conducts electricity. What makes the difference?*

Separating sodium from chlorine

There is plenty of salt in the sea and, in some places, in the ground. Salt has its uses – for adding to food and for treating roads in icy weather, for example. And the sodium and the chlorine are raw materials for very many useful materials.

Metal plates, with a voltage between them, pull sodium ions one way and chlorine ions the other way. The ions separate. Electrical separation of ions is called **electrolysis**. Electrolysis of salt solution (brine) is the first stage in the manufacture of many materials.

▶ *In a liquid which is conducting electricity, why do some ions go one way and some ions go the opposite way?*

Electrical forces on dissolving ions

A water molecule has its positive and negative charges effectively concentrated in different places within the molecule. That makes one end of the molecule positive and the other end negative. So water molecules can exert electrical forces on ions of sodium and chlorine. The forces are strong enough to eat away at a crystal which is put into the water. The crystal dissolves.

Electroplating

Shiny chromium handlebars look good on a bike. The thin layer of chromium and nickel on the surface of the handlebars protect the steel underneath and stop it going rusty. Chromium is shiny but it will not stick to steel. So handlebars first get a coat of nickel. The nickel provides a protective layer for the steel, and chromium atoms will stick to nickel to provide the final shiny coating.

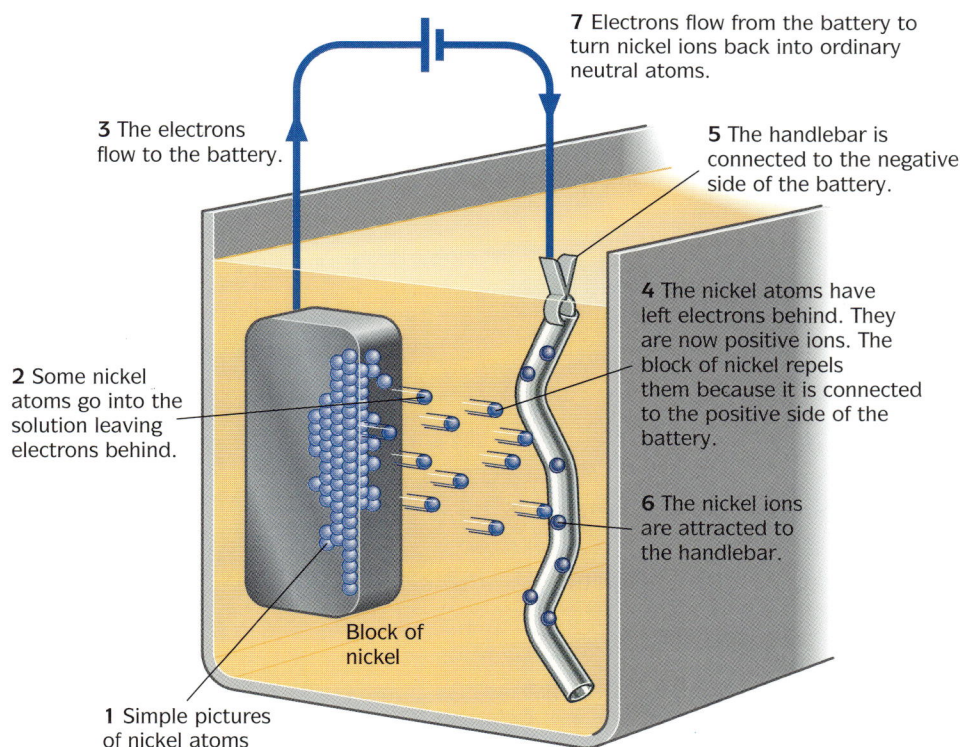

7 Electrons flow from the battery to turn nickel ions back into ordinary neutral atoms.

3 The electrons flow to the battery.

5 The handlebar is connected to the negative side of the battery.

2 Some nickel atoms go into the solution leaving electrons behind.

4 The nickel atoms have left electrons behind. They are now positive ions. The block of nickel repels them because it is connected to the positive side of the battery.

6 The nickel ions are attracted to the handlebar.

Block of nickel

1 Simple pictures of nickel atoms

🔺 Seven steps to make a nickel coating on steel.

To get their nickel coating, the steel handlebars are dipped into a bath of liquid. Also in the bath is a block of pure, solid nickel. The handlebars and the nickel block are connected to the two terminals of a DC power supply, such as a battery.

Nickel atoms gradually dissolve away from the nickel block. They travel through the liquid as ions. Then they stick to the handlebars as neutral atoms again. Electrons flow in the connecting wires to allow the nickel atoms to turn into ions and back again.

It takes about 20 minutes to put a coating of nickel onto the handlebars. Then the process happens over again in a bath with a block of chromium.

▶ *Why does the block of nickel get smaller?*

Summary

- Atoms contain electrons which have negative charge and protons which have positive charge.
- Negatively charged particles repel each other. Positively charged particles repel each other.
- There is an attraction between negatively charged particles and positively charged particles.
- Neutral atoms contain equal numbers of electrons and protons.
- Protons are in the nuclei of atoms, and it is very difficult to change the number of protons in an atom.
- Electrons are in the outer layers of atoms, and atoms quite easily lose and gain electrons.
- An atom with an excess of electrons is a negative ion.
- An atom with a shortage of electrons is a positive ion.
- An object can be charged by adding or removing electrons.
- Friction can transfer electrons from one object to another.
- A flow of electrons or ions is an electric current.
- Charge is measured in coulomb and current is measured in amp.
- It takes huge numbers of electrons (negative charge) or protons (positive charge) to provide 1 coulomb of charge.
- Current is rate of flow of charge, or

  current = charge flowing per second

  and

  $$\text{current} = \frac{\text{total charge flowing}}{\text{total time taken for it to flow}}$$

- Any material which contains charged particles which are free to move is an electrical conductor.
- Any material with no free charged particles is an electrical insulator.
- In metals it is electrons which flow.
- In liquids (solutions) it is ions which flow.
- In a liquid, positive ions and negative ions flow in opposite directions. This is used to separate ions in the process called electrolysis.

Revision Questions

1 Why does your hair sometimes stand up a little bit when you comb it very hard? What happens to electrons when you comb your hair?

2 Neutral means electrically balanced. How does an object lose electrical balance?

3 What is ionisation? What can cause it?

4 If you were a farmer, why would you want to cut down the amount of pesticide spray that you use? How does electrical charge help you?

5 What does electrolysis do to ions:
   a in hair roots (at a beauty parlour)
   b in treating salt to obtain sodium and chlorine?

6 What disagreement was there about cathode rays, among scientists in the 1890s?

7 Describe the journey of an electron in a television tube.

8 Why is there a force of attraction between a wall and a charged balloon? What does 'charged' mean?

9 Why are metals good conductors of electricity?

10 Sodium atoms all have 11 protons. How many electrons are there in a neutral sodium atom? What kind of ion is formed if a sodium atom loses an electron?

11 Why do droplets of pesticide gain positive charge in a spray gun?

12 Describe the scene inside a metal, on the scale of electrons.

13 Describe the different ways in which electric current flows in metal wire and in salt solution.

14 It is not possible to plate steel with nickel using an AC power supply. Explain why.

15 Explain what is happening to electrons in each of these pictures.

a

b

c

16 Explain what is happening to the ions in this picture.

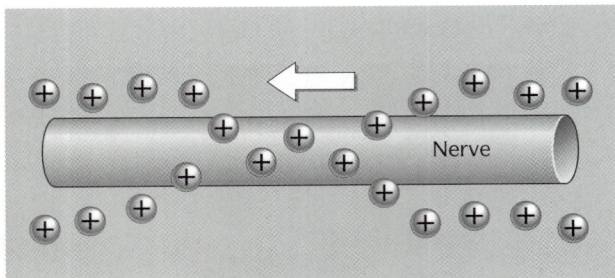

17 The Sun is very hot. It does not contain neutral atoms. Why are the atoms all ionised?

18 Explain how the periodic table is related to the numbers of protons and electrons in atoms. You may have to check your Chemistry for this.

19 In a spark, air suddenly conducts.
  a What makes the air start to conduct?
  b What makes it stop conducting again?

20 Describe how you can use a gold leaf electroscope to show that two plastic rods have opposite charge to each other.

21 Look at page 197. Why are electrons more evenly distributed through the metal of a negatively charged gold leaf electroscope after the charged plastic rod is taken away?

Electromagnetism

■ Keeping hospitals running

Hospitals use electricity as a life-giving support in heating new-born babies' incubators in the maternity ward. They use it to detect the life signs from seriously ill patients in the intensive care unit. It runs the computers that feed essential information to doctors. It sterilises the operating theatre and the instruments the surgeons use. It cooks the food for special diets. It works the signal that calls the nurse to an uncomfortable patient. It turns the motors for the lifts and works the television that keeps the patients' minds off their problems.

But imagine what happens during a power cut, when all the electricity supplies from the National Grid fail. All the lights go out, the babies get cold, the seriously ill are unwatched, patients are left uncomfortable and cannot get from floor to floor.

It can't be allowed to happen. When the National Grid cuts out then the hospital's own emergency generators cut in. They take over and provide the power to keep all the essential functions going. This chapter is about the principles of electromagnetism.

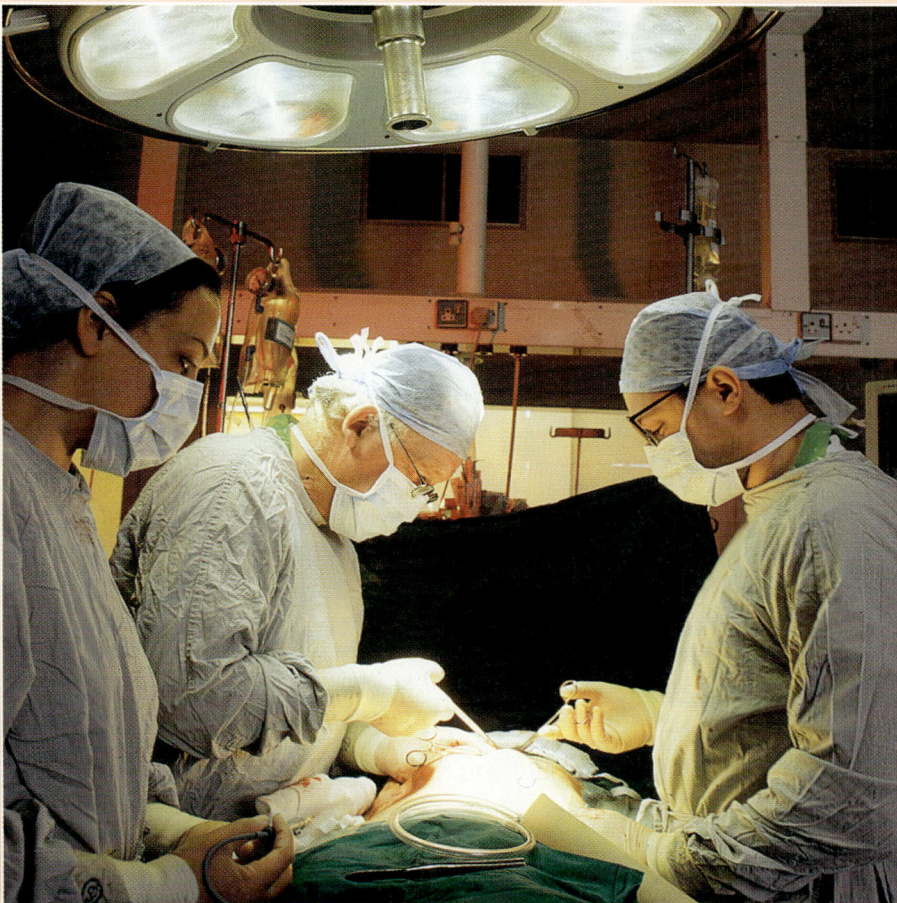

Review

Before going any further, read this page and attempt the tasks. Write the answers in your notes.

In the space surrounding a magnet, magnetic materials experience force. There is a magnetic field in the space.

By placing a compass in different places in the magnetic field, you can find out the direction of the magnetic force at different places. The directions join up to make a pattern of lines, called field lines. You can also compare the size of the forces at different places. The magnetic field is strongest where the lines are packed close together and weakest where the lines are spaced well apart.

Magnetic force can be attractive or repulsive. Every magnet has two ends, or poles, which we call north and south. North poles repel each other. South poles repel each other. But north attracts south and south attracts north.

A coil of wire makes a very useful magnet, because its magnetism can be switched on and off. It is an electromagnet, and there is only a magnetic field around it when there is electric current flowing through it. The pattern of field lines around a long coil is very similar to the pattern around a permanent magnet. Electromagnets are strongest when they have an iron core inside them.

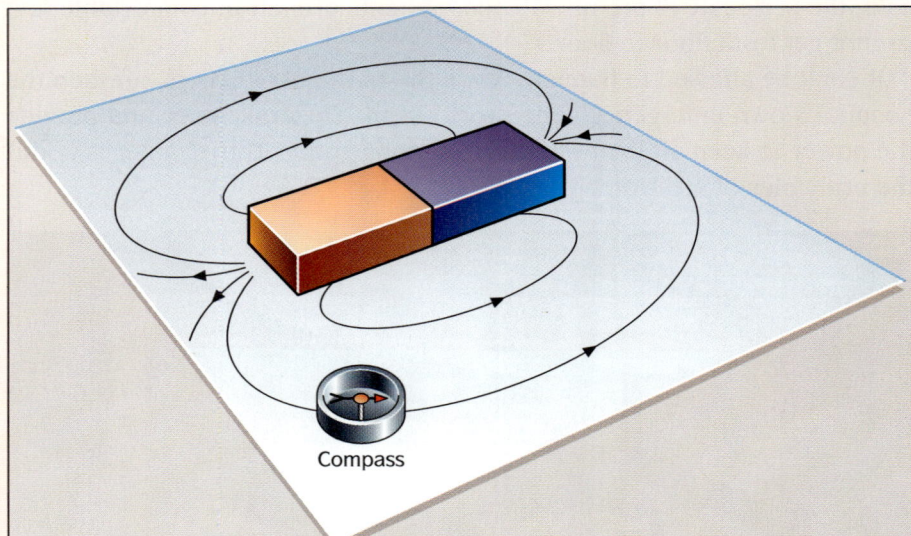

Compass

▲ Patterns of field lines show the direction of magnetic force in different places around the magnet.

CHECK FOURTEEN

1 Solve these anagrams.

so scamp – a swivelling magnet that shows direction
clean gromette – it needs a current to make a field
sort ng – a magnetic field where the force lines are close together
thorn – a pole that attracts a south pole
if led – space in which force acts
shout – a pole that repels a south pole

2 Why would you expect field lines to be closest together near to a magnet, and to get further apart as you move away from the magnet?

3 In words and pictures, make up a way of making it easier to remember which poles attract and which repel each other.

4 How would you make a simple electromagnet?

5 Where might you find an electromagnet being used?

The Earth's magnetic field

The Earth has an iron core which is magnetic. So the Earth has magnetic field, and the pattern of the lines of force is similar to the pattern that would be made by a huge bar magnet inside the Earth. The Earth's poles do not stay in exactly the same place and sometimes the direction of the magnetism (its **polarity**) reverses completely.

▶ *The diagram on page 206 shows a magnetic field around a bar magnet. How do the shapes of the lines of force compare with the Earth's magnetic field?*

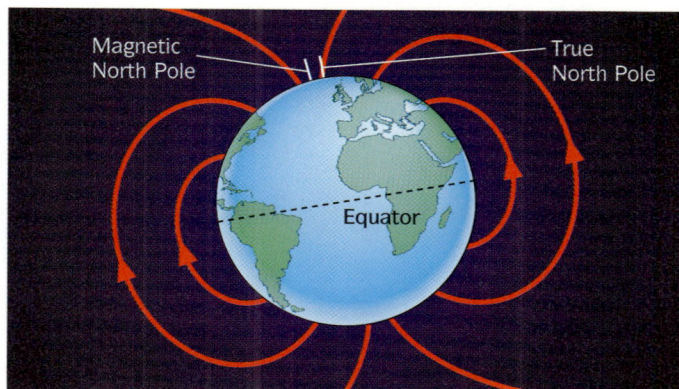

🔺 The lines of force of the Earth's magnetic field do not follow the Earth's surface.

MAGNETIC VARIATION

The Earth's magnetic poles move day by day and year by year. Annual variation in their average positions is about 10 km, and daily variations around the average can be even bigger.

Over longer periods of time, thousands of years, the polarity of the Earth's magnetic field appears to turn around completely. Evidence for this exists in rock continuously being formed from hot material that bubbles up onto the mid-ocean floor. The rock holds iron within it and as it solidifies the orientation of the magnetism of the iron is 'frozen' into that of the Earth's magnetic field.

There are alternating bands of magnetism of the rock at the bottom of the Atlantic Ocean. The rock has become solid at different times, and when it solidified it's magnetism matched the direction (or 'polarity') of the earth at that time.

🔺 Some rock is magnetised one way round and some the opposite way, depending on the polarity of the Earth's magnetism at the time the rock became solid.

It was this discovery, following ocean surveys in the 1960s, that led to the acceptance of the idea that ocean floors are spreading. This supported the notion that sections of the Earth's crust can move relative to one another. This is now known as plate tectonic theory.

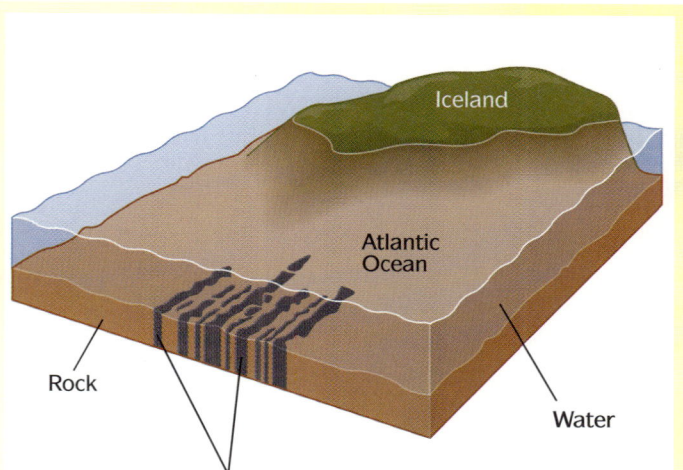

🔺 A survey ship detecting the magnetism of rock on the ocean floor.

Magnetic force

We experience gravitational force all of the time. We know about electrical force – it is what holds material together. That makes it very important in our lives, though we do not feel the force directly ourselves.

Magnetic force is a third type of force. It is related to electrical force. We know this because a wire which is carrying an electric current has a magnetic field around it. If you have ridden on a vehicle today, listened to the

PHYSICS

radio or watched television, you have already made use of the magnetic effect of electric current. You can find out more about magnetic force later in this chapter. Meanwhile, this is a summary of what we know about forces of gravity, electricity and magnetism:

Gravitational force	Acts between all masses	Is always attractive	There is only one kind of mass
Electrical force	Acts between all charges	Can be attractive or repulsive	There are two types of charge, called positive and negative
Magnetic force	Acts between moving charges	Can be attractive or repulsive	There are two types of magnetic pole, called north and south

With electrical force, we have to believe that there are two types of charge, because that is how we can explain that electrical force is sometimes attractive and sometimes repulsive. Charges that are the same repel each other, while charges that are different attract. We say that like charges repel, unlike charges attract. A similar rule applies to magnetism. North poles repel each other, south poles repel each other, but north and south attract. Like poles repel, unlike poles attract.

▶ *You hold two magnets so that they attract each other. What will happen if you:*
a *turn one magnet around*
b *turn both magnets around?*

Electromagnets

An electromagnet is a magnet that can be turned on and off. You can make one by winding insulated wire round a piece of magnetic material, usually iron. The wire is wound round so that you get the current flowing through the same region lots of times. This greatly increases the magnetic effect. The iron in the 'core' of the coil also increases the strength of the electromagnet.

▲ Lift = on. Drop = off.

Investigating electromagnets

You may be given a worksheet to help you find out which variables affect the strength of an electromagnet.

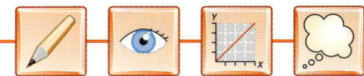

Lines of force around electromagnets

The pattern of magnetic lines of force round a wire are circles centred on the wire. You can remember the direction of the magnetic field by using the left-hand grip rule. Point the thumb in the direction of *electron flow* in the wire and the curl of the fingers gives the direction of the lines of force.

The magnetic fields from the individual wires of a coil reinforce each other inside and outside the coil. This gives a field pattern very similar to the

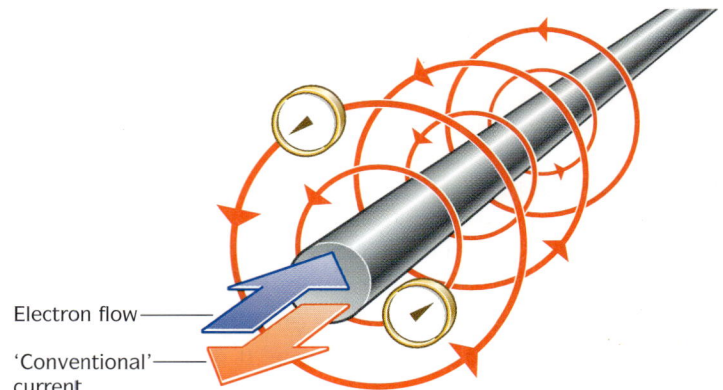

Electron flow
'Conventional' current
▲ The lines of force around a straight line.

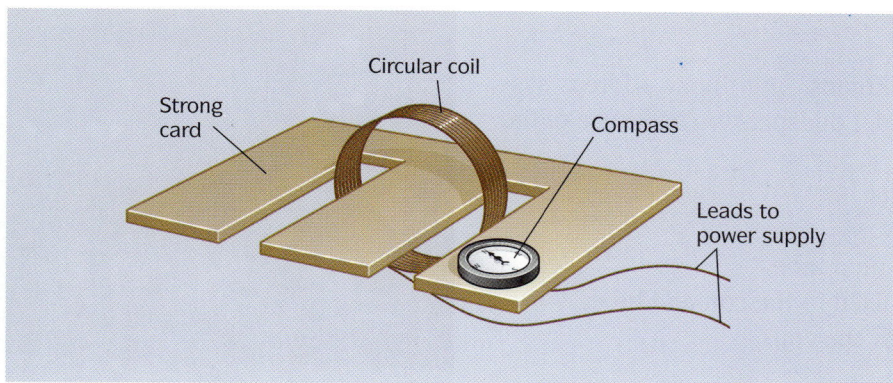

▲ Plotting compasses can be used to show the shape of the lines of force around different shapes of coil.

pattern around a bar magnet. The end of the coil, where the electrons flow clockwise in the coil, acts as a magnetic north pole. The other end, where the electrons flow anticlockwise, is a south pole.

Relays

Heavy electrical machinery often uses very large electric current of tens or even hundreds of amps. Thin wires would soon overheat and melt or cause a fire. The cables needed for big currents are thick and expensive. Switches connected to the wires would have to be very heavy.

A good example is in the starter circuit of a motor car. The current needed to turn the starter motor can be as high as 200 amps. But the current needs to be controlled by the driver from the ignition switch. The wires in the starter motor are very thick, but the cables that connect the starter circuit to the ignition switch are quite thin.

A **relay** switch provides the link. It is an electromagnet that can create a quite strong magnetic field with only a small current. When the driver turns the ignition switch, current flows in the electromagnet. That operates the switch in the heavy-duty starter-motor circuit.

▶ *Why does the cable from the battery to the starter motor in a car need to be so thick?*

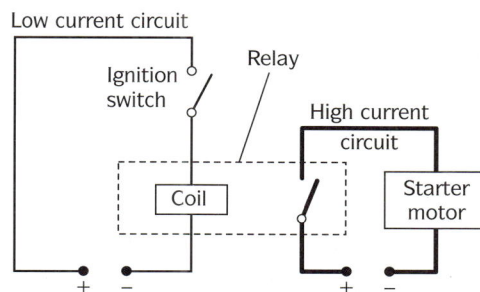

▲ Ignition switch and starter motor circuits in a car. The driver turns a key and closes the ignition switch. A current flows in the coil. The magnetism of the coil is strong enough to attract the relay switch. That turns on the big current in the starter-motor circuit. The thick wires in the starter-motor circuit do not need to be very long.

Jumping wire

A magnet and a straight wire carrying a current both create a magnetic field. When these two magnetic fields try to occupy the same space, there is a force between the magnet and the wire. The push on the wire is at right angles to the current and the lines of force of the permanent magnetic field. This is called the **motor effect**.

▶ *Why is there a force on two DC wires side by side?*

Loudspeakers

Cassette players, hi-fi systems, radios, walkmans, and public address systems all use loudspeakers to make the sound. Loudspeakers make use of the motor effect.

A loudspeaker consists of these main parts:
- a heavy permanent magnet
- a very light coil of insulated wire wound on a tube
- a paper cone (usually thick black paper) fixed to the coil and tube
- a metal frame with insulated terminals for the coil.

The electrical signal fed to a loudspeaker is a varying current, with a frequency that changes to match the frequency of the music. The current goes through the coil.

The current signal turns the coil into a very weak magnet. Because it is a varying current, the strength of the magnetic field of the coil keeps changing. So the force between the coil and the heavy permanent magnet also keeps changing. The coil vibrates with the same frequency as the signal. It moves the paper cone in and out. The movement sends the vibration through the air as a sound wave.

▶ *Suggest why good loudspeakers have their paper cones attached to a heavy metal frame.*

🔺 Loudspeakers use electromagnetism to make vibrations.

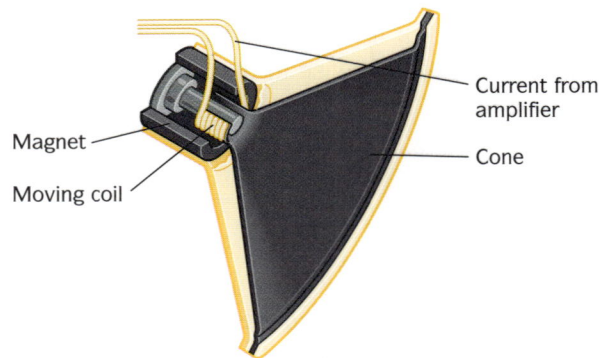

Magnet

Moving coil

Current from amplifier

Cone

🔺 The parts of a loudspeaker.

Electric motors (DC)

▶ *Make a list of all the electrical devices in your home that have electric motors in them.*

An electric motor consists of a coil wrapped around a frame or **armature**. It is free to spin around a spindle. A current must flow around the coil to create its magnetic field. The electric contacts to the coil have to allow the coil to spin. This can be done using a segmented or split ring metal **commutator** that spins with the coil. It touches fixed **brushes**.

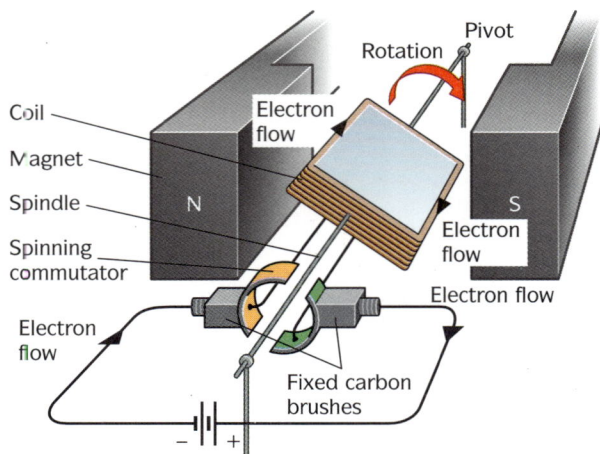

Coil

Magnet

Spindle

Spinning commutator

Electron flow

Rotation

Pivot

Electron flow

N

S

Electron flow

Electron flow

Electron flow

Fixed carbon brushes

🔺 Both sides of a coil of a simple electric motor experience force so that the coil turns.

🔺 Electric motors produce no fumes themselves, so they are very suitable for city transport systems, like this one in Newcastle.

Stages in the rotation of a coil of a motor:

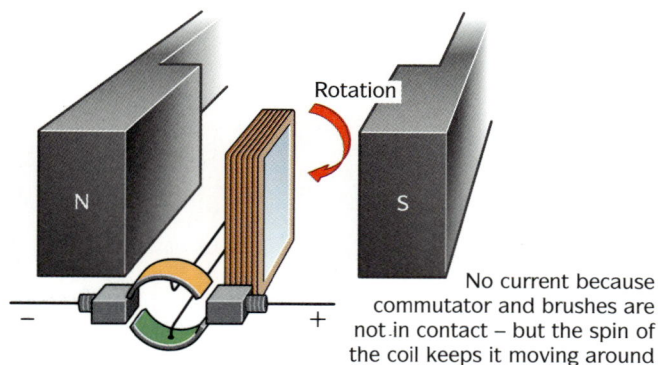

Rotation

No current because commutator and brushes are not in contact – but the spin of the coil keeps it moving around

▲ The coil flips round so that the brushes are no longer in contact with the commutator. As it does so, the current is cut off so that it has no magnetic field.

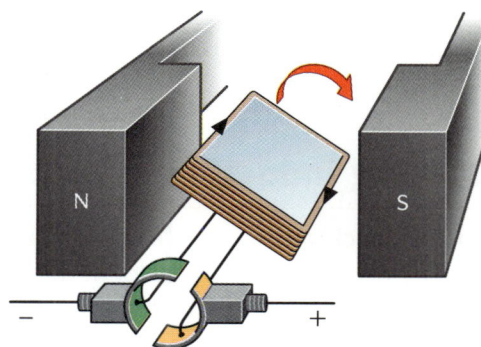

▲ When it reaches half a turn from its original position the commutator is again in contact with the brushes and the current flows. This makes it flip round again. The movement is not smooth but made up of a flip every half a turn.

The brushes and split ring commutator serve two purposes:

■ they make a sliding contact so that the wires do not get twisted as the coil turns
■ they make the current flow round the coil first one way then the other. If the current was not switched round like this, the coil would turn for a short way and stop with its north pole facing the magnet's south pole.

You could increase the forces turning the coil in any of these ways:

■ have more turns of wire on the coil
■ increase the current flowing round the coil
■ use stronger magnets
■ use a coil with a bigger area.

Faraday's induction

Faraday was the man who started the Royal Institution Christmas Lectures that are on television every year. He did a lot of the discovery work that enables us to have hi-fi systems and electric hair dryers.

Generating and transmitting electricity makes use of **electromagnetic induction**. (You can read more about generators in Chapter Twelve – Mains electricity). It was Faraday who discovered how induction works.

The diagram shows a circuit with no battery but with a very sensitive ammeter. Whenever the wire is moved so that it cuts through the magnet's invisible lines of force, the ammeter needle twitches. A current is being **induced** in the circuit. The energy comes from the person pushing the wire.

▲ Michael Faraday did experiments on electromagnetic induction and demonstrated them to big crowds.

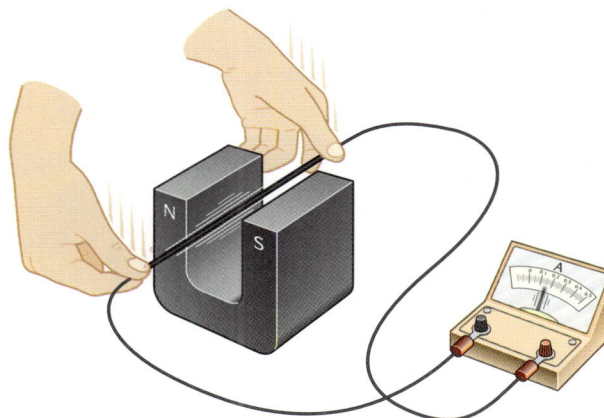

▲ A current is induced in a circuit when a wire cuts through lines of magnetic force.

It does not matter whether the magnet moves or the wire moves. The important thing is that magnetic lines of force move through the wire.

▶ *Look back at the information about generators in Chapter Twelve (Mains electricity). Summarise in one sentence what the principle that generators work by is.*

Investigating induction in a coil

A magnet moved quickly in or out of a coil will induce a current in the coil. In the data below, the reading on the meter in the circuit is the dependent variable. Using the same magnet all of the time, there are three variables that can be controlled. These are the number of turns the coil has, the speed of movement of the magnet, and the direction of the motion. The table shows some sample results.

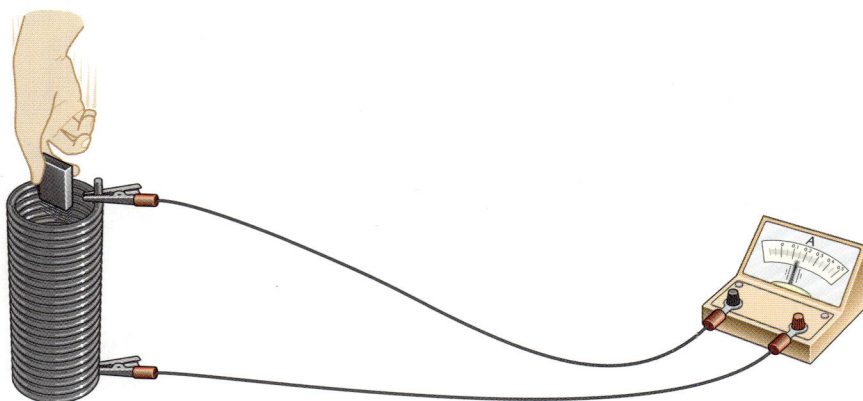

▲ Inducing a current in a circuit.

Number of turns on coil	Speed of movement	Direction of movement	Highest reading on meter scale (in scale units)
600	slow	up	+6
600	fast	up	+20
600	slow	down	−6
600	fast	down	−19
600	slow	sideways	0
600	fast	sideways	0
300	slow	up	+3
300	fast	up	+11
300	slow	down	−3
300	fast	down	−10
300	slow	sideways	0
300	fast	sideways	0
1200	slow	up	+12
1200	fast	up	+38
1200	slow	down	−13
1200	fast	down	+40
1200	slow	sideways	−1
1200	fast	sideways	0

▶ *Use these data to write a conclusion for the investigation. Include in your conclusion the effect of number of turns, speed of movement and direction on the meter reading produced.*

Here is the output of a data logger and graphing programme. A long thin magnet has been dropped through a coil of wire.

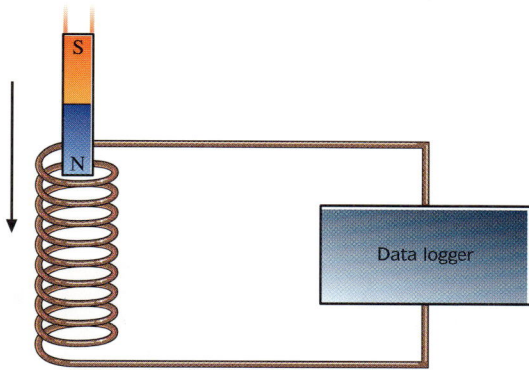

A data logger measures the induced voltage.

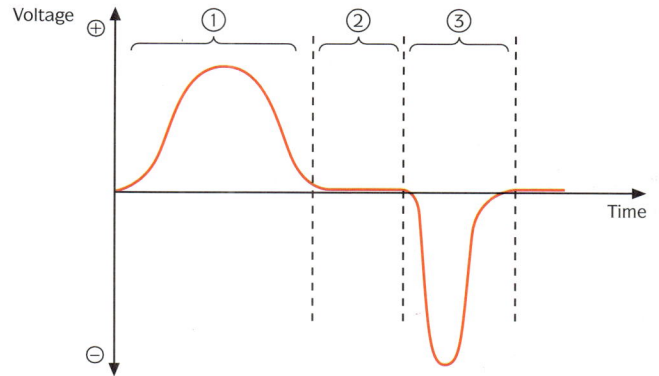

A graph of the voltage at different times.

▶ *Copy the graph into your notebook. Explain the shape of the graph for each of the sections 1, 2 and 3.*

▶ *Explain why the induced voltage is greater as the magnet leaves the coil than it is when it enters.*

This is the output of the same data capture system when it is attached to the set-up shown below.

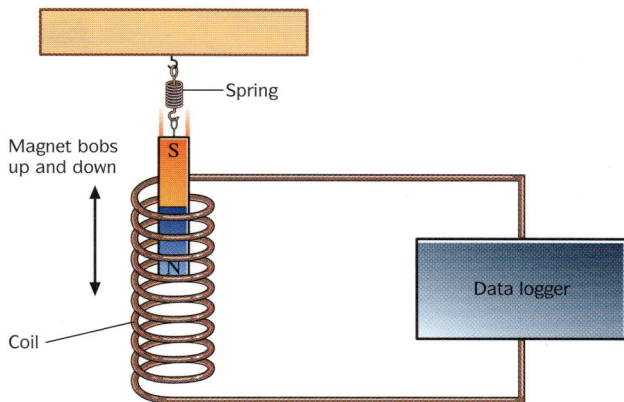

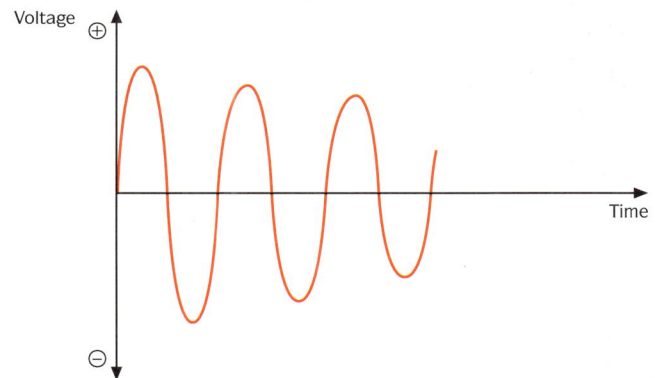

▶ *Copy the graph into your notebook and explain the changes that happen in the shape of the graph.*

▶ *How could a device like the one in the diagram be used to generate electricity from sea waves?*

Induction without motion

A current is induced in a circuit whenever a part of the circuit is in a changing magnetic field. The change in the magnetic field can be caused by moving a magnet near to a wire in the circuit, or by moving a wire near to a magnet. But motion is not always necessary.

An electromagnet can provide the magnetic field. If the current in the electromagnet changes, then the strength of its magnetism changes. Then the invisible lines of force grow and shrink around the electromagnet. The lines

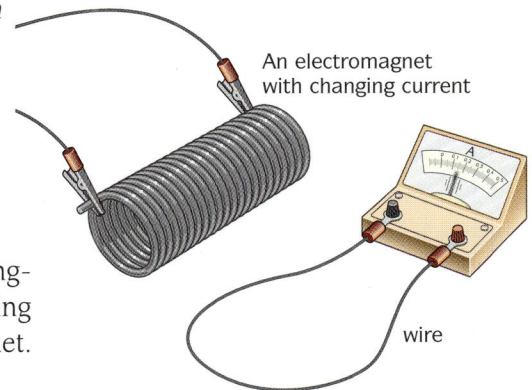

An electromagnet with changing current

wire

An electromagnet with a changing current can induce a current in a nearby circuit.

of force will cut through a wire which is near the electromagnet. If the wire is part of a circuit, a current will be induced in it.

In a DC circuit, it is generally difficult to change the current in an electromagnet very quickly. When the current in the electromagnet is steady, its magnetic field is not changing. It usually only provides a changing magnetic field when it is switched on or off. But if AC flows in an electromagnet, the current in it is continuously changing. Then it provides a continuously changing magnetic field. That can be useful for inducing current in nearby circuits.

▶ *Why does an electromagnet connected to a battery induce no current in a nearby circuit?*

Transformers

AC is just as effective as DC for lighting and heating. And alternating voltages have one major advantage – they can be increased or decreased very easily using transformers.

All the 'low voltage' power packs that students use in laboratories contain transformers. They change the 230 volt mains to lower values that can be used safely with bare wires.

A simple transformer has an iron core with two coils wound around it. When a current flows in one coil the core becomes strongly magnetised. When the magnetic field changes it induces current in the second circuit.

🔺 Computer circuits do not work with 50 hertz, 230 volt mains AC. So computers contain transformers, which convert the AC voltage into voltages suitable for the circuitry.

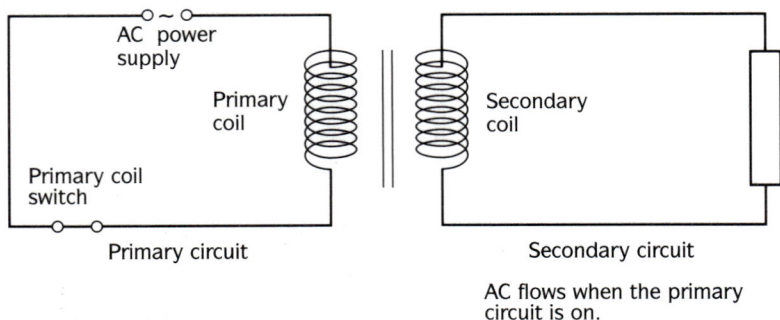

No current flows except for a very short time while the primary coil switch is being switched on or off.

🔺 When the switch is closed a current flows in the primary coil and a magnetic field builds up rapidly. This changing magnetic field induces current in the secondary circuit. But very soon the current in the primary circuit becomes steady, so the magnetic field is steady. Then no current is induced in the secondary circuit.

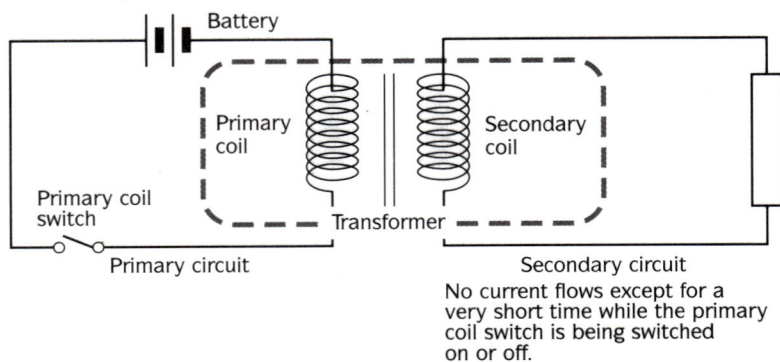

AC flows when the primary circuit is on.

🔺 An alternating current through the first coil is constantly changing in size and direction. That induces an alternating current in the second circuit.

PHYSICS

Voltage up and down

When the primary and secondary coils of a transformer have exactly the same number of turns the output voltage is the same as the supply voltage. When they have different numbers of turns the voltage is changed. The voltage can be increased or decreased.

The primary coil behaves as an electromagnet and produces a varying (alternating) magnetic field around the iron core. The secondary coil experiences a changing magnetic field which induces a voltage between its ends.

The more turns on the primary coil, the greater its magnetic field. The more turns on the secondary coil, the more wire there is in the changing magnetic field and so the greater the induced voltage. So the voltage from a transformer depends on the number of turns on the primary and secondary coils.

There is a formula which predicts how the voltages are related to the numbers of turns in the coils:

$$\frac{\text{voltage across secondary}}{\text{voltage across primary}} = \frac{\text{number of turns in secondary coil}}{\text{number of turns in primary coil}}$$

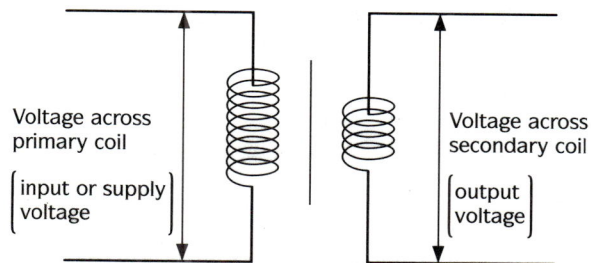

🔺 An AC supply through the primary coil is constantly changing in size and direction. That induces an alternating current in the second circuit.

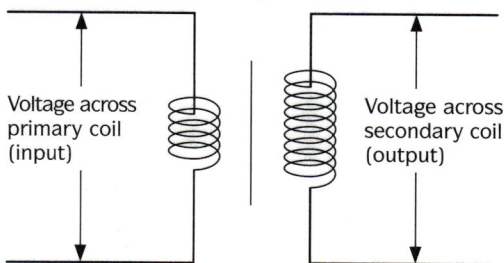

🔺 To increase a voltage we use a step-up transformer. This has more turns on the secondary or output side.

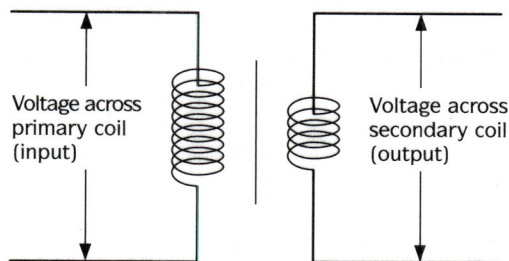

🔺 A step-down transformer has fewer turns on the output side. This gives an output voltage which is lower than the input voltage.

▶ *A transformer has 200 turns on the input side and 1000 turns on the output side. Does the transformer step voltage up or down?*

Transformers at home

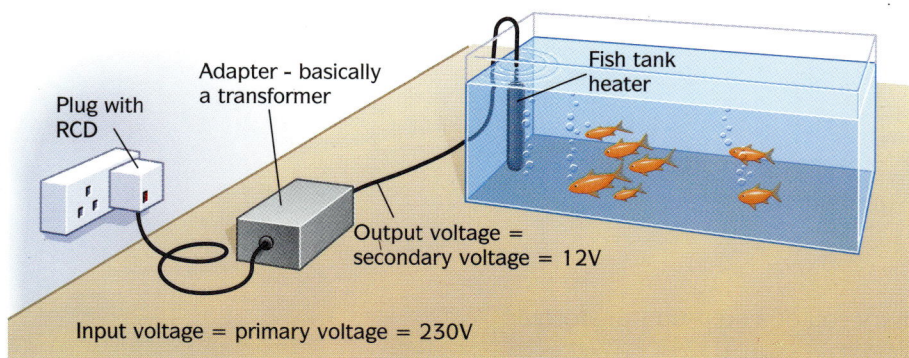

▶ *A transformer in a cassette recorder converts 230 volts into 23 volts. Which coil should have more turns, the primary or the secondary? What should be the ratio of the numbers of turns?*

PHYSICS

Energy transfer by transformers

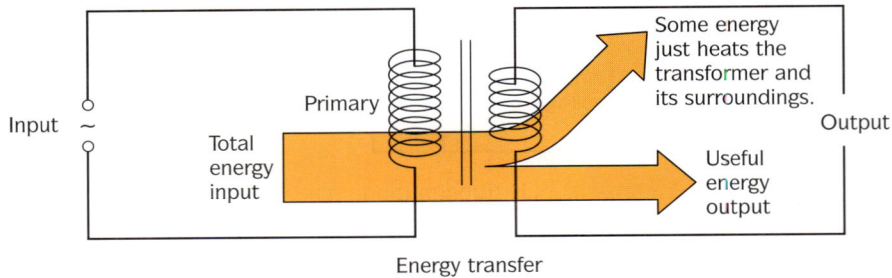

Energy transfer

▲ Transformers transfer energy from one circuit to another.

▶ *Why is the energy output of a transformer less than the energy input?*

Transformer efficiency

You can get more voltage out of a step-up transformer than you put in. But transformers do not give you energy for nothing.

energy = current × voltage × time

If energy output equals energy input, then if the voltage goes up the current must go down.

A perfect transformer gives exactly the same output energy as the input energy.

But real transformers are not this efficient. Transformers waste some energy heating their surroundings. That is partly caused by currents that are induced inside the iron core. To reduce these 'eddy currents' the core is laminated. This means that it is made out of thin sheets of iron rather than a solid piece of iron.

We do not always want to be bothered measuring the time for which a transformer works. So *power* can be a more useful quantity than energy:

$$\text{power} = \frac{\text{energy}}{\text{time}} = \text{current} \times \text{voltage}$$

The efficiency of a transformer is a useful way of comparing power output with power input:

$$\text{efficiency} = \frac{\text{power output}}{\text{power input}} \times 100\%$$

You can read about the principles of measuring energy, power and efficiency in Chapter Seven (Energy measurements).

Example

The input to 60 turns of wire on the primary coil of a step-up transformer was 1.00 volt and 3.44 amp.

The output from 1200 turns of wire on the secondary coil of the transformer was 19.9 volt and 0.156 amp.

Find the energy efficiency of the transformer.

Input power = voltage × current = $1.00\,V \times 3.44\,A = 3.44\,W$

Output power = voltage × current = $19.9\,V \times 0.156\,A = 3.10\,W$

Efficiency of transformer = $\dfrac{\text{output power}}{\text{input power}} \times 100\% = \dfrac{3.10\,W}{3.44\,W} \times 100\% = 0.901 \times 100\% = 90.1\%$

So the transformer is 90.1 per cent efficient.

Transformers in the National Grid

The National Grid is the network of cables that joins power stations to places where people want electricity. The Grid transfers energy. The cables that run from pylon to pylon have low resistance, so that they do not wastefully transfer huge amounts of energy by getting very hot.

But the current in the cables does heat them up a little bit. In thousands of kilometres of warm cable, a lot of energy can be lost. So the power companies keep the current as low as possible. The current in the cables can be low provided that the voltage between the cable and the ground is high.

A power station generates alternating current at a voltage of 25 kilovolt. At the power station, transformers step up the voltage to 275 kilovolt or 400 kilovolt. Long-distance cables have these voltages. Then, near to a town, a sub-station steps down the voltage, first to 132 kilovolt. Other sub-stations provide smaller and smaller voltages, down to the 230 volt that we use in schools and houses.

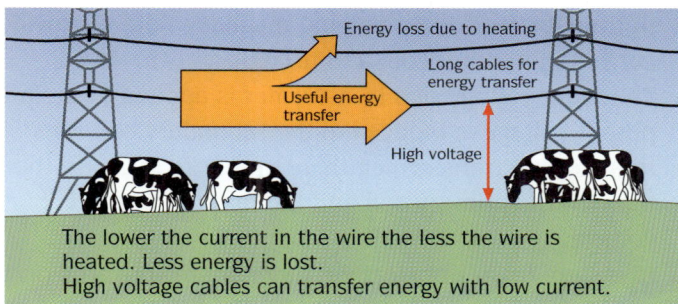

The lower the current in the wire the less the wire is heated. Less energy is lost.
High voltage cables can transfer energy with low current.

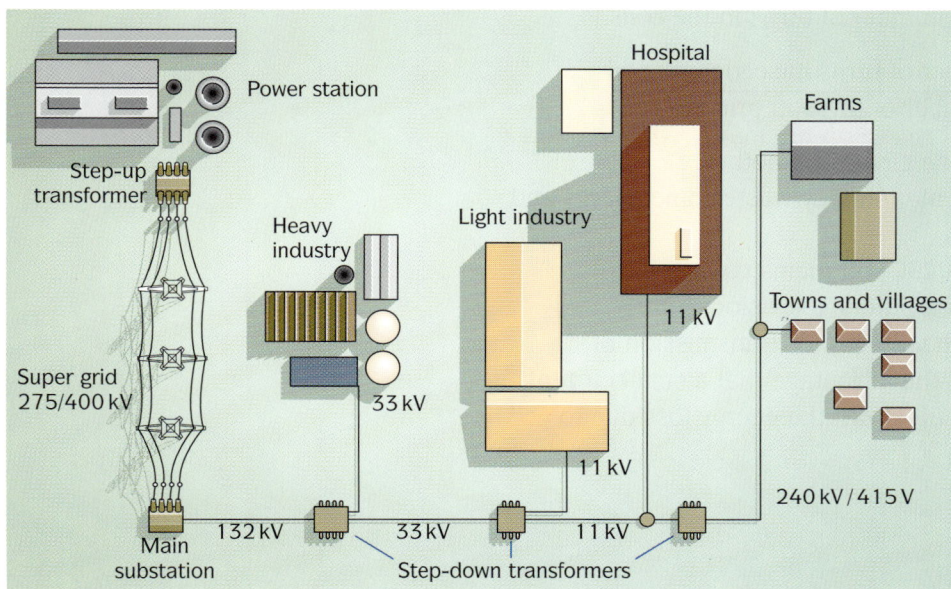

⬧ Transformers in use. Factories and hospitals have their own step-down transformers which are not shown here.

▶ *Do power stations have step-up or step-down transformers?*

▶ *Why do power companies prefer using overhead cables rather than cables underground?*

PHYSICS

The power business

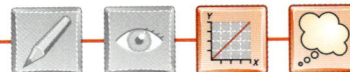

You may be given a worksheet to help you think more about how electricity is generated and transmitted.

Summary

- Like magnetic poles repel and unlike poles attract.
- In the region around a magnet there is a magnetic field in which other magnetic materials experience force.
- There is a magnetic field around a wire which is carrying a current.
- Electromagnets are coils carrying current.
- Electromagnets are used in relays, loudspeakers and motors.
- These devices make use of the force between a coil (electromagnet) and another magnet, which can be a permanent magnet or an electromagnet.
- Motor coils are connected to their power supply by brushes and commutators.
- A current is induced in a circuit when part of the circuit lies in a changing magnetic field.
- In generators, the changing magnetic field is provided by motion of a coil relative to a magnetic field.
- In transformers, the changing magnetic field is provided by changing current in another coil, and no motion is involved.
- The input voltage of a transformer is applied to the primary coil. The output voltage is induced in the secondary coil.
- In a step-up transformer, there are more turns on the secondary coil than on the primary coil and the output voltage is bigger than the input voltage.
- In a step-down transformer, there are fewer turns on the secondary coil, and the output voltage is smaller than the input voltage.
- The formula relating voltages to the number of turns in the coils is:

$$\frac{\text{voltage across secondary}}{\text{voltage across primary}} = \frac{\text{number of turns in secondary coil}}{\text{number of turns in primary coil}}$$

- Transformers transfer energy from one circuit to another.
- Transformers are not perfectly efficient, and they waste some energy and heat their surroundings.
- Step-down transformers can convert 230 volt mains voltage into voltages suitable for hi-fi systems, computers, televisions, etc.
- Step-up transformers can create high voltages for transmission of energy over long distances. This has the advantage that a small current flows in the transmission cables. It cuts down the energy loss due to heating of the cables.

Revision Questions

1 What is inside the Earth that makes it magnetic?

2 a What is the rule for remembering when magnets attract and repel?

b Which of these diagrams show repelling magnets and which show attracting magnets?

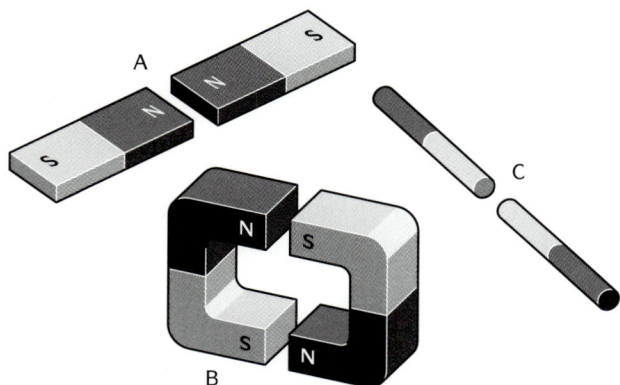

3 a How many loudspeakers have you got at home?

b What are the main parts of a loudspeaker?

c Why does a loudspeaker need a permanent magnet *and* an electromagnet?

4 a Do you think that cars in cities should have petrol engines or electric motors? Explain your answer.

b What are the advantages and disadvantages of the two types of car?

5 a How could you assemble this equipment to make the meter needle twitch?

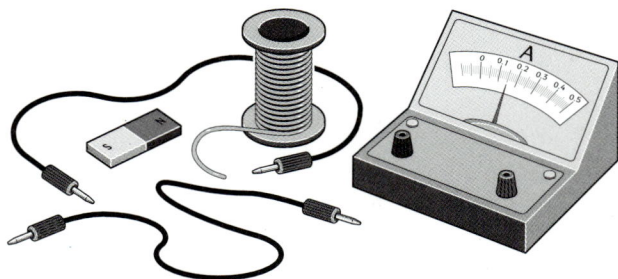

b What is the name of this effect?

c What is the name of the scientist who made discoveries about this?

6 What are the differences between generators and transformers? Mention how they are made and what they are used for.

7 Name one appliance in your home that has a built-in transformer. Why does it need it?

8 Is magnetic force more like gravitational force or electric force? Explain your answer.

9 What difference does it make to an electromagnet when you put an iron core inside it?

10 Copy the diagram. Add arrows to your lines of force to show the direction of the force that would act on a small north pole, such as a compass needle.

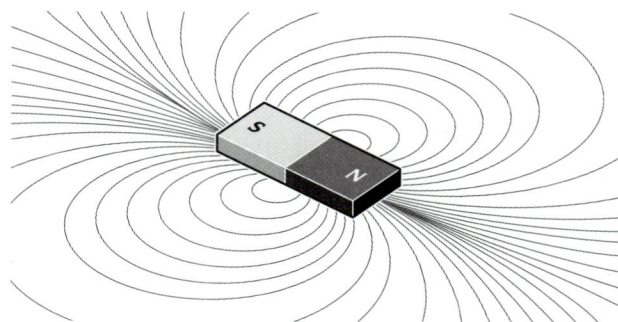

11 What are the purposes of the brushes and commutator in an electric motor?

12 a In electromagnetic induction, what is the useful outcome?

b What causes electromagnetic induction:
  i in a generator
  ii in a transformer?

13 A transformer has 20 turns on the primary coil and 100 turns on the secondary coil.
  a Is it a step-up or step-down transformer?
  b Predict the output voltage when the input voltage is 5 volts.

14 Give two reasons for using AC rather than DC for transmission of electricity from a power station.

15 What is the ratio

$$\frac{\text{number of turns on primary coil}}{\text{number of turns on secondary coil}}$$

for a substation which steps voltage down from 33 kilovolt to 11 kilovolt?

16 Explain why there are stripes in the pattern of magnetic polarity of the rocks under the Atlantic Ocean.

17 In a car, how does a relay:
  a improve safety
  b reduce cost?

18 What kinds of pollution are caused by operation of an electrically powered city transport system? Where does the worst pollution occur?

19 Explain how it is possible for a cardboard cone inside a loudspeaker to make sounds like a human voice.

20 Why does a DC electric motor rotate continuously and not flick one way and then the other?

21 Imagine that you are designing motors for
  i an electric car
  ii a hair drier.
  a Do you design the motors for AC or DC?
  b How important is the size of the turning force on the coil or coils in the motor?
  c What variables could you use to set the size of the turning forces?

22 The diagram shows the plate from a transformer.

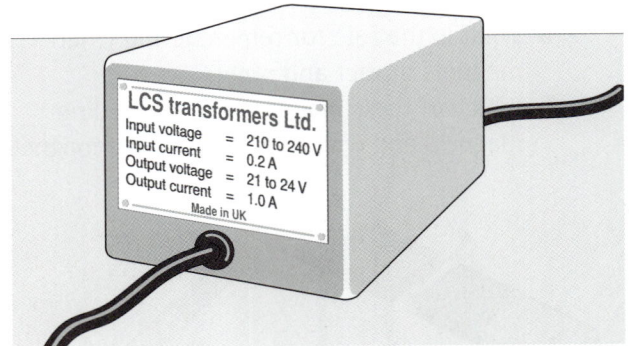

LCS transformers Ltd.
Input voltage = 210 to 240 V
Input current = 0.2 A
Output voltage = 21 to 24 V
Output current = 1.0 A
Made in UK

  a Is it a step-up or step-down transformer?
  b What is the ratio of primary coil turns to secondary coil turns?
  c Estimate the transformer's efficiency.

23 These are two possible systems for delivering power to some theatre lights. Which is better? Explain your answer.

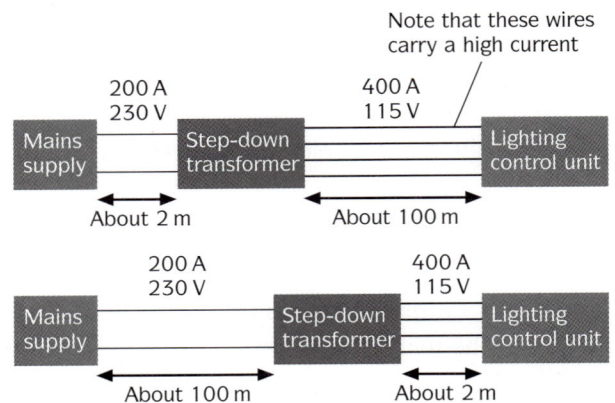

Note that these wires carry a high current

200 A
230 V
Mains supply — Step-down transformer — 400 A 115 V — Lighting control unit
About 2 m   About 100 m

200 A
230 V
Mains supply — Step-down transformer — 400 A 115 V — Lighting control unit
About 100 m   About 2 m

24 A transformer has inputs of 230 V and 0.4 A and outputs of 23 V and 3.0 A. What is its efficiency?

Radioactivity

▪ Nuclear reactions

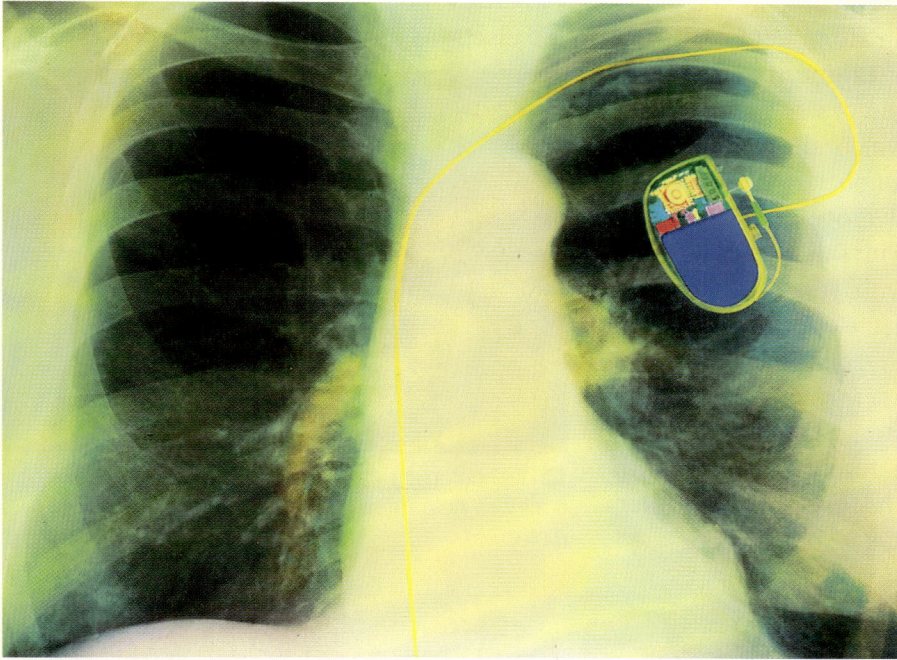

Nuclear reactions can provide safe and long-lasting power sources, like in this heart pacemaker.

Nuclear reactions are responsible for the release of energy in a nuclear explosion.

A lot of people make use of nuclear reactions at home. Smoke detectors contain a small amount of radioactive material.

Review

Before going any further, read this page and attempt the tasks. Write the answers in your notes.

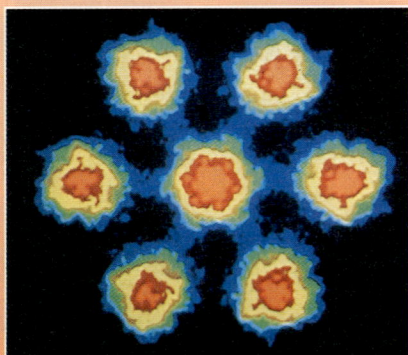

▲ Electron microscopes can pick out individual atoms.

Smaller than atoms

This book, your chair, your breakfast and you are made of **atoms**. Atoms are the building blocks of all material. Every atom is made up of three types of even smaller particles.

Two kinds of particle, the **neutrons** and the **protons**, pack themselves tightly together in the centre of an atom. This centre is the **nucleus**. **Electrons** are the third kind of particle, and they make up the outer layers of an atom. Neutrons, protons and electrons are **sub-atomic** particles.

Elements are substances with atoms which all have the same number of protons. Hydrogen is the element with the smallest atoms – with just one proton in each one. The nuclei in oxygen atoms each have 8 protons. Uranium atoms are the biggest natural atoms on Earth, and every one of them has 92 protons.

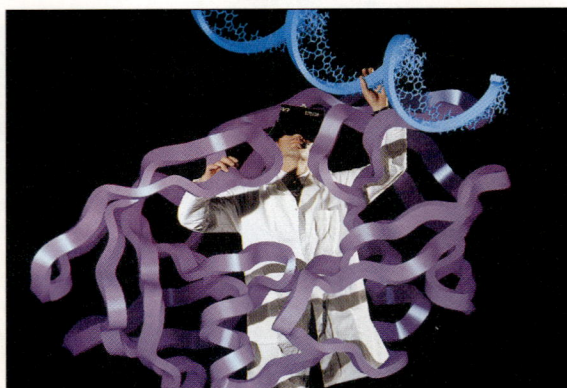

▲ Technologists develop new drugs using virtual reality to help them to picture the atoms in large molecules.

It's hard to imagine atoms. A simple picture of an atom is just a tiny ball, but inside they're probably a lot more complicated than that.

JJ Thomson thought that the electrons must come out of the atoms of the cathode (see Chapter Thirteen (Particles, charge and current)). He tried to imagine what an atom might be like on the inside. His idea is called the 'pudding model' because he imagined that the electrons were spread about like fruit in a sponge of positive charge.

Even today, it's still not easy to picture atoms. One modern model shows the positive 'nucleus' of an atom with electrons round it in fuzzy clouds.

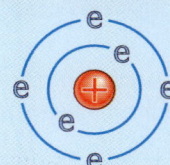

A tidied up version of this model shows electrons in neat orbits round the nucleus. This atom is electrically neutral. The number of units of positive charge in the nucleus matches the number of electrons in the atom.

▲ There are different ways of imagining atoms. This chapter is about nuclei, the compact centres of atoms.

CHECK FIFTEEN

1 Solve the anagrams:
sun clue – the centre of an atom
steel corn – particles from the outer layers of atoms
top ron – one of the kinds of particle in a nucleus
meet len – substance with atoms all holding the same number of protons
um, a ruin! – an element with 92 protons in every nucleus

2 What are the names of the two kinds of particles in the nuclei of atoms?

3 What other kind of particle makes up a complete atom?

4 Look at your hand. Do you believe that it is made of atoms? What evidence do you know about that supports the idea that all substances are made of atoms?

The first pictures from radioactivity

More than a hundred years ago, Henri Becquerel checked some photographic film that he had kept stored in the dark, wrapped in thick black paper. He was surprised to find that a patch of the film had become foggy, as if it had been in the light. There had been a small sample of uranium ore next to the film. The only explanation of the fogginess was that uranium ore had affected the film.

Whatever had caused the fogging of the film must have been able to pass through paper. People began to use the word *radioactive* to describe the uranium ore.

▶ *Ordinary light and the radiation from uranium can both fog photographic film. How did Henri Becquerel know that it wasn't light that had fogged his film?*

Radiation

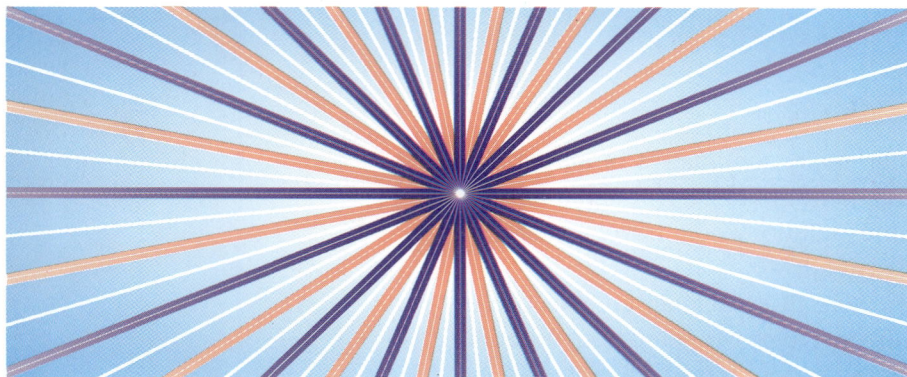

▲ Anything that 'radiates' spreads out from a centre or source. That is what happens with radioactive effects – radiation from a source.

▲ Marie Curie discovered more radioactive elements – radium and polonium.

Radiation from a radioactive substance affects materials that it travels through. It causes ionisation. That is how we detect radiation. You can read more about ionisation on pages 226 and 227.

Detecting the radiation

▲ This man is wearing a 'film badge'. He is exposed to low levels of radiation every day. The more radiation, the more the film inside the badge is affected.

▲ A GM tube provides a measurement of the level of radiation coming from a particular place.

PHYSICS

Three different penetrating effects

Materials absorb, or stop, radiation. Scientists discovered that the radiation from different radioactive sources could travel different distances through air and other materials before being absorbed. Some radiation penetrates further, and some not so far. From studies of different radioactive materials, scientists identified three distinct levels of penetrating ability.

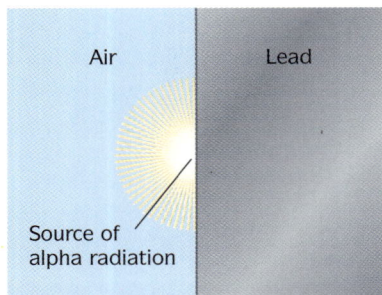

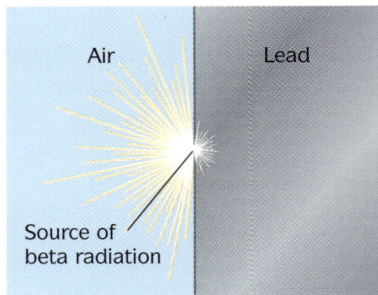

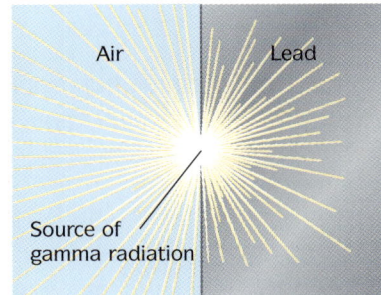

⏶ Three types of radiation.

Some of the radiation could travel through many centimetres of air and even through a few centimetres of solid lead. Some could get through a few centimetres of air, or thin layers of lead. Some radiation could travel a short distance in air, but could not get through lead at all.

The scientists concluded that since there were three distinct abilities to penetrate material, there must be three distinct types of radiation from radioactive sources. They called them **alpha** radiation, **beta** radiation and **gamma** radiation.

▶ *Which is better at absorbing radiation, lead or air?*

Observing penetrating abilities

Your teacher might show you the different penetrating abilities of alpha, beta and gamma radiations.

The distance between the source and the GM tube can stay the same. Different thicknesses of absorber have different effects on the three types of radiation. Graphs can show the patterns.

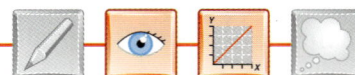

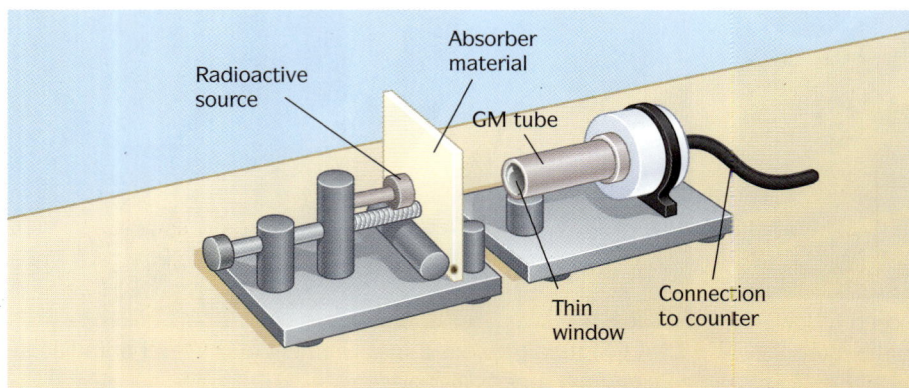

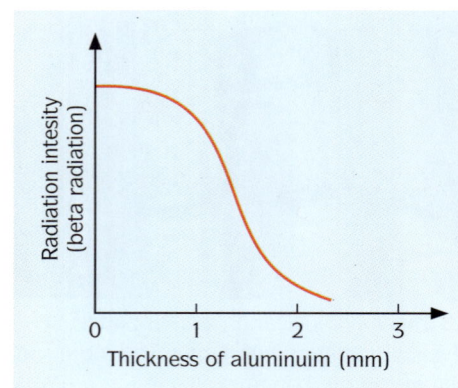

PHYSICS

Thickness control

Radioactive materials can be used in industrial processes, like paper-making, to control thickness of material. Radiation can penetrate through the paper but if the paper becomes thicker, less radiation gets through. A detector can measure the radiation that penetrates sheets of new material, and the information can be used to control the pressure of rollers being used to make the sheets.

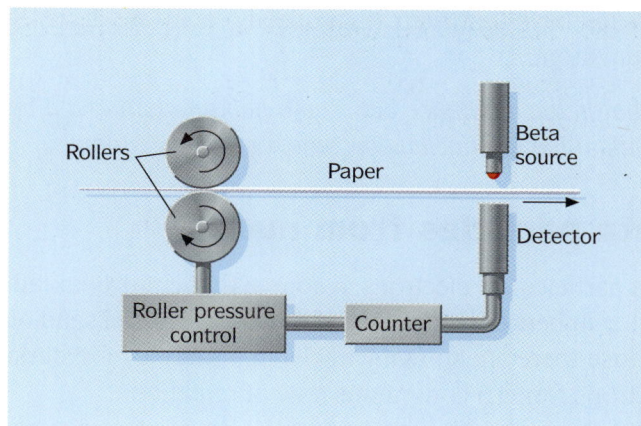

Three different responses to magnetism

Just as alpha, beta and gamma radiations can travel through different distances, they also behave differently when they travel through magnetic fields.

Magnets have no effect at all on gamma radiation, just as they have no effect on light or X-rays. But magnets bend the paths of alpha and beta radiations – in opposite directions.

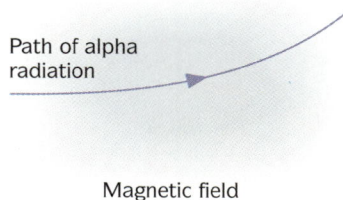

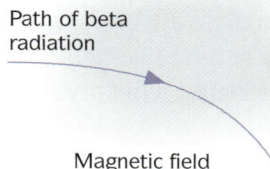

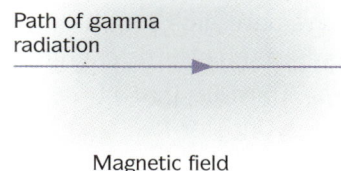

Path of alpha radiation — Magnetic field

Path of beta radiation — Magnetic field

Path of gamma radiation — Magnetic field

The paths of moving electrons are affected by magnetic fields. Beta radiation is affected in exactly the same way. That is evidence for saying that beta radiation is a flow of fast-moving electrons out from a radioactive source. The electrons in beta radiation are often called **beta particles**.

Electrons, or beta particles, all have negative electric charge. Alpha radiation is bent in the opposite direction, because it is a stream of positively charge particles. These are **alpha particles**.

▶ *The paths of alpha and beta particles are bent by a magnetic field. Why are they bent in opposite directions? Why do gamma rays keep going in a straight line?*

Identifying alpha particles

If you leave some material that emits alpha radiation inside a closed container for a while, you will find that helium very slowly builds up. Helium is the element with the second smallest nuclei, with only two protons in each one.

A small cluster of neutrons and protons can break free from a large nucleus. That is what happens when a nucleus emits an alpha particle. Once alpha

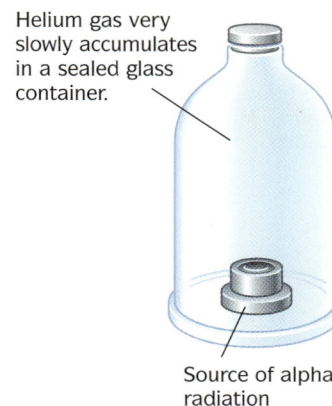

Helium gas very slowly accumulates in a sealed glass container.

Source of alpha radiation

PHYSICS

particles have lost their high speed, each one is just a nucleus of a new helium atom.

▶ *What is the difference between a helium atom and a helium nucleus? How could a helium nucleus become a complete atom?*

Beta particles from nuclei

Beta particles are electrons. A source that emits beta radiation is made up of huge numbers of nuclei. One at a time, the nuclei send out the electrons. It is because there are so many nuclei in a sample of material that the stream of electrons forms a continuous flow of radiation.

But there is a problem with the idea of electrons coming out of nuclei. Nuclei do not have any electrons inside them. What seems to happen is that a neutron can change into a proton and an electron. The proton stays inside the nucleus and the electron flies out at high speed.

▶ *What happens to the number of protons inside a nucleus when a beta particle is emitted?*

Gamma rays

Gamma rays have high penetrating ability but they are not affected by magnets. They have no electric charge and no mass. They behave like radio, light and X-rays. They are part of the electromagnetic spectrum, which you can read about in Chapter Two (A spectrum of light).

Ionisation

Alpha, beta and gamma radiations can all ionise material. As they pass through the material they knock electrons out of atoms. Neutral atoms in the material become positive ions. The three main types of radiation have different abilities to ionise.

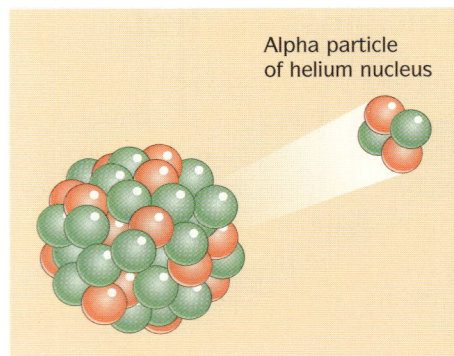

🔺 Alpha radiation consists of helium nuclei emitted from larger nuclei.

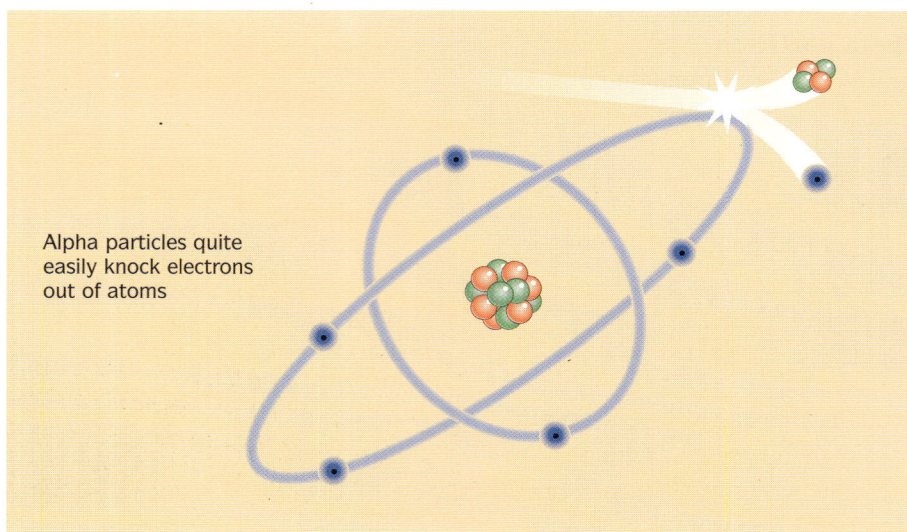

Neutron		Proton		Electron
🟢	Changes into	🔴	Plus	•

🔺 Beta particles are formed from neutrons.

🔺 Gamma rays are electromagnetic radiation.

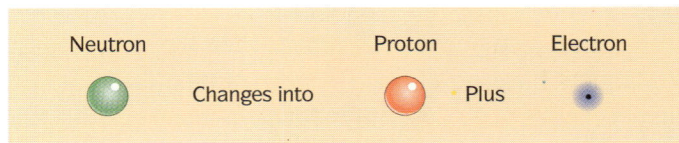

Alpha particles quite easily knock electrons out of atoms

🔺 Ionisation by radiation.

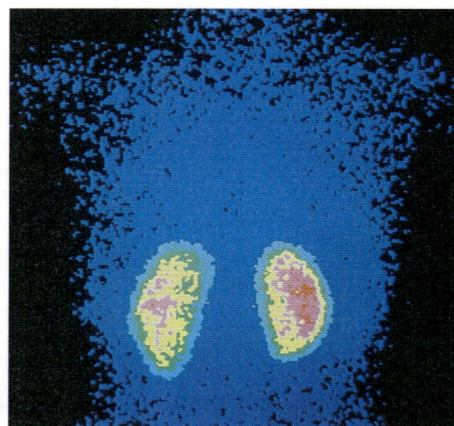

🔺 We can make use of the fact that gamma radiation can penetrate material. A source of gamma rays inside a body provides radiation that can still be measured on the outside, using a gamma camera.

Alpha particles are big and heavy compared to other types of radiation. They easily knock electrons out of atoms. They are strongly ionising. That is why they do not travel very far through materials. They lose energy every time they cause an ionisation of an atom, and they soon run out of energy and slow down.

Beta particles pass more easily between atoms and exert smaller forces than alpha particles do. They do not knock electrons out of atoms so easily. They do not ionise so much, and keep their energy for longer.

Gamma radiation ionises weakly. A gamma ray can pass many atoms without interacting with electrons at all. Just occasionally a gamma ray will give some of its energy to an electron to knock it out of an atom.

The ionising ability of radiation can damage and even kill living cells. In radiotherapy, radiation kills cancer cells. Ionisation in the cells stops the normal chemical reactions from going on.

▶ When an alpha particle ionises an atom, what happens to:

   a the alpha particle
   b one of the electrons of the atom?

It is sometimes helpful to use a story to help to picture how small things behave. Imagine a forest as a material. Then imagine a bus as an alpha particle, a motor cycle as a beta particle and a golf ball as a gamma ray. The bus quickly crashes into trees, does a lot of damage, and does not get very far. The motor cycle travels further and does less damage on each collision. The golf ball is likely to travel the furthest, and have the least effect.

Counting protons and neutrons

Different elements have nuclei with different numbers of protons, starting with hydrogen. Hydrogen is element number one because it has only one proton per nucleus. Helium, with two protons, is element number two.

The chemical behaviour of an element depends on how many protons it has in its nucleus. Protons have positive electric charge. In neutral atoms there are just the right number of negatively charged electrons to balance the positive charge. Chemical reactions happen because of electrical forces between atoms. You can read more about this in Chemistry, Chapter Nine.

Carbon, for example, always has six protons per nucleus. Most carbon atoms also have six neutrons, but some have seven and some have eight. Neutrons do not affect the electric charge of an atom, so they have no influence on electrical forces or on chemical reactions. The number of protons in a nucleus is called its **atomic number**. The total number of protons and neutrons is called its **mass number**.

The forms of an element with different numbers of neutrons are called **isotopes** of the element. Carbon has several isotopes.

🔺 Radiation can kill bacteria in food, so that it can be stored for long times without going rotten or causing food poisoning.

🔺 John Wayne – was it smoking or ionising radiation that killed him?

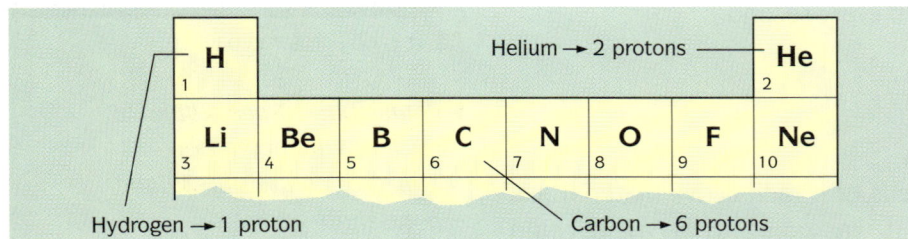

🔺 Part of the periodic table, showing the number of protons in the nuclei of each element.

Isotope	Number of protons (atomic number)	Number of neutrons	Number of protons and neutrons (mass number)	Abbreviation
Carbon–10	6	4	10	$^{10}_{6}C$
Carbon–11	6	5	11	$^{11}_{6}C$
Carbon–12	6	6	12	$^{12}_{6}C$
Carbon–13	6	7	13	$^{13}_{6}C$
Carbon–14	6	8	14	$^{14}_{6}C$

🔺 All carbon atoms have six protons but they don't all have the same number of neutrons.

Some nuclear decays

The process of giving out radiation is sometimes called **decay** or **disintegration**. But the nucleus does not fall apart, it just changes. Once a nucleus has changed in a particular way, it can never repeat exactly the same process. It happens only once for that nucleus.

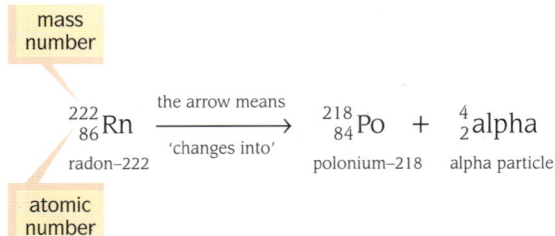

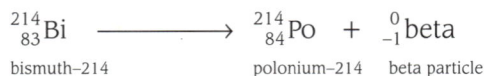

mass number

$$^{222}_{86}Rn \xrightarrow{\text{the arrow means 'changes into'}} ^{218}_{84}Po + ^{4}_{2}\text{alpha}$$

radon–222 polonium–218 alpha particle

atomic number

$$^{214}_{83}Bi \longrightarrow ^{214}_{84}Po + ^{0}_{-1}\text{beta}$$

bismuth–214 polonium–214 beta particle

▶ Nuclei of polonium–218 (symbol $^{218}_{84}Po$) give out alpha particles and turn into nuclei of lead–208 (symbol $^{208}_{82}Pb$). Write down the nuclear change showing the atomic numbers and mass numbers of each particle.

Stability, instability and randomness

Most of the nuclei in your body are stable. They will never emit radiation, or decay. But a small proportion are unstable. These are nuclei of radioactive material.

One radioactive material in your body is potassium–40. It has unstable nuclei. They emit beta radiation. There are enough potassium–40 nuclei for about 4000 of them to decay in your body in every second.

This is the process involved:

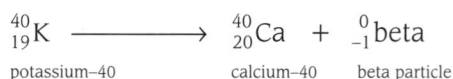

$$^{40}_{19}K \longrightarrow ^{40}_{20}Ca + ^{0}_{-1}\text{beta}$$

potassium–40 calcium–40 beta particle

If we could pick out an individual nucleus of a radioactive material like potassium–40 we could never say when it was going to decay. It could happen within a fraction of a second, or not for billions of years. In a sample of the material, nuclei decay at random.

▶ How many neutrons are there in a nucleus of carbon–11?

Alpha particles have an atomic number of 2 (matching the number of protons in each one) and a mass number of 4 (matching the total number of protons and neutrons). We write them as $^{4}_{2}$alpha. Beta particles have no neutrons or protons, so they have a mass number 0. They have a negative charge, so we say their 'atomic number' is –1. We write them as $^{0}_{-1}$beta

🔺 This object is radioactive.

▶ Potassium–39 has stable nuclei. Write down how atoms of potassium–39 and potassium–40 are:

a the same
b different.

Fall in activity

Carbon–14 is a radioactive isotope. It has unstable nuclei which emit beta particles and change into nitrogen nuclei. The nitrogen nuclei are stable.

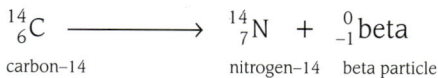

$$^{14}_{6}\text{C} \longrightarrow {}^{14}_{7}\text{N} + {}^{0}_{-1}\text{beta}$$

carbon–14   nitrogen–14   beta particle

Each carbon–14 nucleus can only decay once. In a small sample of carbon–14 the nuclei, one by one, turn into nitrogen. After a very long time (many thousands of years) nearly all of the carbon-14 nuclei will have decayed into nitrogen. Then the sample will no longer be radioactive.

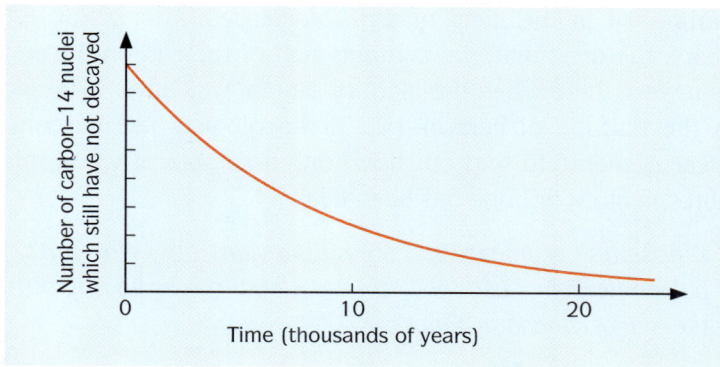

Half-life

Half-life is the time taken for half of the nuclei in a sample of a radioactive isotope to decay. Different isotopes have different half-lives, varying from fractions of seconds up to billions of years. The more unstable the nuclei, the shorter the half-life of the isotope.

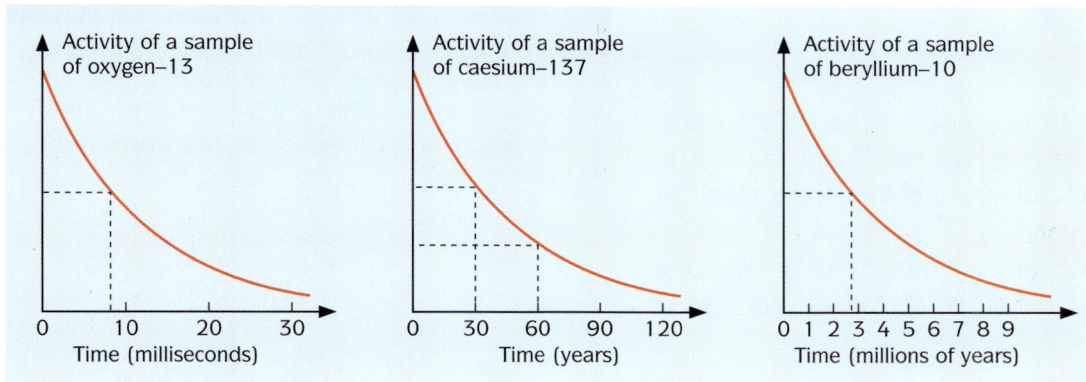

🔺 Carbon–14 nuclei, one by one, turn into nitrogen–14.

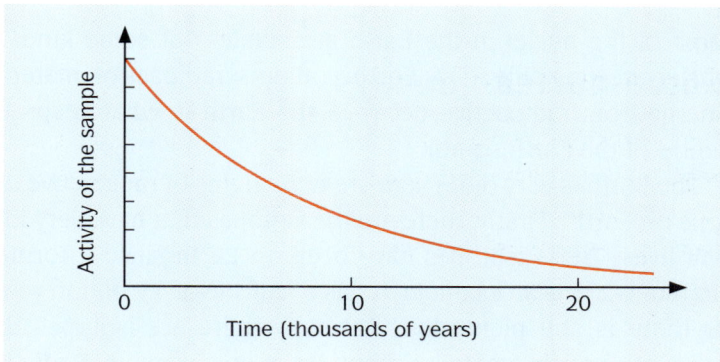

🔺 A sample of carbon–14 becomes less and less radioactive.

🔺 Spot the difference.

▶ *Which graph shows the shortest half-life?*

▶ *How long does it take for a sample of caesium–137 to lose three-quarters of its original activity?*

Computer simulation of decay

Computers can simulate the randomness of radioactive decay. They reproduce data with patterns that are similar to those produced by real decay.

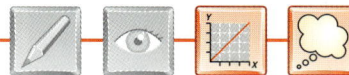

Radioactivity and the age of things

Living things contain a lot of carbon. Most of it is carbon–12, which has nuclei with six protons and six neutrons. The nuclei are stable. But carbon-14 nuclei are not stable. Carbon–14 is radioactive.

Living plants take in carbon from the air. Animals take in carbon from plants. When a living thing dies, it stops taking in any more carbon–14. As time goes by, carbon–14 nuclei turn into nitrogen nuclei. The amount of carbon–14 in the dead material decreases. After about 5700 years, the dead material contains half of the carbon–14 nuclei that were there when the plant or animal was alive. 5700 years is the half-life of carbon–14. Archaeologists use carbon–14 measurements to find out how long a sample of wood, plant fibres in cloth or bone has been dead.

▶ *Dinosaurs became extinct 65 million years ago. Why can't palaeontologists use the carbon–14 method for finding out the age of dinosaur bones?*

Radioactivity of the Earth

Most of the nuclei in the Earth are stable. But some kinds of nuclei are unstable. The Earth contains radioactive material. Energy from radioactive decay in the Earth is what keeps the centre of the Earth so hot.

The Earth is very old. There are two origins of radioactive isotope on Earth. Firstly, there are the isotopes that have very long half-lives. These isotopes have been on Earth since it formed. Uranium–238 is an example. It has a half-life of 4.5 billion years, so there is still plenty left. Secondly there are isotopes that are continuously created. Carbon–14 is one example. Radiation from space produces nuclei of carbon–14 in the air.

Dating rocks

Rubidium is a metal found in the rocks of the Earth's crust. Most rubidium on the Earth is rubidium–85 and the rest is rubidium–87. Since the two isotopes are chemically identical they always exist together.

Rubidium–87 is radioactive, but only just. It has a very long half-life of 47 billion years, and so its activity is very low. It decays to strontium–87 by beta decay:

$$^{87}_{37}Rb \longrightarrow ^{87}_{38}Sr + ^{0}_{-1}beta$$

rubidium–87   strontium–87

Wherever solid rock holds rubidium–87 there will also be some strontium–87 produced by radioactive decay. In molten rock the rubidium and strontium can easily separate and spread out. But solid rock traps the strontium as well as the rubidium. The amount of strontium–87 and rubidium–87 in a rock sample shows for how long the strontium has been accumulating. It shows how long the rock has been solid.

▶ *Why does the amount of strontium–87 in a rock increase at exactly the same rate as the amount of rubidium-87 decreases?*

▶ *When a rubidium nucleus decays, why does the total number of particles in the nucleus stay the same?*

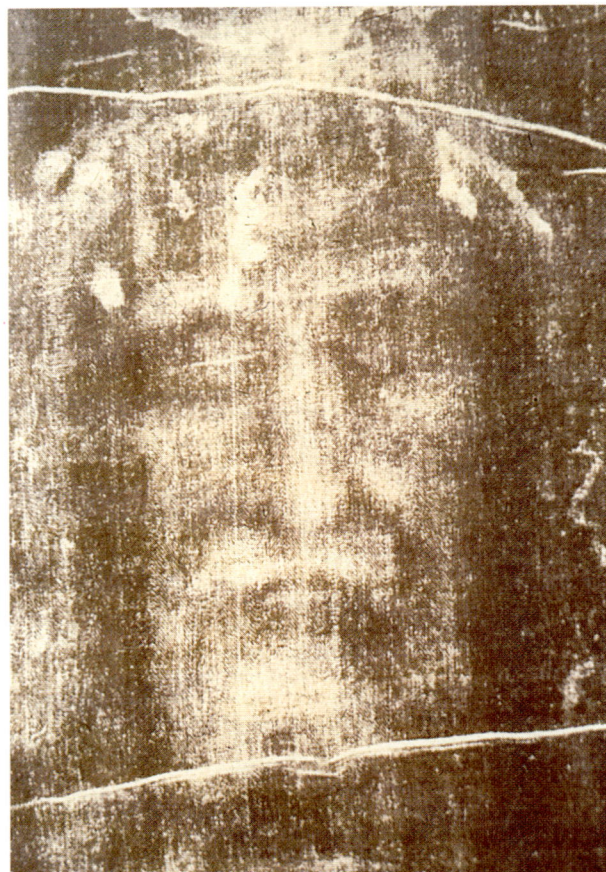

▲ Some people have wondered if the Turin shroud was wrapped around the body of Christ, about 2000 years ago. The level of radioactivity of the cloth shows that it is made of material that was living and growing about 800 years ago.

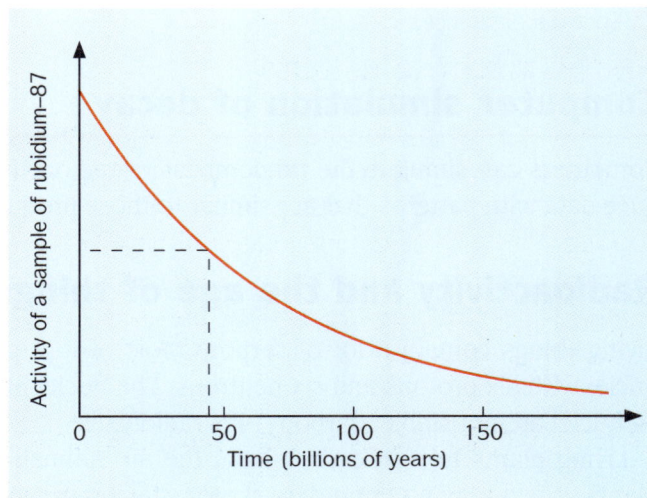

▲ A graph showing the decay of rubidium–87

Natural background radiation

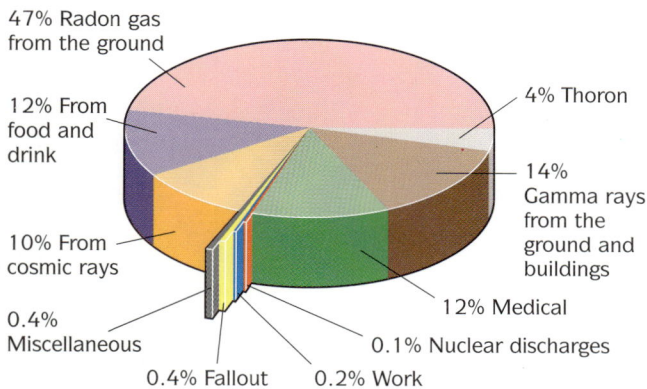

47% Radon gas from the ground

12% From food and drink

10% From cosmic rays

0.4% Miscellaneous

0.4% Fallout

0.2% Work

0.1% Nuclear discharges

12% Medical

14% Gamma rays from the ground and buildings

4% Thoron

81% Radon gas from the ground

4.0%

3.2%

4.0%

6.3%

1.3%

<0.1   <0.1   0.1   0.1

🔺 Radiation dose to people is measured in millisievert. The average annual dose to people in the UK is 2.5 millisievert. Nearly all of the radiation comes from radioactive material which is naturally around us all of the time. It is called **background radiation**.

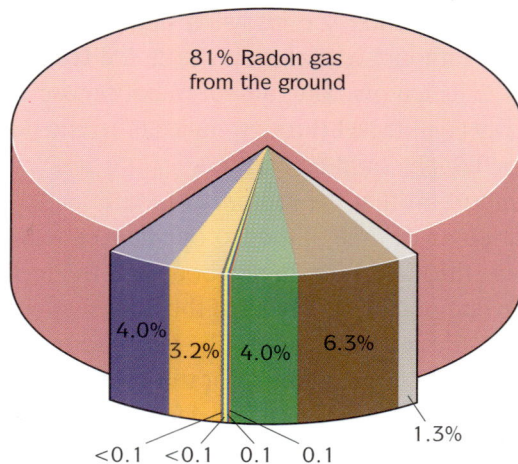

🔺 In Cornwall the yearly radiation dose to people from natural background radiation is three times higher than in the rest of the UK. That is because of radioactive gas called radon that seeps out of the rock.

Measuring background count

You can use a GM tube connected to a counter to obtain a radioactivity count for a one-minute period. Different one-minute counts give slightly different results. So it is necessary to make several measurements, and work out the average.

▶ *If you measured background count on the ground and then in a high-flying aircraft, what difference would there be?*

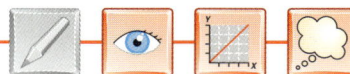

Variation in background count

You can investigate whether background count varies during a 24-hour period. A data-logger will record the counts over 24 hours, for several days. Graphs of the results will help to identify the variations, if there are any.

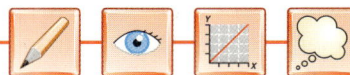

Radon and leukaemia

In Cornwall, the granite rock contains a lot of radioactive uranium. Decay of this uranium produces nuclei of radon, which is also a radioactive material. Radon is a gas which seeps up through the rock and accumulates inside buildings. In Derbyshire, radon easily gets to the surface because the limestone rock has many small holes and cracks for the gas to move through. People in Cornwall and Derbyshire are (slightly) more likely to develop leukaemia. You may be given a worksheet with some data to analyse.

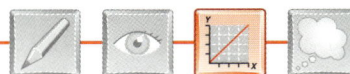

Choosing isotopes as medical tracers

In hospitals, medical staff can give radioactive material to people to drink, or in injections, or to breathe into their lungs. Then the radiation can be 'traced' from outside the body, to build up pictures of what is going on inside. The radioactive materials are called **tracers**.

Isotopes which give off gamma radiation are usually best as tracers. The gamma rays can travel through material to the outside, and they cause less ionisation which could be harmful.

It is important that the radioactive material stays in the person's body for the right length of time. If the isotope has a short half-life then by the time it has spread through the patient's body and the medical staff have set up their detecting equipment, nearly all of the nuclei will have decayed. If the half-life is too long the material will not be very radioactive, so that the patient will need to take in a large quantity for the detectors to pick up enough radiation. Half-lives of a few hours or a few days are most suitable.

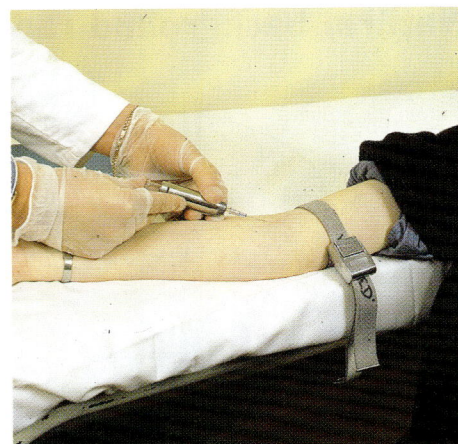

Radioactive isotope	Half-life	Radiation emitted
calcium–45	165 days	beta, gamma
cobalt–60	5.26 years	beta, gamma
strontium–90	28 years	beta
xenon–133 (gas)	5 days	gamma
iridium–192	74 days	gamma
polonium–210	138 days	alpha

▶ *What are the important factors for choice of medical tracer isotopes?*

▶ *Why is polonium–210 not suitable for medical use?*

▶ *Which isotope would you use to trace an outline of the inside of a person's lungs?*

Energy from nuclear changes

In a chemical reaction, the total mass of substances does not change. But when a nucleus decays, the total mass of the particles decreases. The 'disappearance' of mass makes energy available. Einstein's famous equation, $E = mc^2$, predicts how much energy (E) is available from a certain amount of mass (m). (C represents the speed of electromagnetic waves.)

Radioactive decays inside the Earth provide energy to keep it hot. Radioactive decays inside heart pacemakers supply the energy to keep them going. Very large amounts of energy are made available by completely splitting large nuclei. That is what happens in a nuclear power station. The process is called **nuclear fission**.

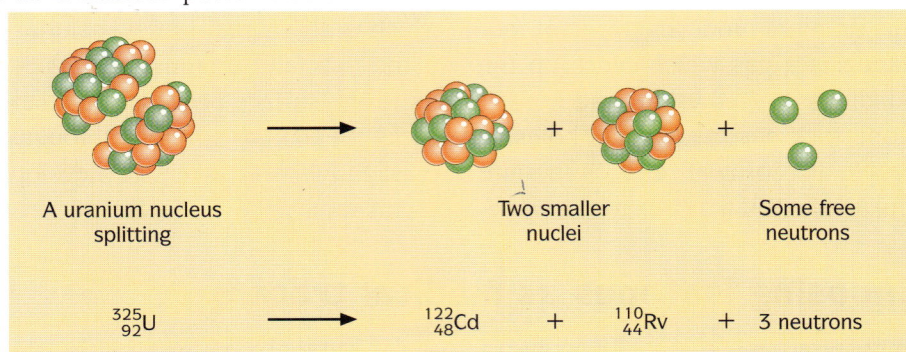

▲ Inside a nuclear reactor.

Fission of a uranium nucleus has to be set off by a neutron which enters the nucleus. So in a power station there must be a supply of neutrons to keep uranium fissioning. When a uranium nucleus splits, it also sets a few neutrons free. These neutrons can go into other uranium nuclei and cause them to split, provided that the neutrons have the right speed.

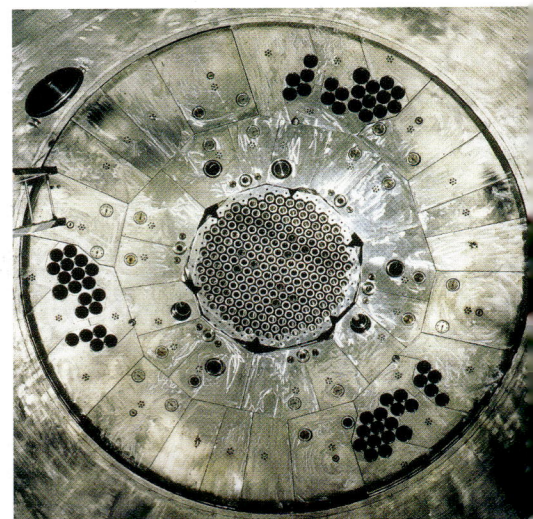

A uranium nucleus splitting	Two smaller nuclei	Some free neutrons
$^{325}_{92}U$	$^{122}_{48}Cd$ + $^{110}_{44}Rv$	+ 3 neutrons

▲ Nuclear fission.

The uranium fuel in a nuclear reactor is inside metal cylinders. Neutrons with high energy speed out of these 'fuel rods' into the surrounding material. They bounce around among the atoms of the surrounding material, losing energy and slowing down. Their speed has been 'moderated'. Eventually some of them go back into the fuel, and cause fission.

▶ *What does moderator material surrounding the fuel rods do to neutrons?*

Chain reactions

A neutron is needed to set off the fission of a uranium nucleus. But the nucleus breaks up into two smaller nuclei plus a few free neutrons. These free neutrons can cause fission in more nuclei. It is a **chain reaction**.

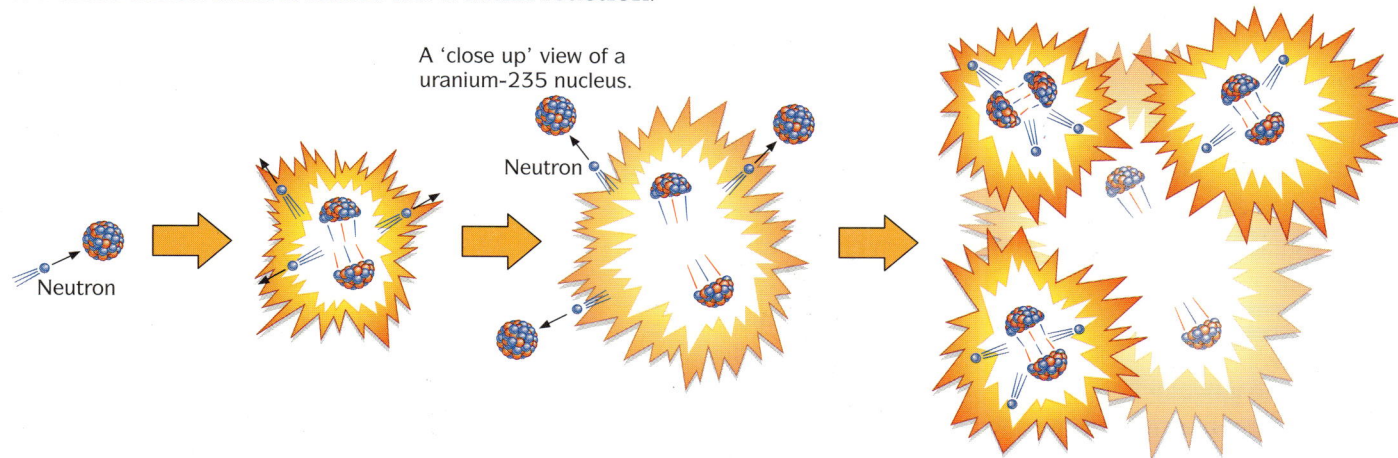

A 'close up' view of a uranium-235 nucleus.

Neutron

Neutron

In a nuclear bomb, the chain reaction is allowed to run wild. More and more nuclei are made to split, so that vast energy is transferred in a very short time. But in a nuclear power station the energy release must be steady and continuous. Only one neutron from each splitting nucleus, on average, must be allowed to split another nucleus.

To help to keep the chain reaction under control, nuclear reactors have **control rods**. They are made of elements which have nuclei which easily take in neutrons. The control rods can be pushed further into the reactor to soak up more neutrons, or pulled out to allow more neutrons to go back into the fuel.

▶ *What would happen to the chain reaction in a nuclear reactor if the control rods absorbed too many neutrons?*

Problems with nuclear power stations

A nuclear power station cannot become a nuclear bomb. The fuel is not of the right kind. But there can be accidents which spread radioactive waste into the environment.

Nuclear reactors produce waste in two ways. Firstly, the two small nuclei produced when a bigger nucleus splits are usually unstable – or radioactive. Secondly, neutrons coming from the fissions are often soaked up by nuclei in the material of the reactor. This change in the make-up of the nuclei can make them unstable.

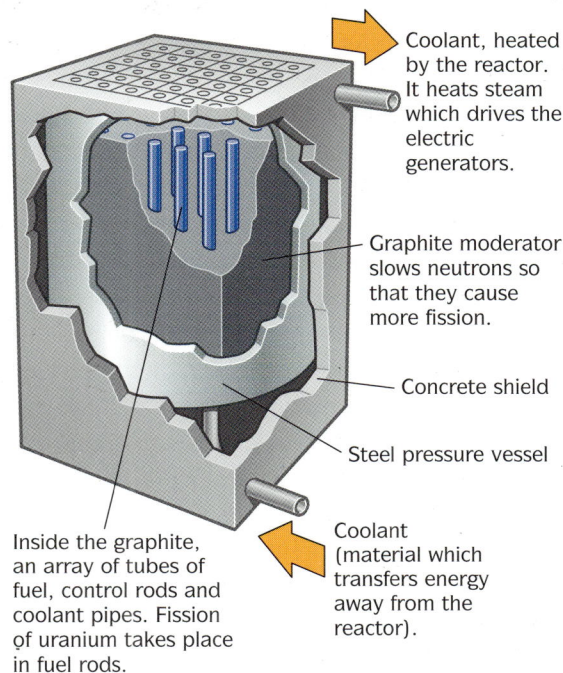

Coolant, heated by the reactor. It heats steam which drives the electric generators.

Graphite moderator slows neutrons so that they cause more fission.

Concrete shield

Steel pressure vessel

Coolant (material which transfers energy away from the reactor).

Inside the graphite, an array of tubes of fuel, control rods and coolant pipes. Fission of uranium takes place in fuel rods.

At Chernobyl in the Ukraine, a reactor caught fire, and tonnes of radioactive material spread across Europe, as far as the UK. The material was spread thinly across a vast area. But plants absorbed the material, and animals ate the plants. Sheep farmers in places like North Wales could not sell their sheep for months, because of the high levels of radioactive material in the sheep's bodies.

When a nuclear power station grows too old to be useful, it has to be closed down. The problem then is that the material in and around the reactors is radioactive. Safely sealing the reactors so that material cannot escape is very expensive.

▶ *How do nuclear reactors produce radioactive waste material?*

▶ *How is the waste material a hazard to health?*

Summary

- Radiation from radioactive sources can ionise material.
- Most elements around us are not radioactive but are made of atoms with stable nuclei.
- Some nuclei are unstable, and material which contains unstable nuclei is radioactive.
- Radioactivity involves emission of particles (alpha and beta) or electromagnetic radiation (gamma) from unstable nuclei.
- Some radioactive material can be found naturally in the environment.
- Some radiation arrives from space.
- The continuous radiation from natural material, from space, and from material generated by people, and dispersed into the environment, is called background radiation.
- Alpha radiation is a flow of alpha particles or helium nuclei. These ionise strongly but do not penetrate very far through materials.
- Beta radiation is a flow of beta particles or electrons. These ionise and penetrate moderately.
- Gamma radiation is a flow of gamma rays, which are a type of electromagnetic radiation. They ionise weakly but penetrate strongly.
- A radioactive material gradually loses its activity as its nuclei decay.
- The time taken for half of the nuclei in a sample of radioactive material to decay is the half-life of the material.
- Ionising radiation can cause cancer but can also be used to cure cancer.
- Gamma radiation can be used to inspect inaccessible places, like inside the human body or in pipelines, because it can penetrate through material.
- The level of radioactivity of ancient plant and animal material can be used to find out how long it is since the material was alive.
- The amount of certain radioactive materials in rock can be compared with the amount of materials produced by radioactive decay to find out how long the rock has been solid.
- Radioactive decay releases energy, as do the process of fission (splitting of large nuclei) and fusion (joining of small nuclei).
- Fission of uranium provides the energy source in nuclear power stations.
- Fusion of hydrogen and other small nuclei provides the energy source in the Sun.

NUCLEAR FUSION – THE POWER OF THE SUN

The Sun is a nuclear furnace, where hydrogen nuclei are squeezed so hard together that they join to form bigger nuclei. This joining together of small nuclei is **nuclear fusion.** Fusion of hydrogen nuclei is the source of the Sun's energy.

On Earth people have succeeded in fusing hydrogen nuclei together, but only by creating huge temperatures. In a 'hydrogen bomb' an ordinary fission bomb creates the high temperature that pushes the hydrogen nuclei together. A hydrogen bomb is the most destructive thing ever made by people.

It is possible that some time in the future fusion will be used for peaceful purposes, in a new kind of power station. Such power stations would produce very little nuclear waste, and very little pollution in the form of gases like carbon dioxide. The problem that scientists have is that hydrogen nuclei are protons, and they all have positive electric charge. They repel each other until they get very close together. Only at high temperatures do the protons have enough speed to overcome their electrical repulsion and get close enough together to join.

Revision Questions

1 Copy this table and use information in the chapter to fill in the gaps.

Type of radiation	Penetrating ability	Electric charge	Ionising ability	What it is
Alpha	weak			
Beta	medium	negative	medium	electrons
Gamma		none	weak	high frequency electromagnetic radiation

▲ Properties of alpha, beta and gamma radiation.

2 Why are gamma rays more useful than alpha particles for medical examinations?

3 Name one difference between a proton and a neutron.

4 a What is background radiation?
  b Name two isotopes in your body which make it radioactive.

5 Why are your chances of getting cancer increased slightly if you:
  a become an airline pilot
  b live in Cornwall?

6 What is the difference between fission and fusion?

7 Copy and complete this table of isotopes.

Isotope	Atomic number (no. of protons)	No. of neutrons
Helium–4	2	
Nitrogen–15		8
Sodium–24	11	
Chlorine–32		15
Stronium–88	38	

8 a What is the link between 'penetrating ability' and 'ionising ability' of different types of radiation?
  b Why is this link very important when choosing sources of radiation as medical tracers?

9 Draw a diagram of a neutral atom of lithium–7, showing the protons, neutrons and electrons. (Lithium–7 can be written as $^{7}_{3}Li$.)

10 Strontium-90 has a half-life of 28 years. How long will it be before a sample of strontium-90 has one-quarter of its original radioactivity?

11 A GM tube and counter were used to measure the activity of a radioactive source at 5-minute intervals. These are the results:

Time (minutes)	0	5	10	15	20	25	30	35	40	45	50	55	60
Count rate (becquerel)	14	13	9	6.5	5.5	4.8	4	3.5	3.4	2.7	2.3	2	1.9

1 becquerel = 1 count per second

  a Plot the results on a graph, with time on the horizontal axis (x-axis).
  b Which point looks like a mistake?
  c Use the graph to find out the half-life of the material.

12 What is the difference in the make-up of ^{12}C and ^{14}C?

13 Why does a magnetic field affect alpha and beta radiation but not gamma radiation?

14 Why does the amount of strontium–87 in some rocks increase as time goes by?

15 In a nuclear power station:
  a how are fast-moving neutrons slowed down
  b how are neutrons 'mopped up' to keep their numbers under control?

16 Summarise the evidence for the existence of three distinct types of radiation from radioactive sources.

17 Explain how it is possible for beta particles to be electrons, when there are no electrons inside nuclei.

18 A local council engineer wants to locate a leak from an underground pipe which passes under your school playing fields. The engineer intends to put some radioactive material into the pipe. Where the material leaks, its radiation will be more strongly detectable from above by using a GM tube. Select one of the isotopes from the table, for the engineer to use. Explain your choice.

Liquid	Half-life	Radiation emitted
A	0.001s	alpha
B	5 hours	gamma
C	25 days	alpha
D	100 years	beta
E	10 hours	beta

19 You have started work in a factory which supplies radioactive isotopes to hospitals.
  a What material would you use for transporting beta sources?
  b One customer wants a radioactive source with an activity of 200 becquerel at 9.00 am on Monday morning, but you want to deliver it at 5.00 pm on Friday evening. The half-life of the material is 8 hours. What activity should the material have when you deliver it?

CHAPTER SIXTEEN

Physics help

■ What Physics gives us

Physics gives us the power to predict the behaviour of materials and their motion.

Physics gives us help in imagining things that are too small to see.

Physics gives us access to the wider Universe.

This section of the book is about the principles of Physics. You can study this section on its own or you can look up things when you need help while you are working on other chapters.

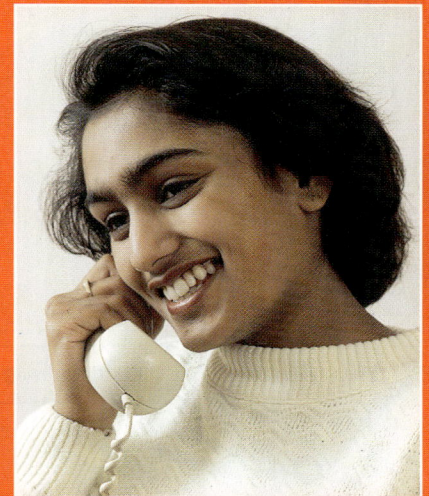

Physics gives us many ways to communicate.

The European story of technology, Physics, and how people live

Ideas and applications of Physics

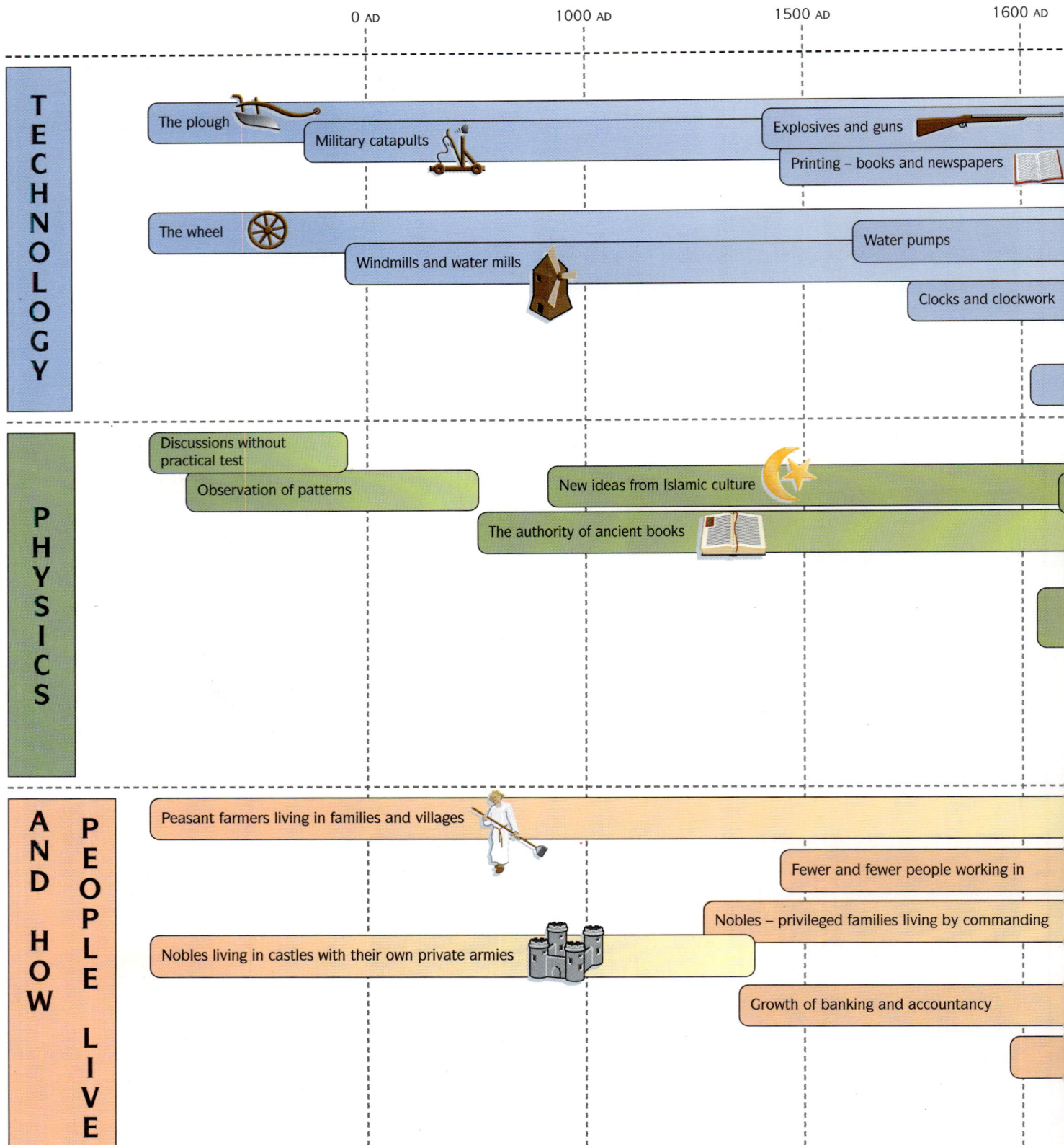

0 AD   1000 AD   1500 AD   1600 AD

T E C H N O L O G Y

- The plough
- Military catapults
- Explosives and guns
- Printing – books and newspapers
- The wheel
- Windmills and water mills
- Water pumps
- Clocks and clockwork

P H Y S I C S

- Discussions without practical test
- Observation of patterns
- New ideas from Islamic culture
- The authority of ancient books

A N D H O W P E O P L E L I V E

- Peasant farmers living in families and villages
- Fewer and fewer people working in
- Nobles – privileged families living by commanding
- Nobles living in castles with their own private armies
- Growth of banking and accountancy

Nitrogen fixation

Nuclear bombs

Radio

TV

Steam engines for driving pumps

Steam engines for transport

Steam turbines

Electric cells

Electric motors, generators and transformers

Vacuum pumps

Internal combustion engine

Telescopes and microscopes

Computers

New ideas from other cultures

New ideas of things that are very big (in space) and things that are very small (such as micro organisms)

People daring to ask questions and try out their ideas

Use of Mathematics for accurate and reliable predictions of how things behave

- The Sun, not the Earth, is the centre of the Solar system

- Gases could be made of particles

- All substances could be made of particles

- Most of the electromagnetic spectrum is invisible

- There are many things that can never be precisely predicted

- Electricity and magnetism are two versions of the same thing

- The energy of light waves is lumpy

- A vacuum can exist

- Light travels in the same way as waves

- Some of the small particles inside atoms are clusters of even smaller particles

- We can predict motion of bodies using the idea of 'force'

- 'Energy' is the ability to do useful work but it can also raise temperature

- Atoms are clusters of even smaller particles

- The Universe began in a 'Big Bang'

agriculture but more and more people working in jobs which help to make agriculture more productive

the work of villagers

International industries

Rapid population growth and European invasion of other parts of the world

Growing environmental problems

Health and safety

The most common laboratory accidents:

- burning by hot items and corrosive liquids
- poisoning by gases, liquids and powders
- eye damage by hot materials, corrosive liquids or sharp points
- cuts from glass and sharp instruments
- falls due to obstacles or spills on the floor
- electric shock.

You can find out about possible dangers by looking at hazard warnings on labels, from laboratory rules, from your teacher and from your own experience.

Hazard warning labels

You can read about hazard warning labels and carrying out risk assessment in Chapter One (Experiments and investigations).

HIGHLY FLAMMABLE   RADIOACTIVE   RISK OF ELECTRIC SHOCK (DANGEROUS VOLTAGE)

DANGER   LASER RADIATION   NON-IONISING RADIATION

EXPLOSIVE   OXIDIZING   CORROSIVE

HIGHLY FLAMMABLE   HARMFUL or IRRITANT   TOXIC

🔺 These signs tell you of hazards in a laboratory area.

🔺 These signs on bottles warn you of hazards of the material inside.

Laboratory rules

Every laboratory in schools, hospitals and factories has clear safety rules.

MODEL RULES FOR LABORATORY STAFF

Much of the work in the laboratory is concerned with the handling of specimens that may be infectious. Office staff are not required to come into direct contact with these materials but may accidentally do so when handling bags and packages containing specimens. Such workers, in addition to following the general precautions outlined above, should also take the following safety measures.

1. If you work in an office that has direct access into the laboratory, wear a coat or gown, like the other laboratory staff.
2. Wash your hands after you have been into the laboratory and may have come into contact with laboratory items or materials that could be infectious.
3. Never lick stamps or labels. Use a roller pad, damp sponge or self-adhesive labels.
4. If you are required to package specimens, only do so if the containers are in a sealed transport bag. If there is any sign of breakage or leakage do not touch the bag. Report it to your supervisor immediately.

If you obey these simple rules you will be as safe as anyone else who works in the hospital, BUT if you are ill tell your doctor where you work.

🔺 A set of rules in a hospital laboratory published by HMSO.

North Western High School

Lab Safety Rules

1. Do not eat in the labs.
2. Do not run in the labs.
3. Keep bags out of the way.
4. Wear eye protection.

🔺 School labs have some of the same hazards and some that are different.

Risk assessments

Before you do practical work your teacher or your instructions will tell you whether you need to do a risk assessment. A risk assessment involves making a list of everything that could possibly be dangerous, and how you can reduce the risk as much as possible.

Quantities and units

Measurements are an important part of any science, but especially Physics. The table shows some of the most useful quantities that we can measure. It also shows the international unit that we use for each one.

The basic quantities and units

Quantity	Unit
Length, l, or distance, d	metre, m
Mass, m	kilogram, kg
Time, t	second, s
Electric current, I	amp, A
Temperature, T	kelvin, K

Other quantities and units

Quantity	Unit
Area, A	square metre, m^2
Volume, V	cubic metre, m^3
Speed, v	metre per second, m/s
Velocity, v	metre per second, m/s
Acceleration, a	metre per second per second, m/s^2
Density	kilogram per cubic metre, kg/m^3
Force	newton, N
Pressure	pascal, Pa
Work and energy	joule, J
Power	watt, W
Electric charge	coulomb, C
Electric potential difference (voltage)	volt, V
EMF (voltage)	volt, V
Electrical resistance	ohm, Ω
Frequency	hertz, Hz
Radioactive count rate	becquerel, Bq

Some special quantities and units

Quantity	Unit
Energy transfer by electrical equipment in homes	kilowatt-hour, kWh (1 kWh = 3 600 000 J)
Distances between stars and galaxies	light year (1 light year = 9 500 000 000 000 000 m)

Small numbers

A measurement of 0.000 000 05 m is troublesome to write down. So we call it 50 nanometre, or 50 nm.

1 centimetre	= 1 cm	= $\frac{1}{100}$ m	= 0.01 m
1 millimetre	= 1 mm	= $\frac{1}{1000}$ m	= 0.001 m
1 micrometre	= 1 μm	= $\frac{1}{1\,000\,000}$ m	= 0.000 001 m
1 nanometre	= 1 nm	= $\frac{1}{1\,000\,000\,000}$ m	= 0.000 000 001 m

The same naming pattern is used for other quantities, like time and current:

1 μs (microsecond) is a millionth of a second, or 0.000 001 s.
1 mA (milliamp) is a thousandth of an amp, or 0.001 A.

Big numbers

The distance from London to Edinburgh is about 650 000 m. It is easier to use kilometres for this measurement. London is 650 km away from Edinburgh.

1 kilometre = 1 km = 1000 m
1 megametre = 1 Mm = 1 000 000 m

Again, the same naming pattern works for other quanities, such as force and power:

1 kN (kilonewton) is a thousand newton, or 1000 N.
1 MW (megawatt) is a million watt, or 1 000 000 W.

▲ When an apple falls from a tree, energy transfer takes place and there is some heating of the apple and the ground. The rise in temperature is about 1 millikelvin (1 mK = 0.001 K).

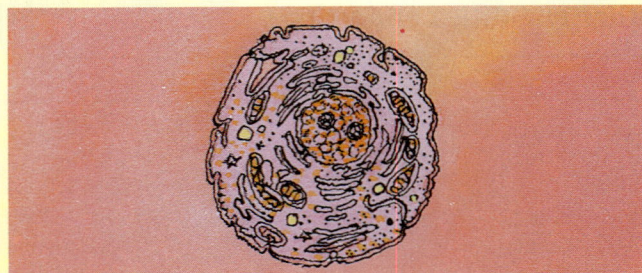

▲ The diameter of a human cell is about 10 micrometres (10 μm = 0.000 01 m).

▲ The temperature at the centre of the Sun is about 10 megakelvin (10 MK = 10 000 000 K).

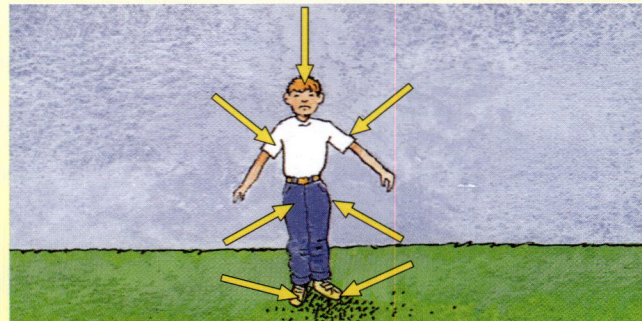

▲ The pressure of the atmosphere acting on your body is about 100 kilopascal (100 kPa = 100 000 Pa).

Making measurements

Reading scales

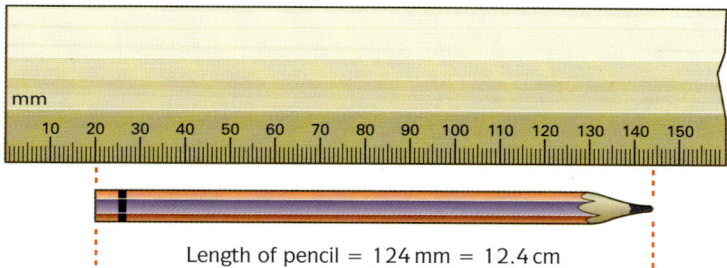

Length of pencil = 124 mm = 12.4 cm

🔺 On a ruler.

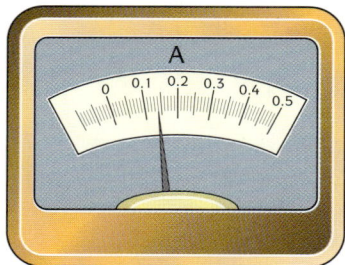

Current = 0.14 A

🔺 On an ammeter.

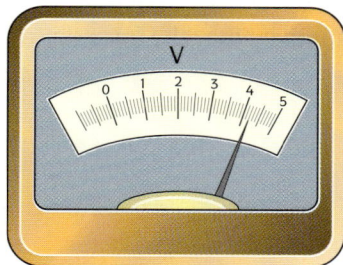

Voltage = 4.2 V

🔺 On an voltmeter.

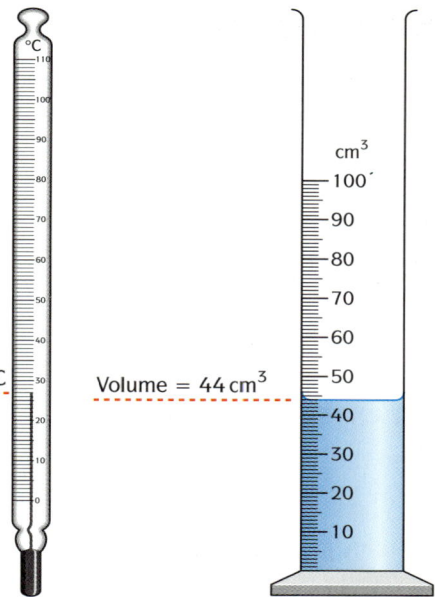

Temperature = 27 °C

🔺 On a thermometer.

Volume = 44 cm³

🔺 On a measuring cylinder.

Choosing the best instrument for the job:

This can measure to the nearest 0.1 cm³. It is precise.

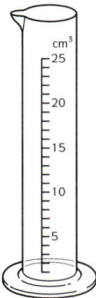

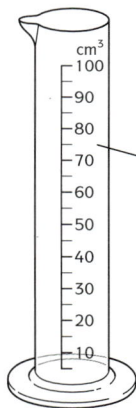

This measures a wide range of volumes.

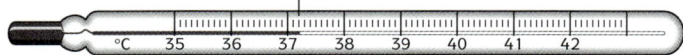

Normal body temperature

A clinical thermometer provides measurements to the nearest 0.1 °C, but it only measures a narrow range of temperatures.

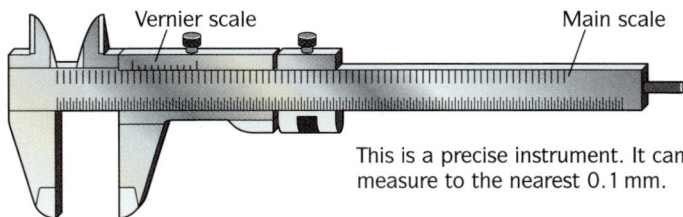

Vernier scale   Main scale

This is a precise instrument. It can measure to the nearest 0.1 mm.

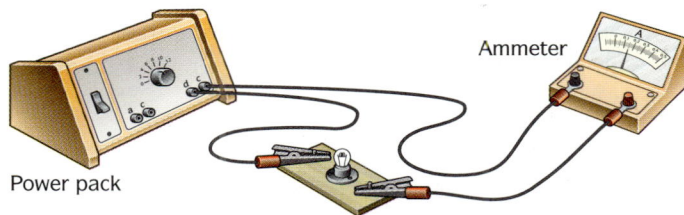

Power pack   Ammeter

An ammeter is connected in series in the circuit so that the current it measures flows through it.

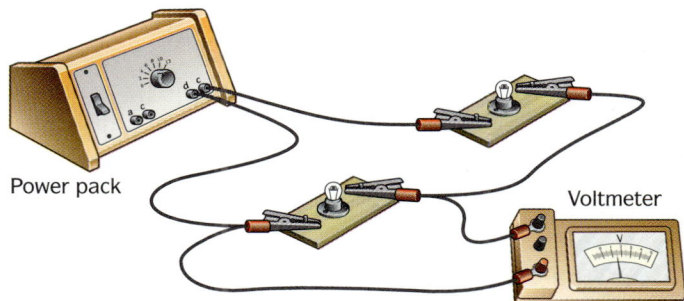

Power pack   Voltmeter

A voltmeter measures the voltage (the potential difference) between two points in a circuit. It is connected in parallel, not in series.

🔺 Ammeter or voltmeter?

🔺 Some instruments have the advantage of measuring a wide range of values. Other instruments are precise

Using formulae

v = speed
d = distance
t = time

We can work out the average speed of an object if we know how far it has travelled and how long it has taken. We use the 'formula' for speed:

$$\text{speed} = \frac{\text{distance}}{\text{time}}$$

It is quicker to write the formula using letters for each quantity:

$$v = \frac{d}{t}$$

An example

Find the average speed of a 400 m runner who finishes the race in 50 s.
 We know that d = 400 m and t = 50 s. We can put these numbers into the formula:

$$v = \frac{d}{t} \quad \text{the formula}$$

$$v = \frac{400\,\text{m}}{50\,\text{s}} \quad \begin{array}{l}\text{distance}\\ \text{the same formula with the numbers}\\ \text{time}\end{array}$$

A calculator will do the rest for us if we need it:

$$v = 8\,\text{m/s} \quad \text{the answer is } 400 \div 50, \text{ with the correct unit}$$

Another example

How much force would you need to give a mass of 3.5 kg an acceleration of 4 m/s²?
 The procedure is the same as before. First, choose the formula you need, and write it down:

$$F = ma$$

Now put the numbers in:

$$F = 3.5\,\text{kg} \times 4\,\text{m/s}^2 \quad \begin{array}{l}\text{mass} \quad \text{acceleration}\end{array}$$

$$= 14\,\text{N} \quad \text{the answer with the correct unit}$$

Note that it is important to write down the unit of force in the final answer. Otherwise anyone who reads your work will not know whether the force is in newtons or kilonewtons, for example. To an engineer working out forces in a new bridge, a mistake like that would be very expensive.

Rearranged formulae

Suppose that you know what your average speed will be for a journey, and how far it is. You can use the formula for speed to estimate how long it will take. But you need to use the formula in a rearranged form.

If $v = \frac{d}{t}$ then rules of logic (see page 246) will tell you that $t = \frac{d}{v}$.

You can use this rearrangement of the same formula to work out time.

Rearrangements of the most common formulae

Formula in words	Formula in letters	Rearrangements	
speed $= \dfrac{\text{distance}}{\text{time}}$	$v = \dfrac{d}{t}$	$t = \dfrac{d}{v}$	$d = vt$
acceleration $= \dfrac{\text{change in velocity}}{\text{time}}$	$a = \dfrac{v-u}{t}$	$t = \dfrac{v-u}{a}$	$v = u + at$
force $=$ mass $\times$ acceleration	$F = ma$	$m = \dfrac{F}{a}$	$a = \dfrac{F}{m}$
work $=$ force $\times$ distance	$E = Fd$	$F = \dfrac{E}{d}$	$d = \dfrac{E}{F}$
power $= \dfrac{\text{energy transfer or work}}{\text{time}}$	$P = \dfrac{E}{t}$	$E = Pt$	$t = \dfrac{E}{p}$
kinetic energy $= \dfrac{1}{2} \times$ mass $\times$ velocity squared	$E_k = \dfrac{1}{2}mv^2$	$m = \dfrac{2E_k}{v^2}$	$v = \sqrt{\dfrac{2E_k}{m}}$
change in potential energy $=$ mass $\times g \times$ change in height	$\Delta E_p = mgh$	$m = \dfrac{\Delta E_p}{gh}$	$h = \dfrac{\Delta E_p}{mg}$
pressure $= \dfrac{\text{force}}{\text{area}}$	$P = \dfrac{F}{A}$	$A = \dfrac{F}{P}$	$F = PA$
force $=$ force constant $\times$ extension	$F = kx$	$k = \dfrac{F}{x}$	$x = \dfrac{F}{k}$
resistance $= \dfrac{\text{voltage}}{\text{current}}$	$R = \dfrac{V}{I}$	$V = IR$	$I = \dfrac{V}{R}$
voltage $= \dfrac{\text{energy}}{\text{charge}}$	$V = \dfrac{E}{Q}$	$E = VQ$	$Q = \dfrac{E}{V}$
electrical power $=$ voltage $\times$ current	$P = VI$	$V = \dfrac{P}{I}$	$I = \dfrac{P}{V}$
price of electricity $=$ power $\times$ time $\times$ cost per kWh	price $= Ptc$	$P = \dfrac{\text{price}}{tc}$	$t = \dfrac{\text{price}}{Pc}$
current $= \dfrac{\text{charge}}{\text{time}}$	$I = \dfrac{Q}{t}$	$Q = It$	$t = \dfrac{Q}{I}$
wave speed $=$ frequency x wavelength	$v = f\lambda$	$f = \dfrac{v}{\lambda}$	$\lambda = \dfrac{v}{f}$

Rearranging your own formulae

In an electric circuit you might have a 100 ohm resistor, and you might want to know how much current will flow in it when the voltage is 6 volt.

The formula $R = \frac{V}{I}$ has got the right three quantities in it, but it is most useful for working out resistance, not current.

To work out current it is much easier to have current I on its own on the left hand side of the formula. That means you have to remember the rearranged formula, or you have to look it up, or you have to work it out for yourself.

So, start with

$$R = \frac{V}{I}$$

We can change both sides of this equation in the same way. Provided that we do the same to both sides, we can do anything we like. But multiplying both sides by I turns out to be most useful:

$$R \times I = \frac{V \times I}{I}$$

There is no point in multiplying V by I and then dividing by I. The answer would be V (since $I \div I = 1$). So the equation is now:

$$R \times I = V$$

Note that this rearrangement would be useful if you wanted to know V. But that does not help you to work out I. You must get I on its own. The way to do that is to move R, by dividing both sides of the formula by R:

$$\frac{R \times I}{R} = \frac{V}{R}$$

As before, multiplying I by R and then dividing by R is a waste of time. You know what the answer will be before you do it – the answer is just I.

$$I = \frac{V}{R}$$

This is the formula that we wanted, for working out current.

If you practise rearranging formulae you will get much more confident and much better at it.

To work it out for yourself you have to remember one logical rule:

If two things are equal then if you change them both in exactly the same way they will again be equal to each other.

Graphs and relationships

Patterns at a glance

In practical work you often put results into tables. That is a neat and easy way of recording information. But patterns in the results can be hard to see in rows and columns of numbers. A graph will show the pattern 'at a glance'.

The table shows some results from an activity on a resistor in a circuit.

Voltage (volts)	0.3	0.9	1.5	1.8	2.4	3.0	3.6
Current (amps)	0.1	0.2	0.5	0.7	0.7	1.0	1.2

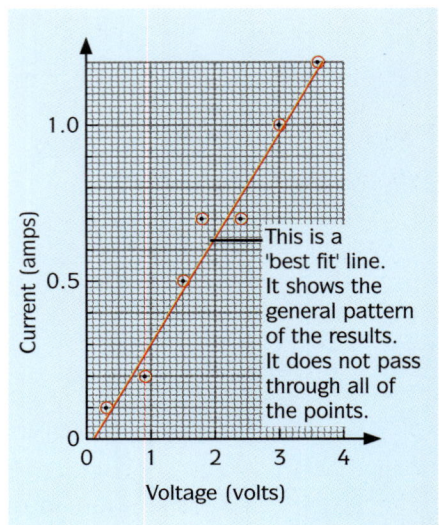

This is a 'best fit' line. It shows the general pattern of the results. It does not pass through all of the points.

PHYSICS

The graph on page 246 shows that as the voltage gets bigger, the current gets bigger. The overall pattern of the points is a straight line. The line starts at the 'origin', the point where voltage and current are both zero.

Note that some points do not lie exactly on the line. Individual measurements are never perfect. It is the general pattern made by all of the measurements together that is important. We draw a line that is the 'best fit' to the overall pattern.

Not all patterns are simple straight lines

The table shows some results for an activity on some water cooling in a test tube.

Time (minutes)	0	1	2	3	4	5	6	7	8
Temperature (°C)	88	64	52	44	36	30	28	24	22

The graph shows the pattern 'at a glance'. The graph is steep at first – it has a large gradient. That is when the water was cooling fastest. The gradient of the graph becomes smaller and smaller. The line will become flat when the water stops cooling.

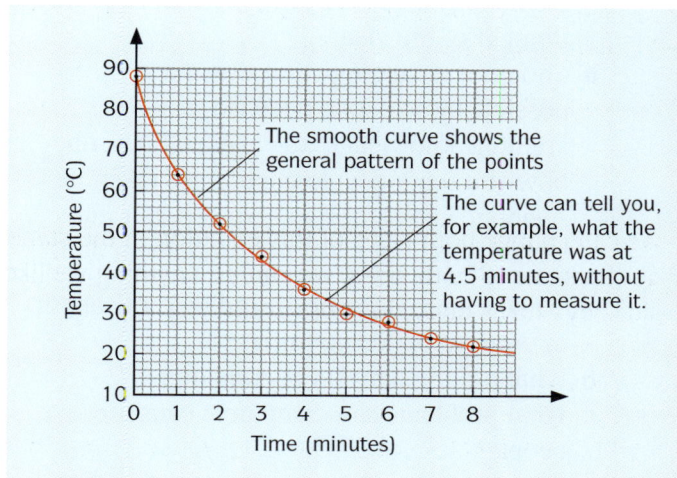

Proportionality and gradients - some conclusions from graphs

Look again at the graph for current against voltage on page 246. When the voltage doubles, the current doubles. When the voltage gets four times bigger, so does the current. In fact, whatever happens to the voltage, the current always changes by an identical **proportion**.

That means that the link (or relationship) between current and voltage in this circuit is quite simple. We describe this relationship as a proportionality. In this resistor, current is **proportional** to the voltage.

If we measure the gradient of a graph it can give us useful information. Graph A shows how the distance travelled by a cyclist changes with time.

The gradient is a measure of 'steepness', and we can work it out by dividing a change in distance by a corresponding change in time.

$$\text{gradient} = \frac{\text{change in distance}}{\text{change in time}}$$

$$= \frac{50\,\text{m}}{5\,\text{s}}$$

$$= 10\,\text{m/s}$$

What we have worked out is the speed of the cyclist. More complicated graphs, like graph B, have gradients that change. A graph for a whole journey of a cyclist shows where speed was highest and lowest.

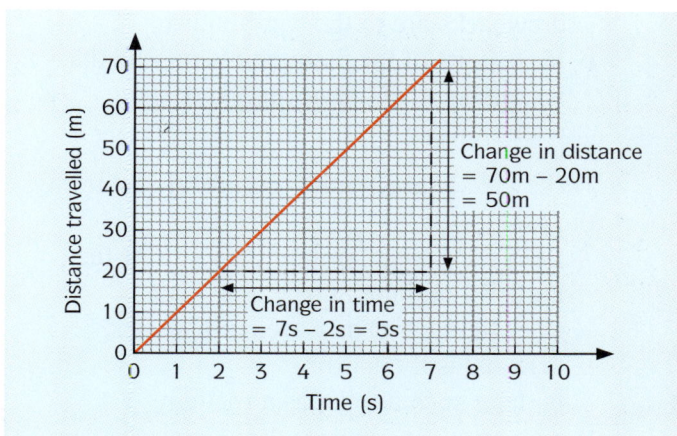

The smooth curve shows the general pattern of the points

The curve can tell you, for example, what the temperature was at 4.5 minutes, without having to measure it.

Change in distance
= 70m – 20m
= 50m

Change in time
= 7s – 2s = 5s

🔺 Distance – time, graph A.

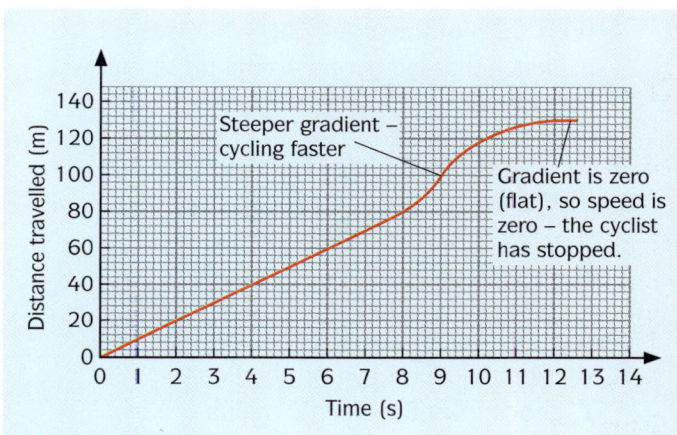

Steeper gradient – cycling faster

Gradient is zero (flat), so speed is zero – the cyclist has stopped.

🔺 Distance – time, graph B.

PHYSICS

Questions

1 Wheels are a technology that was developed from practical experience and not from scientific knowledge.
   a Choose another 'practical experience' technology. Describe how you think people thought of the idea.
   b Choose a technology that was made possible by scientific knowledge. What scientific knowledge was needed? Describe how you think people might have taken the scientific knowledge and converted it into working technology. What made them do it?

2 a What science do people need to know about in order to build computers?
   b What are the benefits of computers?
   c What problems can computers cause to people?

3 a How does television affect the quality of your life? Say what the benefits and drawbacks are to the way you live.
   b Make a list of the main points of scientific knowledge that are needed to design televisions.

4 These are some scientific 'controversies' from the past:
   ■ Does the Sun go around the Earth or the Earth around the Sun?
   ■ Does light travel as waves or particles?
   ■ How old is the Earth?
   ■ Is there such a thing as a vacuum?
   You may have read about these controversies in this book. Choose two of them, and for each one make a list of the evidence that supports both sides of the argument. What was the evidence that led people to the ideas that we have now?

5 Name one way to reduce risk of accidents involving:
   a corrosive liquids like acids
   b poisoning by gases
   c eye damage by splashes of hot liquid
   d cuts from snapping glass tubes
   e tripping over a bag on the floor
   f shock from the electric mains.

6 Design your own hazard symbol to warn people of the danger of bags on the floor.

7 Are the safety rules from the hospital laboratory easy to understand and remember? Could you make them easier – for example, by using a set of simple pictures? Design your own set of illustrated safety rules for this lab.

8 What is the unit of:
   a mass   b temperature   c volume
   d density   e work   f resistance
   g frequency?

9 Write down the quantity to match each of these units:
   a m   b A   c m/s^2 d Pa
   e V   f Ω   g Bq

10 Write down these measurements in metres. The first one is done for you:
   a 5 mm = 0.005 m
   b 6 mm
   c 2 mm
   d 12 mm
   e 1 μm
   f 8 μm
   g 1 nm
   h 4 nm
   i 40 nm

11 a How many μs are there in 1 s?
   b What time of year will it be in 1 Ms (one megasecond) from now?
   c If a thousand small ants can exert a combined force of 1 mN, what is the average force per ant?

12 These are some values jotted down in a student's book:

time = 30 s
current = 2 A
area = 0.4 m^2
speed = 10 m/s
power = 100W
resistance = 30 Ω
force = 6N

These are some questions that the student has been set:

Homework

a Work out the voltage applied to the resistor.
b Work out the pressure on the area.
c Work out the distance travelled.
d Work out the energy transferred in the electric circuit.

Do the student's homework.

13 If $x = y \times z$, work out a formula that begins $y =$

14 These are the results of an experiment on stretching a cable to be used for a bridge.

Force in newton	0	200	400	600	800	1000	1200	1400	1600
Increase in length (mm)	0	0.06	0.11	0.18	0.26	0.30	0.35	0.40	0.49

a Plot a graph, with the independent (controlled) variable on the x-axis and the dependent variable on the y-axis.
b Does the graph show proportionality?
c What is the gradient of the graph?
d Why would an engineer find the gradient of the graph to be useful information?

Index

absorption 23, 66
AC *see* alternating current
AC generators 185
acceleration 117, 131–5, 132–3
  downward 128
  force 135–6
  gravity 133–4
  mass 135–6
  sideways 129
  vector quantity 131
adding velocities 129
air brakes 136
air resistance 117–18
alpha particles 225–6
alpha radiation 224
alternating current (AC) 176, 214
altitude 151
ammeters 161–2, 165, 243
amp 162
amplitude 20
analysing evidence 3, 9–10
anode 191
appliances, energy transfer 173
archery 135
armature 210
asteroids 53–4
astronauts 134
atmospheres 47, 116, 149–50
atmospheric pressure 151
atoms 1, 192, 222

background count, radiation 231
balanced forces 128–9
balanced vectors 128
balloons 192–3
balls 106
bats 32
batteries 158, 167, 168, 181
beauty treatment 201
Becquerel, Henri 223
beta radiation 224, 225, 226
Betelgeuse 57
bicycles 126, 153, 184, 202
Big Bang 68–70
big numbers 242
biomass 78
Boyle's law 154
braking 102, 136, 149
bridges 120
Bruno, Giordano 55
brushes 210
bungee jumping 109–10, 120, 122
Burnell, Jocelyn Bell 72

cables 176
caesium-137 229
cameras 26, 226
car safety, kinetic energy 100
carbon-14 229
cathode rays 191
chain reactions 233
changes of state 82–3
charge 183, 189–204
  current 199
  electron control 192
  friction 192
  measurement 198
Chatsworth House 146

chemical reactions, electrons 194
Chernobyl 234
chimneys 196
chromium plating 201–2
circuit breakers 180
circuit diagrams 158, 159
circuit set-ups 159
circuits 157–72
  current generation 184
circulation, electrons 159
city transport, motors 210
clocks 238–9
coil induction, investigation 212–13
comets 53
commutators 210
compasses 206, 209
compression, gases/liquids 147
computers 136, 214, 229, 239
concave 17
conclusions 3, 10
conduction 84–5, 158
conservation of energy 105
constellations 56–7
control rods 233
convection, gases and liquids 85–6
conventional current 163
convex 17
cooker circuits 178
cooling 79, 83
Copernicus (Nikolai Koppernick) 55
cosmic background radiation 70
coulomb (C) 183, 198
critical angle 18
CT scan 25
Curie, Marie 223
current
  alternating 214
  big/small 162
  flow 181
  generation 184
  induction 211–14
  magnetism 161
  parallel circuits 166
  particles/charge 189–204
  resistors 160
  series circuits 166
  thermistors 166
current-temperature graphs 166

dams 147
dating, radioactivity 229–30
dating rocks 230
decay
  computer simulation 229
  radiation 228
  rubidium-87 230
density, liquid pressure 145–6
dependant variables 7
desalination 200–1
diamonds 18
diesel engines 174
diffraction 34, 35–6
diffuse reflection 15
digging machines 148
diodes 164
direct current 176

disc brakes 149
disintegration 228
distance 115–16
distance-time graphs 113, 119, 247
diving 117, 133–4, 145
downward acceleration 128
drag 98, 118–19, 128
drum brakes 149
dynamos 184

ears 30
Earth
  age 63
  gravity 104
  magnetic field 207–8
  origins 64–5
  population 198
  radioactivity 64, 230
  space 45–92
  temperature 80
  tilt 46
  waves 38
earth circuit 177
earth wire 176, 177
earthquakes 39, 40
echoes 31
eddy currents 216
efficiency, energy 89, 97–8
electric cells 239
electric circuits, energy transfer 160–1
electric current 199
electric generators, nuclear 233
electric motors 210–11, 239
electric quantities 183
electric shock 181–2, 193
electrical balance 193
electrical charge 190
electrical force, dissolving ions 201
electricity
  demand 93
  generation 88, 184–5
  home 175
  live connection 175–6
  mains 173–88
  payment 182
electroacupuncture 162
electrodes 191
electrolysis 201
electromagnetic induction 211–12
electromagnetic radiation
  at home 23
  diffraction 34
  speed 23
electromagnetism 205–20
  communication 24
  medicine 25
  spectrum 22
  waves 37
electron beam 191
electron control 192
electron flow 163, 198–9, 208
electron microscope 222
electronic components 157–72
electrons 192–4, 222, 226
  circulation 159
  ions 191, 194
  movement 84
  shock 193

technology 191
  vacuum 150
electroplating 201–2
electroscopes
  charging 197
  gold leaf 197–8
electrostatics 192–4, 195
elements 222
energy
  absorption 14
  conservation 105
  efficiency 88–9, 217
  flows 88–9
  fossil fuels 78, 89
  kinetic 94, 100, 101–2
  measurements 93–108
  nuclear changes 232–3
  passenger transport 99
  potential 94, 103
  resources 77–92
  temperature 82
energy transfer 79–88, 105
  appliances 173
  detection 81
  electric circuits 160–1
  electricity 173–88
  power 99
  transformers 216
  work 95–6
energy-efficient homes 90
engines 96–7
environmental problems 239
epicentres 40
equal/opposite forces 137
equipment 7–8
European story 238–9
evaluation, evidence 3, 11
evaporation 83
evidence
  analysis 3, 9–10
  collection 3
  evaluation 11
experiments 1–12
extension 119–22
extension-tension graphs 121, 122
eyes 22

fair test 3, 154
fairgrounds 174–5
falling 109–25
Faraday, Michael 211–12
feet 143
filament lamps 160
film badges 223
fire hazards 199
fission 232
fluorine atoms 192
focal lengths 17
force 116
  acceleration 134–6
  direction 127–8
  lines 209
  motion 127
  pressure 143
  weight 144
  work 96
forces
  balanced 128–9
  collisions 136–7
  electrical 190, 208
  equal/opposite 137
  gravitational 208
  magnetic 208
  vectors 127

formulae 244–6
fossil fuels 78, 89
fountains 146
freezing 82
frequency 20, 36, 37
friction 126, 137, 190, 196
fuel gauges 164
fuels 78, 89
fuses 175, 176–8, 180
fusion 72, 73

galaxies 46, 57, 62
Galileo Galilei 55
gamma radiation 25, 26, 224, 226
gas flame lighter 184
gas supply, pressure 152
gas syringe 153
gases
  absorption 66
  pressure 153–4
generators 174, 233
geology 63
glass 16
GM tube 223, 224, 231
gold leaf electroscopes 197–8
graphite 233
graphs 9–10
  current/temperature 166
  extension 121, 122
  motion 115–16
  pressure/volume 154
  relationships 246–7
  tension 121, 122
  velocity/time 132
gravity 46, 133–4

half-lives 229, 232
health and safety 4, 240
hearing tests 167
heart pace makers 221
heating 79, 214
  work 96
helium 66, 73, 225–6
high pressure 144
high voltage cables 217
high-speed motion 118
horse power 99
hospitals 205, 240
hot air balloons 85
house wiring 175
hydraulics 148
hydrogen, fusion 73
hypothesis 3

ice dancing 137
ignition switch 209
incubators 77, 205
independent variables 7
induction 211–14
industries 239
infra-red radiation 22, 23, 24, 25, 86
insulation 87, 88, 176
internal combustion engines 239
international industries 239
interstellar travel 56
inverse proportion 135, 154
investigation
  liquid pressure/depth 147
  sports shoes 144
investigations 1–12, 8
ion flow, liquids 200

ionisation 25, 194
   radioactivity 223, 226–7
ions
   attraction 195
   electrons 194
   salt solution 200
   sodium 200
iron, fusion 73
iron core 216
isotopes 227–8
   medical tracers 231–2

joule 182
jumping wire 209
Jupiter 49, 54, 55

kettles 160–1
keyhole surgery 19
kilowatt-hour (kWh) 182
kinetic energy 94
   car safety 100
   loss/gain 101
   speed/mass 101–2
kWh see kilowatt-hour

laboratory rules 240
LDR see Light-Dependent
   Resistor
lenses 17
leukaemia 231
lie detectors 181
light
   brightness 7
   control 18
   dispersal 21
   spectra 13–29, 67
   speed 14, 57
   stars 66
   waves 20
light year 57
Light-Dependent Resistors
   (LDR) 165
lighting 5, 178, 214
lightning 162, 195, 214
lines of force 209
liquid pressure 144–9
   density 145–6
   depth 145, 147
   direction 145
live connection, electricity
   175–6
longitudinal waves 38
loudspeakers 174, 210
Love waves 39–40
'low voltage' power packs
   214
luminous objects 14
magnetic fields, Earth
   207–8
magnetic force 206, 207–8,
   211
magnetism
   current 161
   radiation 225
magnets 206
mains electricity 173–88
manometer 152
Mars 45, 54
mass 135–6, 144
Maxwell, James Clerk 22
measurements 7–9, 243
   motion 113–15, 125–40
measuring cylinders 243
medicine 25, 32
melanin filters 24
melting 82
Mercury 52, 150–1
metals 197, 198–9
meteorites 64
meteors 53–4
microphones 174

microscopes 222, 239
microwaves 22, 23, 24
Milky Way 57
miniature circuit breakers
   (MCB) 180
mirrors 15, 16
models 2
molecules, pressure 153
Moon 49–50, 116
motion 46, 109–40
motor effect 209
motors, electric 174, 209
mountains 63, 150–1
moving energy 37

National Grid 205, 217
natural background
   radiation 231
nervous system 200
neutral wire 175
neutrons 222, 226, 227, 228
Newton, Isaac 127
newton (N) 142–3
nickel coating 201–2
nuclear bombs 239
nuclear decay 228–9
nuclear fission 232
nuclear fusion 72, 73, 234
nuclear power stations
   233–4
nuclear reactions 221, 232
nuclei 222, 226
numbers 242

optical fibres 19
orbits 49
ozone layer 24, 47

P waves 39–41
pace makers 221
parachutists 118–19
parallel circuits 163, 168
particles 189–204
pascal (Pa) 142–3
passenger transport, energy
   consumption 99
patterns, graphical 246–7
periodic table 227–8
permanent repulsion 197
personal power 100, 104
perspex refraction 18
plane mirrors 15
planets 52, 65
planning investigations 3,
   6–8
plate tectonic theory 207
polarity, Earth's magnetism
   207
polonium 223, 228
positive ions 226
posters 2
potassium-40 228
potential difference 167
potential energy 94
   gain 103
   water 103
power 99–100
   acceleration 134
   electricity 183
   weightlifting 104
power lines 161
   see also voltage cables
power packs 243
power stations 77, 184–5,
   217, 233–4
   efficiency 89
precision 8
prediction checking 10
presentation 9
pressure 141–56
   altitude 151

bicycle pumps 153
forces 148–9
gases 152, 153–4
liquids 144–9
molecules 153
shoes 143
trends 151
volume 153–4
primary coil 214–16
prisms 21
protons 222, 226, 227, 228

radiation
   background 231
   bending 225
   detection 223
   magnetism 225
   penetration 224–5
   types 87, 224
radiation intensity-
   thickness, graph 224
radio waves 22, 24, 37, 239
radioactive material 221,
   223, 232
radioactivity 25, 64, 221–36
radioactivity-time graphs
   229, 230
radium 223
radon 231
rays 17
RCD see residual current
   devices
reactions 200
reactor, nuclear 232
real world representation 4
rearranged formulae 244–6
recording measurements 9
red shift 67–8
reflection 14, 15–16, 19, 31
   P and S waves 41
refraction 14, 16–18, 19, 21
   P and S waves 41
   sound waves 33
refrigerators, energy
   transfer 83
relays 209
renewable resources 89
research 6–7
reservoir systems 103
residual current devices
   (RCD) 180
resistance 160, 168
results, reliability 11
revolutionary ideas 54–5
ring mains 178
risk assessment 4, 240
rockets 137
rocks, dating 230
rubber 120, 121
rubidium-87 230

S waves 39–41
safety 4, 121, 240
   cars 100
   earth wire 177
   stage lighting 5
salt 200–1
satellites
   communication 48
   images 48
   motion 49
   observations 45, 48
   television 111
Saturn 51
scalar quantities 127
sea breezes 86
secondary coil 214–16
seismic waves 39–42
seismograms 39
sensation 30
series circuits 163, 168

shoes, pressure 143
skaters, pressure 142
skiing 142
small numbers 242
sodium/chlorine separation
   200–1
solar system 45–6, 55, 62
   collisions 54
sonar 31
sound 30–3
   diffraction 35, 36
   speed 32
sound waves
   reflection 31
   refraction 33
space 45–92
spacecraft 137
   solar system 51
sparks 195
spectrum, light 13–29
speed 118–19, 130
   calculations 111–12
   measurement 113
   units 111
speed-time graphs 114,
   115–16
speedometer 113
springs 121
stars 56–7, 71–3
   classification 71
   colours 67
   death 73
   life 72
   material 61
   shooting 53
starter motors 209
static build-up 199
Steady State 69
steam 184–5
steam engines 97
stopping distances 102, 136
streamlining 98
stretching 109–25
sub-atomic particles 222
submarines 141
sun 61
   fusion 73, 234
   temperature 243
   thermal radiation 86
   warmth model 53
sunlight 66
super grid 217
supernova 71, 73
suspension bridges 120
switches 176–7

technology
   electrons 191
   history 238–9
   motion 126
telescopes 55, 239
television 111, 191–2, 239
temperature 80–2, 242, 247
tennis 127
tension 119–22
   bungee jumping 120
terminal velocity 118–19
thermal conductivity 85
thermal equilibrium 79
thermal imaging cameras 87
thermal insulation 87
thermal radiation 86–7
thermionic emission 192
thermistors 165, 166
thermometers 243
'Thermos' flasks 88
thickness control 225
Thomson, JJ 191, 222
three-pin plugs 177, 179
thrust 128
ticker-timers 114

time 61–76
tracers 231–2
transformers 214–17
transport, efficiency
   comparison 99
transverse waves 38
travel 50–1, 56
turbines 88, 174, 184–5
tyres 126

UK energy resources 93
ultrasound 31, 32
ultraviolet radiation 22,
   23–4
unbalanced forces 128–9,
   133
units 241
universe
   centre 54
   expanding 68
   lumpy 70
   origins 69
uranium 223, 232

vacuum 149–50
   pumps 239
Van de Graaff generators
   190, 194, 196
variable resistance 164, 165
variables 3, 154
vectors 127–31
vehicle stopping distances
   136
velocity 129–31
   vectors 129–30
velocity-time 132, 133, 134
Venus 45, 50–1, 52
Vernier callipers 243
vibrations,
   electromagnetism 210
virtual reality 222
voltage 167–8
   cables 217
   high 196
   up/down 215
voltage-time graphs 213
voltmeters 167, 243
volume, pressure 153–4
Voyager 1 & 2 51

water
   experiments 149
   flow 159
   pumps 238–9
   spouts 146
   waves 19, 36
watt (W) 183
wavelength 20, 36, 68
waves 19, 29–44
weather 6, 150
weight 118–20
   force 144
weightlifting 104
whales 33
wheels 238–9
windmills 238–9
work 95–6
world energy resources
   89–90

X-rays 34, 48, 86
   magnetism 225, 226
   medicine 25, 32
   spectrum 22
   voltage 167

WYKE MANOR SCHOOL